ALISTAIR MOFFAT was born [...]
country. He took degrees at [...]
Edinburgh and London and p[...]
universities. In 1976, he took charge [...]
fringe, which burgeoned into the largest arts festival in the
world. After a period as Scottish Television's arts correspondent,
he was appointed Controller of Features and then Director of
Programmes. Until recently he was Managing Director of
Scottish Television Enterprises. He is the author of four previous
books: *The Edinburgh Fringe, Kelsae: a History of Kelos from
the Earliest Times, Remembering Charles Rennie Mackintosh* and
Arthur and the Lost Kingdoms.

THE
SEA KINGDOMS

THE STORY
OF CELTIC BRITAIN
AND IRELAND

Alistair Moffat

HarperCollins*Publishers*

HarperCollins*Publishers*
77–85 Fulham Palace Road,
Hammersmith, London w6 8jb

www.**fire**and**water**.com

Published by HarperCollins*Publishers* 2002
3 5 7 9 8 6 4 2

A catalogue record for this book is available from
the British Library

ISBN 0 00 653243 8

Chapter headings show the Galley of Lorne,
from the tomb of Alexander MacLeod,
St Clement's Church, Rodel, Harris. © RCAHMS

Maps by Leslie Robinson

Set in PostScript Linotype Minion with Photina display
by Rowland Phototypesetting Ltd,
Bury St Edmunds, Suffolk

Printed and bound in Great Britain by
Clays Ltd, St Ives plc

CONTENTS

ACKNOWLEDGEMENTS

Donnie Campbell was a passionate football fan. In his office at Sabhal Mor Ostaig, the Gaelic-medium further education college on the Isle of Skye, a small television was showing Scotland playing in a World Cup qualifier in the late 1980s. With his eyes constantly flicking to the screen, Donnie was trying to concentrate on talking to me in English about something or other, but when Scotland scored a goal, he immediately leaped up and roared. '*A steach!*' – 'It's in!'

In extremis, even exultation, Gaelic sprang first to his lips. It occurred to me that for some people, albeit a rapidly diminishing number, Gaelic was not simply a colourful facet of Scots culture, but still existed as an entirely different way of seeing Scotland, of understanding our national identity – and even of coping with the continuing tragedy of our football team. In his gentle and straightforward manner Donnie told me a great deal about Gaelic, about the West, and the links with Ireland and the south. His early death in a car accident was a sore loss and I am glad to remember him and his quiet kindness, and acknowledge both. *Moran taing a' charaid.*

Christeen Combe taught me Gaelic and had immense patience with my impatience. She not only guided me successfully through public examinations, but in introducing me to her family also offered an unselfconscious means of understanding better the Gaelic speech community of the Western Isles. Christine's teaching was translated into practical use by Rhoda Macdonald, who insisted that we speak Gaelic at work in Scottish Television and who lent me books, tapes and insights. Through talking to Rhoda I began to see that Gaelic Scotland had much in common with Ireland, Man, Wales and Cornwall, and that some of this sonorous talk about culture hides a great deal of fun and laughter.

Like the good teacher he is, Norman Gillies, the principal of Sabhal Mor Ostaig, has always encouraged my interests. When the college began to create links with Ireland and Irish Gaelic speakers, it began to seem less like an outpost on the edge of Scotland and more like a cultural entrepôt in the middle of the Celtic west. Norman will find the arguments in this book very familiar.

When we came to film a ten-part series of *The Sea Kingdoms* for Scottish Television I had to rethink the book as spoken words and moving pictures. My director, Anne Buckland, demanded clarity and endless rewrites – some of which have found their way into the book. She may even have stamped her foot once or twice. John Agnew, Ken MacNeill, Anita Cox and Adam Moffat helped greatly to make our long journey from Stornoway to Penzance a creative one.

At HarperCollins Michael Fishwick and Arabella Pike created the means for me to write this book and I am grateful for their faith in it. To Kate Morris fell the unenviable task of editing the text and managing it through to publication. Because of her hard work, diligence and tact, *The Sea Kingdoms* is undoubtedly a better book.

It is simply a pleasure to work with David Godwin, my agent, a lovely man with a sharp eye for a good project and a softly spoken word for an agitated author. Thank you David.

Finally, I want to thank the scores of people who stopped what they were doing, took the time and sat down to talk to me in Scotland, Ireland, Man, Wales and Cornwall. It was grand.

LIST OF ILLUSTRATIONS

Stonehenge (The Art Archive)
A druid (The Art Archive)
The Wicker Man (The Art Archive)
The Bard, Thomas Jones (National Museums and Galleries of Wales)
'Lindow Man' (The British Museum)
Ogham alphabet (From *Celtic Connections* by David James and Simant
    Bostock, Blandford. Illustration by Anthony Rees (Blandford/Cassells
    Publisher)
St Brendan and the whale (The Art Archive/British Library)
Book of Kells (Trinity College Library, Dublin, Ireland/Bridgeman Art Library)
Oseburg Ship (© University Museum of Cultural Heritage – University of
    Oslo, Norway)
Bjornson cross (Manx National Heritage)

Lewis Chessmen (© The British Museum (Iv. Cat. 122.119.121))
St David's Cathedral (© Philip Craven)
Edward I (The Art Archive/British Library)
Gregor MacGregor (© The British Museum)
Henry Joy McCracken (© National Museum of Ireland)
Theobald Wolfe Tone (© National Museum of Ireland)
Captain Swayne (© National Museum of Ireland)
Rebels piking prisoners on Wexford Bridge (© National Library of Ireland)
Dr William Price (From *Gwylellis yn Nayd* (The Will of My Father), 1871,
    reproduced by permission of the National Museum of Wales, Welsh
    Folk Museum, Cardiff)
'Caradog' (By permission of the National Library of Wales)
The Dowlais Temperance Choir (By permission of the National Library of
    Wales)

Tynwald in session (Isle of Man Newspapers)
A curragh (Collections/Brian Shuel)

Iona (© Murdo Macleod)
Cornish wrestlers (Cornish Picture Library/Paul Watts)

The 'Obby 'Oss (Collections/Brian Shuel)
A funeral at Dalmore (© Murdo Macleod)

MAPS

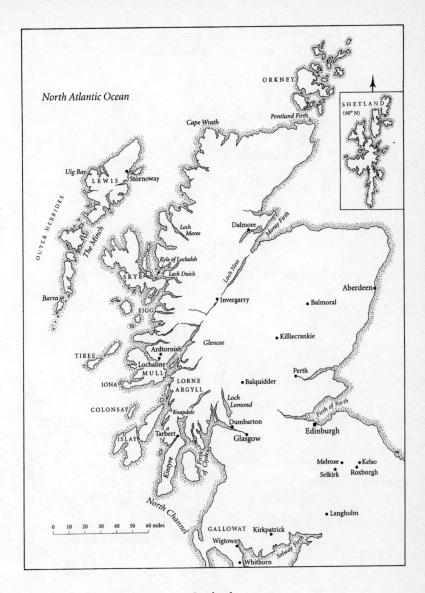

North Atlantic Ocean

ORKNEY

SHETLAND
(60° N)

Pentland Firth

Cape Wrath

Uig Bay

LEWIS Stornoway

Dalmore

Loch
Maree

OUTER HEBRIDES

The Minch

Kyle of Lochalsh

SKYE

Loch Duich

Loch Ness

Barra

Invergarry

Aberdeen

Balmoral

EIGG

Killiecrankie

Glencoe

TIREE

Ardtornish

Lochaline

MULL

Perth

IONA

LORNE

Balquidder

ARGYLL

Loch
Lomond

COLONSAY

Knapdale

Firth of Forth

Dumbarton

Edinburgh

ISLAY

Tarbert

Glasgow

Melrose Kelso

Selkirk Roxburgh

Kintyre

Firth of Clyde

North Channel

Langholm

0 10 20 30 40 50 60 miles

GALLOWAY Kirkpatrick

Wigtown

Solway Firth

Whithorn

Scotland

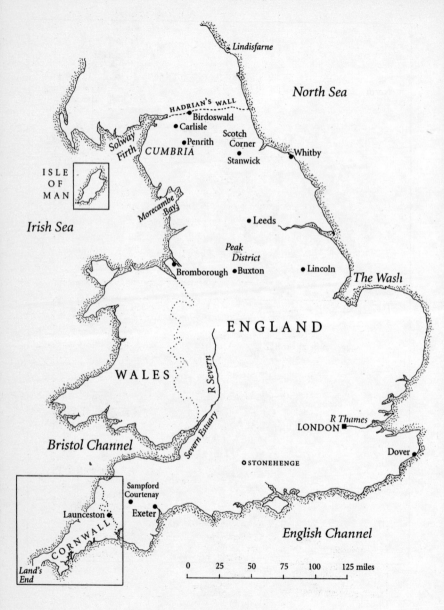

England

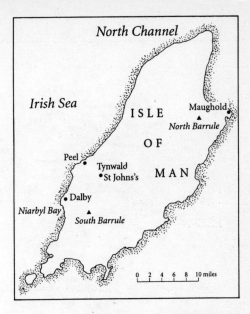

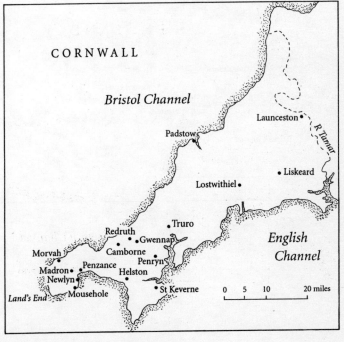

Isle of Man and Cornwall

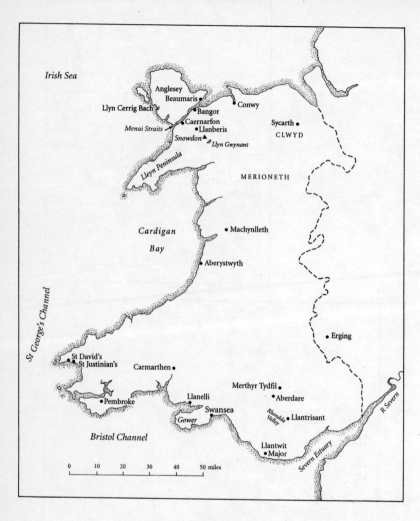

Wales

North Atlantic Ocean

Lough Swilly

North Channel

Ballycastle

CO DONEGAL

Derry CO
LONDONDERRY

Ballymena
Slemish
Antrim

Carrickfergus

U L S T E R

Donegal

CO TYRONE

Belfast

CO FERMANAGH

Portadown

Armagh

CO ARMAGH

Ardglass

Mayo

CO CAVAN

Irish Sea

C O N N A U G H T

Clew Bay

Kells

R Boyne

CO MEATH

Clonard

Dublin

Galway Bay

R Liffey

Kildare

Wicklow

Portlaoise

L E I N S T E R

Glendalough

R Shannon

Durrow

Carlow

Tullow

Aughrim

Limerick

Kilkenny

Enniscorthy

Oulart

Tipperary

Tara

New Ross

Rosslare

M U N S T E R

Waterford

St George's Channel

Dingle Peninsula

Skellig
Michael

BLARNEY
CASTLE

Cork

Kinsale

Bantry Bay

0 10 20 30 40 50 60 miles

Ireland

The Music of the Thing
As It Happened

THIS IS A HISTORY of whispers and forgetfulness, a story of how the memories and understandings of the Celtic peoples of Britain and Ireland almost faded into inconsequence. It is also a story of the struggle for control of these islands, of those who lost it, and how they continued to interact with the eventual winners, the English and the British. It attempts a lengthy definition of what it means and meant to be Celtic, to think and behave in ways that are different from the British habits of mind – and also often different from the simply Welsh, Irish, Scots, Manx, Cornish and English traditions. With the creation of parliaments in Scotland, Wales and Northern Ireland, it is timely to draw up a catalogue of cultural difference, a list of half-forgotten reasons for some of the tensions which have led to the break-up of Britain, the creation of a new and evolving union between England and her old Celtic colonies, and new relationships between those regions.

Two thousand years ago these tensions lay in the future. The farms, fortresses and harbours of these islands echoed to the speech of Celts who recited their history, managed their politics and conducted their business in recognizable versions of old Welsh and early Gaelic. Over the face of England and parts of lowland Scotland where the old Welsh language has long fled, ancient place names evoke those people who first described the rivers, lakes, mountains and marshlands of Britain. Another history of these islands, a Celtic history, often unclear but just catchable, can be heard in the quiet words and phrases of Welsh and Gaelic. For language is the most important yet elusive definition of what 'Celtic' meant then and means now: it is a matter of understanding and listening, and is certainly not a question of race or place of birth. First and foremost, the Celts of Britain are a speech community. At the time when an older version of Welsh was spoken over much of the island of Britain, Irish was the common tongue from Belfast Lough to Bantry Bay: Irish Gaelic and Welsh are cousin languages, sharing syntax and vocabulary, although over time they have become mutually unintelligible.

Sadly, and perhaps inevitably, the once-mighty languages of the West are dying: Cornish and Manx are whispered only in the mouths of a few enthusiasts; within a single generation Scots Gaelic will wither into a lexical curiosity; and Irish suffers from the lip service of a familiarity which hides wholesale decline and absence of interest. Only in Wales is there real strength and even resurgence. But the important observation is that these isles were once all Celtic, and even though politics continually pressed the autonomous Welsh and Gaelic speech communities ever farther westwards, they have survived. The languages which described Britain and Ireland more than 2,500 years ago still describe these places now, in a continuity unique in western Europe. As much as the decline of Celtic languages is to be regretted, their resilience ought to be marvelled at too. But it is not the languages themselves that matter, although to my ear their lyrical beauty is unmatched: it is the culture that they embody, the way of thinking about the world that they shape, and the stories they hold inside them that are crucial. These stories are beginning to slip quickly away into silence, and, worse, into a sickly mixture of cliché, quaintness, myth-history and something known as 'local colour'. Soon, perhaps by the middle of the twenty-first century, the history of Celtic Britain might depend so heavily on translation as to lose much of its texture, and become a thing seen through glass.

To find a way of seeing that history better we first need to forget national boundaries. Scotland, Ireland, the Isle of Man, Wales and England all make artificial distinctions across Celtic Britain and Ireland that blur the bigger picture and pull the focus in misleading directions. The cultural reality we need to see is that Stornoway and Penzance once had, and in many important ways still have, more in common with each other than they do with either Edinburgh or London. There is a unity of experience down the western edge of Britain which makes it a distinctive place, another country inside the one we think we know.

The sea is the unbroken link that binds this experience together, and the reason this book is entitled *The Sea Kingdoms*. For most of the last 3,000 years the sea was a better highway than any on land. This has created a cultural coherence which is is very old and far more widespread than is often realized. From around 500 BC Celtic languages were spoken down the length of the Atlantic littoral of Western Europe, and dialects of a common Celtic language were understood from as far south as the Algarve up to the northern coasts of Scotland. Celtiberian in Portugal and Spain, and Gaulish and Lepontic in France and central Europe all disappeared during Roman rule and subsequent barbarian invasions, but for at least 500 years and probably much longer there existed a common Celtic sea-going culture along the Atlantic coasts which also reached deep inland.

Archaeologists have confirmed that for at least two millennia before the Romans began to expand their empire, there was regular maritime trade on a well-established series of networks within Atlantic Europe, particularly around its subsidiary gulfs and seas such as the Bay of Biscay, the Brittany coast, Portugal, the English Channel, the Severn Estuary and the Irish Sea. Artefacts traded in these areas were transported up major navigable rivers and, passing through several pairs of hands, have sometimes been found more than a thousand miles from their point of manufacture. Pottery, axe-heads, weapons and much that was perishable made journeys on a scale which surprises us now. In the wake of these early ships a great deal followed: not only a commonly understood language, but also ideas about politics, religion and technology.

So that the dynamic of Celtic culture – and its survival in modern versions in the west of Britain and Ireland – can be better understood, this story needs to be seen from a vantage point not on the land, looking out to sea, but from the sea, looking towards the land. And so that it is easier for us to understand how the Sea Kingdoms of the West understood themselves, this tale takes the form of a double journey: through geography from the Isle of Lewis to the Cornish coast, and through history from earliest times to the present day.

*   *   *

Looking back over the immense sweep of all that has happened in these islands, a constant theme insists on its place. For a multitude of reasons, some of them accidental, the story of the Celtic peoples is the story of the war for Britain, and of those who lost it, again and again. The Romans, the Anglo-Saxons, the Normans, the English and the British (including many Scots, Welsh and Irish Britons) won that war, and by the eighteenth century had colonized all of these islands. Their version of history was bound to dominate and be believed – even by the defeated. And because the Celtic peoples of Britain and Ireland had comparatively little written culture until recently, an alternative version of events can be difficult to find. This book is not an exhaustive and wearying recital of defeat, or a tear-stained harking back to a black list of injustices, but rather a journey through what remains and a search for another way of seeing the past. The story of the Celts of Britain and Ireland is still whispered, can still just be heard if we push aside our misconceptions, look again at the map of Britain, and see it differently. For too long our history has consisted of London talking to Britain, and the inevitable outcome is that the United Kingdom is too readily seen as a natural point towards which all narratives should flow. Celtic Britain did not die when the Angles, Saxons and other Germanic tribes invaded and settled most of what is now England and lowland Scotland: it was only defeated, marginalized and ignored.

In order to understand better why British history has been skewed in this way, we should never forget that the early Celtic society of Britain was non-literate, not illiterate (for that implies something deficient) and that it relied on memory and recital. For a hundred generations, stories were told in the circle of firelight: the early peoples of Britain listened to their history. Spoken and heard rather than written and read, many of the stories of the men and women who were here before the English have disappeared into the night air. The tales of Celtic Britain, of the west, seem now to be of the twilight, of dying languages and minorities, of emigration and loss, of quaintness and yesterday. And of derision, for to prejudiced eyes the Celts of Britain have also become comic figures: hicks from a rural margin bewildered by the sophistication of the modern world. The term 'Irish' for a way of saying or doing something implies eccentricity at best and stupidity at worst, while the Scottish Highlanders are sometimes viewed by urban Scotland as reservation Indians, much given to drink and idleness. There is no word in

Gaelic, joke the Lowlanders, which adequately describes the urgency of mañana.

But in Scotland, Ireland, Man, Wales and Cornwall a new future is dawning. The old imperial monolith of the United Kingdom is rapidly crumbling as England's first colonies rediscover what they were and realize what they might become once the corrosive habit of blaming the English for everything has withered into disuse. There is a new hunger for a different history, one which is not refracted through a metrocentric prism, and seeks a new telling of the stories of old places. With only the annual passions of international rugby matches, the interminable and inexplicable shedding of Irish and British blood, and occasional surges in the popularity of step-dancing and Gaelic music to go on, the English, by contrast, have every right to their indifference or bafflement. With at least a millennium of resentment to draw on, the Celts of Britain, the losers, have wasted much time in defining themselves primarily as un- or anti-English.

Better surely to seek out and piece together the stories of this largely non-literate, politically marginalized society. Power passed to those who wrote down their history and had an interest in ignoring the stories of the Celts or changing them into a new shape to fit their purposes, or condemning them to a minor posterity. Because it is difficult to read about the history of the west of Britain, we need to listen hard for its whispers, intuit connections and try to remember what has almost been forgotten. In a translation of a Gaelic phrase, we should listen for the music of the thing as it happened.

For at least ten years I have kept notes of what seemed to be phrases of incidental music: not a diary, but more a set of memos to remind me of incidents, places and anecdotes that seemed to be significant, often because they told a familiar story from a different viewpoint, often the viewpoint of the defeated. The battle of Culloden has an iconic place in Scottish and Celtic history. In 1746 the handsome, charismatic and romantic figure of Bonnie Prince Charlie led his army of Highlanders to a disastrous defeat, what a Scottish aristocrat called 'the end of an old song'. Much of the romance was attached to Prince Charles himself and the failure to restore the Jacobite dynasty, and too little attention was paid to the fate of the men who fought for him on the moor near Culloden House.

In May 1990 I went to visit the Gaelic Further Education College at Sabhal Mor Ostaig in the Sleat Peninsula in Skye and made a note of a long conversation with the late and much-missed Donnie Campbell, who used to work there. What follows is an outline of the story he told me about what happened before the battle at Culloden. It appears in no written version I could find but that does not dim its power or damage its authenticity.

When the Highland army reached Inverness in April 1746, it was pursued by government forces commanded by the Duke of Cumberland and supported by Rear-Admiral Byng's fleet in the Moray Firth, a well-equipped, properly provisioned modern army which, throughout the Jacobite Rebellion, had never managed to stand its ground and resist the furious charges of the regiments of clansmen raised by Prince Charles Edward Stuart. It seemed that elemental savagery had won at Prestonpans and Falkirk and would continue to win. Even though his generals advised a guerrilla campaign in the mountains, the Prince chose to turn his undefeated army and fight on Drumossie Moor, near Culloden House. It was to be the last pitched battle fought on British soil.

At about eleven o'clock in the morning of 16 April, lookouts from Clan Cameron and Clan Chattan peered through the sleeting rain and saw the columns of the government army advancing to the moor. The waiting ranks of Highlanders stood to and watched the march of the scarlet and white silk standards, listened to the fife and drum and the tramp of soldiers forming up in lines abreast to face them. The government commanders rode up and down the line to encourage their men, some of whom had run for their lives as the Highlanders charged at the battle of Falkirk only three months before. They reminded them of their tactics and implored them to stand fast. Some government soldiers began to shout abuse at the enemy who stood across the moor, 500 yards away.

The clansmen shouted their own taunts and some clashed their broad-swords against their targes, but mostly they watched and waited. Standing in family groups, fathers with their sons behind them, uncles with their nephews at their shoulder, cousins side by side, many were silent, knowing what was to come. Leaders of a Gaelic army which relied entirely on the terrifying power of a furious charge always set the most experienced and older men in front, culminating in the chief of the name. The Gaels believed that courage flowed down the generations. As they stood in the heather and watched the redcoats prepare for battle, some men sang the Twentieth Psalm but, as Donnie emphasized, others did something entirely unique for a Highland army. They recited their genealogy: '*Is mise mac Ruari, mac Iain, mac Domhnaill.*' Some men could go back through the generations for hundreds of years. While the government soldiers were shouting abuse and challenges, listening to their officers and checking their equipment, the clansmen were remembering why they had come to fight. For their families, for their history and the land from which neither was divisible, they stood quietly on the moor with only their shields and broadswords and all their courage.

Once the government army had set up their artillery, they began a murderous cannonade. Round shot ploughed through the Highland lines, but Prince Charles would not give the signal to attack. For more than an hour the clansmen shouted over their shoulders begging for '*Claidheamh Mor!*', the order to charge. Unable to stand still any longer under the incessant cannon fire, Clan Chattan finally broke away. Mackintoshes, MacBeans and McGillivrays roared their war cries '*Loch Moy!*' and '*Dunmaglass!*' as they raced towards the redcoats. And when they saw that Clan Chattan was away, Clan Cameron, the Atholl Brigade and then the Appin Stewarts broke into the charge. Donald Cameron of Locheil raised his broadsword and shouted, '*Is sinne clann Thearlaich!*', 'We are the children of Charles!'

As Prince Charles peered through the smoke he saw his clan regiments blown to bits by disciplined musket fire and grapeshot. Few Highlanders reached the government lines. Of the handful who broke through, John McGillivray killed twelve men and then ran on to meet the battalions in the rear where he died. Gillies MacBean, an officer of Clan Chattan, was repeatedly stabbed by bayonet thrusts and his leg broken by grapeshot, but he still broke through the front line before the second cut him down. But they were too few and quickly isolated. When the charge failed the Stewarts and Camerons retreated, walking backwards and glaring at the redcoats in defiance.

Gaelic Scotland began to die at Culloden. The repressive aftermath of the battle was the beginning of a long end for the clans, their culture and their language. But what struck me forcibly about Donnie Campbell's story was that the significant difference between the two armies was not their equipment – modern against medieval – or their tactics – discipline against a furious charge – but their reasons for fighting. One took the field for the maintenance of a Protestant and increasingly constitutional monarchy, for a version of progress and for regular pay and rations. The other fought for its sense of itself. Behind the clansmen who recited their genealogy stood the ghosts of their past, and in their war cries were the names of their places. Within a generation of Culloden the great emigrations to the New World had begun to convert the Highlands from a working landscape into mere scenery, and with them the departure of memory and understanding began to convert the Highlanders' stories into riddles or pastiche, as a drowsy nostalgia was substituted for a badly understood past.

Culloden was a decisive moment in the war for Britain. The Duke of Cumberland's victory finally killed off the possibility of a Jacobite monarchy and all it stood for, and it secured the Hanoverian progression towards an ever more compliant kingship. It was not the last battle, by any means, to be fought between Celtic soldiers and British armies, but it was the last time that cultural difference and political and military opposition stood glaring at each other across a battlefield on British soil. In thinking of the clansmen reciting their genealogy, and the government army shouting abuse and listening again to their battle orders, determined to stand their ground, it is not difficult to hear the music of Celtic history as it happened.

Culloden offers a partial definition of what it is to be Celtic, but when a history of the Celtic peoples of Britain is promised, it is only sensible at the outset to offer a basic framework for a broader definition of 'Celtic'. It can be an elusive and often useless description sliding between items as diverse as brooches, beer, music, dancing, harps and languages, and it needs to be better focused and more carefully assembled if it is to serve any useful purpose. The immediate difficulty is that the question of what Celtic means has often been asked and answered from the outside with a set of observed and sometimes even imposed defining qualities. In an implied and sometimes overt contrast with their own culture, Roman historians listed and repeated Celtic characteristics over a long period. Several consistent themes are obvious, as is a noticeable tendency to convert what might be thought of as virtues into excesses or even vices.

The Romans recognized, with awe, two often related Celtic capacities, for drink and sex. It appeared (and still appears) to commentators that the Celts' appetite for alcohol was extraordinary, limited only by its supply in some recorded cases. Allied to that was a parallel fondness for love-making, mostly between men and women, and at certain times in the year between men and women who were barely known to each other. Sadly, this last has not survived down the centuries, and Celtic Britain has become markedly more straightlaced as time has gone on. This appears to be a direct consequence of the splutterings, thunderings and fulminations of strict Presbyterians and Nonconformists against such abandonment.

Religious devotion joins the list, but in a less obviously traceable way. The early Celts of Britain were seen as devout and their Druidical faith (its details albeit imperfectly understood) inspired and thoroughly informed their culture. Celtic soldiers were fabled for their bravery on the battlefield, an attribute encouraged by their absolute belief in the afterlife – the Otherworld. That all-pervading devotion was later transferred to Christianity. When the Reformation replaced the Catholic church with a Protestant faith that could be adopted by each Celtic nation as its own, this devotion resurfaced in Presbyterian Scotland and Northern Ireland, Nonconformist Wales and Cornwall. The present-day fundamentalists of the Western Isles and Ulster, and the Baptists and Methodists of Wales and Cornwall are a persistent witness to a long tradition.

The links between the Celts and their land are another central trait of their culture. When the clansmen in the Highland army at Culloden recited their genealogy and roared their war cries, they showed how tightly bound up people and families were with the land they lived on and the seas that lapped its shores. To say that the Celts of Britain have a close affinity with the land and the sea is to underplay a near-umbilical connection. The huge skies of the Atlantic shore, the rose and gold of sunsets dying in the west, the bleakness of the land and the majesty of land and sea together pierce the hearts of those who are born there. Even if they leave, the west never leaves them.

Julius Caesar offered one of the first assessments of the Celts in his influential *De Bello Gallico*, written to glorify his successful campaign to subdue Gaul between 58 and 54 BC. Like many Roman writers, he commented particularly on the eloquence of the Celts. Often using highly coloured language, flecked with the devices of poetry, Celtic orators could construct long passages in their heads and deliver them without a break, a note, or a reminder of any sort. Much later, during the reign of the Emperor Constantine I (305–337 AD), a Celtic prince from the tribe of the Aedui in Gaul came to ask the Roman Senate for military help against invaders. A contemporary historian offered a sense of how comfortable he was when he addressed the Conscript Fathers: 'the Aeduan prince, haranguing the Senate, leaning on his long shield'.

Such sustained eloquence was made possible by a prodigious memory, also recognized by the Romans as peculiarly Celtic. Clearly, an organized and instantly accessible store of knowledge is required by the likes of the Aeduan prince, or anyone speaking at length without notes. Nowadays we find it difficult to comprehend the sheer quantity of material remembered by the Celts, since we are surrounded by stored knowledge in every conceivable form, but they could remember vast amounts, much of it in precise detail. Until the modern period and the beginning of publishing in Celtic languages, culture was to be found almost entirely in an oral form which was, in turn, sustained by a memory underpinned by a particular arrangement of ideas and facts. With its devices of metre, rhyme, repetition, alliteration and onomatopoeia, we forget that poetry was originally no more than an aid to memory and better story-telling. Gaelic, Welsh, Manx and Cornish are still full of everyday poetry, and accurate descriptions of what might seem to us non-essential detail. Remnants of these habits still exist in English, and we use mnemonics to remember lists and rhyme to remind us of the most everyday things. For example, who can remember how many days are in each month without beginning inwardly to recite, 'Thirty days hath September, April, June and November'? And in popular music we continue to use the ancient story-telling device of the chorus. When Sir Walter Scott was collecting previously unrecorded ballads in the 1790s for his *Minstrelsy of the Scottish Border*, some had as many as seventy-five verses, but between each one the chorus was always repeated by the listeners. Part of the reason for that was to allow time for the reciter or singer of the ballad to remember what came next, and his or her memory was cued by hearing the rhythm and metre of the chorus.

Genuine Celtic eloquence, sadly, is no longer seen as a virtue. During the long period when England grew into Britain, oral culture became gradually discredited and was replaced with the perceived greater certainties of ink and paper. Not only did Anglo-Saxon historians like Bede of

Jarrow commit an English version of history to writing, thereby giving it permanence and authority, but the engines of government also came to depend on signed, witnessed and dated texts. The Doomsday Book of 1086 is a thumping affirmation of the view that nothing is true unless it is written down. We have inherited that approach to the world, and in our courts a written and signed statement will always be preferred to reported speech, or hearsay.

But some remnants of a different way of thinking are still observable in the west. On 5 July 2000 I went to the Isle of Man to attend the annual meeting of Tynwald so that I could listen to the oldest parliament in Europe do as the name originally meant – talk.

About six miles inland from the little town of Peel on the west coast of the Isle of Man, there is a grassy mound. Shaped like a tiered wedding cake with steps cut into one side, it rises in a series of circular terraces up to a small dais at the top. Sitting at a natural north–south, east–west crossroads for the island, it is known in Manx Gaelic as Cronk y Keeillown, the Hill of the Chapel of St John, by very few people, and by very many as Tynwald. A Norse word meaning 'assembly-field', the grassy mound is where the Isle of Man parliament meets in ceremonial session on 5 July, the date of Old Midsummer.

Norsemen began to raid the coasts of Britain and Ireland in the late eighth century and, quickly understanding the key strategic position of the island, they removed and almost obliterated the Celtic hegemony and established the Kingdom of Man. The Norse settled all over the Sea Kingdoms and their Tynwalds survive as place names as far apart as Galloway and Dingwall, the old county town of Ross-shire. Even though ultimate political control of the Western Isles and Man remained nominally, and occasionally actually, with the kings of Norway into the thirteenth century, the Norse settlers were absorbed into Celtic society, and began to speak Celtic languages. They added powerful ingredients to British Celtic culture. One of these was the Lochaber axe used at Bannockburn in 1314, and another was the Tynwald.

The occasion of the annual meeting of the Isle of Man legislature is mostly for show now, but before 1919 it had a real purpose. For many centuries previously, the Tynwald had listened very closely to two men talking from memory. They were the Deemsters, or judges, and, until forced to write it down in 1690, they retained all the common law of Man in their memories. Each year they recited it in Manx Gaelic and added any new measures which had been agreed in the interim. Until 1919 no new law in Man could be enacted unless it had been recited at Tynwald by the Deemsters. It was called 'Breast-Law' because that it where it was learned and locked for safe-keeping. Although these ancient functions have been mostly forgotten, the phrase 'to learn by heart' is a memory of what they did, as is the verb 'to deem', or to judge.

The survival of an oral recital of the law as a functioning part of government until 1919 is remarkable, particularly in an area of life where written title and written proof are seen as absolutely integral. The Deemsters still perform a truncated version of their ancient role at Tynwald and Manx is still spoken; its use is now nominal, but ceremonies and symbols can still be powerful. At the Tynwald for 2000 Prince Charles sat on top of the little hill, under a prudent tented canopy, as the titular presiding presence. He had only a few formulaic phrases to utter but, to the great embarrassment of the Manx government sitting below him, his microphone refused to work, and, seen but not heard, the Prince took no part in the proceedings. Some Manxmen expressed great satisfaction that allegedly faulty technology had prevented the participation of someone who should in any case have no part in Tynwald, since it was pressure from the English crown which had long ago forced their oral legal culture to be set down on paper.

This cultural shift also radically changed attitudes over a long period. Julius Caesar and other Roman commentators believed Celtic eloquence to be a great virtue and were regularly impressed by the fluency and power of the Celts who spoke to them (presumably using Latin as a second language). Nowadays, we have almost wholly converted this virtue into a vice. English-speaking society not only mistrusts eloquence but has little time for it. Telling phrases like 'he talks a good game' or 'running off at the mouth' show how deep these attitudes now go. Blarney Castle near Cork gave its name not to eloquence or witty speech but to a vapid flow of verbiage that amounts to very little of substance, according to the Elizabethans who coined the term. In recent years the press treatment of the former Labour Leader, Neil Kinnock, was instructive. A Welsh politician and public speaker of genuine passion and colour in the tradition of Aneurin Bevan and David Lloyd George,

Kinnock was regularly pilloried by the Anglo-Saxon press as a 'Welsh Windbag'. It struck a chord and stuck.

For many centuries English and English speakers legislated, punished, discouraged or ignored those who preferred the languages of their fathers to that of their eastern or southern neighbours. For those who held fast onto their Gaelic and Welsh and quietly passed them to their children, their sense of their own languages became ever more intimate and inward, specific to places and to people, and the bonds of family and shared memory. They turned towards the Atlantic and away from the east. More than English, written down everywhere, Celtic languages were, for many speakers, written down nowhere. Even now, older Welsh and Gaelic native speakers with wide vocabularies have great difficulty in spelling and writing all but the most everyday words, because Celtic languages live most vividly in the minds and the mouths of their speech communities and far less in cold print on white paper. Consequently they have a sensual love of the words and phrases for themselves: the mouth-filling syllables of simple vocabulary, the everyday dramas of cadence, onomatopoeia and rhythm. The Celts of Britain truly love their ancient languages, call them mighty and beautiful, and have fought hard to keep them alive.

On 27 January 2000 there was a story on the leader pages of the *Independent* that exemplifies the power of English as a language. Recently released statistics showed that because the Internet and virtually the entire information revolution is being conducted in English, the performance of national economies is likely to improve or worsen in direct relation to how well their populations understand the language. Obviously the USA, the old Commonwealth countries and Britain were best placed, but not far behind were the Scandinavian nations and the Low Countries because they have a long-standing educational policy of teaching English as a second language. In the greatest difficulty, predicted the analysts, would be the Far Eastern economies like Japan and China (with the important exception of Hong Kong), because both their languages and methods of writing are most distant in every way from English.

Driving through the countryside of north Wales I began to marvel at rather than mourn the state of the language that lives nearest to English. Welsh has not only survived its dangerous proximity but its speech community is large, numbering more than 500,000. Bilingual road signs with the Welsh names printed above the English are only the most visible evidence of what amounts to a triumph of stubbornness and love. Of all the Celtic parts of Britain, Wales has the longest border with England and it is very near to large English-speaking population centres, from Liverpool and Manchester down to Birmingham and Bristol. Significantly, Wales became the first thoroughly colonized part of Celtic Britain when the Anglo-Norman Kings of England determined to make it their own.

Edward I was an implacable enemy of the Celts, determined to conquer the Welsh, who bitterly resisted him in a series of wars. In 1282 Llywelyn II, Prince of Wales, rose for a second time in rebellion. Edward was anxious to avoid another expensive punitive invasion, and he allowed John Pecham, the Archbishop of Canterbury, to intervene and to see if he could secure a negotiated peace. Pecham spent three days at Llywelyn's headquarters, near Caernarfon, but failed to find any common ground. Finally, he offered to attempt to persuade Edward I to grant Llywelyn a pension and an honourable position at the English court if he would only yield all his territory to Edward. Given the probable outcome of any war, it might have seemed to the English negotiators like a generous offer. It did not seem so to the Welsh. Not only did Llywelyn refuse but, lest there be any doubt, the leading men of North Wales wrote this letter to Pecham:

> The Prince should not throw aside his inheritance and that of his ancestors in Wales and accept land in England, a country with whose language, way of life, laws and customs he is unfamiliar . . . Let this be clearly understood: his council will not permit him to yield . . . and even if the Prince wishes to transfer [his people] into the hands of the king, they will not do homage to any stranger as they are wholly unacquainted with his language, his way of life and his laws.

Written in 1282, it is a defiant and eloquent letter, but its significance is not so much in its dignity but the fact that even at this early stage the Welsh are in no doubt about the importance of their language. In the passage above it comes emphatically first, before way of life, customs and laws – twice. The Welsh have long understood that without their language their nation will fade from the map of history. In recent times they have gone to extremes of violence, civil disobedience and even the threatened suicide of the Plaid Cymru MP, Gwynfor Evans, to protect it.

It is an extraordinary survival. The Celtic languages of Britain have outlasted the Roman occupation, the invasions of the Anglo-Saxons and the Normans and now, it seems, the onslaught of the Internet and a global economy driven by an understanding of English. Because Welsh is such an old language and because it described Britain first, it carries a version of the history of the whole island inside it. The words in *Y Geiriadur Mawr*, *The Big Dictionary*, are the quiet transports of memory, and if we listen hard to what the Welsh say, we can hear an echo of Britain talking 2,000 years ago.

From Caernarfon I drove down through Wales, crossed the Severn Bridge into the West Country and made for north Cornwall and the little fishing village of Padstow. It was 1 May, the date of an ancient fertility festival. There, I discovered immediately that Celtic Britain today is sometimes far from quiet, but even aggressive and exuberant, and certainly defensive.

'Fuck off! Why don't you people fuck off out of here? We don't want you. This is our day. This is our thing. Fuck off!' The young man might have been eighteen, certainly no older. Clutching a bottle of American lager and clearly very drunk, he put his face so close to mine I thought he was going to head-butt me or even pull out a knife. Instead, he began to sway slightly and was easily persuaded by his mates to back off.

It was nine o'clock in the morning and the narrow streets of Padstow were jammed with people. Perhaps more than 5,000 had come to celebrate the festival. Each year on May Day, out of the door of the Golden Lion pub, a creature comes back from the past. This is the 'Obby 'Oss, and he has made the long journey from an ancient culture to dance for a day around Padstow. Although he is accompanied by supporters and musicians, the 'Obby 'Oss really dances to the music of time, for this is a fertility festival of a sort that used to be celebrated all over Britain but has survived nowhere as completely as in Padstow. There is a wildness, a strangeness and a sense, often fuelled by drink, of abandonment which seems not to fit, to be oddly un-British in such a traditional setting as this, a Cornish fishing village. Yet in truth, the 'Obby 'Oss could not be more of this place, could not be more essentially British. It is much older than many of the ceremonies we now think of as traditional, like the coronation or the state opening of parliament. For the 'Obby 'Oss comes spinning out of the labyrinth of Celtic memory. More alive, vivid and noisier than any solemn royal or parliamentary ceremony acted out in London, the 'Oss is a Celtic ritual played in the streets and lanes of today's Padstow.

Padstow is an old harbour town that tumbles down to the sea on the west side of the Camel estuary in north Cornwall. During the winter it huddles around the quays from where a few fishing boats sail out in search of an inshore catch. It makes its real money from tourists, but the annual dance of the 'Obby 'Oss is not put on for their benefit.

On 1 May the centre of the village is decked out in swags of greenery, mainly the cut boughs of the sycamore tree and cowslip and bluebell flowers. The old country rhyme 'Here we go gathering nuts in May' has long baffled naturalists, since there are no nuts to be gathered in May, it being much too early in the year. The phrase is a corruption of what still goes on in Padstow and should read 'Here we go gathering knots in May' – knots or bunches of leaves and flowers. The English phrase 'to go a-maying' means approximately the same thing.

The 'Oss dances under the knots of sycamore, lunging and swerving in front of the press of people. The costume is made from a large circular hoop covered in black canvas with skirts reaching down to the ground, and it is worn by a strong and agile man. Fitted on top is a strange pointed head that looks African in origin, like a witch-doctor's mask, and is decorated with red-and-white ribbons, the colours of spring and resurgent life.

The 'Oss dances three times around different parts of the village and, as the day goes on, the pubs do better and better. By five o'clock there are hundreds of people, perhaps a thousand, a good deal the worse for drink. Or perhaps better. In the twelfth century a clerical historian called Gerald of Wales listed eloquence, stubbornness, bravery and an immoderate love of intoxicating drink as Welsh characteristics. He could easily have extended his definition to cover all the Celtic regions of Britain, definitely including Cornwall and Padstow on May Day. The resentment of the drunken young man shown to me on the morning was extreme but not untypical. The 'Obby 'Oss is their festival, it is something they do for themselves and for their own reasons. It is most emphatically not quaint or something performed by the natives for the charabanc trade. The 'Oss is not a comfortable, categorized hunk of heritage. It is not nice, and very Celtic in its feel. With all its abandonment and energy, it is probably the one event in all Britain and Ireland most resembling a Celtic festival day: 1 May is the date of the ancient festival of Beltane. When it falls on a weekday there are many fewer visitors: Padstow prefers that because the 'Oss has always danced for them, and for no-one else.

Reckless bravery allied to a fiery disposition is yet another combination of characteristics applied to the Celts, although it is not exclusively applied to them. Spanish footballers, Italian prima donnas and even some southern French film actors are sometimes believed to be governed by a Latin temperament, which amounts to much the same thing. The English do not see themselves like that: they find the solid and unflappable figure of John Bull a far more satisfying self-image. Altogether cooler and less impulsive, they believe that dogged determination, consistency and calculation make them different and, without often stating it bluntly, more successful as a culture. One English rugby commentator recently made a good joke about an Irish player who kept giving away penalties and points through persistent flashes of anger. 'A temperamental fellow', he remarked, '50% temper and 50% mental'.

From their earliest contacts the Celts were admired by the Romans for their courage in battle, but that was often tempered by criticism for being 'war-mad' and needlessly provocative and bellicose. This was a persistent observation made throughout British history: in the medieval period, during the Jacobite rebellions and by the English commanders of the late-eighteenth-century British imperial armies that were overwhelmingly recruited from the Celtic west. P. G. Wodehouse's crack that it was not difficult to tell the difference between a Scotsman with a grievance and a ray of sunshine still has, with its mixture of lofty condescension and accuracy, the power to produce precisely the reaction that confirms it. The Romans and Greeks agreed with the rugby commentator and, in the face of Celtic excess, were just as phlegmatic as the English. The historian and geographer Strabo, writing about the Celts of Europe at the beginning of the first century AD, stated:

The whole nation that is nowadays called Gallic or Galatic is war-mad, and both high spirited and quick for battle although otherwise simple and not uncouth. Because of this, if the Gauls are provoked they tend to rush into a battle all together, without concealment or forward planning. For anyone who wants to out-wit them, they are therefore easy to deal with, since it is enough to provoke them into a rage by any means at all, at any time and in any place. It will then be found that they are willing to risk everything they have with nothing to rely on other than their sheer physical strength and courage.

Approximately 1,800 years later Strabo's observations were born out almost to the letter. The rebellion of 1798 is little known outside Ireland and yet it was a remarkably savage event. Lasting only five weeks of the early summer and focused mainly in Leinster and Ulster, it saw 30,000 people killed out of a total Irish population of 5 million. This compares to the contemporary French Revolution where, between 1789 and 1804, 25,000 people died out of a total population of thirty million. The guillotine, the Reign of Terror and the Storming of the Bastille are all properly famous and powerful symbols, but the astonishing concen-tration of carnage in the green summer fields and roadside ditches of Leinster and Ulster has been virtually forgotten beyond the Irish Sea, even though Ireland suffered a comparable reign of terror, during which its people were forced, by extreme provocation, to echo Strabo's descrip-tion of reckless bravery.

Partly inspired by the French Revolution and the American Revol-ution of 1776 before that, the Irish Rebellion of 1798 arose out of deep political dissatisfaction. Since the Elizabethan conquest, the Catholic majority and the Presbyterian minority had been progressively disenfran-chized to the extent that almost all power lay in the hands of a Protestant minority which made up less than 10 per cent of the population. A Presbyterian called Theobald Wolfe Tone and others formed the Society of United Irishmen in the 1790s not only to argue a political case but also to promote the idea of unity across a growing sectarian divide. At about this time the Irish tricolour became popular. It was an imitation of the French Revolutionary tricolour, but the choice of colours reflected the ideals of the United Irishmen: green and orange were for Catholic and Protestant, while the white band between them was for peace.

In the years leading up to the rebellion of 1798, there was little enough of that. It seemed as though the colonial government in Dublin Castle was deliberately attempting to spark a popular rebellion so that it could put it down severely and thereafter establish a tighter grip on Ireland. Through a well-organized network of informants, the government knew a great deal about the plans of the United Irishmen, and either to provoke or discourage thoughts of an uprising, troops embarked on a horrifying reign of terror. When they caught suspected rebels a favourite prelude to interrogation was pitch-capping. First, gunpowder was sprinkled on the suspect's head. Then a canvas skull-cap was soaked in tar, his hands were tied and the cap was crammed onto his head and set alight. When the cap was ripped off the victim was scalped. An Irish historian told me that he had listened to recorded interviews with old ladies recalling men who had suffered pitch-capping being allowed by the clergy to keep handkerchiefs on their scarred heads while in church.

Events were driven hard by such excesses, and in the early summer of 1798 the long-awaited rebellion finally erupted. The core organization of the United Irishmen had been betrayed in Dublin by informers, and without proper co-ordination, decent equipment or French support, the rising was bound for ultimate failure. However, the rebels had some initial success in Leinster, south of Dublin. Huge but poorly armed rebel forces gathered on hilltops. One of the key battles was fought on Vinegar Hill, above the town of Enniscorthy in Leinster. The rebels were commanded by a priest, Father John Murphy from nearby Boolavogue, who had great leadership qualities but a limited knowledge of strategy or tactics. His camp was quickly surrounded by a very large government army. On 21 June more than 20,000 troops attacked the rebels and, moving their cannon expertly up the slopes, they raked the hill with devastating volleys. Although the Irish rebels had a handful of cannon and some muskets, they relied, like the Highlanders at Culloden fifty years before, on the ancient tactic of an all-out charge. Armed only with 12-foot pikes, they launched desperate downhill charges at the cannon and lines of redcoats. Women and children fought alongside their men on Vinegar Hill but their undoubted physical courage could make little impression on the advance of the disciplined troops below them. After two hours of slaughter, Father Murphy directed a retreat. A gap in the encirclement was found and, fighting a rearguard action, the rebels poured through it, leaving more than 500 dead on the hill.

Soon after the battle at Vinegar Hill, Father Murphy was captured. In the market square in Tullow, County Carlow, he was tied to a triangle, the shirt was ripped off his back, and he was lashed repeatedly as officers interrogated him for his identity. Murphy refused to say anything and was taken from the whipping frame and hanged on a mobile gallows. When his body was taken down, his head was hacked off. Some soldiers set it on a spike in the railings outside the court-house and then stuffed his torso in a tar barrel which they set alight. One of the houses in Tullow market square was occupied by a prosperous Catholic family, the Callaghans. The soldiers set the blazing barrel outside their house and, pushing past their children, went inside. 'There could be no objection in this house to the incense of a priest,' they shouted as they forced open all the windows to let in 'the holy smoke'.

The Callaghan family still live in Tullow. The appalling cruelty meted out to Father Murphy happened on their doorstep. The story of these dreadful events is vivid, and part of a personal history, part of a real inherited memory rather than a background text from a distant past. The terror happened not to historical figures in a misty landscape long, long ago but to real people, many of whose descendants still live in the same places and whose family memories are sharp. In short, the practice of pitch-capping is not just a barbarity from a primitive and less civilized age, it affects the present. In Ireland the past is not another country, it happened near at hand, in the fields and hills of Leinster, in the market places of small towns in Carlow.

By contrast, in England a Celtic past is certainly thought to have happened in another country. Despite the unquestioned fact that Old Welsh was spoken all over England (and southern Scotland), many English historians have some difficulty with this and argue that the language should be called Cumbric, British or Romano-British and so on. This academic diffidence obscures the fact that Welsh is the modern language much the closest to the old speech of Britain, and that it offers more than an echo of how our ancestors talked and sang. For that reason, and for clarity, Old Welsh is the most straightforward label. It is also a handy reminder that not everything told in Welsh happened in Wales.

In the middle of England the Peak District is the geological full stop at the southern end of the Pennine Chain. Place names often remember periods of history recorded nowhere else, and Pennine comes from the Welsh word *pen* for head. Only fifteen miles from the edge of the

Manchester conurbation, Buxton sits at the heart of the Peak District and is a spa town well known for the waters of its therapeutic well. Nowadays Buxton water is bottled and marketed all over the world and its production is an example of a long historical continuity. The Romans called the little town Aquae Arnemetiae, which translates as the 'waters of She who stands out before the Sacred Grove'. The well itself is now named after St Anne, but its derivation is probably from a Christianized version of Anu, a Celtic goddess name. The Celtic peoples of Britain venerated wells, believing that gods and goddesses inhabited them and also that, springing naturally from the bowels of the earth, they were portals to the Otherworld.

In the Peak District, and particularly in the Wye Valley below Buxton, ancient Celtic wells are venerated every summer in the rituals of well-dressing. Sanitized and Christianized, these are ceremonies more than 2,000 years old which still take place in twenty-one towns and villages. It is a clear and unambiguous survival of Celtic culture in the sort of difficult upcountry where Celtic customs and language lasted longest in England. The wells are adorned with garlands of flowers, and in some places women go out at dawn on May Day to tie simple posies and swags of greenery on the trees and shrubs around them. As in Padstow, the white-and-red ribbons of reawakening life are also tied on. Throughout the summer the wells are dressed in different ways: some villages build large 10-foot-high panels which are covered with elaborate patterns of living plants and flowers and erected behind or at the side of the spring. After the flowers have been put in place, there are often small festivals and local events to celebrate the coming summer and welcome the return of the sun.

Buxton and the Peak District are rarely included in any description or definition of Celtic Britain, but the survival of well-dressing and other rituals argue strongly that they should be. Much of England retains some connection, however elusive, with the culture that existed over most of Britain before the Romans, the Anglo-Saxons and the Normans came. Again, place names show this: London, Dover, Leeds and Lincoln are all Celtic in origin. The part played by England in the stories of the Sea Kingdoms is both overwhelmingly obvious – it would be perverse and also impossible to tell the stories without near-constant reference to the interaction between the Celts and their powerful and populous neighbours – and complex and subtle. There is a Celtic England which is not the England we know, a layer of experience not often seen as part of a traditional sense of Englishness.

Although it would be easy to allow a description of the dynamic of this relationship to slide into a maudlin recital of cultures crushed and lost, it is neither the most informative nor the most accurate approach to take. England's role is not simply that of the island bully ruthlessly imposing an Anglocentric uniformity on the enfeebled Celts of the west. History is rarely so simple. It is essential to remember that some of England's native culture has its roots in a half-forgotten past often obscured by a Christian overlay or ignored in an over-emphasis of an identity based on the role of London as its capital city. Beefeaters, Westminster and Buckingham Palace are important components of England's culture, but so is the fact that Cumbria comes from Cumber, the name used by the Anglo-Saxons for the British Celts, or the fact that early forms of morris dancing owe much to the way in which the four annual Celtic festivals were celebrated. England has a part in the stories of the Sea Kingdoms as a ruthless oppressor, but it also has a Celtic culture of its own.

Added to the paradox of Celtic England is the clear historical development of non-Celtic Scotland, Wales and Ireland. The distinctions between Celtic and non-Celtic inside these so-called Celtic nations are very clearly present, and if each had to be sifted and weighed, the telling of this story would take on a bewildering complexity. Common sense advises that each nation, including England, ought to be judged by the degree of its Celtic identity. Obviously Glasgow is more of a Celtic city than, say, Wolverhampton. Not only does it have a Celtic name, but very many of its inhabitants have either Scots or Irish Gaelic backgrounds at a distance of only one or two generations, and Gaelic is still spoken by a few thousand of its citizens. More important than that, Scottish history – all of it – has been highly coloured by a Celtic past and its culture made distinctive by a Celtic present.

While this positions Scotland, Wales and Ireland (as well as Man and Cornwall) in a Celtic atmosphere, it is important not to ignore or underplay the tensions inside these countries. The Welsh speech community is large but it comprises only a sixth of the total population of Wales, and if language has been the central tenet of Welshness since the age of Llywelyn II, how does the five-sixths majority express its sense of Welshness?

*   *   *

The foregoing examples and arguments are intended only as an opening set of impressions of clear similarities and shared experiences which exist between apparently distant places in Britain. What follows is the diary of a long journey through the Sea Kingdoms of Celtic Britain.

TWO

In The Dreamtime

THE RAGE-FIT WAS UPON HIM. He shook like a bulrush in
the stream. His sinews stretched and bunched, and every huge,
immeasurable, vast ball of them was as big as the head of a
month-old child. His face as a red bowl, fearsomely distorted,
one eye sucked in so far that the beak of a wild crane could
scarcely reach it, the other eye bulged out of his cheek. Teeth
and jawbone strained through peeled-back lips. Lungs and liver
pulsed in his throat. Flecks of fire streamed from his mouth. The
booming of his heart was like the deep baying of bloodhounds,
or the growl of lions attacking bears.

In virulent clouds, sparks blazed, lit by the torches of the
war-goddess Badb. The sky was slashed as a mark of his fury.
His hair stood about his head like the twisted branches of red
hawthorn. A stream of dark blood, as tall as the mast of a ship,
rose out of the top of his head, then dispersed into dark mist,
like the smoke of winter fires.

These are the brilliant images of a story told in the circle of firelight. This was the way in which the Irish hero Cuchulainn inflamed
himself for battle as, in a translation of a Gaelic phrase, he became
'beside himself with rage', to ride out and defend Ulster against the
armies of Connaught. His rage-fit was seen as a transcendence, when
he came out of an ordinary state of being to grow into something
other, a terrifying figure from a world next to us, invisible but sensed.
As the warp spasm pulsed through Cuchulainn, his everyday self

watched it happen, not in a normal place or time, but in a Celtic dream-time.

> Cuchulainn's war chariot was both broad and fine, shining like white crystal, with a yoke of gold, great panels of copper, shafts of bronze, wheel-rims of white metal, light-framed. It could reach the speed of a swallow or a wild deer racing over the plains of Mag Slebe. The chariot was drawn by two well-yoked horses, swift, strong, roan-breasted and long-striding. One was supple, hard-pulling and great-hoofed. The other was curly-maned, slender-hoofed and sleek. They were harnessed in inlaid golden bridles and pulled a chariot carrying a blue-mantled man whose hair was like the yellow of bees when the sun shines on a summer's day. In his clenched fist there was a spear, red-flaming. Around his eye was the shining of a great fire.
>
> This is how Cuchulainn's war chariot appeared to the servant of Fer Diad, his opponent in single combat.

These passages are from a tale called the *Tain Bo Cuailgne*, the *Great Cattle Raid of Cooley*. It existed for many generations as an orally transmitted story, written down nowhere and constantly embellished and changed. The *Tain Bo* is very ancient, perhaps 2,000 years old. When it was first transcribed in the eleventh century by Irish monks, one of the copyists was not much impressed and he wrote in the margin: 'But I, who have written this history, or rather fable, am doubtful about many things in it. For some of them are the figments of demons, some of them poetic imaginings, some true, some not, some for the delight of fools.'

Perhaps the most surprising thing is not that the copyist had forgotten what he needed to believe, or not, but that these medieval monkish renditions were made at all. The *Tain Bo* is a gorgeous, blood-soaked memory of pre-Christian Ireland, offering an abundance of pagan imagery from which monks might well want to avert their eyes. As well as a plethora of violence, there is plenty of sex, sensuality and erotic symbolism. At an early stage in the tale Queen Maeve of Connaught attempts to avoid the need for warfare by offering 'her own friendly thighs' in order to get what she wants. In another story in the *Tain Bo* cycle Cuchulainn meets a girl he likes and she says to him, 'May your road be blessed!' He replies, 'May the apple of your eye see only good,' and then, peering down her cleavage, says, 'I see a sweet country. I could rest my weapon there.'

If the story is to be taken as a piece of documentary realism, then the monkish copyist was not unfair in his assessment: there are many truly fantastical episodes, and throughout Cuchulainn (like Batman or Superman) performs impossible feats. But it was never intended to be taken as a piece of reportage: instead it is a virtuoso celebration of fighting skills, courage, weaponry and, above all, the hero-cult. Offering precious and unique insights into the atmosphere of the early Celtic culture of Ireland, it tells what these people admired and thought important. The overwhelming impression echoes exactly what the Greek historian Strabo observed – the Celts did seem to be 'war-mad'.

The *Tain Bo Cuailgne* is part of a series of tales known as the Ulster Cycle and cousin to another group, the Fenian Cycle, which features different hero, Finn MacCool. Through archaeological evidence showing that Ulster was indeed defended by a series of oak ramparts placed at a series of strategic points, and some certainty about the time when chariots went out of use in warfare, it is possible to settle on an approximate date for these stories. They were probably first told some time after 100 BC. Apart from the classical literature of the Greeks and Romans, that makes the *Tain Bo* one of the oldest stories still surviving in Europe. The Fenian and Ulster cycles represent the western residue of a culture and language which was common over much of Atlantic Europe. The stories survived because Ireland remained outside of the Roman Empire, and no substantial invasion took place until the ninth century, when the Vikings attacked the coastlines of the east.

At an early stage the Romans and the Greeks knew a great deal about the Celts because they encountered them first in central Europe. Archaeologists have found substantial numbers of Celtic artefacts, many in lakes and wells, in an area immediately to the north of the Alps. They show a culture capable of brilliant metalwork, particularly in iron but also in gold and silver. Around 1000 BC the Celts began to move all over Europe. Place names trace the extent of their journeys. The rivers Danube, Rhine and Rhone all rise in their homeland in the uplands of Europe, and all have Celtic names. The root word *gal*, cognate to the modern Gael, shows where they or their influence reached. Beginning as far west in mainland Europe as it is possible to get to, Celtic culture stretched to Portugal, Galicia in northern Spain, Gaul (the Roman name for modern France), Cisalpine Gaul in northern Italy, Galicia in southern Poland and Galatia in central Turkey. On the Bosphorus, Gallipoli means 'the city of the Celts'. In addition, there are many other names unconnected to *gal* but which are Celtic in origin all the same, such as Lyons, London and Leyden, which are all combinations of the name of the Celtic god, Lugh, and their word *dun* for a fort.

Expertise in metalwork allowed the Celts to forge the kind of weaponry so lovingly described in the *Tain Bo*, and at the time unparalleled elsewhere. The quality of their spears, swords, chariots, darts and axes gave warriors an advantage which persuaded them to challenge and defeat any who stood in the way of their migrations. In 390 BC the Celts sacked Rome, and in 279 BC they attacked the shrine of Greece's sacred oracle at Delphi and crossed the Bosphorus into Asia Minor. They were the first masters of Europe. And even after others had taken their place, Celtic warriors retained their prestige and turned up in unlikely places. Queen Cleopatra was protected by an elite bodyguard of 300 Celts, and when she died they sought and gained employment with Herod the Great.

When the Greeks first encountered them in the sixth century BC, they called these new people Keltoi, probably because, when asked, that is what they called themselves. Many of their tribal names have straightforward origins, particularly for those who understand Celtic languages. For example, the Selgovae of southern Scotland got theirs from something they did: *seilg* means to hunt, and made them simply the Hunters. But Keltoi is a difficult name. One of the most plausible and engaging theories is that it comes from the Indo-European root *kel*, meaning hidden, which in turn may derive from the early Celtic habit of writing down nothing in order to preserve their store of knowledge and religious lore as a secret. Given the events of the last 1,500 years, the derivation of the name for the Celts from the Hidden People could scarcely be more appropriate.

In his *De Bello Gallico*, Julius Caesar added a complication which eventually developed into a conundrum. He used 'Galli' or 'Gaul' as an alternative name for those 'who are called Celts in their own language'. Its meaning is even more obscure than Celt and over time it changed radically. From being a term used to describe Gauls or Gaels, it gradually came to mean the opposite. The Irish used Gaul or Galli as a label for all those who were not Irish, and this became mutated into 'Gall' for strangers or foreigners. The surprising result is that in Scots Gaelic the Celtic homeland is now known as the Gaidhealtachd while the English-speaking lowlands are known as the Galltachd. A long time ago both names would have meant much the same thing.

Caesar also compiled a very useful sketch of Celtic society. It was evidently a steep-sided pyramid, with a warrior class on top, then a supporting professional group including priests, prophets, bards, physicians, lawyers and artists, and finally a broad base of people called plebs by the Romans, a large and sometimes unfree agricultural proletariat whose produce supported everyone. Kings sat on the pinnacle and were thought of as being close to divine. The Gaelic word *righ* for king is related to the verb 'to reach' and the adjective 'rich'. Cuchulainn was a member of the warrior class who fought against and on behalf of kings and queens, and although Caesar was describing the Gauls of what is now France, there is no reason to doubt that a similar social structure was maintained in Britain and Ireland before the Roman invasions.

Kings and their tribes or nations often set great store by the stories of their foundation or the exploits of their ancestors. The hero-tales of the Ulster and Fenian Cycles are home to many big names whose prestige was borrowed by the royal and less than royal for centuries. Genealogies resound to the reputations of men like Conchobar macNessa, Niall of the Nine Hostages and Conn of the Hundred Battles. The use of their names retained a tremendous iconic power for millennia. At the battle of Harlaw in 1411, when the army of the Lords of the Isles was met by the Earl of Mar and his mounted knights and men-at-arms near Aberdeen, the bard Lachlan Mor MacMhuirich walked out in front of the great crescent-shaped lines of the clans. He turned to face them and to recite the long genealogy of the Lordship, and, putting steel and pride into the Highlanders' sense of themselves, he implored them:

> Sons of Conn remember
> Hardihood in time of strife!

Although Conn of the Hundred Battles was an Irish hero, this epithet mattered less than the fact that the name of a Gael was used as an incitement to battle against the Gall, the hated Lowlanders of eastern and southern Scotland.

The names of heroes and ancient kings and the celebration of their exploits conferred antiquity, legitimacy and dignity, and any question of historical accuracy was much less important than the magic power of the grand name. These attributes were not diminished by the passing of the centuries. In 1320 the Scots were particularly anxious to persuade Pope John XXII that their new king, Robert Bruce, had a rightful claim to the throne of Scotland, and the Abbot of Arbroath, Bernard de Linton, wrote to the Vatican in these terms:

> The which Scottish nation, journeying from Greater Scythia by the Tyrrhene Sea and the Pillars of Hercules, could not in any place or time or manner be overcome by the barbarians, though long dwelling in Spain among the fiercest of them. Coming thence, twelve hundred years after the transit of Israel, with many victories and many toils they won that habitation in the West, which though the Britons have been driven out, the Picts effaced, and the Norwegians, Danes and English have often assailed it, they hold now, in freedom from all vassalage; and as the old historians bear witness, have ever so held it. In this kingdom have reigned a hundred and thirteen kings of their own Blood Royal, and no man foreign has been among them.

Commentators have often dismissed the journeys of the Scots as classical myth-history with no basis in anything concrete. But if the expansion of the culture of the European Celts out of its original homelands north of the Alps is looked at carefully, Bernard de Linton's recital of prehistory begins to look more substantial. The genealogy of 113 kings begins with Fergus Mac Erc, the first King of Dalriada. The Dalriadic Scots crossed from Ireland in the fifth century and for a long time the terms Scots and Irish were confusingly interchangeable. In the eleventh century, Irish copyists transcribed the oral tradition of their national foundation story as *An Leabhar Gabhala*, the *Book of Invasions*. At one point it includes a central account of a Celtic people who came to Ireland from Spain. The European migrations of the Celts certainly took them both to Scythia on the western shore of the Black Sea, and also to the Iberian Peninsula, the location of Portugal and Galicia. It is by no means impossible that a folk memory of a people who made a long journey from the Black Sea to Spain and Portugal, to Ireland and thence to Scotland persisted until the early fourteenth century. The Declaration of Arbroath of 1320 may well be more history than myth.

In order to bolster Scotland and Robert Bruce's claims to genuine antiquity and consistency, Bernard de Linton added some precision: 'twelve hundred years after the transit of Israel'. This may be a rare spurious element. The Celts did not reckon time in the same way as medieval abbots or popes, and the early stories never bother with details of dates or years – events themselves were important, not the times when they took place. History was passed down the generations, although as time unfolded, earlier years began to drop out of memory. The longest detailed span retained was generally thought to be fifty years, on a rolling basis. This habit of memory is still found in the Western Isles and the west of Ireland, where older people deal with ideas of time in a wholly concrete and non-abstract fashion.

In Gaelic usage there is the notion of a continuing present tense which often corresponds with a speaker's own lifetime and experience, and history is not measured in a back-calculation of years and dates, but overwhelmingly by the use of genealogy. Just like the clansmen at Culloden, Hebrideans and Irish speakers can recite their genealogy back through the generations, moving rhythmically from one name to another using only a Christian name. Where, as often happens in families, the same Christian names are repeated in succession or close to one another, adjectives or nicknames are attached which bring life to the long lists. And so Iain Ban (fair-haired Iain), the son of Iain Mor (big Iain), the son of Domnhall Ruadh (red-haired Donald), the son of Iain Lom (Iain with no hair) begins to sound less like a series of names anonymous to an outsider and look more like an impossible family photograph. Compared to the conventional flow of history, which starts from panoramas of great events and their dates, and focuses on individuals only when they are actors in those great events, the way that Celts consider the past is very different. In any talk of long ago, a genealogy is laid out first and established as a determinant framework within which the sweep of politics is considered only if it impacted on a family or a set of relationships. A genealogy could clearly be affected by a war, if a life was shortened and a generation half-skipped, but it is the individual who is important in Celtic reckoning, not the event itself. By extension, the wider group, linked by family bonds, becomes a vitally important. For Scottish Highlanders, the clan was not a background but a world inside which they lived and died. The recital of genealogies at Culloden and the battle of Harlaw was not a ritual but a reminder and a powerful motivator: it marks a real difference between the way in which we now think about history and how it was once understood down the western edges of Britain and in Ireland.

In the imaginations of the listeners to tales like the *Tain Bo*, perhaps 100 years after the death of a warrior with a name and attributes like those of Cuchulainn, the context of events but not the person will have outrun living memory. It will all have taken place, simply, a long time ago, and because no date could be attached to it, no distance could exist between the listeners and the heroes which would encourage searching, factual questions to be asked. The deeds of Cuchulainn became part of the lives of the peoples of the north of Ireland, part of their continuing history transmitted down the generations (Cuchulainn was a favourite subject for muralists on both sides of the sectarian divide in Belfast and Derry), and part of that near-uncatchable thing, the atmosphere of a culture. When and if these things happened were matters which interested them little, if at all.

The Celtic way of reckoning time on a more immediate basis was also very different from our modern method of dividing a year into months, days and hours. A Celtic year was arranged around four quarter-day festivals which took their cue not from the date on the calendar but from the weather, the landscape and the behaviour of animals. At Imbolc, around the beginning of March in our modern reckoning, ewes began to lactate in anticipation of lambing. That meant a new source of fresh food in the lean times after the hungry winter months and was the occasion for a festival: fires were lit on hilltops and people celebrated. The old Gaelic translation of February, Ceud Mhios an Earraich, the First Month of Spring, remembers these hopeful first signs of the end of winter. May Day was called Beltane: it marked the return of real warmth and the time when flocks and herds were moved from lowland pasture up-country for the summer. It was also the festival when the 'Obby 'Oss came out to dance. Lughnasa occurred at the beginning of August, and it focused on the Celtic god, Lugh, and the time when first fruits could be harvested. Finally Samhuinn, at the end of October, saw the end of summer.

Like many early peoples, the Celts of Britain did not count days, but rather measured the passage of the year in nights. A remnant of that way of thinking is the term fortnight, something completely incomprehensible to an English-speaking American, just as the seven-night version, 'sennight', is now lost to us. A telling if distant example that helps us to understand how the Celts thought about time is a body of recent research done with North African tribesmen. The Scottish Gaels have at least two words, *aimsir* and *tide*, which can mean both time and weather, and although this is difficult to demonstrate, it is likely that the use for weather came first. Something of the sense of this remains in the English phrase 'time and tide wait for no man'. Similarly, the African tribesmen have no use for a word that only means time: it always has to mean something else first, like milking time or flood time. There is no separate word for time and therefore it is difficult to waste it or save it. Instead, Africans traditionally reckon the passage of time to be nothing more than a succession of events, mainly natural rather than man-made, distinguished by their differing impact on the life of the tribe rather than any sense of how long they took or which year they occurred. Like the Celts, the African tribesmen are pastoralists, and what marks out change in a run of years is how each affects their cattle or their goats: whether there are floods, disease, good or sparse grass and so on. Although the chief business of the *Tain Bo Cuailgne* is to celebrate and elaborate the hero-cult of Cuchulainn, the story uses cattle as a pretext for all its fighting, and, bluntly, its English translation of its title is, after all, the *Great Cattle Raid of Cooley*. It is very probable that Celtic time was like African pastoralist time: what one historian has called the Cattle Clock.

The seasonal turns of the year are clear to all pastoralists, including the Celts. Like the African tribesmen who do not even need a word for time, they would have had little use for the painstaking precision with which we measure out our time. More pointedly, the weather was not something merely of interest, a topic for idle discussion as it is in our centrally heated modern times, or a conventional greeting. To the Celtic peoples of Britain, it could be a matter of life or death for them or their animals. It is equally important to recognize that the seasons affected early rural life profoundly, and that the measurement of time inside the span of a day is only a matter of convention – it is definitely not a cultural difference which marks levels of relative sophistication. Partly because fine measurements of time were of little importance to the agricultural peoples of the west, we tended to adopt them ready-made from others, primarily the civilizations of the Near and Middle East. Following the annual rhythm of the floods of the river Nile, always measured at the same place at Heliopolis for the sake of consistency, the Egyptians devised a calendar of twelve months of thirty days each, adding five on at the end of the year to make 365, so that the lunar and solar cycles were in agreement. The Egyptians also evolved the twenty-four-hour divisions of the day, but following Babylonian mathematical precepts they divided the hour into sixty firsts, which we now call minutes, and sixty seconds, which we still call seconds.

Not only would this precision have been lost on the European and island Celts, but it was originally of little interest to the Greeks. Before the histories of Herodotus and Thucydides in the fifth century BC, the Greek past was peopled by heroes rather than dated events. On the plains of Troy, Achilles and Priam fought each other both with and without the interference of the Gods. In a Hellenic dream-time, Odysseus took twenty years to return to Ithaca to prevent the Lady Penelope from falling into the arms of persistent suitors. The exact time was unimportant: twenty years simply meant 'a long time'. Nevertheless, historians have founded much on the Greek hero-stories, perhaps because they were first written down more than 2,000 years ago, in languages which still command academic prestige. Excavations at Troy and Mycenae have uncovered evidence of settlements which thrived and may have been at war with each other before the time, carefully reconstructed by historians, when Homer composed the great stories, but nothing related to their heroes or their deeds has ever been found. Nonetheless, the *Iliad* and the *Odyssey* have coloured much of the manner in which we write and think about the Greeks, and the power of the stories is such that their historically insubstantial protagonists are the best-known classical Greek figures, perhaps the best-known Greeks of all. Helen of Troy, Achilles, Hector and Odysseus come more readily to the popular mind than Pericles, Themistocles or Leonidas.

Both in terms of general awareness and its use by British and European historians, the status of the *Tain Bo Cuailgne* and the other Irish and Welsh tales is, by contrast, very lowly, even though the tone, the brilliant use of language and the subject matter are all strikingly similar to the Homeric epics. Rather than scouring the Irish texts for information about early Celtic society, the peoples whose language and culture spread over much of Europe and who defeated and humbled both the Romans in 390 BC and the Greeks in 279 BC, historians, with very few exceptions, have either ignored the stories or asked questions first. Can the events described be proved? When did they happen? Where is the evidence for war between Ulster and Connaught? And so on. The fact is that the *Tain Bo Cuailgne* is unique, a window on a society which did not record its history in writing. The primary reason for the overwhelming interest in the stories of Homer and the virtual dismissal of the Ulster and Fenian Cycles is an academic preference for the doings of a literate, and assumedly sophisticated, culture over against those of a non-literate, assumedly primitive, one. It seems to matter little that the Celts form the bedrock of British history and that the Trojans and Greeks do not. Indeed, histories of Britain have traditionally begun with the appearance of people who were not British at all. Because the Romans left reasonably reliable written records their invasions are habitually presented as a sensible starting point for our history, even though their actions were the result of an imperial, Mediterranean policy which had almost nothing to do with the native British. Inevitably, the Celts of Britain are made to look passive, primitive, and definitely second to the dynamic Romans. There is the faintest whiff of snobbery, and perhaps something worse, around these preferences: the Celts lost the war for Britain and left little or no trace of their triumphs in Europe, and therefore, literally, their stories are of no account.

Today, anyone interested in reading modern texts of the *Tain Bo Cuailgne*, the Fenian Cycle or the *Mabinogion* (a collection of ancient Welsh tales) is confronted by a surprisingly persistent literary habit. Many bookshops categorize tales like these under the likes of 'Mind, Body and Spirit' (this appears to be some sort of euphemism for New Age daftness), while the early heroic stories of ancient Greece and Rome are often to be found on the history shelves. The Greek invention of history helped to create attitudes like these.

When the Persian Empire began to expand westwards through modern Turkey, and the Greek cities of the Ionian coast were attacked, a series of events of huge importance began to unfold. The period between the fall of the Greek city of Sardis, the battles at Marathon (490 BC), and Salamis and Thermopylae (480 BC), and after these unexpected reverses, the final retreat of Xerxes, the King of Persia, formed a single episode which broke into a cyclical sense of time and demanded telling in a different way. Not only did the Greeks wish to glorify their ability to withstand the surging power of a huge empire which stretched eastwards to the banks of the Indus, they also wanted to record what actually happened with some precision. Herodotus managed to establish a sequence of events and give a sense of the intervals of time between them, but as a historian he enjoyed detail and excursus too much to pin down many dates and places, at least by current standards. Thucydides then went a stage further in his history of the war between Athens and Sparta, which raged in the fifth century BC. In order to set down exactly what happened and when, he began to use the years of office of the officials in each city as a guide. By this method he built up a sequence of dates over a lengthy period that included many events, some of which took place simultaneously. He had developed a new means of recording and writing history which was very influential. Its precision about time demanded that it be written rather than remembered, recited and made fabulous as with the *Tain Bo* and the *Iliad*. Although this forensic approach took a long time to become general, the setting of events in a well-understood time frame was a determining factor in the formation of modern attitudes, particularly towards to the history of the Celts.

An interesting side-effect of this more precise recording of history was the formation of a new approach to foreigners. The dramatist Aeschylus had fought in the Athenian army at the battle at Marathon against the invading Persians in the fifth century BC. In his tragedy *The Persae* he drew characters which are unmistakable renditions of slant-eyed Asiatics – utterly immoral, cruel, arrogant and barbarian – compared to the superior Greeks. Coming from the east, the source of much that was poisonous, uncivilized and destructive in his eyes, they also spoke incomprehensible and base languages. The word 'barbarian' derives from the dismissive gesture of drawing the fingers across the lips while making a guttural noise to produce 'bar-bar-bar', or in an English idiom, 'blah, blah, blah'.

Before the wars with Persia and Aeschylus's tragedies, the Greeks had shown few negative feelings about outsiders, and sometimes they could be made into gods or heroes much in the way that the Aztecs first regarded the Conquistadors. In the *Iliad*, Homer treated the Trojans and the Greeks as equals. The Persian wars changed all that by inventing a cultural fault line enthusiastically adopted by the Romans that did not fade for 2,000 years, and which still casts an occasional shadow over Europe.

The Greeks began also to move into abstract conventions of time-keeping which have, again, entered the core of our lives and influenced profoundly the way in which we understand our history. In Athens, this near-obsession with the measurement of time is exemplified by a ruin known as the Tower of the Winds. Built in the first century BC, it was a water-clock whose accuracy depended on a steady and measurable flow from one tank into another over a twenty-four-hour period. Allied to a weather vane and a series of sundials on the eight walls of the tower, the water-clock allowed the whole building to tell a cross-checked time very accurately at any time of the day or night, and whether or not it was cloudy or bright. The Tower of the Winds must have been a dazzling sight, and a monument to a collective Greek will to measure and thereby understand the passage of time.

By contrast, faced with the certainties of dates, events, causes and effects, a Celtic sense of history has undoubtedly perished. The power of stories like the Ulster Cycle in Ireland and the *Mabinogion* in Wales is today much diminished, and their content often dismissed as rambling, repetitive and predictable. Not really stories as we understand them now, they often confuse and conflate the names of the actors and rarely bother to arrange their actions in a linear narrative. Historians search through the medieval copies of these tales, analysing lush metaphor and hyperbole, scouring the ground for explanation, and something, anything, provable. In their anxiety they forget that the substantial surviving corpus of Celtic stories and poems is far more informative if facts are left to themselves and an atmosphere is allowed to grow and colour the imagination. Readers of such poems as the Welsh *Culhwch and Olwen* should remember that they were never meant to be read, and that their structure evolved for recital – to be listened to, changed, added to and perhaps, like traditional pantomime, attracting topical references from the time and place where they were told.

The tales of the Celts are entirely distinctive, and in telling the story of Celtic Britain and Ireland it is essential to avoid the double trap of according too much importance to written sources and mistrusting an orally transmitted tradition. This is a history of a culture which lived in the memories of its people for most of its existence – stories not documented anywhere but surviving only in memory are sometimes brought to the foreground, and understandings and habits not listed in written history are sketched in, while the brute forces of politics are included only when unavoidable, or when guidance from no other source is available. The music of the thing as it happened does not always bang and clash like the *1812 Overture* – sometimes it sounds like a lullaby whispered on a winter's night.

THREE

The Islands of the Evening

FOR THE PASSENGERS, landing in an aeroplane on the little island of Barra, in the Outer Hebrides, is a unique experience. There is no airport, not even a runway. Aircraft hop over the high sand dunes and land on a beach at low tide. Instead of loose yellow sand, it is a cockleshell beach where billions of white shards pack tight into a hard surface. Once down, the plane taxis to a large shed where the more experienced travellers wait for the props to still and then go around to the luggage hold to collect their suitcases from the baggage handler/airport manager. Even though I had been told what to expect, it was more than a relief to be on nearly dry land. As we threaded our way down the sunlit single-track road, my taxi driver was quiet. We came to a T-junction and I asked which way to Castlebay. 'Both,' he said. After a moment's puzzlement I remembered that Barra was a small island with one circular road which led to the village and my hotel. It was only a question of distance, and he took me the short way.

I needed to make a phone call and the hotel receptionist directed me to the public bar. The view over the bay and Kismuil Castle at its centre is stunning, and yet the bar seemed to have no windows. In the gloom it was easy to pick out the only customers: three fisherman in orange oilskin trousers. They had been out in their boat since dawn and were in for a celebratory dram. 'Hello there,' said one, 'You'll join us in a dram.' It was not yet noon. 'No thanks, I'm fine. Thank you.' 'Well,' he persisted, 'what about a soft drink, like a beer?'

We compromised on a tomato juice, with lots of Worcester sauce, and I sat down to talk. They were lobster fishermen, and 'anything else we can get', and they sent all of their catch to Glasgow and the posh restaurants for 'the yuppies to toy with'. None of them fished full time and Shony Alec, who insisted on buying me a drink, worked in a local shop most afternoons as well as running a croft. Before he began to sound like an extra from *Local Hero*, he was quick to point out that it was not an easy life. Even though he and his friends rarely ventured out of sheltered waters, they never failed to be careful, to remember the huge power of the mighty Atlantic. 'There is nothing between here and America but water,' said Shony Alec, 'and if you go out when the wind and the tide are coming from the wrong place, you could end up going there. Except you wouldn't get there.' He explained that anyone who fished for a few laughs and said that they were not afraid of the sea was likely soon to be drowned. And even those that were afraid sometimes drowned anyway. By way of illustration, he told me the story of the *Iolaire*.

On 31 December 1918, at the end of the First World War, hundreds of Hebridean servicemen reached the railhead at Kyle of Lochalsh on their long journey home to Lewis. There were so many demobbed soldiers and sailors that the regular mail boat, the *Sheila*, was unable to take them all. At the last minute the H. M. yacht *Iolaire* was brought alongside the quay and it was decided that the soldiers should go back to Lewis on the mail boat and the sailors on the yacht. As both vessels made their way into the Sound of Raasay and then out of the lee of the Isle of Skye, the weather began to worsen until a blinding storm blew. Having made the journey many times, the captain of the *Sheila* guided her carefully across the Minch and into safe harbour at Stornoway. In the huge seas, the *Iolaire* missed the narrow entrance and was thrown and smashed against the rocks known as the Beasts of Holm. Only a few yards from shore, the sailors, 'Sailors, mind, all sailors who knew what to do and had just gone through a war,' tried to lower boats but the mountainous seas made it impossible. Land was so close that many tried to swim for it, but they were driven back and pulled down by the irresistible undertow. Some men were lucky to be washed up alive, but many of the survivors owed their lives to John F. MacLeod of Port of Ness, near the Butt of Lewis. An immensely strong man, he jumped from the deck of the yacht with a line which he had thought to attach to a hawser. Wedging himself between the boulders on the beach, he hauled the cable ashore and secured it. Most of the seventy-five men who survived pulled themselves along MacLeod's hawser, but even some who took hold of it were torn off by the power of the tempestuous waves rolling back off the beach. Two hundred men died in the wreck of the *Iolaire*. Within sight of Stornoway harbour, where their families waited, the rage of the sea pulled them under. Some small villages were decimated: Liurbost and North Tolsta lost eleven men each and some families suffered more than one casualty.

The point Shony Alec was making in the hotel bar was a simple one. The sea unites the Hebridean communities, and also offers links with others to the north and south, but often these shared experiences are bitter. The sea is a provider, a highway and an enemy never to be trusted. No-one has affection for the sea in the way they might for a piece of land, and sailors have understood this paradox for thousands of years. Perhaps because of the vastness of the oceans, the elemental threat of the deeps and their enduring ability to drown even the careful and well equipped, we are somehow unwilling to believe that the early peoples of Europe ever embarked on long voyages. But they undoubtedly did. Given reasonable weather, sound boats and common sense, a voyage between, say, northern Spain and the Rhine estuary was much faster, safer and more comfortable by sea than by land.

The Greeks developed a Mediterranean trading empire which had only coastal colonies because they operated almost all of their business by ship and avoided land transport (which cost more and reduced profit margins) wherever possible. These colonies ran all along the northern shores of the Mediterranean, from Cyprus in the east to what is now Valencia in southern Spain. A mixture of commerce and curiosity prompted a man called Pytheas to travel from Marseilles, probably over-land, to the Gironde on the Biscay coast, where he then took ship for Britain and Ireland. Even at that early stage, around 300 BC, the Cornish tin industry was a magnet for traders from the Mediterranean. Pytheas's own account of the journey is lost but parts of it were reproduced by other, later writers – enough to piece together where his ship took him. Beyond Biscay the sailors first sighted a smaller more westerly island which they called Ierne, and which later Romans changed to Hibernia. Unmistakably Ireland, the original name came from a Greek rendition of a Celtic name, something close to the modern version, Eirinn. Next to the westermost island was the much larger Nesos Albionon, the Island of Albion. Now, Britain has never lost the name of Albion and it was memorably used by Napoleon's recruiting poster in the phrase 'Perfidious Albion', but its derivation is less clear-cut. It probably comes from the Indo-European root *alb* which generally means white. The Latin *albus* still appears in English words like albino and, more remotely, in names like the Alps. All geographers after Pytheas who repeat a variation of the name Albion approached Britain from a southern perspective: the first and most dramatic geological features obvious to those making the shortest crossing of the English Channel, or even on a clear day to those standing on the French coast, are the white cliffs on either side of Dover. Britain was probably first called Alba, or White-Land by the Celts living in what is now the Pas de Calais (another place name with *gal*). While the use of Albion has withered in English, it has remained in Celtic languages, but in a different, more localized sense. Alba is the Gaelic word for Scotland because that is what the Irish called it. They lived on Ierne and in the sixth century some of them migrated to Albion or Alba. It is the cause of some pain for patriotic Scots to accept that Scotland is named in our most Scottish language after a geographical feature romantically associated with England.

Pytheas had a third name which gathered up Ierne and Albion into one: he called them 'Pretanike'. This came from another Celtic word which meant the Painted People or the People of the Designs, a likely reference to a widespread use of tattoos. In modern Welsh, Pretanike has mutated into Prydein, but more tellingly it became the Latin, Britannia, and the English, Britain. While it may have passed through several pairs of Mediterranean hands in the process, it is more than salutary to note that the Celts' names for the place have at least endured.

Most of the information about the early tin trade with Cornwall comes from Pytheas, or rather the fragments of his work surviving in later texts. Britain was important to the Greeks because it was a reliable source of tin, a vital ingredient in several alloys, including bronze. Much European tin came from Cornwall, where the ore was panned from streams and smelted into large astragal-shaped ingots which weighed around 80 kilograms. Trade was conducted at the easily found landmark of St Michael's Mount, near modern Penzance. There the Greeks beached their ships, loaded up with ingots and then waited for high tide to refloat them. The phrase 'coasting along' comes from the sensible maritime practice of taking the easy way of navigating by keeping land in sight, which is exactly what the tin ships did. They coasted up the English Channel to a landmark like Portland Bill and then turned south towards the Cherbourg Peninsula. When they saw Cap de la Hague, at 600 feet high not easy to miss in good weather, they made straight for it and the French coast. Then the Greeks made their way up to Le Havre and the mouth of the River Seine. Depending on how deep or shallow their draught and how much tin they had aboard, the ships would be poled, rowed or possibly pulled from a tow-path as far up the Seine as it was possible to go. At that point the tin was loaded onto pack-horses. Two astragal-shaped ingots could be easily lashed together and slung either side of a pack-saddle, and the usual total load of 160 kilograms was exactly what the average horse could manage. Slowly, and at great expense to the Greek merchants, the string of pack-horses was led up over the watershed of central France and down to the headwaters of the Rhone. There the tin was reloaded onto boats and, with a strong current behind them, it reached Marseilles very quickly. The shortest time taken for this journey was thirty days, and to work properly and profitably, it required a range of shipping skills and a great deal of organization.

The expensive land route taken by the tin may have been forced on the Greeks by the colonizers of the southern Mediterranean shore, the Phoenicians. They held harbours either side of the Straits of Gibraltar at Cadiz and Lixou, and to protect their trade probably enforced a blockade. The Greeks called the Straits the 'Pillars of Hercules' and in their stories of the Gods there lay beyond them a garden of golden apples guarded by nymphs called the Hesperides. They got their name from Hesperus, the planet Venus, which was to be found due west in the summertime. One of the later geographers who borrowed from Pytheas wrote about a scatter of islands that lay beyond the Pillars of Hercules, beyond the islands of Ireland and Britain, and under the Evening Star. He meant the Western Isles or the Hebrides, but we should call them in the way the ancients thought of them: the Islands of the Evening.

We think of them now as remote, on the edge of Britain and Europe with, as Shony Alec said, nothing between them and America but the vastness of the mighty Atlantic. We think like this because we have rapid means of moving overland: roads, cars, railways as well as aeroplanes. All of these means of travel are new, and so is our way of thinking about the islands off the west coast of Britain. As late as the fifteenth century and probably later, ordinary people living near the sea will have known much more of the outside world than a peasant living fifteen miles from London. Because sailors from many parts of the west coast of Britain and northern Europe docked regularly on the islands, these people heard stories and languages, and saw goods, that came from far beyond their immediate experience. And they themselves sometimes travelled to other islands or had family who went even further. In many of the small ports of the west there are exotic street names – Baltic, Jamaica, Spanish – which remember a wider world.

The facts of the geography of the coasts of the west are eloquent. With more than 500 islands of every size, the Hebrides is a huge archipelago, although only thirty-two are large enough to support significant populations. They arc from north to south in two main groups, the Outer and Inner Hebrides, but are never more than fifty miles from the mainland and most are much closer. Nowhere is far from the sea. The Isle of Skye is cut so deeply with sea lochs that no-one can get more than five miles from the ocean, and on the Isle of Lewis there is only one village, Achadh Mor, where the inhabitants cannot see the sea. The long fingers of the Atlantic reach so deeply into the heart of Argyll that, even though it is part of the Scottish mainland, nowhere is more than twelve miles from the coast. The common western place name of Tarbert recalls how inconvenient pieces of land were not permitted to inhibit the flow of sea travel. Tarbert or Tarbet is from *tairm-bert*, meaning an 'overbringing', and it is almost always to be found between two lochs. The long peninsula of Kintyre is almost an island where West Loch Tarbert gets within a mile of East Loch Tarbert, and it was here that King Magnus Bareleg of Norway did what the name Tarbert means. At the end of the eleventh century, King Edgar of Scotland agreed to cede control of all of the islands off the west coast to Norway in return for a peaceful frontier. Magnus promptly sailed to Kintyre and had his sailors drag their boat across the narrow neck of land to prove that Kintyre was an island and that it should therefore belong to him.

There are Tarberts on the narrow waist of the island of Jura and on Gigha, a few miles to the south, a Tarbet between Loch Nevis and Loch Morar, and another at the neck of South Harris where the Minch and the Atlantic almost meet. There is even a place called Tarbet which does not connect two sea lochs but rather the sea with an inland loch. At the head of Loch Long, which reaches far into the mountains north of

Glasgow, Tarbet sits on a sliver of land linking the sea with Scotland's largest loch, Loch Lomond. More than twenty-two miles long and five miles across in the south, it is the largest expanse of fresh water in Britain. Its bonny banks once created large opportunities for raiding and trading, and its long coastline and thirty islands are as much a part of the Sea Kingdoms as the Hebrides. Once a boat had been dragged over to Loch Lomond, the network of inland lochs to the east and the Trossachs opened up journeys whose logic was to avoid the dangerous and time-consuming business of moving overland. There is a good illustration of this when motorists drive up the twisting modern road on Loch Lomondside, often behind a fish lorry, and they look out to their right and see stately craft gliding on the wide, calm and uncluttered surface of the great loch. The heart of Ireland was also accessible to boats in the same way. The River Shannon is navigable for much of its length through a network of lochs which can take sailors more than fifty miles from the seashore.

The North Channel between the Mull of Kintyre and the Antrim coast of Ireland is only twelve miles wide, and, despite the treacherous tide race as the Irish Sea fills up and empties each day, it was a busy highway. From early times it was much easier to sail from Ballycastle to Campbelltown than it was to turn south and travel inland to Ballymena, another, entirely different twelve miles away. Nowadays almost no-one thinks like that.

Like the many Tarberts, place names remember the business of sea travel well. Even though the winter seas can boil around it, the northern Cape Wrath has nothing to do with anger. It means 'turning point' in early Norse. When sailors from the north were bound for the Hebrides and they saw the cliffs of Wrath, they knew to bear to the left, to the port side. A long way south, the Isle of Man carried an equally practical label. Much has been made of its supposed naming after the Celtic sea god Manannan macLir but more likely, in the tradition of the Tarberts, it was given a name that reflected its importance to sailors. Man is probably derived from the Gaelic root *meadhon*, which simply means 'middle'. Not only does the Isle of Man sit almost exactly in the centre of the Irish Sea, equidistant from Galloway in the north, Lancashire in the east, Angelsey and Wales in the south and Ireland in the west, but it also has a wider geographical significance. On a line drawn between two famous landmarks important to sea farers, John O' Groats and

Land's End, Man is precisely halfway. Early sailors could measure how far they had travelled and how long it took and they knew that Man was in the middle – the Midway Island. The Isle of Man was equally valued for its shelved beaches which allowed boats to be easily dragged up above the high-tide mark, its safe harbours and a fertile agricultural hinterland that could provision ships bound for onward destinations.

While sailing within sight of the coastline was the safest and most reliable course, early navigators sometimes took more direct routes. The Irish Sea is only sixty miles across at the narrowest points between Ireland and Wales. The western coasts of Britain and the eastern coasts of Ireland presented big targets for sea captains to aim at, and with a wealth of knowledge passed on from generations of mariners, they will not often have missed. There is a substantial body of evidence to show that this crossing was made frequently, and in both directions.

The Irish Sea could equally have been called the Holy Sea. Described by some historians as obscure, a man came to Galloway at the end of the fourth century to do something of absolute clarity. St Ninian founded a church, arguably the oldest Christian site in Britain still in continuous use. At Whithorn he chose a place to build situated very close to the shores of Wigtown Bay – on a fertile peninsula and at the hub of a busy sea-borne trading area. Within sight of the Galloway coast, across the tides of the Solway Firth, lies Cumbria. Such sources as there are suggest that the area around Carlisle retained a strong sense of the Roman past long after the last legionaries left in 410. Some time in the early fifth century Sucat, a young boy from Cumbria, was captured by a raiding party and sold in Ireland as a slave, but after escaping to Gaul he took the name Patrick on being received into the church and sailed back to Ireland to begin a mission of conversion in the north. Further south, on the Pembroke peninsula of Wales, St David established a monastery close to the sea and a cult founded on his exemplary life began to attract pilgrims, many of whom arrived in ships and small boats. Ninian, Patrick and David are only the most famous, but there are many early mentions of hundreds of Celtic saints criss-crossing the Irish Sea and creating a network of coastal monasteries where the light of God burned brightly. In much of eastern and inland Britain, the light burned not at all and the Celtic saints of the west made many voyages to rekindle it.

Faith took these courageous and resourceful men great distances, but they needed technology and skill to make sure they arrived safely. What were their boats like and how did they sail them? Sadly the evidence is scarce. Unlike buildings on land, the ships of the sea have left little trace. Maritime archaeology has revealed little of substance before the era of the great Viking ship burials of Scandinavia and eastern England. The boats of the holy men were small and made of entirely perishable materials, but, given what early sources do say, it is not difficult to visualize them. They are still being built today: enthusiasts and traditional craftsmen are still making curraghs and coracles in the Dingle peninsula of Ireland and in the city of Cork. There is little doubt that the saints sailed in curraghs. On the western side of the tiny island of Iona there is a bay where St Columba is said to have made landfall. Maps show it as Port na Curraigh, the port of the curragh.

These boats were made out of ox-hides sewn together, stretched over a wooden frame and sealed with wool grease. Now, they are made from canvas and used for coastal fishing and for racing. They are very versatile: able to go up rivers as well as on the sea, they take a very shallow draught, needing less than a foot of water to float them. Mostly rowed now, they could be driven along by a small sail and some were large, more than 40 feet long by 8 feet wide.

I went to the city of Cork in southern Ireland to watch a curragh being made and to talk to its builder, Padraic O' Duinnin. In a small boatyard by the River Lee, opposite the Beamish brewery, cluttered with half-finished repairs to rowing boats, bundles of tree branches and sheets of canvas, Padraic had assembled two curved lengths of timber into an oval frame. In what would become the gunwales he had bored a dozen holes on each side. Taking a bunch of green hazel rods, 'magic wood', he untied them and set them down beside a wooden machine. Ingenious in its design, it gripped the rod tightly using the weight of his body on a set of levers and allowed him to adze off the bark and finely hone the cut end so that the whippy hazel branch fitted exactly into the holes in the gunwale. Then, taking another, he pushed and screwed it into a hole exactly opposite on the other side and bent both pieces of green wood into the curve of what would become the hull of the curragh. The two rods were tied tight with twine, and, when all twenty-four were in place (Padraic constantly measuring and adjusting by eye alone), the skeleton shape of the boat became clear. Lathes were then tied lengthwise from bow to stern and black canvas stretched like a thick membrane over the frame. So that the boat stayed fairly rigid and did not simply fold in half under pressure, benches were fitted inside to act as thwarts. Only wood, twine and canvas was used, and no metal fittings of any sort were needed.

A fluent Irish speaker, Padraic flecks his talk about curraghs with Gaelic words which seem to him to cope better with describing the business of sailing and rowing them. Full of jokes and self-deprecation, he nonetheless senses the immensity of the past as he builds a new boat, and the presence of its ghosts beside him as he works. When he tells of voyages made in the curragh there is an intensity to his tone, because he knows that on the open sea, with three or more other rowers, he is doing exactly what Irishmen have done for 2,500 years and more. The experience is exactly the same, utterly authentic. Unlike battle re-enactors with cars waiting by the side of Marston Moor or centrally heated homes to go to after Hastings, the men in a fragile canvas boat on the face of the mighty ocean have only themselves, their courage and millennia of sea lore to rely on. When the waves are high and the boat is in a trough, there is no difference between what Columba, Ninian, Patrick or David saw and felt and what Padraic and his crew experience.

'When the sea is big,' he told me, 'you must have faith, must not panic or move around. At times like that I imagine a seagull sitting quiet on the waves, letting the swell carry it up and down. The curragh is so light that it sits like a bird on top of the water.' Padraic talks of calmer waters and of how the crew of a curragh can become of one mind, rowing together in metronomic synchronicity. When a landmark is sighted and made for, the bow oarsman often says nothing, just pulling harder for a few strokes to change course.

Sea voyages were well within the compass of larger curraghs, and in good weather they could have managed the journey from Lewis to Cornwall without trouble. This is not a matter of conjecture or deduction from the scanty evidence but a clear fact: curraghs were resilient and widely used craft capable of sailing immense distances. An Irish saint claimed to show the way and an English sailor proved that he was telling the truth.

St Brendan the Navigator lived between 490 and 570 AD, almost exactly contemporary with St Columba when he sailed his curragh to Iona. Like many of the Celtic holy men, Brendan had travelled extensively, visiting the Orkney Islands, Shetland and Iona itself, but his chief distinction is that he wrote an account of a long voyage. Called *Navigatio Sancti Brendani Abbatis*, it first appeared more than 200 years after his death and became immediately popular. Copyists reproduced many Latin versions, and ultimately it was translated into several European vernaculars: it appeared in German, Dutch, French and Danish.

The subtitle of Brendan's book is 'The Journey to the Promised Land', which describes what the saint set out to find. He and fourteen other monks made a large wooden frame for their curragh and covered it with ox-hide tanned in oak bark solution. Once the hides had been lashed with leather thongs to the frame, the joints were plastered with wool grease. The monks took on board forty days' supplies and also stowed enough wood and hide to make two additional boats. A mast and sail were fitted out and a steering paddle fixed to the bow.

Brendan set his course for the west, and, at the summer solstice, he would have known to aim for Hesperus, the Evening Star. At first all went well and a favourable wind blew them along in the direction they had navigated, but then the sea became calm and the brothers were forced to row until they dropped exhausted over the oars. After a time they came to an island. It was rocky, with high cliffs rising sheer out of the sea and no obvious place to beach the boat. Then Brendan noticed a steep-sided cleft in the cliff face which opened out into a narrow channel leading to a small port. After this first landfall the story develops into a succession of visits to islands: one is covered with grazing sheep, another with sea birds, another turned out to be a friendly floating whale called Jasconius, another had volcanoes, yet another a pillar of ice crystal, until finally the curragh reached a dense bank of fog. St Brendan penetrated this and came upon the Promised Land. After a short stay, he sailed home, apparently with much less incident.

Some of the islands described by St Brendan have clear links with real places: St Kilda is home to hundreds of thousands of sea birds, Faroe supports many flocks of sheep, Iceland has volcanoes and the fog banks might correspond with the frequently fog-bound Grand Banks off Newfoundland. Even though the story shows real navigational knowledge, the fabulous elements such as the whale have discouraged historians from attaching much importance or credence to it. And those who believed that St Brendan's voyage is an account of the discovery of North America a thousand years before Columbus were indulging in wild conjecture: it could not be possible for a skin boat to sail clear across the North Atlantic in the sixth century.

Not possible, that is, until someone did it. In 1976, Tim Severin set sail from south-western Ireland in a leather boat, named the *St Brendan*, made according to the information in the text of the *Voyage of St Brendan*, and he reached North America. Not only was it possible to make lengthy voyages with nothing more than the width of an ox-hide between a man and the ocean, but Severin and his crew also rediscovered much of the long-lost navigational skill needed to move confidently on the seas around Britain.

Meteorologists have shown that the climate was significantly warmer between *c.*400 and *c.*800. There may have been fewer storms, longer summers, and the Arctic ice pack retreated far enough northwards to allow ships to sail unhindered in higher latitudes. The Viking settlements established in Iceland, Greenland and Newfoundland were first made possible by a kinder climate, and then became untenable as the weather generally worsened into the medieval period. Tim Severin believed that the islands in St Brendan's text often referred to real places and that their sequence showed him taking a stepping-stone route in an arc around the North Atlantic to reach North America. This was, and remains, the sensible way to go. The direct route on a modern map is longer because of the curvature of the Earth, and it also fights the prevailing winds which blow from west to east. The northern route is both shorter and faster, with more favourable ocean currents.

The Irish monks knew that the world was round, 'like a well-formed apple', and were aware of islands lying to the north of Scotland. After the collapse of the western Roman Empire, they gathered and rescued a large corpus of classical scholarship, much of which was scientific and geographical, including the work of Strabo and Ptolemy. Ireland was also a focus for scholarly refugees who brought important works with them, which were copied in the monasteries and then reintroduced to Europe.

There is strong evidence to support the idea that Irish monks not only knew of the islands of the north-eastern Atlantic, but also founded monasteries on them. By 700 AD Irish monks had established a settlement on the Faroe Islands, where the story of St Brendan is well known, even to schoolchildren. His visit is remembered at Brandersvik, while *papars* in Faroese means Irish monks. On Iceland there are several place names – Papos, Papey and Papafjord – which refer to an ancient Irish presence, and there are clear references to the monks in the Norse sagas. By the time Iceland was colonized in 870 AD by Hebridean Vikings, the Irish monks living there had gone, but they left traces of their monastery, including some artefacts.

It looks as if Brendan knew where he was going and was by no means the first to make the journey. The islands would have been of immense help in navigating the open sea, a long way from the comforting coastline. In the twenty-four-hour summer light of the North Atlantic, their outline on the horizon could be seen at any time, and during the day the location of an island could be seen before it was visible. Tall columns of cloud often stack up thousands of feet high above even a small landmass, and they can be picked out from 50 miles away, long before the island itself comes into view. Early mariners understood these phenomena well and kept a sharp lookout for them.

More surprising than the tell-tale clouds is something that can only be observed in northern latitudes. When a stable mass of clear air sits over a colder surface it begins to behave like a lens, bouncing the light to allow sailors a sight of land which actually lies over the horizon. This is called a superior or Arctic mirage, and the bounced image appears as though it is floating upside down in the sky above its actual location, making it visible from much longer distances. Arctic mirage is often observed on a northern passage.

Next to violent storms, early mariners feared dense fog, because it blotted out almost all reference both during daylight and at night, when a view of the stars might have helped to plot a position. Because Tim Severin's curragh, the *St Brendan*, sailed in the summer of 1976, the weather was often clear and the crew noted in the log that in the 250-mile interval between Iceland and Greenland the height of the mountains in both places ensured that they were only out of sight of land for one or two days.

There were other simple aids to navigation derived from observation, which were passed on by one generation of early mariners to another. They looked over the sides of their curraghs for shoals of fish to give them guidance. Particular species, such as cod, were usually found near the Continental Shelf where the ocean was shallow, and even if land had not yet been sighted, that was a sign that it was close. Experienced sailors could also smell land before they could see it, if the wind was in the right quarter. Perhaps the most reliable aid to navigation was the sounding lead. In order to drop reasonably straight and measure the depth of the ocean accurately, leads needed to be heavy and some weighed more than 7lbs. Knowing the depth over a distance was important because the Continental Shelf rose gradually as land neared, and as a boat travelled out to sea, it fell away precipitously into the deeps. Captains knew that if they hit bottom with a lead at about 100 fathoms, that was the edge of the Shelf. When it was hauled aboard, the lead was carefully examined for materials dredged up from the seabed. Sailors knew places where the sand and mud was a particular colour or texture, and that could help to plot a position. The sounding lead was frequently used by early sailors: Herodotus knew of it and examples from the second century BC have been turned up by marine archaeologists.

Once the Continental Shelf had been found, experience had taught that certain pieces of land would come into view – given reasonable visibility – at certain times. Low-lying coastlines were obviously harder to detect from long distances out at sea, but a 300-metre hill or cliff could be seen from 35 nautical miles away.

Tim Severin had charts, compass, chronometer and a radio, but for the daily business of sailing a skin boat, he had no handbook. The skills needed to handle a curragh on the open sea had been long ago forgotten. Early in the voyage he discovered that the *St Brendan* was extremely fast over the water when a brisk wind filled the leather sails. Because it drew less than a foot of water, it scudded over the sea at speeds of 12 knots, faster than some modern yachts, but because there was no external keel and deeper draught, it could not hold the sea, and if she turned side-on to big waves, there was a great danger of being knocked down and capsizing, or filling with water. The *St Brendan* was an undecked open boat, and big seas meant constant pumping and bailing.

Equally, the fact that the curragh was made entirely out of sixth-century materials like wood, flax ropes, ox-hide, and held together with leather thongs, meant that she could flex considerably without damage when battered by big waves. And, crucially, could be repaired. Severin found that modern equipment often rusted or simply failed in extreme conditions, but that organic kit was both durable and reparable. At a late stage in the voyage the *St Brendan* strayed into the Labrador ice pack and was holed below the waterline. If the boat had been made of metal or wood, the consequences would have been disastrous and possibly fatal. As it was, a member of the crew, admittedly with great difficulty and showing tremendous fortitude, cut a spare ox-hide and, leaning over the side and under the surface, was able to work with a colleague inside the hull to fit and sew a life-saving patch over the hole.

Not only was the voyage of the *St Brendan* a remarkably courageous undertaking, but its achievement also added a great deal to the sparse store of knowledge about early Celtic seamanship. The matter of whether or not America was discovered a thousand years before Columbus might have made a dramatic headline but it was not really the point. Crossing the Atlantic in a leather boat simply showed that these apparently fragile craft were capable of almost anything, and that far from being disabled by poor technology, Celtic sailors could and did go where they pleased. Or, more precisely, where God was pleased to allow them to go. Tim Severin is convinced that the monks' faith was an important component of their seamanship. While accepting that their skills were considerable and that navigation was far from an exact science, he believes that many long voyages were attempted not in a spirit of daring or even recklessness, but because the monastic sailors trusted absolutely in God's mercy and prudence. Walking along the cliffs of the County Cork coastline near his home, Severin told me that it occurred to him more than once on the *St Brendan* voyage that a powerful faith might have been a comfort.

While monks, missionaries and mystics sailed around the coasts of Britain in search of converts and marvels, sea lords looked for plunder and conquest. Amongst the earliest records in Scotland, Ireland and Man are those related to naval warfare. The sea kingdom of Dalriada straddled both coasts of the North Channel, and on the Scottish side it had three kindred groups. There is a table in the *Senchus Fer nAlban*, or the *History of the Men of Alba*, compiled some time in the sixth century, which listed how many seven-bench war-boats each group should supply for a sea expedition (incidentally it is likely that these were large curraghs, and St Brendan took fourteen monks to sail his boat, enough for a seven bencher). In total the kindreds were expected to provide what amounted to a Celtic navy: 141 ships. It is clear from these and other records that wars were settled by admirals, sea lords and naval engagements, although nothing is written about how they fought. Much later, large numbers were still involved in warfare at sea, and in a medieval naval levy for the Isle of Man more than 600 sailors are demanded to row twenty-four galleys with twenty-six oars or sixteen larger ships.

While archaeological, oral and written records may be quiet about the conduct of Celtic naval warfare before 800, from around that date they resound to the clash of battle and slaughter from a new and terrifying direction. In 793 the Vikings sailed into history and attacked the monks of the defenceless island monastery of Lindisfarne off the coast of Northumberland. In all the written records there is a real sense of shock and outright terror at the sudden appearance of what seemed like an elemental force. Here is a telling piece of marginalia found in a ninth-century Irish manuscript:

> Fierce and wild is the wind tonight.
> It tosses the tresses of the sea to white.
> On such a night as this I take my ease,
> Fierce Northmen only course the quiet seas.

The savagery of the first attacks seems extreme, and that impression is fed by the fact that the Vikings were for a long time pagans who worshipped gods of war and thunder, and did not hesitate to slaughter monks like the man who wrote the verse above and steal their sacred treasure. In reality the Vikings employed no new tactics and invented no devastating weapons. Except one. What made the Vikings truly terrifying was their ships. They called them the *dreki*, or dragon-ships, and for the time they were unequalled in design and construction. Fast, adaptable and durable, the *dreki* gave the Vikings a priceless military advantage: the element of surprise. They could attack virtually any place without warning and get away quickly.

Developed to a sophisticated stage before they ever appeared off the coast of Britain, the *dreki* were decidedly superior to the leather boats of the Celts. Very large, sometimes measuring 80 by 17 feet, they were able to carry a crew of up to seventy and a load of 18 tons. The speed and size of the *dreki* could deliver a large war band quickly to a vulnerable target. Made of wood sawn into long planks or strakes, nailed together so that they overlapped and then lashed with pliable and springy spruce tree roots and caulked with horse hair and grease, the dragon-ships were light and flexible. Since the keel was often made out of a single oak tree, that helped to make the whole construction so elastic that the gunwales could twist 6 inches out of true and still remain watertight.

The Vikings appear to have been the first to use a large sail, and when a dragon-ship ran before the wind, it must have made tremendous headway. From earliest times, sailors had built up a substantial lore about the behaviour of the wind and classified it into different types. Classical writers gave the wind names and Homer characterized them: the north wind was cold, the west wet and the south hot and dry. Outside the Mediterranean the Vikings will have made different judgements, but their knowledge will have been very sophisticated and extensive.

Like the Celtic curraghs, the draught of a dragon-ship was shallow, and this allowed the Vikings to row the boats very close to a beach and then drag them up quickly above the tidemark, and also to make way up small rivers. If the river-course was only a foot or two deep, the load could quickly be lightened by taking all but two or three men out and having them row with only one or two pairs of oars pulled from the middle of the narrow ship, like a very large rowing boat.

For voyages out of the sight of land, the Vikings had no charts or compasses, and, like other early sailors, they relied on observation, sea lore and common sense. Distances were estimated on the basis of days under sail, or, if there was no wind, the number of shifts at the oars. A floating log was also used to measure the speed of the boat: it was attached to a line which had knots tied in it at regular intervals. This method was in universal use by the fifteenth century, and it gave us the names of two characteristic items of maritime technology: the ship's log and its speed measured in knots.

When the night sky was clear, the Vikings understood enough astronomy to use the stars as direction finders and an aid to plotting position. On cloudy days they sometimes brought out what the sagas called a sunstone, a piece of feldspar whose minerals polarize sunlight and change colour as the stone is turned towards where the sun might be. Such devices were much less reliable than what the Viking sea lords could observe. The presence of sea birds and seals generally indicated that land was not far away, and the regular, seasonal behaviour of larger creatures like whales could also help to confirm a position. Less obviously, the Vikings could work out directions relative to the sea swell and its patterns. In the Norn language, a dialect of Norse used in Shetland until the nineteenth century, there is a word for the 'Mother Wave' which shows how closely northern sailors observed the sea, in ways that seem almost mysterious to us now.

Even though the summer journey from Norway to Shetland could be managed in less than thirty-six hours with a following wind, life on board must have been harsh. The open-decked boats offered virtually no shelter and men were often cold and wet. For the sake of some protection, the Vikings treated the skin side of fleeces with cod liver oil in an attempt to make them waterproof. These first oilskins were probably very smelly, but no-one will have cared if they kept men dry.

Dragon-ships were designed for raiding and war but behind them sailed a name now remembered only on soup packets and stock cubes. The *knorr* was a cargo boat, wider, deeper and slower than the *dreki*, usually powered by sail and steered by a large paddle lashed to the bow end. This was the steerboard, a word which eventually mutated into starboard to mean the right hand side of a ship. The *knorr*s plied trade over an immense area. The early Vikings penetrated as far as Greenland and the shores of what is now Canada in the west, as far east as Kiev in Russia and south of there to Constantinople, which they called Micklegarth. One of their staples was the slave trade, and when the Vikings set up Dublin as a market, one of its prime values was as a central location for processing British captives into slavery. *Thrall* is the Norse word for 'slave', and it changed meaning somewhat as it passed into English as enthralled. The Vikings also controlled another lucrative commodity, as their colonies in Iceland and Greenland had a monopoly on walrus ivory. This was much sought after in Europe, particularly when the Moslem takeover of the southern Mediterranean and the Crusades cut off sources of elephant tusks.

One of the most beautiful examples of walrus ivory carving was found in a sand dune at Uig Bay on the Atlantic shore of the Isle of Lewis. Ninety-three chessmen were taken from a small stone-lined chamber dug into the sand and covered over. Four sets can be made up from the pieces, and microscopic examination reveals that some of them were stained red. The figures are compact for ease of play and storage, and had no projecting parts which could be accidentally be broken off – as a result, they are in excellent condition. With their pointed caps and hunched shoulders, the Lewis chessmen prompted a generation of children to see the Vikings in a very different light. Peter Firmin, the artist who created the images for the cartoon series *Noggin the Nog*, took them as a model for his drawings. Perhaps the figures animated so well because the originals have tremendous energy in their carving, looking as though they had just burst out of the walrus ivory ready to fight.

The chessmen were found in 1831 by a Lewis crofter, Calum MacLeod. It was appropriate that a man bearing this name should find such a powerful and beautiful reminder of Lewis's Viking past. MacLeod means son of Lod, a Viking name, as is MacAulay (son of Olaf), MacIver (son of Ivar), MacSween (son of Sweyn), MacAskill (son of Asgeir) and many others. When Calum MacLeod picked up a particular chess piece from the sand dune at Uig Bay, he will have seen an image come racing across the centuries to confront him. The rooks or castles are carved with staring eyes and bared teeth. They are berserkers, the crazed Viking warriors whose savagery was never forgotten.

As the list of Gaelic surnames suggests, the Viking settlers in the Hebrides, Ireland and Man were ultimately absorbed into Celtic culture. One of the earliest shifts to demonstrate this was caused by the emergence of an extraordinary man. Called Somerled the Viking, he was in fact no such thing, although he did have Celto-Norse parentage. He was the leader of a Gaelic revival which rolled back the power of the Vikings. In the early twelfth century Somerled emerged as a charismatic Hebridean admiral who used a modified naval technology to great effect. His name derives from Sumar-lidi, Norse for Summer Traveller, and it refers to the season when sea battles and raiding traditionally took place. Somerled's base was at Dunyvaig on the island of Islay and, like his personal name, it tells something about what he did. Dunyvaig means the Fort of the Little Ships. The Gaelic sea lords sailed craft which were smaller and even more manoeuvrable than the traditional dragon-ships. The little ships were built by a caste of boat wrights whose skills were passed on down the generations, and the widespread incidence of the surname MacIntyre may remember them, since it comes from Mac an t-Saoir, son of the carpenter. Around the time of Somerled's dominance, Hebridean boatwrights replaced the crude bow paddle, the steerboard of the *dreki* and the *knorrs*, with a hinged rudder which allowed ships to go about in a smaller and more controlled turning circle. In addition, Somerled's designers added a deck which acted as a fighting platform for archers and other, more close-quarter, soldiers. These new ships were called birlinns, or galleys, and they came to dominate naval warfare for a long time.

The *Aileach* is a beautifully made reconstruction of an early Hebridean birlinn, and in August 2000 I watched it being rowed up the Sound of Mull and into the harbour at Lochaline. The evening sea was calm and glassy, and the sun was still glowing golden over the hills of Mull as the oarsmen slid the little wooden boat alongside the pier. Once the rumbustious and thirsty crew had disembarked in search of a bar, the skipper, Susie Strachan, invited me aboard to have a look around. She runs the ship as a historical resource sustained by donations and covenants, and sails it as a piece of working maritime heritage. Open-decked, tough and highly seaworthy, lovingly crafted with its edges rubbed smooth by use, the *Aileach* has a surprising inner homeliness. Sitting on the rowing benches in the evening sunshine, Susie agreed that maritime archaeology had little to say about birlinns and that most of the information about their structure came from representations on funerary sculpture. Some of the best examples are on the tombs of Hebridean noblemen which are now displayed in the cloister of Iona Abbey, but the experience of sailing the *Aileach* in the Western Isles and the Atlantic littoral had allowed Susie some highly informed theorizing about naval warfare of the period. The construction of birlinns makes a particular method of ramming a likely tactic. Under oars, with a shallow draught, these ships can skim fast over the top of the water, and Susie believed that it was possible for an attacking boat to ram an opponent amidships. This would not sink the enemy ship by holing it below the waterline, as Greek and Roman galleys did, but the shape of the birlinn's hull would enable it to splinter oars, climb up on top and use its weight to push the other boat down and under the water, and perhaps crack the gunwales and break her in two.

Fighting platforms were built onto Somerled's birlinns, but a large fleet could also defend itself by rafting boats together. Tying several in line, side by side, would allow an admiral a much larger fighting platform which could beat off sporadic attacks by moving small groups of marines quickly to vulnerable points. While rafting will have largely immobilized a dozen or more birlinns, they could use the wind and the tide as well as their much-reduced rowing power to move slowly into the midst of an enemy fleet, where they could act like an aircraft carrier amongst smaller ships. There is no documentary evidence that Somerled or any other Hebridean admiral used precisely these tactics, but Susie Strachan's practical experience in sailing a birlinn makes their feasibility and likelihood persuasive.

Although he never used the title, Somerled was in effect the first in a line of leaders who called themselves the Lords of the Isles. Over time they built up a huge maritime empire which stretched from Lewis and the north-west mainland right down to the Isle of Man. It was held together by sea power and an unusual network of castles. Built on coastal sites so that they could service and be supplied by a navy rather an army, some, like Ardtornish in Morvern, have no roads leading to them and can only be reached by boat. There were more than thirty sea-castles in existence by 1400 and many were placed in line of beacon-sight so that signals could be passed quickly down the chain. Given the speed of the birlinns, communications in the Lordship of the Isles must have been much faster than in landward areas.

The greatest British sea poem is not a hymn to the exploits of Sir Francis Drake or Horatio Nelson, and it was not written in English. Alasdair macMhaighstir Alasdair composed *The Birlinn of Clanranald* some time around 1750 and recited it to the Chief of Clanranald soon after the disaster at Culloden. A schoolmaster turned captain in the Clan Donald regiments of the Highland army of the 1745 Rebellion, Alasdair macMhaighstir Alasdair caught the elegiac mood of a dying Gaelic society and turned his gifts to look back at the great sea culture of the Celts.

The Birlinn of Clanranald takes the narrative form of a voyage and begins with the blessing of the boat, a habit that reaches back across millennia to Columba and the pagan Celtic priests before him. Then the weapons of the sailors are blessed, and in Alexander Nicolson's superb translation no-one is allowed to forget that the sea itself is the greatest enemy:

> God's blessing be upon . . .
>
> Our polished bows of yew-tree,
> That bend in battle's din,
> Our birchen shafts that split not,
> Cased in grim badger's skin.
>
> Bless thou our dirks and pistols,
> Our good kilts in their folds,
> And every kind of warlike gear
> McDonell's bark now holds!

Be ye not soft or mild of mood
To face the war of weather,
While four planks of bark remain,
Or two sticks cling together.

While 'neath your feet she swims, while one
Thole-pin hold up its head,
Yield not to the ocean's frown,
Whate'er ye see of dread.

For the first part of the voyage the galley was rowed to the sailing place, where the wind would fill her sails. The sailors were urged to take hold of:

The smooth-handled oars, well-fashioned,
Light and easy,
That will do the rowing stout and sturdy,
Quick-palmed, blazing,
That will send the surge in sparkles,
Up to skyward,
All in flying spindrift flashing,
Like a fire-shower!
With the fierce and pithy pelting
Of the oar-bank,
That will wound the swelling billows,
With their bending.
With the knife-blades of the white thin oars
Smiting bodies,
On the crest of the blue hills and glens,
Rough and heaving.

And when all the oarsmen were seated, Malcolm, son of Ranald of the Ocean, began the boat-song.

Now since you're all chosen,
And ranked in good order,
With a bold stately plunge send her forward!
With a bold stately plunge send her forward!

A plunge quick and handy,
Not reckless, nor languid,
Keeping watch on the grey briny storm-hills
Keeping watch on the grey briny storm-hills

With a plunge of full vigour,
That will strain bone and sinew,
Let her track gleam behind her in glory!
Let her track gleam behind her in glory!

And to stir up your neighbour,
Raise a song light and cheery,
This good chant from the mouth of your fore-oar,
This good chant from the mouth of your fore-oar.

While rowlocks are grinding,
Palms blistered and shining,
Oars twisting in curls of the billows,
Oars twisting in curls of the billows.

Let your cheeks be all glowing,
Hands peeled skin all showing,
Great drops from your brows quickly falling,
Great drops from your brows quickly falling...

Pull clean, as one man,
Cleaving waves at each span,
With hearty goodwill and not tardy,
With hearty goodwill and not tardy.

Strike even and steady,
Looking oft to each other,
Wake the life in your sinews and arms,
Wake the life in your sinews and arms...

Clear the point there before you,
With brow-sweat fast pouring,
Then hoist sail from Uist of wild geese!
Then hoist sail from Uist of wild geese!

At sunrise on the Feast of St Bride (1 February, or the Celtic festival of
Imbolc) the birlinn nosed its way out of the mouth of Loch Eynort in
South Uist and on into the Minch:

The sun bursting golden yellow
From his cloud-husk;
Then the sky grew tawny, smokey,
Full of gloom;

It waxed wave-blue, thick, buff-speckled,
Dun and troubled;
Every colour of the tartan
Marked the heavens.
A rainbow 'dog' is seen to westward –
Stormy presage;
Flying clouds by strong winds riven,
Squally showers.

The storm tossed the birlinn on the ocean and beat hard down as it
made way south until:

The sea cried peace with us at length
At Islay Sound Cross,
And the harsh-voiced wind was bidden
To give over.
She lifted us to high regions
Of the heavens,
And the sea, a smooth white table,
Ceased from barking.
Thanks we gave to the High King
Of the elements,
Good Clanranald who preserved
From death horrid;
Then we took down the thin sails,
Speckled canvas,
Let down the fine smooth red masts
Along her floor,
Shoved out the slim, shining oars,
Smooth and coloured,
Of the far McBarras cut
In Finnan Island;
And we rowed with steady swinging,
Without failing,
To good harbour 'neath the heights
Of Carrick Fergus.
We cast anchor at our leisure
In the roads there,
And took meat and drink in plenty,
And abode there.

Even though Alasdair macMhaighstir Alasdair was looking back from the middle of the eighteenth century, his great poem catches brilliantly the atmosphere of medieval Celtic sea culture in the days of its pomp. With sailors as experienced and intrepid as those in the birlinn of Clanranald, it is not difficult to understand why and how the Lordship of the Isles grew so powerful and ambitious.

Elsewhere down the western edge of Britain, geography was shaping politics. At approximately the same time as Ardtornish Castle was being fortified, the English kings were building sea castles. When Edward I of England invaded north Wales in 1277 and 1282, he understood the importance of the local geography immediately, and that Llywelyn's principality of Gwynedd was protected by a combination of mountains and sea. Tidal estuaries on both northern and western coasts made advance difficult, and Anglesey was divided from the mainland by the powerful currents of the Menai Straits. Edward I and his military advisors had considered these problems and they planned a ring of sea castles to hold Wales in an iron grip. Like the fortresses of the Lords of the Isles, Conwy, Caernarfon, Beaumaris and the others are designed to be supplied by sea, and each has a small, fortified harbour for easy and safe access. Edward's grasp of sea power was sure, and when his huge armies tramped along the coast road to Gwynedd, they were guarded and provisioned by fleets sailing out of Dublin and Chester.

As the English colonized more and more of the Sea Kingdoms and the Scottish crown succeeded in bringing the Lords of the Isles under closer control, the importance of naval power in the west began to decline. Large navies were increasingly hard to maintain, and maritime warfare moved more and more towards the use of artillery which was difficult to manufacture in the predominantly rural western littoral, and difficult to acquire. But the spirit of the early sea lords had one last triumphant hurrah in the unlikely shape of the Irish Pirate Queen, Grace O'Malley. Her story supplies a cheerful coda at the end of the long story of Celtic sea power.

The proper version of her name is Granuaille and she was born in 1530, the only child of Dudara O'Malley, King of Umhall, the area around Clew Bay on the western coast of Ireland. The real kingdom of the O'Malleys was not on land: they were the lords of the seas around

Ireland. On Dudara's death, in an early witness to Grace's determination, she overturned Ireland's kin-based system of inheritance to beat off male contenders and assert her own right to the succession.

When Grace took over her father's fleet, it mostly traded in raw materials such as hides, tallow, salt beef and salt fish, but it did so in such a way as to avoid paying customs due at ports like Galway and Cork. Granting spurious licences to Scottish, Spanish, English and French fishermen, it sounds as though she also ran a protection business, but increasingly Grace spent her time in piracy. When the English sent a force to besiege her castle in County Clare, she repulsed them with some ease and such was her captains' knowledge of the reefs and rocks off the Atlantic shore that government ships were powerless to control the Queen of Pirates. Her ships seem to have been highly developed versions of Hebridean birlinns, and Grace's flagship was a very manoeuvrable galley 'rowed with 30 oars and sail and had on board ready to defend her 100 good shot'. This was not a small-time operation.

Grace wore out two husbands and chose a third, Richard Bourke, on a trial basis, reviving the old Celtic custom of handfasting. Still observed in country places in nineteenth-century Scotland, this was a sort of trial marriage whereby partners agreed to live together for a year to see if a close relationship might also become a happy one. If this temporary union produced any children, they could be the responsibility of either partner, but importantly, no social stigma was attached if things did not go well and the couple parted. At the start of a handfasted year a simple oath was sworn, and the 'marriages' supervised by the blacksmith at Gretna Green are a remnant of the ancient tradition. Grace moved into Rockfleet Castle with Bourke, but after a year she locked him out of his castle and harangued him from the battlements. Surprisingly, they reunited and Grace became pregnant. She gave birth on board one of her pirate ships the day before it happened to be attacked by Algerian corsairs. When the fight was at its fiercest, the First Mate came below to ask Grace, who was nursing her new-born son, if she could come on deck. 'What!' she roared, buckling on her cutlass, 'Can you not do without me for one day?' Grace appeared on deck and urged her sailors on to victory. To commemorate the day and its deeds, she named her son Tibbet na Long, Tibbet of the Ships.

Much later the O'Malleys undertook a contract to ferry mercenaries to Ireland to fight for the native kings against the Elizabethan colonists.

Tibbet was taken hostage and threatened with an indictment for treason and the appalling death that would follow his certain conviction. His mother petitioned Elizabeth I, who not only granted a pardon but also sent '18 articles of interrogatory' to be answered by 'Grany Ni Maly', a much better than usual rendition of her Gaelic name. The Queen was curious about Grace and had heard many tales. They were exactly the same age and both mature women who had made their way in a man's world. In 1593 Grace sailed her flagship from Clew Bay to Greenwich to have an audience with Queen Elizabeth. They were both sixty-three and nearing the ends of eventful lives. Apparently entirely unattended, they spent several hours closeted together, and although there is nothing but circumstantial evidence to support the judgement, it is very likely that they found a great deal to talk about. The upshot was that Grace was given a letter allowing her 'to hang the Queen's enemies' wherever she found them. Like Sir Francis Drake's notorious commission, it was tacit permission to return to piracy. The English Governor of Ireland, Sir Richard Bingham, was horrified to discover that Queen Elizabeth had neglected to extract a promise of good behaviour from Grace, and to make her triumph entirely complete, Bingham was recalled to London in disgrace eighteen months later.

Elizabeth and Grace both died in 1603, and Grace O'Malley was buried in the graveyard at the abbey on Clare Island, out in the Atlantic, surrounded by the sea on which she had lived her life.

The traditions of the navies of the Sea Kingdoms gradually faded into memory and the seamanship turned itself to piracy and to smuggling. Both in Cornwall and the Isle of Man, the attentions of the excisemen were often avoided, and the Manx perfected such an efficient quasi-legal method of laundering contraband that the British crown was forced to incorporate the island by purchasing it from the Dukes of Atholl for £70,000 in 1765.

Sea lords, fleets of warships and pirates may no longer sail from the ports and harbours of the west of Britain, but fishing boats still hunt in these waters, and many of the traditions of the Sea Kingdoms are still whispered in their unwritten habits and superstitions. Because the sea is so unpredictable, fishermen are creatures of routine. It provides certainty amongst potential chaos, and some of these certainties are very ancient.

When a new boat was built everything possible was done to make it lucky. The choice of wood was important and she-oak (a tree with more female than male flowers – males stand up on stalks and females hang down in tresses, of course) was greatly favoured and may be the reason why ships are called 'she'. If a woman came on board it was considered unlucky because the boat might become jealous. New craft were never commissioned on a Friday, just as keels were never laid that day, and the lore of omens and weather signs would fill a large directory. Perhaps the most telling fact is that fishing boats were where Celtic languages were spoken last and longest. Both Cornish and Manx were stubbornly used by fishermen long after English had triumphed on land. Because they were traditional, and because they formed part of an unbroken routine, they persisted in the mouths of skippers and deckhands, the descendants of the sailors who rowed the curraghs, dragon-ships and birlinns of the west of Britain.

Conceptualizing the maritime culture of the Sea Kingdoms is difficult. Land empires like Rome have pulled our attention away from the sea with ideas like 'all roads lead to Rome', and successors such as the dominions of Charlemagne and the concept of Christendom have kept the focus to landward. But now and again there are occasional flickers of the old ways of thinking. A group of young people in Ballycastle on the Antrim coast of Northen Ireland recently decided to go to a party. Since some of them were fishermen, they thought of it as only going across the road. In fact the party was on the island of Islay, twenty miles across the sea to the north. They sailed over, had a grand time, slept in the boat and came back home the following morning.

FOUR

The Islands of the Mighty

SCOTLAND IS ENGLISH FOR ALBA, Wales is English for Cymru and means the Land of the Foreigners, the Isle of Man is English for Ellan Vannin, Cornwall is English for Kernow and it means the Land of the Cornish Foreigners. At least Ireland retains an element of Eirinn in the first syllable. All five Celtic languages use the same word for the English. The Scottish and Irish Gaels, the Manx, the Welsh and the Cornish call them the Sais. It means the Saxons. Even though England and the English took their names from the Angles, the other part of the main composite group to settle in Britain in the middle of the first millennium, the uniform use of 'Saxon' by the Celts is striking.

All of the names hint at incomprehension, on both sides. Most European languages had more than one neighbour and those at the edges of speech communities often had an ability to understand something of each other and, over a period, exchanged borrowings. But when the Angles, the Saxons, the Jutes, the Frisians and others arrived on the island of Britain, the Celts had no idea what they were saying, and the Germanic tribes were similarly nonplussed. Each incoming group was just as unintelligible as the next, so they were all lumped into the one category, the Sais. It became a heavily loaded description and the Scottish term Sasunnach and the Welsh use of Sais are still mildly abusive. In their turn the Sais called the Celts the Welsh (the Foreigners), even though they were quite clearly the natives.

English has absorbed very few words from Britain's Celtic languages despite long-term proximity, and while that might arise for any number

66

of reasons, it does not imply harmony and frequent interchange. The linguistic traffic in the opposite direction has been a little more brisk, but that is hardly surprising when the later dominance of the English speech community is taken into account. A surprising footnote is that there is a small but fascinating group of Celtic loan words that have made their way into English by a very circuitous route. For example, moccasin is not a North American Indian word: it comes from the Gaelic *mo chasan,* meaning my feet. And when the increasing popularity of jazz and blues music helped to import black American slang, devotees were often asked, 'Do you dig it, man?' Dig has no agricultural associations but comes from the Gaelic root, *tuig,* which means to understand. There is a variant in Cockney with the use of the word 'twig'.

The journeys of Celtic words may be long, colourful and surprising, but place and people names offer a stronger sense of contemporary historical attitudes. Recorded events are relatively easy to arrange in an intelligible sequence, but attitudes offer a more pungent understanding of the past and how it shaped the present. The long relationship between the Celts of Britain and the English is now, more than ever, a distillate of historical attitudes, and it must be instructive for our future to find out where they came from – some understanding of linguistic borders is a good place to start.

The Welsh did not call themselves Welsh for a very long time. Until the twelfth century they called themselves the British, the Brytaniaid. As the independent remnant of the Britons, the people who were here before the Romans, the Anglo-Saxons and the Normans, they clung to an ever-diminishing hope that their nation might return to its ancient glories, and that Welsh-speaking kings might rule again in the place they called the Island of the Mighty.

Eventually reality wore out romantic aspiration and the Welsh gave up the name of the British and began to call themselves the Cymry. It is an interesting word that sheds more light on their national self-awareness. Cymry comes from Combrogi, which translates literally as 'the people who share the same border/region'. A looser but better rendition is Compatriots, a name which allowed the Welsh to link themselves with the Celtic people of southern Scotland (called Yr Hen Ogledd, the Old North), Cumbria, Cornwall and the hills of northern England. Cumbria also derives from Combrogi, and Welsh was still spoken around Carlisle and in the mountains of the Lake District until at least 1000, and in Strathclyde and the Southern Uplands for even longer. These northern Compatriots were subsumed into an expanding Kingdom of the Scots, but before they lost their separate identity, they bolstered a Welsh sense of a British past.

The Welsh word for England remembers the old politics: it is Lloegr and it means the Lost Lands. There is a historical moment when that loss began to become clear to the Brytaniaid. Around the year 610 a holy man called Beuno was walking on the Welsh bank of the Severn when he heard a man on the other side of the water calling his dogs in a language he did not understand. Beuno knew at once that the Sais had reached the frontiers of the Cymry. 'Listen,' said the saint, 'I hear the heathens coming.'

In time the heathens became Christians and then eventually a unified English polity which pressed hard on its Celtic neighbours for more than a thousand years. At every turning point in the long process of colonizing the rest of Britain and Ireland, the English never failed to understand the power of Celtic languages and how they gave real cohesion to the Welsh, the Scots, the Irish, the Manx and the Cornish. They intuited that the Celts are not a racial group but one bound together by language. To conquer, dominate and exploit, it was essential to strike hard at that cultural core and destroy or enfeeble the mighty languages of the Celts. The war for Britain was as much a war of words as of blood and steel.

In their modern versions the five Celtic languages fall into two main groups, and in order to understand their centrality to the story of the Sea Kingdoms, the differences between them need to be understood. Welsh and Gaelic are not mutually intelligible, although they share clear connections. P-Celtic and Q-Celtic are the handy philological labels given to each. The Welsh word for head is *pen*, a place-name prefix found, for example, in Penrith, Penicuik and Penarth; the Gaelic equivalent is *ceann*, found in places like Kintyre or Kincardine. Other words show the differences equally well: *map* and *mac* for son of, or *pedwar* and *ceithir* for the number four. P-Celtic place names reached far to the north of what is now Scotland, and there is strong evidence that it was spoken on the Isle of Man before Manx became established. A small group of loan words in Irish Gaelic also suggest that P-Celtic may have been spoken there first. These whispers of evidence imply two clear waves of Celtic settlement in Britain and Ireland. However that may be, there are unmistakable indications that the P and Q groups were fully differentiated by 400 AD. The northern Q-Celtic group comprises Irish Gaelic and its two dialects of Scots Gaelic and Manx, while in the southern P-Celtic group are Welsh, Cornish and Breton.

While these distinctions inside the Celtic speech group are important, the differences between Celtic languages as a whole and English will continually inform all of this story, and show why some of the clashes between the two took on a particular colour. What strikes a listener first and most forcibly is how different English and, for example, Gaelic sound to the ear. Unlike other European languages occupying neighbouring territory, they share no obvious vocabulary and have a completely separate syntax. When it is explained to a non-Gaelic-speaking listener that Gaelic has no word for no or for yes, he or she understandably wonders how a language can function without such basic equipment. To confuse further, Gaelic often changes the beginnings of words as well as their endings depending on the context in which they are found.

The most elementary observation is also the most telling: the sound and the rhythm of the two languages are very different, and this is a telling observation which needs explaining. Here is a Gaelic poem, often performed as a beautiful song, written about Uig Bay, coincidentally the place where the Lewis Chessmen were found, on the Atlantic coast of the Hebrides:

> An ataireachd ard,
> Cluinn fuaim na h-ataireachd ard,
> Tha torunn a' chuain,
> Mar a chualas leums' e nam phaisd,
> Gun mhuthadh, gun truas,
> A' sluaisreadh ganneimh na tragh'd,
> An ataireachd bhuan
> Cluinn fuiam na h'ataireachd ard.

And here is an English translation:

> The high surge of the sea,
> Listen to the high surge of the sea,
> It is the sound of the ocean,

As I heard it when I was a child,
Without cease, without pity,
It washes back and forth on the sands of the beach.
The eternal surge of the sea,
Listen to the high surge of the sea.

This is not a bad rendering in English, if somewhat literal, but the differences between the versions are instructive. No-one could reasonably expect English to follow closely the rhythms of the original, but for the language of Shakespeare and Cranmer, it fails, disappointingly, to catch much of the magic of the poem. The first reason for this is obvious. Although it is difficult for a monoglot English speaker to perceive it without hearing the pronunciation, there is a rhythm to 'An Ataireachd Ard' which plays in harmony with its subject. The words, the lines and their cadences sound like the waves rolling in off the Atlantic. The individual words help to sound a steady beat. With the emphasis overwhelmingly on the first syllable, 'ataireachd' (pronounced 'aatairochg') mimics the build-up and abrupt crash of a breaker. 'Torunn' means not only sound but a particular thump as a wave hits the tideline, and the verb 'sluaisreadh' (pronounced 'slewashrigh') is a beautiful onomatopoeia of the action of the tide washing in and out over the sand. Ataireachd and sluaisreadh have no English equivalent and it is hard to avoid clumsy translation. Not only does English lack the lexical scope to describe the ocean like this, but it has also lost the vocal range needed to do justice to a whole range of the sounds of the natural world.

Difficult to express on paper but worth doing nonetheless, both Welsh and Gaelic contain standard consonants and vowels not found in English. In fact, the bafflement caused by Welsh consonant clusters where w and y are used as vowels and the number of redundant d's and h's in Gaelic make it very awkward for English speakers to find a way into these languages because they find the pronunciation so difficult. It may be a familiar observation that the word 'loch' presents great problems to an Englishman who almost invariably pronounces it as 'lock' while having no difficulty with the name of the German composer Johann Sebastian Bach, but the picture is a good deal more complex than that.

Superficially the alphabets of English, Welsh and Gaelic look similar, with the last-named having only eighteen letters. There appears to be no j, k, q, v, x or z in either Welsh or Gaelic, but in fact these sounds are produced by compounds and variable pronunciations of other letters. S can work differently in Gaelic, from a hissed sibilant to the 'sh' sound both found in *sluaisreadh*, and v is represented in Welsh by f and mh in Gaelic. Celtic languages demand a greater range of sounds from the speaker than English does. In everyday words the ll which appears twice in the place name Llanelli is difficult, and the Gaelic *dhomh* meaning 'for me' or 'to me' is almost impossible to communicate in the standard alphabet. The basic form is like the word 'gong' but with the g's further back in the palate so that it almost sounds like 'young'. But doesn't really.

Scholars of linguistics point out that the vocabulary of modern urban Europeans is often much smaller than that of allegedly primitive peoples. The reason for this is straightforward: those who live in and depend on the natural world need to describe it accurately and retain an extensive range of terms (not just adjectives) to cope with the ways in which the landscape changes with the seasons, the weather and the actions of men and women. The Celtic languages of Britain are old and share a good deal with those of the Masai of eastern Africa, the Amazonian Indians and the Australian Aborigines. They are also rural and coastal, and describe a life far from what the Gaels call Abhainn mor an t-Sluaigh, the Great River of People. A weather forecast given in Gaelic, for example, would contain much precision and colour. *Tioradh* means a dry period between bands of rain seen coming off the Atlantic. There are four words to describe different sorts of squall, and one, *tioram*, for a dry day with low humidity. Not only would weather forecasts in Gaelic be shorter, they would also be more precise – at least in their use of language.

Welsh is described affectionately as Yr Hen Iaith, the Old Language of the country, whereas English is Yr Iaith Fain, the Thin Language. While this presents a partial view of the picture, it does give a sense of an absorbent, elastic and comparatively rule-free English compared with a formal and frankly archaic Welsh and Gaelic. Always playing linguistic catch-up with pale imitations like *facs* and *fon* on a letterhead, or, even more disappointing, *computair* for 'computer', or the ridiculous *feareolais tomhas is aireamh*, which lumbers literally into English as 'the man with knowledge of measurement and number', but really means mathematician, Celtic languages do not cope well with technology or indeed with urban life. Where their richness lies is in the natural and domestic worlds and the eternal subtleties of human nature.

The Celts of Britain and Ireland see colour differently from English speakers and take care to describe its nuances with some precision. The unhappy vagueness of 'creamy-white' or 'pinky-red' or the dithering of a recent television presenter's description on a DIY show of 'a sort of Tuscan quarry tile ochrey sort of light red . . . ish colour' is not tolerated in Celtic languages. A much broader range of colour names was developed to cope with and accurately label colour differences as they occur throughout the natural world. Despite the boom in interior decoration, particularly on television, where discussions about colour can be heard most evenings, English has not revived the richness of its pre-Industrial Revolution vocabulary and it now rarely uses 'brindled' for 'streaked with irregular dark shades', whereas Gaelic has kept the equivalent *riabhach* in currency. There is nothing now in English for a colour at a point in the spectrum between parchment and porridge, and nothing for 'dark and blotchy', but Gaelic still has *odhar* and *lachdann*.

This versatility is characteristic of old and rural languages. Latin used two words for black (*ater* for matt and *niger* for shiny) and for white (*albus* for matt and *candidus* for shiny) because it never lost its links with the countryside. All of the Gaelic adjectives noted above developed as descriptions of the hides of cattle. When questions of ownership and pastoral rights arose, it was important to be clear what your cows looked like. In that context it is hardly surprising that the interior designers who inflict their colour schemes on a nervously grateful couple each week no longer possess the vocabulary or perception to describe what they have done with anything more than a vague sweep of the hand and a few quotes from a paint manufacturer's catalogue. When an Englishman declares that sunsets are simply red, a Gael smiles and remembers the power of his mighty language.

English originated in the speech of small groups of Anglo-Saxon settlers in eastern Britain in the fifth and sixth centuries. As the linguistic and political frontier rolled west over Britain, four main dialects emerged. Northumbrian, Mercian, Kentish and West Saxon all enjoyed periods of primacy as their kings tried to convert the symbolism of the title Bretwalda, or Britain-ruler, into a reality. Under King Ine of Wessex and his better-known successor, Alfred, their West Saxon dialect of English developed sufficient prestige to challenge Latin as the language of law, literature and education. Unparalleled elsewhere in vernacular Europe, the precocity of written, official English contrasts with the overwhelmingly oral life of Welsh and Gaelic. This unwritten tradition survived for a long time. There are very few texts for Cornish, only some religious scraps from the medieval period, and a handful of miracle plays and religious tracts from the seventeenth and eighteenth centuries, while the first substantial dictionary did not appear until 1951. So little sense of continuity exists that those who wish to reconstruct Cornish find it difficult to agree on a standard version, badly hampering any potential revival and one of the reasons why it has fewer than a thousand or so speakers.

In Welsh, the habit of composing poetry entirely in the imagination and thereafter not writing it down but holding it in memory for recital persisted until recently. On a farm near Llanfyllin in Powys a woman called Anne Griffiths created a substantial corpus of poetry in her head which remained only in an oral form until some time after her death in 1805. A religious ecstatic, the act of composition occasionally threw Anne Griffiths into a trance. As she worked in the fields of her farm, the poetry inhabited her mind so powerfully that she would fall to the ground with cries of wonder at what she had imagined. The poems became hymns of huge passion, and were only preserved because Griffiths recited them to Ruth Evans, a woman who helped at the planting and the harvest. Some time after the poet's death, Evans dictated what she could remember to an amanuensis and through his manuscript Anne Griffiths' imagination found its way into Welsh language culture.

At the heart of a comparison between English as a written language of record and the oral tradition of Gaelic and Welsh there lies a striking anomaly. The distinction is broadly correct but not at all clear-cut. Gaelic-speaking scribes produced a phenomenal amount of written material for centuries before much appeared in English. In places now thought to be far from the intellectual heart of Europe, works of extraordinary literary beauty were produced. These did not spring unbidden from a fertile Celtic creativity: they were copied and written in Latin and made beautiful for the greater glory of God. The illuminated manuscripts of the Gaelic west were compiled as devotional objects, but they have something to tell us about the language spoken, and only very occasionally written, by the calligraphers who produced them.

As early Christianity struggled to survive in barbarian Europe, the Irish church of Palladius, Patrick and the other missionary saints took on the role of a beacon. Christianity is a religion of the book. '*In principio erat verbum*' begins a long story which formed the whole basis of Christianity's message, and if worship was to be properly offered and converts made, Bibles, gospels and commentaries were needed. Thousands of Irish copyists met this need, and between 450 and 850, they made more than half of all the biblical commentaries which survive in Europe from that time. Precious unique manuscripts, often secular classical works by the likes of Vergil and Homer, were sent from Rome to Ireland to be copied and therefore preserved.

In addition, the Irish made many individual gospels which were small enough to be portable and easily read from the hand. But their most glorious achievements were the great illuminated manuscripts. The *Book of Kells* is thought to be the most sumptuous of all the Irish gospels and it is certainly the best known. It was probably begun on Iona and, when the Vikings began to raid regularly, brought inland to Kells, in the Irish midlands, to be continued, but surprisingly, never completed. No-one cared much about this because the *Book of Kells* was never intended to be read. Instead, it was opened for display on the altar or elsewhere in the church where it could be seen. There are many mistakes in the text, and one page has been copied twice. Scribes knew that no-one was going to read the gospel and they expended their care and energy on the quality of the decoration. The great books were thought to have magical powers. After the Dissolution of the Monasteries, another gorgeous illuminated manuscript known as the *Book of Durrow* was sold and eventually ended up in the hands of a farmer. He used to dip it into cattle troughs and have sick cows drink the water. Evidently he believed that this could cure them. In more practical gospels the decorated capital letters at the beginning of important sections had more than an aesthetic role. Before the Bible was organized into books, chapters and verses, these pages helped readers find their way around.

The illuminated manuscripts took a long time to make and cost a great deal in resources. The early Irish economy valued cattle very highly and it is no cultural accident that one of the most loving terms of endearment used in Gaelic is *m-eudail*, which originally meant 'my cattle'. Two hundred animal skins were needed to make the *Book of Kells* – a very substantial economic investment. Consequently there was no wastage and every hide, even those with blemishes, was used. The shape of the hide had an interesting effect. Once scrolls had given way to pages, it dictated the shape of the book you are holding now. Because of the need to use as large a surface area as possible for writing and painting, the monks cut the skin in a rectangle running from the points at which the animal's legs joined the body. Then they folded it so that it could be stitched in the middle and written on on either side. That is why almost all books are taller when closed and broader when opened.

Scribes preferred to write on calfskin and the words vellum and veal both come from the Old French *velin* for a calf. The younger the better, and the thinnest pages used the skin of unborn animals aborted for the purpose, while a thicker gauge could be got from calves at two or three months old. Young skins had an ivory colour much prized by the scribes, and the whiter vellum with a reasonable degree of thickness was best for the more heavily decorated pages. Much preparation was involved before a monk could set to work. Skins were first dipped in lime before having all the hair scraped off and then stretched on a wooden frame. Pages were cut to size and then folded and arranged into 'gatherings'. With a very sharp knife, tiny holes were pricked to mark out the overall writing area, then pages were finally ruled out into lines and copying began.

Some of the more elaborate illustrations of the four gospels give a glimpse of how the Irish monks worked. Quills were made from the long tail feathers of geese or swans to allow them to be sharpened more than once and one saint is depicted holding a reed pen for more detailed work. Two styles of handwriting evolved: Irish majuscule for bigger letters and Irish miniscule for smaller. To execute the areas of paint inside the curve of the capital letters and in the places where only decoration was wanted, known as the carpet pages, the monks used brushes made of animal hair. Since it was soft and fine, the winter coat of the pine marten was much sought after. Compasses, rules, set-squares and dividers were all employed to make straight lines and perfect curves, and the blank obverses of heavily decorated pages often show their traces. Inkwells were conical and look as though they were made out of horns which were straight enough to be stuck in the ground or through a hole in a writing board. The *Book of Kells* is written in iron-gall ink, which is made from a decoction of oak-apples and sulphate of iron. For decoration the range of pigments available to the Irish was extremely wide, and while reds, whites, browns and greens could readily be made from minerals, plants and animals found locally, some colours made a long journey. For the ultramarine (the name reveals a distant origin) needed to paint the robes of the Virgin Mary, lapis lazuli was imported from Afghanistan. The extract known as folium came from the Mediterranean sunflower and offered a spectrum from pinks to purples, while a bright red called kermes came from insects caught in southern Europe and North Africa which were dried and then crushed to produce a powder. A natural dark blue was obtained from the indigo plant of the eastern Mediterranean. These colours were available because of a well-organized trade operating between Irish monasteries and merchants who could source them from great distances, deliver them to Atlantic ports and carry them by ship to Ireland. Small, light and precious, pigment was the perfect cargo.

Judging by the evidence from marginalia and archaeology, it seems likely that Irish copyists often worked outside. When the weather was good, the light would have been far better outdoors than in buildings with small windows. Many manuscripts were not made in busy scriptoria but by hermits working alone with a writing board on their knees under a shady tree, listening to birdsong.

A moment's reflection on the amount of organization required for the production of these beautiful gospels will banish any preconceptions about a primitive and unsophisticated society blundering about in the chaos of the post-Roman Dark Ages. The Irish understood well the central importance of copying and preserving Latin, Greek and sometimes Hebrew manuscripts. Their extraordinary output spun a golden thread between the classical period and the Renaissance, and without them much would have been lost. The only pity is that they did not often apply their great skills to recording a native Irish literature. Short marginalia offer tantalizing glimpses of the lives and thoughts of these men. In a ninth-century Latin commentary on Vergil and a list of Greek paradigms – dry stuff – there appears this poem in Gaelic:

> I and Pangur Ban my cat,
> 'Tis a like task we are at:
> Hunting mice is his delight,
> Hunting words I sit all night.
>
> 'Tis a merry thing to see
> At our tasks how glad are we,
> When at home we sit and find
> Entertainment to our mind.

'Gainst the wall he sets his eye,
Full and fierce and sharp and sly;
'Gainst the wall of knowledge I
All my little wisdom try.

So in peace our task we ply,
Pangur Ban my cat and I;
In our arts we find our bliss,
I have mine and he has his.

It sounds like a good and contented life led by a man who had a cheerful sense of posterity, and perhaps also a quiet sense of mission. Two hundred years before, armed with their freshly copied gospels, Irish missionaries had fanned out all over barbarian Europe. Incredibly and often anonymously intrepid, they suffered all manner of privation, even martyrdom, to found a glittering list of monasteries: Iona, St Gall, Bobbio, Fiesole, Regensburg are among the most famous, as Irishmen and women took the word of God as far to the east as Kiev and as far south as Taranto. Many Irish manuscripts survived in these European monastic libraries and in 870 the French writer of a *Life of St Germanus* noted: 'Almost all of Ireland, despising the sea, is migrating to our shores with a herd of philosophers!'

While the intellectual life of Europe was being revived by the Irish, England was suffering first the attentions of the Vikings and then conquest by the Danes. Between 1016 and 1035 the Danish King Cnut ruled a great sea-borne Scandinavian empire and, after invading Britain, presided over years of relative peace before the return of the dynasty of Wessex and Edward the Confessor. Partly because Cnut represented a Norse-speaking and non-English empire, his achievements have been undervalued and less noticed than they deserve. But there is no doubt that the influence of the Norse on England was profound, particularly as regards the development of the English language. So that the Norse settlers and the English could understand each other, the complexities of the native tongue were somewhat smoothed out, and much vocabulary and syntax was imported from Scandinavia. Basic forms like 'they', 'their' and 'them' are Norse in origin. With the advent of more Norsemen, in the shape of French-speaking Normans in the second half of the eleventh century, English once again adapted to external influence. In the interests of intelligibility, its most cosmopolitan dialect, that of London, had become the standard written form by the fifteenth century and the arrival of Caxton's printing press. By that time English had laid down many of the foundations of its elasticity, utility and ability to change and modernize.

The kings of medieval England, who mostly spoke French, understood the power of language and its importance as a political tool: peoples who understood each other were more likely to form a homogenous society which was simpler, if not necessarily easier, to govern.

Between the twelfth and seventeenth centuries English, Scottish and British kings began to use force, either military, legislative or both, to strike at the cultural roots of the Welsh and Gaelic languages. The last 800 years have been the story of slow retreat, with occasional retrenchments, until today there is no-one in Britain or Ireland who is a monoglot speaker of a Celtic language: everyone now speaks English. What follows are incidents in that long struggle, from Wales, Ireland and Scotland, where the languages were attacked and, later, where they sometimes fought back.

As the Plantagenet kings turned their attention to Wales, they showed how well they had grasped the principles of a monoglot state, and amongst their earliest actions was an attempt to banish poetry. When Edward I came to the English throne in 1272, about 45 per cent of the people living on the islands of Britain and Ireland spoke dialects of Welsh or Gaelic. Governed by a French-speaking elite and recorded in Latin by clerks who probably also spoke French, England spoke to itself in a language used by only a narrow majority of the total population of the Isles. The modern picture of Celtic languages as lexical curiosities languishing in Britain's back rooms while English powers the world economy can easily colour our thinking about our past. In the thirteenth century Welsh and Gaelic were strong, the languages of nations and related cultures, and striking expressions of independence and difference.

Edward I was the greatest European warrior of the age: a tall, fearless and occasionally furious man whose fits of temper are recorded in the Exchequer records. There survives a bill for the repair of his daughter Elizabeth's coronet which the king had flung in the fire, and another report of Edward Longshanks literally tearing out lumps of his son's hair in rage at his persistent interest in young men. But this king was no mere hothead or madman. Rather, he was brutally single-minded and highly perceptive about the obstacles that lay in the way of the achievement of his objectives. The Welsh and the Scots got in Edward's

ABOVE Stonehenge rebuilt and visualized as a gathering-place for a 'Festival of Britons'.

BELOW LEFT This seventeenth-century vision of a Druid appears to owe more to the Old Testament than to Celtic history. Holding a book, of all things, he seems to be pondering the identity of a plant while referring to some botanical text.

BELOW RIGHT A seventeenth-century realization of the Wicker Man. How this structure managed to stay upright is not explained in the drawing.

A romantic rendition of Celtic culture – *The Bard* by Thomas Jones shows Stonehenge-like remains in the background and what appear to be dead bodies strewn around the windy landscape.

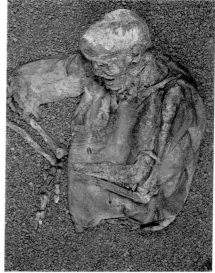

The remains of 'Lindow Man'
show how well the peat preserved
his skin.

A stylized Ogham alphabet with the Gaelic names of trees arranged opposite
each combination of *fleascan*. The initial letter of each word corresponds to
the Ogham letter.

Et belua in mari que grece aspido delone dicat Aspido tit
Laune ũ aspido testudo. Cete etiam dicta. ob cete.
īmmanitatē corporis. est enī sicut ille q̃ excepit

St Brendan's encounter with the whale, Jasconius, from a manuscript of *c.* 1200.

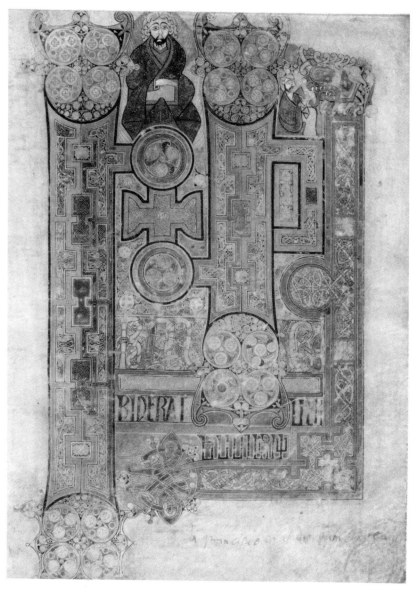

The *Book of Kells* opened at the first page of the Gospel of St John.

OPPOSITE On display in Oslo, the Oseburg Ship was discovered virtually intact in a grave; dated between 815 and 820, it is the oldest dragon-ship yet discovered.

A cross-slab carved with characteristic ring-chain
interleaving by Gaut Bjornson.

way more than once, and although his tombstone in Westminster Abbey describes him bluntly as 'The Hammer of the Scots', it should read 'The Hammer of the Celts'.

A meticulous planner whose administrators recorded, checked and rechecked all that was needed for his campaigns, he was nevertheless aware how a different culture worked – the culture he was determined to extinguish – the culture of Wales. Edward recognized the central place of a spoken language in the life of a non-literate people like the Welsh, and when he exhorted the English to destroy Wales, he made the link absolutely clear. He wanted to obliterate 'lingua Wallensica', the Welsh language, but what he intended was the total destruction of Wales.

History, prophecy and propaganda were all bound together in the oral poetry recited to great men and small alike by Welsh bards. They propounded a sense of history which the English found threatening. As French-speaking imperialists with extensive possessions in Continental Europe, it may be that the Plantagenets were particularly discomfited by the collective memory of the Welsh. Here is an extract from a life of Edward II, written in the early fourteenth century, which shows an extraordinary contemporary awareness of what made the Welsh tick:

> The Welsh habit of revolt against the English is a long-standing madness ... And this is the reason. The Welsh, formerly called the Britons, were once noble crowned over the whole realm of England; but they were expelled by the Saxons and lost both name and kingdom ... But from the sayings of the prophet Merlin they still hope to recover England. Hence it is that they frequently rebel.

Before Edward I invaded and conquered Wales in two massive expeditions in 1277 and 1282, his predecessors had preferred to contain the west by planting powerful magnates on its borders. The Marcher Lords were wealthy and independent-minded. Walter Clifford, who held a castle at Llandovery, deep in Wales to the north of the Brecon Beacons, was enraged when a royal messenger arrived with a summons for him to appear at the court of Henry I at Woodstock. Clifford made the poor messenger eat the summons, wax seal and all.

In August 1170 another Marcher Lord, Richard fitz Gilbert, Earl of Pembroke, landed with an army in Ireland, near Waterford. Nicknamed Strongbow, he fought his way through Leinster and captured Dublin.

Ironically, his war cry was 'Sainte Davide!' but his interest was in conquest to add to his personal estates in Wales and England. More Norman barons followed Strongbow until they controlled large swathes of southern-central Ireland, built castles and settled down to exploit the countryside. As time went on, the Normans became more Irish than the Irish. Not only did they adopt native customs and laws, they also began to speak Gaelic far more than English or French, and ultimately most of them became monoglot. This alarmed the English crown and, believing their hold over Ireland to be patchy and tenuous at the best of times, they promulgated the Statute of Kilkenny through the Irish parliament in 1366. Amongst much else the legislation was concerned with the increasing Gaelicization of the English barons and their families. Inside the areas controlled by them, all were required to use the English language to conduct their business, to call each other only by English personal names and not the Irish equivalent, and, incidentally, to ride their horses in 'the English manner', which apparently required a different saddle and tack from that used on native horses. Efforts were made to enforce the terms of the statute: in 1371 William Power paid a fine of 40 shillings and also went to prison because he could no longer speak English, and was only released if he 'would apply himself diligently to learning' it. Never underestimating the power of language, the English always understood both how it bound the Celtic peoples together and excluded them, but Ireland was comparatively remote and difficult to control from London, and when Henry VIII's coronation was proclaimed in the Irish parliament in Dublin in 1509, only one of the great magnates, the Earl of Desmond, could understand English – a translator had to be found to let the others know what was going on.

Significantly, the Statute of Kilkenny attempted to restrict the access of travelling poets or bards to areas under English control. This was no footnote to the legislation but a piece of real politics. Forty years later, across the Irish Sea, the Welsh rose in rebellion for the last time, and poetry lay at the heart of their actions. On 16 September 1400 a well-connected Welsh nobleman, Owain Glyn Dwr, was proclaimed Prince of Wales at Merioneth. Although he was related to the royal houses of Deheubarth and Powys, he had shown few signs of high aspiration until then, far less insurrection. In 1385 he fought for the English at Berwick Upon Tweed against the Scots, and for the most part lived peaceably on his estate at Sycarth in north Wales. But there were subtle harbingers of what was to come. Owain may have been in the service of an English king but he was still a Celtic nobleman, and when he went to Berwick, he took with him a man called Crach Ffinnant. He was Glyn Dwr's personal bard, soothsayer and advisor, and before the rebellion in 1400 there were no less than six praise poems written about Owain. Even though he was only ranked as a squire, the poems reflected a sense of expectation and a level of attention from bards which added an impetus to events. This was heightened even more in 1400, and afterwards, because the poems sang of heroes and redemption and reflected an ancient messianic tradition. Since the time of the Anglo-Saxon invasions the Welsh had longed for and dreamed of a National Redeemer to lead them back to old glories, because, in the twelfth-century words of Geoffrey of Monmouth, they 'to this day suffer pain and deprivation and exile in their native land'. The sense of disinheritance was intense and Y Mab Darogan, literally, the Son of Prophecy – the man who would be the messianic deliverer – came from a long line. Owain of the old North British kingdom of Rheged, Arthur and Cadwaladr, and, more recently, the Welsh mercenary leader Owain Lawgoch (who was assassinated in 1371) had all been hailed as National Redeemers. The tradition is still alive today, although poorly understood in the London newspapers. When the New Zealander, Graham Henry, was appointed as coach to the Welsh rugby team, he was welcomed as a National Redeemer, but the English press entirely failed to grasp what it meant and berated the Welsh for over-excitement and blasphemy.

Owain Glyn Dwr was proclaimed Prince of Wales in 1404 amidst a blaze of grandiloquence and expectation. He quickly made contact with the other Celtic nations and wrote to the King of Scots about the power of 'the prophecy' and reminded him of their common ancestry and common cause. Walter Bower, the Scottish chronicler and abbot of the island monastery of Inchcolm, wrote what must have sounded like music to Glyn Dwr's ears:

> The Britons shall flourish, in alliance with the Alban people;
> The whole island will bear its ancient name.
> As the eagle proclaims, speaking from the ancient tower,
> The Britons with the Scots rule their fatherland.
> They will rule in harmony and quiet prosperity,
> Their enemies expelled, until the day of judgement.

Even though the English had been on the island for nearly a thousand years, Bower and the Welsh bards refused to see their settlement as permanent, and believed that deliverance might still come if the Celts of the west and north united. The English took a different view. William Shakespeare used Owain Glyn Dwr as a character in *Henry IV Part One*, depicting him as an immediately recognizable stock character. Having portrayed Harry Hotspur as the phlegmatic Englishman, he painted Owain as a fiery, boastful and mystical Welshman, giving him the speech:

> I am not in the roll of common men.
> I can call spirits from the vasty deep.

When the rebellion in Wales broke out, the English parliament reacted immediately and banned poetry. Knowing the central role played by bards in carrying news and propaganda, and inciting rebellion, they wanted to suppress 'wasters and rhymers, minstrels or vagabonds . . . for to make commorthas or gatherings upon the common people, whom by their divinations, dreams and excitations, they draw into the Welsh insurrection and rebellion'. Owain's rebellion lasted a long time and only petered out in 1415.

In Ireland to speak Gaelic was to be anti-British, in Wales to speak Welsh was to be more British than the English, and in Scotland to speak Gaelic was not to acknowledge the existence of the British at all. The first King of Great Britain, James VI and I, was determined to bring the Scottish Gaidhealtachd, the Highlands, under closer control. Both the Gaelic language and those who spoke it were seen as barbarous and as a threat to James' English-speaking British project. In 1608 an expedition was sent to the island of Mull in the Inner Hebrides, where various Highland clan chiefs were invited to board a ship anchored out in Tobermory Bay. They were told that a minister was waiting to preach an improving sermon, but instead of prayers, soldiers were waiting and the chiefs were abducted and imprisoned in the Lowlands. The price of release was their signatures on the Statutes of Iona. Amongst the clauses there was a ban on Highland bards (on pain of being put in the stocks) and their poetry, and an insistence that the eldest sons of chiefs be educated in Lowland schools. The Statutes were quickly followed up by the 1616 Education Act which contained pointed and unequivocal views

on the Gaelic or, as it was fashionably disparaged as being alien to Scotland, the Irish language. One of its aims was:

> that the vulgar English tongue be planted, and the Irish language which is one of the chief and principal causes of the continuance of barbarity and incivility amongst the inhabitants of the Isles and Highlands, may be abolished and removed.

Allied to military weight, the suppression of Celtic languages has been a consistent component of policy in the English drive to colonize the rest of Britain and Ireland. By the eighteenth century there was an unmistakable sense that the languages were slipping into footnotes and quaintness. James MacPherson's confected Gaelic epic poem, known as *Ossian*, was immensely popular, but its appearance strongly reinforced the notion that Celtic languages were from another, remote, even heroic but definitely bygone age. Their time had come and gone. Few reliable statistics exist, but it is clear that by the time *Ossian* was published in 1762, the Cornish language had declined close to extinction. In the fishing villages between Penzance and Land's End there were only a few handfuls of speakers left, and in 1777 the last native speaker of Cornish, according to tradition a woman from Mousehole named Dolly Pentraeth, died. Dolly had refused to speak any English, even though it is likely that she understood it, as Mousehole is only three miles from the busy port of Newlyn and the town of Penzance. There is some evidence that a scatt' of native speakers of Cornish lived on into the early years of the ni teenth century, but after that time the speech community ceased to This early death meant that there could be no record of how Cornish was actually spoken, what it sounded like and consequ' pronunciation for modern learners has had to be conjectur' eighteenth century Manx was under grave threat and the ar' land south of the Highlands where Gaelic had been spo' Carrick, Galloway and eastern Perthshire, saw the beginnir retreat.

In Wales, closest to England and English, the signs w' but a Redeemer of a different sort was at hand. Wha' Welsh language from enfeeblement, if not extinctic Religion. More important in the sixteenth cent' English was the spread of the new faith. Conv' mattered little if they did not speak Englis'

Prayer, the New Testament and finally the entire Bible were translated and published in Welsh between 1563 and 1588. This substantial body of literature allowed the creation, and the shaping, of modern standard Welsh. The Protestant church and the later Nonconformist chapels became fortresses of Welsh language and culture. In the eighteenth century Methodism sent down powerful roots in the hills and valleys, and its combination of egalitarianism and a rejection of the official hierarchy appealed strongly to the Welsh. The adoption of Celtic languages by the proselytizing Protestant churches quickly took them to the heart of communities, and that is where they have stayed. All down the western side of Britain and in Ireland religious passion still burns, while in the Western Isles there is something approaching a Gaelic-speaking theocracy, and in Wales and Cornwall the chapel still counts for much.

The coming together of the Welsh language with great Methodist music particularly caught the popular imagination. Hymn singing was not the lifeless drone heard in today's churches but an exultant and vigorous form of communal worship. Anyone who has heard a Welsh rugby crowd sing the hymn 'Bread of Heaven' cannot mistake the generations of passion behind it. The most glorious child of the union of the Welsh language and Protestantism is without doubt the Welsh male voice choir. The chapels were central to an enormous growth in choral singing in the second half of the nineteenth century. Because South Wales had industrialized so rapidly, thousands came flooding into often jerry-built valley towns to work in mines, mills and factories. In stark contrast to Ireland and Scotland, Wales experienced a net gain of population in the nineteenth century, but there was little sense of community in the rows of houses that lined the hillsides, little to do in what free time people had – the major beneficiaries in this social vacuum were the pubs. Drunkenness and absenteeism from work were considerable problems, and in attempt to combat them the mill and mine owners backed the Temperance Movement. Employers and the Band of Hope also wanted to see Welsh language culture, the informal eisteddfod – or music and poetry festival move out of the pub to a place where drink was not available. Building an already strong popular interest in classical music and romantic ry (the Welsh Christian names Haydn and Byron show where tastes the popularity of choirs in places like Merthyr Tydfil, the Swansea , Rhymney and Aberdare developed quickly.

The work of the Tonic Solfa Movement and the popularity of their new scale – Do, Re, Mi, Fa, So, La, Ti, Doh – markedly accelerated this initial interest. Most traditional Welsh music had been learned by ear and passed on in the same way, but when this new method of learning to sight read music became widely current, the effect was revolutionary. With the publication of sheet music and the development of the ability to read it without help or the immediate need for a tutor, the numbers of people with an intelligent interest in making music rocketed. At the National Eisteddfod in 1865 there was only one choir but by 1911 sixty-nine competed. Many thousands of people from all over south Wales were involved, and when competitions were held, often for substantial cash prizes, rivalry could boil over into fighting and the organized barracking of other choirs as they attempted to sing. But generally the choral movement acted as social glue for communities whose only *raison d'être* was the pit or the steel mill, and also as a great buttress to the power and prestige of the Welsh language. Even though many of the set test pieces, and much of the sacred music, were sung in English, the choirs were run in Welsh.

In 1873 their greatest hour arrived. The South Wales Choral Union decided to form a combined choir known simply as Y Cor Mawr, the Big Choir, and send it to London to compete in the national championships at Crystal Palace. The crucial role of conductor was taken by Griffith Rhys Jones from the Aberdare United choir, and with a fine sense of history he took the name of an ancient Welsh hero and called himself Caradoc. Large amounts of money were raised and many auditions held from all the choirs in the valleys. Finally Y Cor Mawr boarded the train and travelled out of Wales to take on the English. And they won. And they went back the following year and won again. The English were baffled. Only twelve years before, the *Daily Telegraph* had written that the revived National Eisteddfod was 'a national debauch of sentimentality' and to *The Times* it was 'simply foolish interference with the natural progress of civilization and prosperity – it is a monstrous folly to encourage the Welsh in a loving fondness for their old language'.

Caradoc and his Cor Mawr had taken on the English on the fields of high Victorian culture and defeated them twice. He coined a cloying phrase which has stuck ever since when he called Wales 'A Land of Song'. The editor of *Y Cerddor Cymreig* (The Welsh Musician) was Ieun Gwyllt, and when the triumph of Y Cor Mawr was complete, he sharpened his pen:

The vast majority of the English have been accustomed to speak disparagingly, and generally have a low opinion of the Welsh. When it comes to achievement knowledge and imagination, Wales is assumed to be as lifeless as the graveyard. Caradoc's choir demonstrated there is life here, and ability and achievement and the Welsh in Wales are no longer to be despised . . . we are in a new era and the impact of this Welsh choral victory will contribute significantly to raising the standing of the Welsh both here and abroad.

One of the London papers complained of an invasion of Jones, Jones and Jones when the Welsh came to the capital – a variant on the racist 'they all look alike to me'. Y Cor Mawr contained eighty singers, but many fewer surnames. What the English and their newspapers fail entirely to understand when they mock the Welsh for their lack of surnames is that it was they who imposed that duplication in a crass attempt to eradicate another bit of Welshness. Unlike the English, the British Celts did not use nuclear surnames which are attached to every succeeding generation. Because they remember and value their genealogy, they use patronymics (and in the Western Isles matronymics as well) to distinguish themselves. In a society in which people generally died close to where they were born, this system involved no confusion. In a settled community where most people knew your father or grandfather, there is a far more pungent and detailed identity involved in being his son or daughter than in bluntly being called Smith.

When the English administration penetrated deeply into Welsh-speaking Wales and demanded surnames, they got instead sawn-off patronymics, and a small but important piece of Welsh identity drifted away. The Welsh word for 'son of' is *ap* and it turned ap Rhys into Price, ap Hywl into Powell, ap Evan into Bevan and when a simple possessive 's' is added to common Christian names, they become Jones for John's, Roberts, Williams, James and so on. Adjectives initially tended to retain their meaning but acquired an English spelling. *Coch* for red became Gough and *fychan* for small became Vaughan. The widespread confusion sown by this forced mass baptism (to say nothing of the habit of using a limited stock of, generally biblical, traditional Christian names) meant that nicknames were needed almost immediately. Some of them are very everyday, such as Jones the Post and Price the Baker. Dylan Thomas uses several in *Under Milkwood*. Others are more mysterious in their origin, and why John Carreg-Thomas should have the word for a stone in the middle of his name is no longer clear – even to him. This illustrates another effect of the loss of patronymics, and that is the wholesale creation of double-barrelled surnames. Generally thought to be the preserve of the English upper classes, these are applied to all sorts of people in Wales, posh or not. The Cardiff telephone directory is full of Parry-Joneses, Elfed-Thomases, Jones-Hugheses, Vaughan-Thomases and thousands more.

Worse was to come. After a damning report on Welsh education compiled by three young monoglot English barristers, and the establishment of a state system in 1880, the Welsh language was banned from schools. Children who spoke Welsh were fined, thrashed and ridiculed. Persistent offenders had a placard hung around their neck which said 'Welsh not'. Many Welsh people agreed – the language appeared to be a barrier to getting on in the world and a sign of ignorance – but others responded with fire and passion. From more than 100,000 people who gave what they could, cash was raised to found the first Welsh university at Aberystwyth, and Welsh language publishing went into a period of frenzied activity. For the first time the 1891 Census carried a question about language: 50 per cent of the population spoke Welsh, but 50 per cent did not, or believed that they did not have enough to call themselves Welsh speakers, officially. By 1961 it had fallen to the critical level of 25 per cent. Saunders Lewis, one of the founders of Plaid Cymru, the Welsh National Party, came out of retirement to deliver the annual BBC Wales Radio Lecture. He chose to deliver a quietly angry and passionate speech on 'Tynged yr Iaith', the 'Fate of the Language'. Lewis called on the Welsh people to make their language's survival and salvation their only cause, and to be prepared to use any and all means to achieve it. The reaction was instantaneous. A campaign of twenty years of non-violent direct action against road signs, television masts, offices and many demonstrations saw the election of Plaid Cymru MPs, the creation of S4C, the Welsh language TV channel, and the establishment of Wales as an officially bilingual country. While there are real and pressing concerns about the inclusion of the majority who do not speak Welsh, the increase in the number of Welsh speakers, particularly amongst young people, is nothing short of a cultural miracle.

Against all the odds Wales as a nation and the language that defines it have survived oppression. Both of the most powerful empires the world has ever seen invaded and attempted assimilation: first the Romans and then the English tried and failed to erase Wales from the map. Even though English is the most powerful language phenomenon in existence and Welsh its closest and most exposed neighbour, Yr Hen Iaith, the Old Language which described Britain before the Romans or the Sais came, still describes it now. After an innumerable series of protests, refusals, demonstrations and acts of civil disobedience, Welsh has survived and is growing again.

At the National Eisteddfod for 2000 held at Llanelli, the Aberdare United choir sang this song.

R'yn ni yma o hyd	We're still here
R'yn ni yma o hyd	We're still here
Er gwaetha pawb a phopeth	Despite everybody and everything
Er gwaetha pawb a phopeth	Despite everybody and everything
Er gwaetha pawb a phopeth	Despite everybody and everything
R'yn ni yma o hyd	We're still here
R'yn ni yma o hyd.	We're still here.

FIVE

The Ghost Fences

JUST BEFORE SUNRISE ON 21 JUNE 1900 at Stonehenge there was a
scuffle. Despite efforts at conciliation and persuasion, the police were
forced to manhandle the Chief Druid and frog-march him off the site.
Once he had been deposited outside the new fence encircling Stonehenge,
the white-robed Druid turned and publicly and ritually cursed the owner
of the land, Sir Edward Antrobus, which was very unfair. In 1900 Stonehenge was still private property, and earlier that year one of the huge
stone uprights had collapsed. Sir Edward decided to put a fence around
the monument, and, so that he could maintain it safely, he charged a
small fee for entry. The Chief Druid was incensed at what he saw as
desecration. Along with the other members of the Order of Bards, Ovates
and Druids, he believed that Stonehenge was a sacred Druidical site and
the place where, since time immemorial, the Summer Solstice had been
celebrated, and where the religious traditions of the Celtic peoples of
Britain could be carried on into the modern era.

The fact that Stonehenge was erected at least 2,500 years before the
first signs of Celtic culture appeared in Britain, and the fact that the
white robes and the faintly masonic rituals of twentieth-century Druids
were only invented in the late eighteenth century are not the most
important points. Even though there is more than a whiff of suburban
amateur drama about modern Druids, the most interesting thing about
them is their revival. Despite a remarkable degree of daftness, otherwise
sensible people want to believe, want to retain the name of the Druids.

More recently, prodigious quantities of brown rice have been eaten in the name of Celtic religion. Under the general banner of the New Age there has been a return to what some modern mystics want to believe was a better and more wholesome way of life. Because the Celtic peoples of Britain did not build towns or temples, an attractive picture has been painted of a people in harmony with a landscape which they revered and often worshipped.

In May 2000 the first Celyddon Conference was held near Lanark in Scotland and its proceedings and atmosphere were self-consciously Celtic in tone. Set in a tent pitched on a field surrounded by trees, it was partly a music festival, partly a semi-academic conference. Speakers offered lectures on 'Aspects of the Celtic Goddess' or 'Pilgrimage through Sacred Lands' or a talk from 'Jockey, A Traveller who Kens these Lands', or 'Tristan, Gawain and the Goddess', as well as a good deal of Arthurian material. To fend off the evil spirits of sameness, dry-as-dust academe or just boredom, those giving lectures were invited to sing or dance before, during or after their presentation. No-one did, with the Arthurian scholars being particularly appalled at the thought. The historical, Celtic war lord, Arthur, is an important element in this loose network of ideas and beliefs, and the name Celyddon comes from some of the early sources surrounding his famous tale. Originally a P-Celtic or Old Welsh word, it described the great wood that extended over southern Scotland during the first millennium.

Cooking at the Celyddon conference was done in the fields and glades over open fires fed by wood-gathering parties, and visiting speakers were told that the woods would also serve as a toilet 'as they had always done'. Inside the large tent the sound system was state-of-the-art, while outside nature was embraced with great enthusiasm and without a trace of awkwardness. Many of the participants were dreadlocked, scruffy and what a famous Scottish poet would have described as 'adjacent'. But amidst the alcohol and the haze of rollup tobacco smoke, it was possible to detect more than simply a hangover from the hippies of the sixties. These people had a real and attractive belief that they were doing what their ancestors had done before other, more aggressive, less sympathetic cultures intervened. They were comfortable in the landscape and genu-inely seemed to care about it. Many had very few resources, little money and had hitch-hiked great distances to attend the conference, dance, sing and listen to the list of slightly startled academics who turned up to talk to them in their tent. The Celyddon people were peaceful, mystical in the sense of appearing to live in the dream of things, and they certainly had a partial sense of how the Celts thought about the world. Like the 'Obby 'Oss in Padstow, their conference hinted at the atmosphere of the great Celtic quarter-day festivals. But only a partial sense – as often, modern consumers of the stories of the past pick the ones they like best and ignore the rest. The realities of the religious life of the Celts were sometimes far from peaceable and remnants of its more grisly aspects have survived in surprising places.

Archaeology and documentary evidence combine to confirm the central importance of the human head in Celtic belief. In *De Bello Gallico*, Julius Caesar noted that Celtic warriors' certainty about immortality and the afterlife made them recklessly brave and difficult to subdue. For they believed their soul to be absolutely indestructible even in death, and more, that it lived on not in their whole beings but inside their heads. After a Celtic tribe known as the Senones destroyed a Roman legion in a battle at Clusium in northern Italy, the historian Plutarch recorded:

> They cut off the heads of enemies slain in battle and attach them to the necks of their horses. The bloodstained spoils they hand over to their attendants and carry off as booty, while striking up a paean and singing a song of victory; and they nail up these first fruits on their houses . . . They embalm in cedar oil the heads of the most distinguished enemies, and preserve them carefully in a chest and display them with pride to strangers, saying that for this head one of their ancestors, or his father, or the man himself, refused the offer of a large sum of money. They say that some of them boast that they refused the weight of the head in gold.

Excavations of sacred Celtic sites have uncovered many skulls and structures either decorated with them or built with special niches to accommodate them. Hundreds of representations of heads, many carved in wood in a stylized manner, have also been found. Other sources reveal the Celts trying to harness the immense power that they believed resided in the severed heads. To celebrate each of the quarterly festivals great bonfires were lit, often on hilltops. At these turning points in the year the barriers between the temporal and spiritual worlds were thought to be more easily breached. To keep evil at bay priests erected poles with skulls fixed on top, or set an array of wooden heads around the fire. These were the ghost fences, and so long as people believed that they worked, they worked.

Some time after 70 AD the Roman conquerors of southern Britannia moved against the Brigantes, the hill tribes of the north and the Pennine Chain. Under their king, Venutius, the hill men made a stand at their fort at Stanwick, near Scotch Corner in North Yorkshire. Defending an impossibly long perimeter, the Brigantian holy men placed skulls on the stockade, near the gates, sure that their magic would turn back the hard-bitten legionaries facing them. The gods failed, Stanwick was over-whelmed and amongst the debris of fallen ramparts archaeologists have found the remains of a ghost fence.

Before the Romans came, the Celts had controlled Britain and Ireland for a very long time. Having established themselves by 600 BC, their hegemony lasted for nearly 700 years until what is now England became the province of Britannia. Even then they retained mastery over the greater parts of these islands for a further 1,000 years. The persistence of Celtic religious traditions should not be wondered at – it is only the business of recognizing them that is difficult.

In the strictly Presbyterian Gaelic dictionaries of the nineteenth cen-tury, the quarterly festival of Samhuinn is translated anxiously as 'The Feast of All Souls'. In fact it is nothing of the kind. Although the derivation is from *samhradh*, and may mean 'the end of summer', Samhuinn was actually the beginning of the Celtic year. Fat cattle too numerous to feed through the lean winter were killed, and while some were reserved for immediate use for the festival, most of the meat was dried or salted. The night before the Feast of All Souls is much better known as Hallowe'en. It is still called Oidhche Shamhna (the Night before Samhuinn) in Gaelic and takes place on 31 October. The remnants of the Celtic feast of Samhuinn can still be seen, just, in Scotland and parts of England where children still dook for apples, trying to pull them out of tubs of water with only their teeth. Apples were sacred to the Celts. They were thought to be the fruits of the Tree of Knowledge and in Gaelic there is a phrase which equates the act of self-betterment with reaching for the highest apple, '*an ubhal as airde*'. In one Irish story, a Celtic goddess has a tub of sacred apples from the Otherworld, but the most famous association is with Avalon. It means the Island of Apples and was the paradise to which the mortally wounded Arthur was taken.

The great bonfires of Samhuinn have been moved four days later to blur the original overtly pagan focus of Hallowe'en and to accommodate the pyre of the traitorous heretic, Guy Fawkes, but the most potent memory of all is reserved exclusively for the night before the date of the old festival. Turnip lanterns are the direct descendants of ghost fences. As the darkness of winter approached the Celts built them to drive away evil. Nowadays children light candles inside hollowed-out turnips, and having carried them around the streets they set them in windows looking outwards, keeping an ancient tradition unbroken.

The details of the beliefs of the Celtic peoples of Britain are too often a matter of sketchy conjecture. It is better to look at their religious practices, like turnip lanterns, which survive today and at records of the more recent past, and try to build up a picture from them.

The solemn, white-robed gentlemen of the various sects of the modern Druids provide a link with a Celtic priesthood, but only in name. It is possible, even probable, that the Druids used Stonehenge for ceremonies despite the fact that they did not build it – it was and remains a remarkable and magical place – but the historical Druids were very different from the mild mystics who turn out freshly laundered at the Summer Solstice. Roman sources discuss the Druids at length, and during the long process of colonizing Gaul and Britain they believed that their power to stiffen resistance to the advance of the legions was considerable. In essence, they were priests who officiated at ceremonial occasions and who had an ability to communicate with the gods of the Celts. While the Romans knew that these gods had strong associations with natural phenomena such as lakes, rivers, wells and mountains and other features of the landscape, their identity was more problematic. The names of more than 400 appear in the classical sources, but of these 300 are mentioned only once. This implies localized, cultic worship as well as a degree of tolerance. However, there were a number of deities whose incidence is high but whose roles and attributes are often duplicated and far from clear. The Celts did not have a pantheon of important gods in the way that the Greeks and Romans did: an anthropomorphic family with a tendency to squabble and transfer their jealousies and rivalries to the doings of unfortunate mortals. Such unequivocal representations as do exist often show animal/human forms, but even these seem to be interchangeable. The Celtic love of shape-shifting, of seeing gods or goddesses in threes and also the occasional switch of gender presents a cloudy picture of the heavens.

In Britain the most powerful god seems to have been Lugh, who left his name not only on the summer festival of Lughnasa but also on many towns and cities, such as London. Ludgate Hill incorporates it more clearly. Lugh was associated with arts and crafts, and in late Celtic Ireland he became Lugh Chronain, or Little Stooping Lugh, which was eventually Anglicized into Leprechaun.

The feast of Lughnasa is sometimes mistakenly thought to be a Celtic harvest festival, but the date of 1 August makes it too early. Because our habit is to celebrate the successful leading in of the crops, Hairst Hame in Scots, we assume that all country festivals around that time had the same purpose. In fact, the interval between the date of Lughnasa and the modern harvest festivals of mid-September points up a crucial cultural difference. Lughnasa was an act of propitiation. The Celtic gods needed to be pleased, appeased and even distracted, so that when the harvest was later gathered in, it would be a good one. By contrast, our contact with God takes place afterwards, and our harvest thanksgiving recognizes that bringing in the ripened corn depends first on human effort – only later do we give thanks. This shows a general pattern at work. The Celts believed that they were at the mercy of the unpredictable temper of their gods, and everything they did required some preparation of the divine. If proper respect, some sacrifice and careful attention were paid to the perceived needs of the gods, then there was a much better chance of all turning out well. The modern approach is to do one's best and if the gods, or God, can help in that, then thanks are due and should be given.

Lughnasa is no longer celebrated in Britain, and where it still happens in Ireland, its form can be difficult to discern. In Brian Friel's excellent play, *Dancing at Lughnasa*, it is little more than the occasion for a good party. But there are good records of the festival in nineteenth-century Cornwall. At Morvah, on the westernmost promontory of Land's End, the place where the Cornish language survived longest as a spoken vernacular, there was a Lughnasa Fair held in the old way. On the first Sunday in August huge crowds gathered on the granite moorland to please their god, Lugh, and to meet him. Dressed in a black bull skin and carrying a hammer to remember his patronage of arts and crafts, he was called Jack the Tinkard and he danced around the Fair. A local collector of folklore left a description of Morvah:

> The celebration of Morvah Fair connects the giants' age with all the times we well remember, when such crowds came to Morvah from all the parishes round on the August Sunday, to keep up this remarkable holiday, that a three acre field would not hold all the horses ridden to Morvah Fair, so that each horse might have a mouthful of grass and room to toss up his heels; and one may be sure that there were plenty of riders for the number of beasts, from the old saying of 'riding three to a horse, like going to Morvah Fair'. More than a score often got a lift on the same horse, as we should take turns to ride and run, holding fast by the girth, legs or tail of the horse, that we might keep all together. When we arrived in Morvah none but the old folks ever thought of going indoors; we young folk seated ourselves on the hillside, hedges, rocks, anywhere to eat, drink chat and enjoy the fun of Morvah Fair games. Morvah Fair was for us the grand day of all the year, when hundreds on hundreds, from east and west, used to meet to see each other and high-country cousins; and we hope it will never be forgotten as long as a rock remains on Morvah Hills.

One of the features of the Fair was Cornish wrestling and unlike Morvah Fair it has survived, but only just. There are still a few traditional wrestlers in the villages of West Cornwall, championship belts and cups to be won, and a ceremony which shows that the sport is very old. Before men fight they line up opposite their opponents and swear an oath in Cornish: '*Gwary wkek yu gwary tek*,' which means 'Good play is fair play,' a serviceable motto for many sports. At the battle of Agincourt in 1415, Cornish archers marched onto the field under a banner depicting two wrestlers locked in combat. Modern fighters wear short canvas jackets tied at the front with rope and compete in shorts and bare feet on the grass. Surrounding them are three referees carrying long sticks. In perhaps the only phrase from Cornish wrestling to have gone into English usage, these are the Sticklers who uphold the rules. The aim of each bout is to win three 'backs', that is, to throw an opponent in such a way as all points of his back, shoulders and hips hit the ground at the same time. Three Sticklers are needed to make sure that throws are seen from every possible angle, and also to keep back the enthusiastic crowds shouting encouragement. Celtic wrestling has survived all over the Sea Kingdoms probably because it was a highlight of festivals like Lughnasa and Samhuinn. Cumbrian and Hebridean variants prefer a locked backhold to the freestyle of the Cornishmen, but all are still fought in the old languages at county fairs.

Other sorts of embrace were also commonly found at the four Celtic festivals. In the evening at Morvah, fires were lit and the bards began to tell stories: tales of giants and how 'many-skilled' Jack the Tinkard cunningly defeated them. When the flames burned low and children were asleep, lovers sometimes stole off to quiet corners: 2,000 years ago sexual licence was permitted, even encouraged, for the nights of the Celtic quarter days. As the bonfires died down people took the warm ashes and blackened their faces both for luck and for disguise. Promiscuity amongst adults symbolically unable to tell their partners apart was common at festivals until the church finally stamped it out in the eighteenth century. The First Statistical Account for Scotland was compiled in 1796 by parish ministers and it told of efforts to suppress the ancient rites. In the town of Lanark 'a sort of secret society of Guisers made itself notorious in several of the neighbouring villages, man dressed as women, women dressed as men, dancing together in a very unseemly way'.

When the Anglo-Saxons settled in England they changed the name of Lughnasa into Lammas, from *hlaf-maesse* or a 'loaf-feast'. This was not a misdated reference to a harvest not yet in but a reference to an act of propitiation. In the Highlands of Scotland in the nineteenth century, Alexander Carmichael recorded a Christianized version of what the Anglo-Saxons meant:

> Early in the morning of the day people go into their fields and pluck [unripe] ears of corn, generally *bere* [oats], to make the Moilean Moire. These ears are laid on a rock exposed to the sun, to dry. When dry, they are husked in the hand, winnowed in a fan, ground in a quern, kneaded on a sheepskin, and formed into a bannock, which is called Moilean Moire, the fatling of Mary. The bannock is toasted before a fire of rowans or some other sacred wood. Then the husbandman breaks the bannock and

gives a bit to his wife and each of his children according to their ages, and the family raise the Iolach Mhoire Mhathar, the Paean of Mary Mother who promised to shield them, and who did and will shield them from harm to the day of death. While singing thus, the family walk sunwise round the fire.

This is an unmistakably pagan Celtic ritual of propitiation dressed up in the vestments of the church.

The installation of Christian saints in place of Celtic gods was mirrored by the replacement of Druids by priests and ministers, but in fact the functions of the Druids either dissipated amongst other important members of a Christian society, or else completely disappeared. Classical sources list three types of Celtic holy men: Druids, Bards and Vates, who interpreted sacrifices and studied natural phenomena. Julius Caesar believed that Druidic teaching could take twenty years to complete and, to preserve secrecy, it was all taught orally in forest glades far from settlements. The derivation of the name 'Druid' is straightforward: it comes from *drus*, the Greek word for an oak tree and *wid*, the Indo-European root for to know. If the name of Oak-knowers was awarded by the Greeks, it may mean nothing more complicated than the people who conduct their ceremonies in woodland glades and who revere the oak as the king of trees.

Some sense of how the Celts thought about the natural world in general can be gleaned from a strange alphabet compiled by the Q-Celtic speakers of early Ireland. Even though they operated as a non-literate culture, they began to develop the Tree-Ogham. Taking its name from the god, Ogmios, it used the initial letter of the names of different species of trees as a way of reciting and remembering it. In Gaelic it follows the order b for *beith* for birch, l for *luis* for rowan, f for *fearn* for alder and so on. There are eighteen letters. What makes it different from the Roman alphabet of twenty-six is not that there are fewer letters but the way in which they are expressed. Instead of rows of abstract symbols arranged in words to be read from the left, the Ogham takes a tree trunk and its branches as the basic structure. Using a vertical edge to stand for the trunk, the letters are then cut as groups of straight lines which are attached to it, or intersect with it. There are no loops because the alphabet was cut with a knife or a chisel and never written with a pen. Because each letter is represented by a different tree, Gaelic-speaking children used not to follow the tradition of a for apple, b for ball and c for cat, but rather listed trees in the mnemonic. It was a for *ailm* for elm, b for *beith* for birch, c for *coll* for hazel and d for *darroch* for oak. Despite its awkwardness Ogham lasted a long time. The towns of Kilkenny and Tipperary insisted that carters had to have their name on their cart, and in the nineteenth century one owner was prosecuted because it was claimed that he did not. The man objected vigorously, and a priest was found, from a remote part of the county, to attest that the carter had in fact put his name on his vehicle – in Ogham.

The tree alphabet offers a sense of how the Celts organized the natural world intellectually. Trees were conceived of as a hierarchy, with the mighty oak at its head and other species with their particular characteristics arranged below. What Alexander Carmichael observed in the ceremony of the Moilean Moire was the use of the rowan as a 'sacred wood', which has long been thought of as a protective tree important to the home. In many farm places all that remains of demolished cottages are the old rowans which still thrive nearby.

Trees and plants also had medicinal attributes, and this lore survived for many generations in the Highlands of Scotland, while it disappeared throughout the rest of Britain as the sixteenth- and seventeenth-century obsession with witchcraft drove folk medicine out of our culture. Remoteness and lack of understanding prevented the witch finders from discovering and persecuting the Gaelic-speaking people who continued to use herbal cures to powerful effect. A medical dynasty called the Beatons committed much of their encyclopaedic knowledge of plant lore to handbooks in the early modern period. Under the label of alternative or complementary medicine it has recently resurfaced to become part of the repertoire of treatments available to the sick or the nervous.

In addition to a knowledge of the powers of the natural world, Druids also had a judicial function. They were an independent group unattached to any particular tribe, which Julius Caesar viewed as both helpful to their objectivity as judges, and also potentially dangerous to Rome. They were repositories of Celtic history and tradition, and their huge stores of inherited and remembered knowledge made them appear authoritative, if not always leading, figures. As well as dispensing justice, they could also arbitrate in war. 'In former times' wrote one Greek commentator, they could even stop a battle.

What exercised classical writers most was the central role taken by

Druids in acts of sacrifice as a way of propitiating the gods, and in particular their use of human sacrifice. Once again, documentary and archaeological sources are in agreement. During the campaign of 49 BC in the conquest of Gaul, Caesar sent axemen to cut timber for the siegeworks to be built around Marseilles. They came across a Druid sanctuary, and were horrified by it. This was no sylvan glade of the romantic imagination. Branches of tall trees had been interlaced in such a way as to make the centre of the clearing gloomy and sunless. Water flowed from dark springs, and in the middle stood a series of altars heaped with hideous offerings of human body parts and entrails, while blood seemed to be sprinkled on every tree. The description begins to take on a dramatic colour when the axemen are said to have reported trees moving for no obvious reason and that not a cheep of wildlife was to be heard or seen. Images (probably of heads) were rough-hewn out of stumps, the only purpose of which seems to have been to terrify devotees. And Roman carpenters. While it is true that everything Caesar wrote had a propaganda purpose, there is a palpable sense of shock in the description, and too much detail for it to be invented. There is another story closer to home which is also tinged with the needs of politics, but which may equally may represent a typical example of what happened to captives unfortunate enough to fall into Celtic hands.

Julius Caesar was baffled even more by the relative pre-eminence of women in early Celtic society than by the Celts' religious rites. During the Roman conquest of Britain there was a revolt which arose directly from this sharp cultural difference. When the King of the Iceni tribe in East Anglia died, he had no male heir. The Romans immediately decided to end the client status of the Iceni and incorporate their territory into the empire under direct rule. When Queen Boudicca, or Boadicea, objected to this, the Romans reacted by treating her family as soldiers have often treated women. Her daughters were raped and a centurion dragged the Queen out into a public place, stripped her, tied her to a stake and, in front of her people, flogged her. Celtic sensibilities were outraged at what they saw as appalling treatment of members of their ruling family, and what, to the Romans, was acceptable treatment of women. There followed a bloody rebellion, led by Boudicca. The Iceni burned Colchester and London, and were initially very successful. They took many captives. Dio Cassius reports that the Romans' women were led to a grove dedicated to the Celtic god of victory, Andraste. There they were tied to trees, and had their breasts cut off and stuffed in their mouths before having a sharpened stake inserted into their anus and shoved up through their bodies.

One of the most enduring images associated with Druid rituals is the story of the Wicker Man. Having no obvious cultural distaste for public slaughter, and indeed a love for the gory gladiatorial contests in the arena, it is surprising how shocked Roman commentators appeared to be by the Celtic habit of human sacrifice, and the Wicker Man particularly appalled them. A huge structure was made in the shape of a man from the sort of wicker used for baskets. It was then filled with people and animals, and then, as no doubt both humans and beasts screamed in fear, the Wicker Man was set alight. Druids watched the death throes for the purposes of divination: signs that would tell of the temper of the gods and how they might be appeased.

While archaeological evidence attests to nothing as horrifying as these atrocities, it does support the idea of the practice of human sacrifice as part of Druidic ritual. Several bodies found well preserved in peat bogs show unmistakable signs of sacrifice. In 1984 the discovery of Lindow Man hit the headlines. His body was in such a remarkable state of preservation that the police were called in before any archaeologist appeared at the site. Nicknamed Pete Marsh, the man had been buried in Lindow Moss in Cheshire around 2,000 years ago. Because most of his skin and many of his organs had survived so well in the sphagnum, it was possible to carry out a post-mortem which allowed the causes of his death to be analysed in far more detail than is ever possible with a skeleton. Naked except for a band of fox-fur around his upper arm, Pete had suffered a complex triple death. In Celtic tales of antiquity the theme of the triple death occurs several times. First, two poleaxe blows to Pete's head probably killed him, then he was throttled with a sinew until his neck broke, and finally his throat was cut so that the blood drained out of him. Trace elements in his preserved skin show that Pete Marsh was probably tattooed, he had a neatly trimmed beard and hair, and his fingernails were unbroken and polished. Certainly not a manual worker, all the evidence points to him having been a nobleman and probably a Druid. There are no signs whatever of any struggle, his hands were not tied and it is reasonable to conclude that Pete went to his triple death willingly.

Some historians and many romantics recoil at the thought of Celtic culture incorporating acts of such vileness and inhumanity, but that is to apply today's standards and ethics to yesterday. Two thousand years ago people thought differently. Life was cheaper and harsher, but that should not lead to the conclusion that, somehow, the Celts, or the Romans come to that, were more primitive or less intelligent than we are. They were not – they simply believed in different things.

There are the remains of other bodies in Lindow Moss, and their burial indicates a Celtic fascination for watery places. They believed that near water the gods were close and people were in danger, and that wells, bogs, rivers and lakes might be portals to the Otherworld. In order to propitiate the gods, they threw huge quantities of valuable objects into water. Most of this was metalwork and almost all surviving examples of the wonderful craftsmanship of the Celts have been fished out of lakes or rivers. When the Romans invaded southern Gaul they knew that a local tribe, the Volcae Tectosages, were particularly fond of throwing cauldrons, swords, spears, shields and much else into a group of sacred lakes. In their usual breezy fashion the legionary commanders first consolidated their conquest and then sold the lakes by public auction. Two lochs in Scotland and a lake in Anglesey have given up finds of beautifully preserved bronze artefacts. Many of these are weapons, and the peculiarly Celtic habit of throwing swords into lakes is echoed in the medieval versions of the story of King Arthur. When the mortally wounded king is taken to the Isle of Apples, Sir Bedivere takes Excalibur to the edge of the lake and hurls it into the middle, where it is caught by a hand clothed in white samite.

When we throw coins into fountains and off bridges, we remember the beliefs of our ancestors, although when most people are asked why they do it, 'for luck' comes back as the answer. 'Propitiation of the gods for what may appear to be luck in the future,' is more long-winded, but more historically accurate.

Wells are amongst the most mysterious reminders of a pagan Celtic past, particularly what are known as 'clootie wells'. There are hundreds of these still to be found in Britain, some by roadsides and some in remote places. One of the most atmospheric is at Madron in west Cornwall, not far from where the Lughnasa Fair used to be held at Morvah. Off a side road, near nowhere in particular and down a long and heavily shaded, muddy track overhung with thick branches, the curious suddenly come upon bushes covered with thousands of pieces of rags. Difficult to see and almost impossible to reach, they mask a spring which bubbles out of the ground and trickles busily in several streams down a shallow incline. Some of the rags are bits of bandage and lint dressing because Madron has a reputation for curing disease. The symbolism of ordinary rags might also relate to the shedding of disease. Whatever the explanations, the most striking thing about Madron Well is its atmosphere. Enclosed by the overhanging branches and completely shielded by dense foliage from the fields beyond, it has an oppressive sense of otherness – it is a place partly of the world, and partly not. The number of new rags, their patterns not yet washed out by the rain, fresh flowers tied with wool to the twigs and new muddy footprints on the long track in the morning show that Madron is often visited, sometimes daily by people on their way to work, perhaps looking for a place to meditate. The intensity of the ancient well, the way that the bushes and trees seem to protect it, and its sheer power are unmistakable. Madron has a concentrated sense of spirituality to be found in very few churches. Many of the places with sacred associations in the west of Britain are like this: they are magical.

The Roman historian Pliny describes the ceremonies of the Druids in some detail and remarks that the most important were accompanied by the sacrifice of bulls. The animal remains a potent symbol, and this aspect of Celtic practice was very persistent. As late as the 1670s bulls were sacrificed in the Highlands of Scotland. 'Abominable and heathenish practices' were tutted over by the elders of the Presbytery of Applecross, part of the mainland opposite Skye. Men from Achnashellach gathered at an ancient holy place, carried out certain Celtic rituals such as walking sunwise, or *deasail* in Gaelic, and then they killed a bull in sacrifice. In 1678 Hector MacKenzie was harangued in the minutes of the Dingwall Presbytery for taking his sons and grandsons to Eilean Ma Ruibhe in the middle of Loch Maree. The island had been dedicated and named after the early Christian missionary, St Maelrubai, who sailed from Ireland in 671 to convert the Picts, the peoples who inhabited Scotland north of the Forth and Clyde line. Loch Maree is also a smoothed-out version of his name. Missionaries like Maelrubai were well advised to attach themselves to places already seen as sacred and the little island in the loch was unquestionably one of these. However, it is surprising that Hector MacKenzie knew this and, ignoring 1,000 years of Christianity, brought a bull across to Eilean Ma Ruibhe, not a simple matter, and killed it in sacrifice to a god named Mourie 'in ane heathenish manner . . . for the sake of his wife Cirstane's health'.

The traditions, beliefs and even the names of the gods of the Druids died very hard – a tenacious survival given the ruthless manner in which Roman strategists pursued them to extermination. The Romans' apparent shock at the Celtic enthusiasm for human sacrifice gave them a civilizing propaganda motive for their campaign, but it is more probable that they believed that the powerful and seditious influence of the Druids lay in the path of a peaceful colonization of Britain and Gaul. The imperial administration wanted to invade Britain at least partly because they were convinced that that the European centre and fount of Druidism lay there, and they were anxious that Gaul was not unsettled by the influence of priests from across the Channel. More particularly, they believed that Anglesey was where novitiates were trained and sent out to minister to the western Celts. In 60 AD Suetonius Paullinus brought the 20th Legion along the coast road of North Wales. When the hard-bitten veterans formed up in ranks on the Snowdon side of the Menai Straits, many of them paused at the sight which greeted them. In front of the army of the Ordovices, the tribe that lived on Anglesey, wild, black-haired women screamed curses at the invaders. Like Furies, with their bodies streaked with ash, they leaped into the water to hurl insults. Behind the tribesmen and their ghost fences stood their Druids, arms aloft, imploring their sky gods to descend and destroy the Romans, who had dared to challenge their power. The legions came to the Menai Straits because Anglesey was the epicentre of Druid power and the oak groves on the island were their most sacred places. At the bottom of the little lake of Llyn Cerrig Bach on Anglesey, weapons from all over Celtic Britain have been found, pointing to the island as a focus of pilgrimage. Staring across the narrow Menai Straits, the Druids knew why Suetonius Paullinus had come. To destroy them utterly.

When the legionaries splashed into the Straits to attack the Ordovices on the opposite shore, they knew the price of defeat could be horrific, and their enemies knew that their religion was fighting for its grisly survival. The sky gods did not intervene, and after a brief engagement, the disciplined imperial troops scattered the native warriors. They then made their purpose clear by spending some weeks on Anglesey cutting down the groves of sacred oaks and hunting down any who professed the old religion.

Like the bards and priests of the north and west, who were able to continue in their traditions for many centuries longer, undisturbed by the Romans or anyone else, the Druids of the early Welsh-speaking peoples of Britain were the keepers of their history and culture – the guardians and interpreters of their sense of themselves. Nearly 2,000 years ago, with Roman thoroughness, this vital part of P-Celtic culture was all but eradicated.

Human sacrifice, altars heaped with entrails, the impaling of captives and the horrors of the Wicker Man were not mentioned at the Celyddon Conference of May 2000. They represent the unacceptably grisly and fell face of Celtic religion, but none of the foregoing would have dis-comfited Canon Angus MacQueen of South Uist. For a multitude of reasons, Catholic priests are often sanguine about the excesses of the past. Perhaps they hope that, through the goodness of God, these are firmly in the past, and sometimes men like MacQueen make a point of attempting to retain some of the more innocently mystical elements of the Celts' view of the world. He began once:

> One of the things that is wrong with young people today is that they don't have as much sense of the life of the earth as we had. When I was a boy I used to take off my winter boots on the day of the Feast of St Bride in March and not put them back on until the Feast of All Saints at the end of October. Walking over the machair to school I could feel the earth coming alive through the soles of my feet. And in the autumn I could feel it getting ready to die again.

This is much more rhythmic and less pedantic in Gaelic, and Angus MacQueen only smiled when it was pointed out that St Bride's Day is Imbolc, a Celtic quarter-day festival, and that All Saints is another, at Samhuinn. '*Tha fios agam*,' he said, 'I know, I know.'

Beltane is the name for the festival held on 1 May, and it signalled the coming of summer and the return of real warmth. It means 'Bel's fire' and derives from another important Celtic god, Belenos. He left his name on Billingsgate, near Ludgate Hill, but his most indelible mark is on Padstow in North Cornwall. For a day Padstow races back across the centuries to enact a Celtic past with a vigour and élan that is wholly and unselfconsciously convincing. The 'Obby 'Oss comes snorting, neighing and whinnying back from the past to disconcert and remind.

Many traditional events remain locked in their own footnotes, but in Padstow any attempt to analyse is met robustly: 'Bollocks! Celtic bollocks! You don't want to pay attention to all that old rubbish. This is our day, you silly bugger, and that's it and all about it!'

Padstonians wish each other 'Happy May Day' just as easily as we say 'Happy Christmas' or 'Happy Easter', for neither of these are as much a focus of the year as 1 May. On the evening of 30 April, the night before the morning, singers gather in the centre of the fishing village for 'The Night Song'. It banishes winter and looks forward to summer. Simple ideas, but to a rural community that had shivered and hungered through the winter snows, winds and rain, it was an occasion of genuine joy when the days began to lengthen and the cold was in retreat. One of the earliest surviving Irish gospel marginalia is a beautiful poem which leaves little doubt about how the Celts regarded winter, and why Padstow welcomes summer with such abandoned pleasure. Here is a modern translation by the Irish poet, Brendan Kennelly:

> Here's my story; the stag cries,
> Winter snarls as summer dies.
> The wind bullies the low sun
> In poor light; the seas moan.
> Shapeless bracken is turning red,
> The wild goose raises its desperate head.
> Birds' wings freeze where fields are hoary.
> The world is ice. That's my story.

By Beltane, winter is certainly over and summer is greeted with a roar in Padstow. When the 'Obby 'Oss emerges from the Golden Lion pub, the Mayers all dressed in white with red ribbons shout, ' 'Oss, 'Oss!' and the reply comes 'Wee 'Oss!' The last remembers a stallion's whinny of recognition. The procession is led by a Master of Ceremonies in top hat and tails at the head of about forty drummers and accordionists (until the 1950s men in drag were also in the van – a clear reminder of guising). Heard streets away, they constantly repeat the tune of the 'Morning Song'. It sounds much like the 'Floral Dance' from nearby Helston which topped the popular music charts some years ago. Dancing wildly and with little regard for the densely packed lanes of Padstow, the 'Obby 'Oss is pushed and thumped by the Teazer, who appears to be both keeper and exhorter, as it moves around the village. It is the duel of winter and summer and the 'Oss, being unquestionably a stallion and nothing like the sort of Hobby Horse that trots through nursery rhymes, is for aggressive fertility and warmth. A wild beast, the 'Oss lunges and uses its wooden snappers to prod, poke and threaten to bite. But no-one stays out of the way.

The church has long disapproved of the 'Obby 'Oss and other horses like it. As early as the sixth century St Augustine of Hippo preached against horse-magic: 'If you ever hear of anyone carrying out that filthy practice of dressing up like a horse or a stag, chastise him most severely!' More recently the traditional May Games of Celtic England were branded as licentious and orgiastic. Around 1500 there were more elements than simply the Hobby Horse: a parade of the May King and Queen was celebrated, and there was a Robin Hood or Green Man play and morris dancing with blacked-up faces. Called Darkie Days in Padstow, with the term 'morris' dancing coming from Morisco or Moorish, it is nevertheless a mistake to think that these black faces originated with North African models of some sort. They are another echo of guising and the habit of smearing on soot from quarter-day fires for temporary disguise.

Padstow's 'Obby 'Oss not only outlived the disapproval of the church and the Temperance Movement – it also resists the attentions of historians. May Day in Padstow passes so quickly and is so loud and colourful that it can seem less like a real experience and more like a dream. Perhaps that is, and was, the point.

Solemn and wholesome are not adjectives to be safely attached to the religious life of the Celtic peoples of Britain – gory, terrifying, magical, evanescent and profound all are. But perhaps the most telling summary of Celtic religion belongs perversely with the devoutly Christian, even fundamentalist west of Britain. For the Free Presbyterians, Methodists and Protestants and Catholics, there is no such thing as a religious aspect to life. Religion informs all of their lives, and is emphatically not something done only on a Sunday morning. All the evidence points to the Celts having a similar sense of their wholly different religion. It was life and death to them, and nothing less.

SIX

Until the Break of Day

THE SIGN SAYS THAT THE ROAD to Dalmore leads nowhere – a
dead end. Turning west off the main road around the waist of the Isle
of Lewis, I drove down a single blacktop track past empty croft houses
and clachans. The twisting, downward incline of the road kept the
horizon of hummocks and shoulders of hillsides close. And then, as
often in the Highlands and Islands, I turned a corner into a breath-
catching vista, a vast landscape of cold Atlantic beauty made by God to
remind us of the glory of creation. Dalmore is a horned bay, a shelving
beach of white sand and rounded pebbles enclosed by sheer cliffs splintered at the edges into stacks by the crash of the ocean. Above the beach
and below the car park which brings the road to an end, there is a
wonderful thing. The beauty of Dalmore has been left for the dead. No
living person looks out from here each day to the eternity of the Atlantic.
There are no houses here, surely one of the most bleakly beautiful places
in the world, but only a cemetery dug on the machair and studded with
hundreds of headstones. Dalmore is the valley of the dead.

Washed by the breakers of the mighty ocean and softened by the
tears of a thousand funerals, Dalmore is made for memory. Many search
for the ghosts of their pasts in overgrown, thistledown blown cemeteries
in half-forgotten corners of our towns and cities, or seek out a damp
gloom amongst the tumbled tombstones and overwrought mausolea.
Death in cities is an overcrowded business of corruption above and
below the ground. At Dalmore it is eternal. The sea and the big Highland
skies remember a time before there were headstones and funeral

processions, and they will be there long after there are no more. Dalmore seems like a dead end but is a gateway to eternity.

When the Labour Party Leader John Smith died suddenly in 1994, part of the funeral service played on television around the world. It was not the burial at Iona, or the pews of distinguished mourners in an Edinburgh church which caught international attention, but the haunting notes of '*Is e Dia Fein 'sa Buachaille Dhomh*', the Gaelic version of 'The Lord's My Shepherd', sung unaccompanied in the nave of the kirk. There is no music like Gaelic psalmody: primitive yet intricate and complex, it depends on few conventions and is supported not by the music of instruments but by the wash of emotions over the soul. There are very few Gaelic psalm tunes, but each is interpreted so differently that there seem to be hundreds. It is the decoration with grace notes which makes them appear individual. Each psalm is sung by a precentor, *air ceann na seinn*, at the head of the singing, and he throws out a line to the congregation who sing it, hung with grace notes, back to him. It is a form of sublime worship, and as precentor and congregation create each psalm anew, the music soars and swoops. It was that elemental power which caught the rapt attention of the congregation at John Smith's funeral service. Almost no-one understood the words, but everyone felt the sadness it signified.

Smith was a Highlander from Dalmally in Argyll, and it was fitting to hear Gaelic sung at his funeral. For death is a part of life well understood and properly treated in the Western Isles, and mourning is encouraged, even institutionalized. The awkwardnesses of urban funerals are unknown. A three-day wake precedes most funerals on Lewis. Work stops in the township and for two nights the minister holds a service in the house of the deceased. Gaelic psalms are sung and all day visitors come to sit with the bereaved. Sometimes as many as 200 people squash into a croft house: bedrooms, kitchens, corridors are full of people in their Sunday best sipping tea and eating sandwiches. Often the first sign that there has been a death in the village is a tractor pulling a trailer full of chairs from the community hall. Many of those who have lost loved ones find the body warmth of the Lewis wakes very comforting.

On the day of the burial the coffin is carried from the house to the graveyard by relays of male pall-bearers. As many as a thousand men have been known to walk at an interment. Women do not go to the graveside – by tradition they stay back at the house of the deceased and wait for their men to return.

On the island of Barra the graveyards used not to have gates, and each time a funeral procession approached, the dry stone wall was broken down to allow entry into the country of the dead. Because almost all of Lewis's townships are on the coast, the graves are dug in sandy soil. So that the wind cannot take the sand, graves at Dalmore are filled in as soon as the minister has finished the formalities, and the mourners sometimes stamp down the clods themselves. Buried in the loose sand, the people of Dalmore seem to be waiting for the sea to take them. Ministers were traditionally buried facing landward, towards their earthly charges, while their congregations' headstones looked to the minister and past him out to the eternal surge of the sea.

Devotion defines the Celtic west as surely as language and history, and yet, apart from the familiar Sunday rituals, it can be hard to detect any depth of spirituality in a community – except in the details. In cemeteries like the one at Dalmore, there are clues hidden by custom and language. At the foot of many of the gravestones in this beautiful place, there is an inscription in Gaelic. 'Gus Am Bris An Latha' literally means, 'Until the Break of Day', but it needs further translation. It really means 'I'll see you again on the Day of the Last Judgement.' A life, a profound belief, a culture, a whole world is distilled into a simple phrase.

The absolute certainty of an afterlife passed unchanging from the Celtic past to the Christian future. The fundamentalist Free Church of the Highlands and Islands fed that sureness and certainty in all it did: a corporeal life was no more than a necessary prelude to everlasting glory. To some sects who believe themselves elect, life on earth is little more than a prior inconvenience to be borne with fortitude and managed with dignity and little fuss. One of the reasons why church ministers raised little resistance to the pain of the forced clearances of the nineteenth century was because they believed them almost irrelevant. Life could be a vale of tears but it would surely be followed by a hereafter in heaven.

Dalmore joins hands with the spiritual past in another way. Along the western edge of Britain and in Ireland many of the earliest religious foundations were dug in wild places remote by land but accessible by sea. Monks built on small islands, rocky promontories and hilltops and other places where sometimes the old gods still lingered. Columba's Iona, Ninian's Whithorn and St David's in Wales are all difficult to reach overland and have the same powerful sense of sanctity as Dalmore, imparted by the dramatic meeting of earth, sea and sky. The most breathtaking of all the Celtic monasteries is built on the rock of Skellig Michael. The peak of an undersea mountain, the island rises sheer out of the Atlantic, eight miles off the coast of south-west Ireland. Perched 550 feet above the ocean, clinging to the sides of the rock is a group of ancient buildings: six beehive-shaped stone huts and a simple rectangular church. Begun in the eighth century, the little monastery can be reached only by an open stone staircase. Near the top of one of the twin summits of Skellig Michael there sits a tiny hermitage, and those brave enough to attempt the climb need to be very fit and agile as well as foolhardy. What these stone stairs and stone cells were like in the teeth of a winter storm beggars understanding. With only some small, unsheltered terraces where something might have grown in the relentless wind, everything but fish, sea birds for meat and collected rainwater will have had to come from the mainland. Bad weather must have cut off Skellig Michael for months at a time. There can be no starker example of Christian asceticism in Europe.

What impelled these extraordinary acts of privation and effort was an early admiration for the lives of the Desert Fathers. In Palestine and Egypt, in the first and second centuries, hermits set up small foundations in the desert. They wanted to avoid busy highways and towns, and the persecution of Christianity by the Roman government which took place regularly before the Emperor Constantine made it the official religion of the empire in 313. Around the monasteries and hermitages of the Desert Fathers lay the barrier of trackless miles of inhospitable sand and scrub: a barrier between a life of devotion and the life of the world. Adapting to western geography, Celtic monks let salt water take the place of the sand and they favoured places dominated by the wastes of the sea. In this way their lonely hermitages, like Skellig Michael, followed the example of their spiritual brothers in the Near East. Deserts or *diseartan* were found all over Britain and Ireland and place names often recall them: Dysart in Fife, Dyzard in Cornwall, several Dyserths in Wales and many Diserts in Ireland. The word has endured in Irish English and is now used for a retreat or a church building.

How these influences reached the west is a matter for conjecture, but two Gaulish bishops played a dominant role in guiding the early Celtic church in Britain and Ireland. St Martin of Tours was an abbot who presided over his monastery towards the end of the Western Roman Empire. He died in 397, and his teaching lived on in the remarkable figure of his disciple Ninian, the first British Christian of any historical substance. The dates vary considerably, but the burden of the story is that Ninian came to Galloway in 398 to build the church of Candida Casa on what may have been the site of an earlier foundation. This means the White House, and it got its name because, uniquely for the time, it was made of stone, probably bright, or white, stone. Erected at a place now called Whithorn, it is probably the oldest church in Britain, a place where the word of God has been preached for at least sixteen centuries. The town of Whithorn is, incidentally, the oldest town in Scotland. It seems certain that Ninian came from Gaul to the Solway Estuary because it was a place where Christianity had already taken root. Carlisle was still flourishing in the fifth and early sixth centuries, and the memory of the empire was strong in the Eden valley at the western end of Hadrian's Wall. Recent archaeology has suggested that trade links to the south, the Mediterranean and the Near East were not uncommon, and, further, that it is possible that Whithorn was in fact not founded from Rome or Tours or Carlisle but directly by missionaries from Palestine or Egypt. Ninian may have become abbot of a going concern, and there is no evidence that he did anything to change the direction of Christianity in the region. Rather, his work acted as a catalyst, helping to lift Christianity to greater eminence in Britain.

The association of Ninian's name with many early churches and places all over Scotland suggest that his death, around 432, saw the rapid development of a cult. This would have conferred great prestige on his monastery and encouraged missionary activity sailing out of Whithorn, south to Wales and west to Ireland.

It is fruitless to try to discover a precise pattern for the conversion of Britain and Ireland since there are so few reliable records for the fifth and sixth centuries. The best that can be safely managed is a rough sequence which places some figures in a chronological order relative to each other. One of the most tantalizing and pivotal names is that of Pelagius, one of the first Celtic heretics. Roughly contemporary with Ninian, he travelled to Rome around 400, where he got his name.

Pelagius is a Greek/Roman version of his Celtic name, perhaps Morgan, which meant 'Son of the Sea'. For familiar simplicity, his friends called him 'Brito', much in the same way that Scots attract the name 'Jock' in London. Perhaps a country boy with an ascetic training, Pelagius was profoundly shocked by the licentious behaviour of the clergy in the great city.

Clearly a brilliant thinker and theologian, he reacted by developing a series of ideas which had to wait 1,000 years for fulfilment by the Reformation. In essence, Pelagius believed that salvation could be gained by the exercise of the will: it was possible to choose to be virtuous and also to choose to behave sinfully. His advocacy of the power of free will appalled conventional wisdom and forced its clarification. St Augustine of Hippo called the views of Pelagius heretical and insisted on the doctrine of original sin and all that sprang from it. St Jerome was more direct: he called Pelagius 'a fat hound weighed down by Scotch porridge'.

Although Pelagius was twice excommunicated and may have died in exile in Palestine, his theology was influential. The monastery of St Honorat on the Isle de Lerins off the French Mediterranean coast near Cannes supported his thinking and the popularity of his ideas in his homeland of Britain prompted the papacy to act. In 429 St Germanus of Auxerre arrived to return the British to orthodoxy and to preach the doctrines of Divine Grace. The teachings of Pelagius proved persistent and Germanus came back on a second mission in 435. His visits imply a functioning church in fifth-century Britain, because protocol demanded that foreign bishops be invited. Germanus and his Roman correctness had an impact which flickered briefly in the early British church. St Dubricius, better known as St Dyfrig, lived between 425 and 505 and was by tradition a follower of Germanus of Auxerre. Probably a bishop rather than a monastic abbot, he flourished in Erging, an area of present-day Herefordshire which, although Welsh-speaking, lay outside the medieval boundaries of Wales. At around this time the characteristic *llan* began to appear. Now attached to thousands of Welsh place names, the word started life meaning a simple enclosure, probably a sanctified area used for burial. Later it became associated with a church and through that with a saint or founder, or sometimes a distinguishing geographical feature. More than half of the modern parish names of Wales have the prefix Llan.

Much more is known of St Dyfrig's successor, the pre-eminent figure of early Christian Wales. St Illtud was an abbot, and he founded the great monastery on the coast of south Wales, near Cardiff, which today has a silly name: Llantwit Major is a clumsy Anglicized version of Llan-illtud Fawr, the largest and most powerful foundation in Britain in the early sixth century. Although he was described by his pupil, St Samson, as a 'renowned teacher of the Britons, learned in the teachings of the Church, in Latin culture and in the teachings of his own people', Illtud's preference for monasticism over episcopacy reflects a retreat from urban life in Britain, and it may also signal a retreat from the orthodoxy of Germanus of Auxerre and a conscious return to the asceticism of the Desert Fathers.

For some even the regime at Llanilltud Fawr was too luxurious, and St Samson took himself off to a windblown hermitage on Caldey Island in the Bristol Channel before sailing to Cornwall to begin a mission of conversion which finally led him to Brittany. Called St Samson of Dol, he is now revered as the patron saint of Brittany. One of the effects of conversion in Cornwall and Brittany was to pattern the landscape with hundreds of saints' names, most of them unrecognized by the Vatican and unknown outside their localities. In Cornwall this occurred because the area was converted relatively late and in a concentrated period, and a habit quickly developed of calling a church or enclosure by the name of its founding priest and conferring sainthood immediately. The British preference for religious remoteness also meant that there was often no settlement near the church from which to borrow a name. Although the Welsh word *llan* found its way across the sea to Cornwall to reappear as *lan*, it is the widespread use of saints' names which dominates Cornish road signs and the map.

The most famous Welsh saint of all emerged in the generation after Samson. Dewi Sant, or St David, lived between 530 and 589 and the popularity of his cult led to more than a thousand churches being dedicated to him. An ascetic and a vegetarian (at one point he lived on wild leeks, thereby giving Wales part of its iconography), David was also an abbot who took the Celtic church in Wales to the most remote place possible – the peninsula of St David's in Pembroke is as far west as Wales gets. Monks flocked to the place called Tyddewi, the House of David, and to other monasteries, some of which grew very large over the succeeding centuries. They were also, to a great degree, independent.

The effects of Germanus's mission were transient and the Celtic church developed along ascetic, monastic lines without paying much heed to events beyond the Sea Kingdoms. The life of a monk, by its nature, implies the choice of a virtuous existence and a clear interest in the attainment of salvation rather than a reliance on God's grace as the sole route to salvation. Just as at Lerins, where the beliefs of Pelagius survived, it is likely that the Celtic church of the islands and promontories believed that men and women could achieve the kingdom of heaven by their actions, and did not simply submit to the doctrine of original sin. The monks on Skellig Michael chose to shiver in the Atlantic gales because they believed that their suffering would bring them nearer to God. Such regional variety in the development of the early Christian church should not be wondered at. Papal authority then was not the dictatorship it became, and its power seems to have fluctuated. It was more powerful in Britain in the fifth century than it was in the sixth or seventh.

In 431, Celestinus, the same Pope who despatched Germanus, sent Palladius 'to the Irish believing in Christ'. It is reasonable to assume that the Irish Christians also needed to be dissuaded from the doctrines of Pelagius. Even though the propaganda needs of the later cult of Patrick diminished his achievements considerably, it is likely that Palladius was successful, particularly in Leinster, the part of Ireland most open to Mediterranean contact. Two papal sources in Rome, dated after 431, celebrate the success of his mission, but as with Dyfrig in Wales, the orthodox temper of Palladius's teaching did not last.

St Patrick was in many ways Ninian's successor, but there is no record of Ninian entering into theological controversy, unlike Patrick. Patrick's original name was Sucat and he grew up in the late fourth century near the Roman town of Carlisle at a place called Bannavem Taberniae, which may be Birdoswald near Hadrian's Wall. His father, Calpurnius, was a decurion, a Roman civic official and Potitus, his grandfather, had been a married Christian priest. When Sucat was sixteen he was captured by a raiding party which landed on the Cumbrian shore in search of prisoners who could be sold on as slaves. They shipped him to Ireland, where he remained in captivity for six years. After making his escape (on a merchant ship bound for Gaul with a cargo of hunting dogs), he changed his name to Patrick on being received into the faith by the anti-Pelagian St Germanus of Auxerre. He then went to study at the pro-Pelagian monastery of St Honorat on the Isle de Lerins off the coast of the south of France.

Clearly a determined and intrepid man, Patrick sailed back to Ireland to begin a mission of conversion in the north. Establishing a diocesan structure based on Armagh and dedicated to eradicating paganism and defeating hostile Druids, he preached and persuaded energetically. Uniquely for such an early Celtic Christian, Patrick left two pieces of writing which have come down to us. They contain few facts but exhibit a strong sense of conviction. The '*Confessio*' and the 'Letter to Coroticus' show a fearless, direct, caring and totally committed Christian – their power is undiluted over fifteen centuries. His wholeheartedness and complete trust in the power and goodness of God must have impressed many. And, unafraid of controversy, he was the first to challenge the morality of slavery. Not despatched by Rome and with no pre-ordained plan, his was a calling directly from God – he seems to have been a genuinely good man.

While Patrick and his successors at Armagh worked in the late fifth century to bring the north of Ireland into God's commonwealth, some of the Irish were departing. The North Channel is only twelve miles wide at its narrowest point and the view to the north and east from the Antrim Hills takes in Islay, Kintyre and western Galloway. For reasons unclear, whether land shortage, internecine warfare or perhaps nothing more complicated than a taste for adventure, northern Irishmen climbed into their curraghs and rowed and sailed to the place they called Alba. The short crossing can be treacherous and the Corrievreckan whirlpool off the island of Rathlin must have claimed victims, but many made landfall safely, and with women, children, weapons and materials stowed on board, the Irish brought the name of Scotland with them. Throughout the first millennium and into the early Middle Ages, the Irish were often called the Scots, and the Scots were increasingly called so. The name given to their immediate destination by the northern Irish was Argyll, which comes from Ear-Gaidheal and means the Eastern Gaels. Argyll extended much further north than it does now, and some early geographers used the term for places as far north as Cape Wrath on the mainland.

The expansion of the Irish across the North Channel was part of a pattern in the fifth and sixth centuries. They colonized the Isle of Man so completely that their Q-Celtic language replaced the aboriginal P-Celtic, and Manx became a dialect of Irish Gaelic. The names of the Lleyn Peninsula in north Wales and Leinster in south-east Ireland are cognate because the former was settled by Irish-speaking peoples from the latter. In Pembroke in south Wales, the Deisi arrived from the area around Cork and left some remnants of their language behind. The distribution of the word *cnwc*, the same as the Irish word *cnoc* meaning a hillock, exactly mirrors Deisi settlement. In Cornwall, saints arrived from the west, some by way of Wales, and Petroc, who gave his name to Padstow (Petroc's Stow flattened out), has an Irish aura about him. The Ogham stones found in Scotland, Man, Wales and Cornwall are the most concrete legacy of the sea-borne Irish invasions of western Britain. Their spiritual legacy was less tangible but enormously influential.

The Ear-Gaidheal took the name Dal Riata from the parent kingdom in Antrim and for a generation or two the new settlement and the old were ruled as one entity. Eventually Scottish Dalriada became independent under a King Fergus Mor Mac Erc who reigned either side of the year 500, and who is the traditional progenitor, the first name in the long genealogy of kings of Scotland. The other Irish colonies in the west of Britain withered or were expelled, but Dalriada survived and expanded. A remarkable document, the *Senchus Fer nAlban* or the *History of the Men of Alba*, shows how and why. Organized into three kindred groups, the *Senchus* lists the naval obligations of each and their relative sizes. The Cenel Loairn colonized the area north of Loch Fyne, perhaps as far north as Fort William and the southern mouth of the Great Glen. It was the smallest of the kindreds, but at least in the district of Lorne it left its name on Scotland's map. The Cenel nOengusa held the fertile island of Islay and the largest and most consistently dominant group, the Cenel nGabrian, settled much of what is modern Argyll and part of Knapdale and Cowal. The coastline controlled by the Eastern Gaels was watched by a network of sea fortresses at Dunollie, Dunstaffnage, Crinan and elsewhere, and the fleets of the three kindreds were directed by the Ard-Righ, an Overking who usually came from the most powerful group, the Cenel nGabrain. Dalriada was the first true sea kingdom of the west to emerge, and in the sixth century its influence spread, bringing the word of God in the wake of its warships.

The word was first brought by St Columba. He has a Gaelic name, Calum Cille, which should be more widely used. Meaning the Dove of the Church, it is beautiful, but the Latinized version has stuck. He founded two monasteries in Ireland, but it appears that Columba's behaviour was far from dove-like, and he was sent into exile because of his involvement in 561 in the battle at Cul-Dreberne, which was fought over monastic possessions. Coming from an aristocratic background with useful connections, Columba was given the little island of Iona by King Conall of Dalriada. The Reilig Oran is the name of a graveyard there, whose name recalls that the Irishman was not the first priest to step ashore. St Oran founded a Christian sanctuary on Iona, also leaving his name on a small chapel and a ruined cross before dying of plague in 549. There is another, even earlier, shadow of sanctity. It appears that Iona is a misrendering of Iova, which comes from *iogh*, the Gaelic word for the 'yew tree'. Capable of living to an immense age, with examples in Derbyshire and Perthshire more than 2,000 years old, yews were often planted near places of burial. Their great age and evergreen leaves represented immortality, and practically they kept foraging animals away from the graves because every part of the tree is very poisonous. The association of yews with churchyards may have a pre-Christian origin in the practices of the Druids, and indeed there is an Irish source which calls Iona Innis Druinidh, the island of the Druids. There is a tradition of white yew wands being carried at ceremonies of inauguration for Highland chiefs and earlier powerful men.

This had nothing to do with the Christian habit of anointment, a practice Columba understood and used to political effect. Aidan Mac Gabrain became Ard-Righ of Dalriada in 574, he allowed Columba to perform a ceremony of ordainment in the following year which may have involved the use of holy oil to anoint his head. It appears that prior to this Aidan had been exiled to the east of Scotland, and when he returned in force to Dalriada he may have considered the support of the early church a helpful buttress to his legitimacy. In turn Aidan's protection of the new foundation on Iona was doubtless welcome, as was the Ard-Righ's public acceptance of the new religion. During this period missionaries almost always attempted conversion at the highest level of society as a matter of priority. If a king accepted Christ then his people would probably follow. When Columba planned his mission to the Pictish kingdom based around Inverness, he took a direct approach and sought an invitation to the royal stronghold at Castle Urquhart on the shores of Loch Ness, but his biographer tells of initial difficulties:

> When the Saint made his first difficult journey to see Brudei, the proud and arrogant king refused to open his castle gates to the new arrival. On seeing this, Columba went up to the gates, made the sign of the cross upon them and knocked. At once the bolts drew back of their own accord and the gates flew open, whereupon Columba and his companions walked into the castle unhindered. Dumbstruck, Brudei and his court immediately ran out and greeted their visitors with suitable reverence and pacifying words. From this time forward Brudei held Columba in very high esteem.

Later elaborations include a clash between the saint and Brudei's Druid, Briochan. Naturally, in the monastic record, Briochan's pagan magic is overcome by Columba's Christian magic, or miracles, but the reality was rather different. While Iona went on to become enormously influential in Christian Britain, and Europe, founding daughter-houses at Durrow and Hinba, beginning a historical chronicle of great value and probably the first few pages of what became the *Book of Kells*, there are no records of Columba or his immediate successors planting any new monasteries in northern mainland Scotland, the area traditionally known as Pictland. It seems that the Picts stayed stubbornly pagan until the eighth century, when Christian iconography began to appear on their symbol stones, which perhaps that makes the persistence in the Highlands of bull sacrifice and 'other heathenish practices' until the seventeenth century slightly less surprising.

St Columba is said dearly to have loved his island, calling it '*I mo Chridhe, I mo Ghraidh*', 'Iona of my heart, my darling'. He also made it powerful, the centre of Christian life in the Sea Kingdoms: a place described by the Northumbrian historian, Bede, as having primacy over all the west of Scotland and influence further afield. Kings wanted to be buried in the Reilig Oran because they believed that the soil was so sacred that it would expunge all of their sins, and the remains of forty-eight Scottish, eight Norwegian, four Irish and four kings of Man are said to lie there. Sanctity went hand in hand with scholarship, and not only was Columba himself a copyist and bibliophile, but there is a Psalter dated as the oldest surviving manuscript in Western Europe which is said to have been written by the saint himself.

When Columba died in 597, ten out of the first twelve abbots who came after him belonged to branches of his family. This was not uncommon and it helps to explain the great effort invested in the rapid development of his cult. The ninth abbot of Iona was Adamnan, Little Adam, a great figure in his own right who is renowned for promulgating 'The Law of the Innocents', which attempted to protect women, children and clerics from the excesses of war. In an instructive passage he makes it clear that the church disapproves of women who fight alongside their husbands in battle. However, he is chiefly remembered as Columba's biographer. No achievement is too exaggerated, no miracle too improbable in what is an unvarnished piece of hagiography designed to confirm sainthood. It was very effective – Columba was unable to convert the Picts, the people whom Bede called 'the scourge of Britain' – but the prominence of his cult has all but eclipsed the brave men who did. St Donan was active on the north-western seaboard and, despite martyrdom on the island of Eigg in 617 with fifty-two of his companions, he seems to have been successful, particularly in the area of Skye and Loch Alsh. He left his name on Loch Duich and the famous Eilean Donan Castle which features regularly in films and advertisements for new cars. St Maelrubai led a mission to the Picts after Donan's death, and again left his name on the landscape.

All the most famous saints of the early Celtic church benefited from the efforts of enthusiastic biography. St David, St Patrick and St Columba were clearly holy and impressive men, but their concrete achievements were probably no greater than those of St Illtud, St Palladius and St Donan, who did not achieve lasting recognition. What mattered was that their stories were written down and that their cults were quickly established. These were supported by the popular belief in the magic of relics and the related and widespread habit of pilgrimage. Just as sixty kings believed that the soil of Iona had the power to purge their sins, so the remains of saints, however unreliable their provenance, were seen as a tangible link with sanctity, and through that with God in heaven. The Brecbannach, the Speckled Box, can be still be seen in the National Museum of Scotland. Shaped like a miniature Celtic oratory, it was said to contain bones of St Columba, and so potent were they thought to be that Robert Bruce had the box carried in the midst of the Scottish host at Bannockburn in 1314. It worked.

Even a sight of saintly relics was to be prized. Irish monks, anxious about their assets wearing out or being stolen, began to build high pencil-shaped towers, part of whose function was to keep relics safe. From doors placed high above ground level, the relics were solemnly brought out and shown to the pilgrims below. The benefit of setting eyes on sanctified remains and of being in the place where the saint walked was the mainspring for the arduous business of pilgrimage. The church recognized this moneyspinning form of early tourism as a pious act capable of improving the chances of immediate access to heaven. Pilgrimage to St David's, Armagh and Iona is still immensely popular and on Columba's island, where there is no huge medieval cathedral to obscure the surroundings, visitors can still taste some of its original atmosphere, some of the unchanging reasons why the saint called it '*I mo Chridhe, I mo Ghraidh*'. On most days in the summer months there is a pilgrimage made around Iona when groups walk to important places to stand and sing and pray under the Highland sky and look out to the west and the islands and the ocean beyond. At the beach called Port na Curraigh, where Columba is said to have landed, there is a strand of smooth granite pebbles. Pilgrims are invited to pick up two: one as a keepsake, and the other to throw as far out to sea as they can. On the pilgrimage route there is no sign of a church, and every sign of the work of God. Columba would have looked up from his gospel and smiled at that continuity.

Where the hagiographers of the Celtic saints signally failed was in England. Even though missionaries from Iona, Ireland and Wales did much to convert the English, the unpleasant St Augustine of Canterbury has grabbed almost all of the historical credit. In fact, St Aidan came from Iona to found the island monastery of Lindisfarne off the North Sea coast and then complete the conversion of the Northumbrians, the most powerful English kingdom of the seventh century. Its kings often laid legitimate claim to the title of Bretwalda, Britain-ruler. Aidan's disciple, St Cuthbert, entered the Celtic foundation at Melrose in the Tweed valley where he was trained by the saintly Boisil. He then carried on his mentor's work in the north of England until his death in 687. Further south the West Mercians were visited by missionaries from Erging in Herefordshire and the successors of St Dyfrig and St Illtud, while the Cornish unquestionably received Christ's teaching from Ireland and Wales.

St Augustine was installed as the Apostle of the English not only by the excessive importance given to the local politics of the south-east of England where the saint was active and where he planted his church at Canterbury, but also as the result of a fascinating debate. The Synod of Whitby was convened in 664 to decide a date. Easter is the most important festival in the Christian calendar, but it is famously moveable and the method of reckoning its date required general agreement. The compelling reason for this is now forgotten, but it concerned the organization of concerted effort. Early Christians believed that human life involved a constant contest between God and the Devil, and that the fight was at its fiercest on Easter Day, the commemoration of Christ's death and resurrection. The more people who prayed, did good works and celebrated, the larger would be the army of Christ and the better his chances of winning. If large groups of people differed in the way they reckoned the date of Easter, their effort could be critically dissipated.

As set out in the Book of Common Prayer, the date of Easter is calculated as the first Sunday after the first full moon on or after 21 March. A full moon was thought to occur fourteen days after the appearance of a new moon. But if the full moon fell on a Sunday, then Easter Day was moved to the following Sunday. This was to avoid a clash with the traditional date of the Jewish Passover and is the reason why Easter can sometimes be much later in the year. Now, the Celtic church was much less concerned with the date of a Jewish festival than the Mediterranean papacy, and over time the two sets of calculations began to drift apart.

This led to the second, more human reason why the Synod of Whitby was called by King Oswy of Northumbria. He celebrated Easter on the Celtic date but his feast was made much less festive by the absence of his Queen, Eanfleda. Her southern, Kentish priest reckoned in the Roman way and so, while the King and his magnates wined and dined, his Queen was still fasting because she believed that it was still Palm Sunday.

Other matters of ecclesiastical practice were also on the agenda. Unlike the Roman tonsure now seen on modern monks, the Celtic version was cut over the crown of the head from ear to ear with the hair at the back allowed to grow long. There is more than a suspicion that this style owed something to a Druid past. At the same time when the Synod was debating chronological niceties, pagan Ireland was suffering from the institution of the warrior-cult known as the Fianna. These were bands of young, unmarried noblemen who roamed the hills and woods and lived by hunting and looting. They terrified the countryside and they were berated for their Druidic hairstyles: they wore a tonsure cut from ear to ear, the *ceudgelt*, with long hair at the back.

The Celtic cause at the Synod was represented by Abbess Hilda of Whitby, Bishop Colman of Lindisfarne and a man who showed how far south missionaries had penetrated, Bishop Cedd of the East Saxons. Despite their arguments, King Oswy decided that the Roman system of dating should be adopted. His reasoning was straightforward and practical. Even though he had been unable to follow much of the debate, Oswy knew that St Peter held the keys of the Kingdom of Heaven, and that he had been the first Bishop of Rome. The decision allowed St Augustine to accept retrospective credit for much of the achievement of the Celtic church and consigned great men like Aidan, Cuthbert, Columba, David and Patrick to supporting local roles. Even though the churchmen of the north and west failed for some considerable time to implement much of what was decided at the Synod, Whitby paved the way for control of the English church to pass to Archbishop Theodore of Canterbury, and the fissures which had split the British were ignored for many centuries. The ascetic, monastic and partly Pelagian beliefs of the Celts in the west were submerged or ignored until the tide of the Reformation flowed to expose once again the rocks of the faith of Columba, David and the others.

Nine hundred years after the Synod of Whitby, the Church of Rome was itself rejected during the English Reformation, but not every part of the country supported change and a large group of Celtic Christians found themselves expressing their independence in a defence of the Catholic faith – because the Church of Rome was thought to be more in harmony with local belief than the imposed Church of England.

In 1549 the Westminster parliament passed the Act of Uniformity, abolishing the wide diversity of religious observance which had been happily tolerated all over England and Wales. The new Book of Common Prayer was to be in English, in the beautiful English prose of Archbishop Thomas Cranmer, and all of the services formerly said in Latin were to be conducted in that English. The Cornish were outraged and they petitioned the King, saying that the new service was 'like a Christmas game ... we will have our old service of Mattins, Mass, Evensong and Procession in Latin as it was before. And so we the Cornish men (whereof certain of us understand no English) utterly refuse this new English.' Cranmer had failed to understand that from early times Latin had been used for the bulk of the service but the Creed, Commandments and other parts of the liturgy had been celebrated in Cornish. As the petition makes clear, many communicants had no English: estimates put the number as high as 50 per cent of the Cornish population of 69,000. When the new laws were enacted, trouble quickly erupted. A sense of what the Cornish feared to lose can be gained from events at the village of Sampford Courtenay. At Whitsun the congregation forced the old priest to wear his chasuble and read the service in Latin as he had always done. Afterwards, Whitsun ale and cakes were taken outside the church, other neighbouring congregations visited and a game of hurling was played. All of this was done in Cornish, both outside and inside the church.

Men gathered in large numbers at Sampford Courtenay, joined other groups, and eventually a rebel army under the command of two Catholic noblemen, Humphrey Arundell of Helland and John Winslade of Tregarrick, marched to the town of Exeter and laid siege to it. Their artillery could make no impression on the town walls, and so the tin miners in the Cornish army sank a shaft and tried to undermine them. Another miner inside the wall heard the clash of their picks and shovels underground, dug a countermine and then organized householders to tip tubs of water down it so that the gunpowder placed in the Cornish mine was soaked.

The 1549 Rebellion did not last long, and the reaction of the government army was ruthless. Thousands of Cornishmen were killed, prisoners slaughtered and priests hanged. The rebel army had been dissuaded from firing incendiary shot over the walls of Exeter and burning the town by Father Welsh, a priest from Penryn, but when he was captured, he was shown no mercy and immediately condemned to death. As a grisly advertisement to discourage religious dissent, several priests were brought to the foot of the bell towers of their churches, 'having a holy water bucket, a sprinkle, a sacring bell, a pair of beads and such other Popish trash hanged about' them, and a rope was placed around their necks. In front of a terrified congregation Father Welsh was choked to a wriggling death as he was hauled up to hang for weeks at the top of his church tower.

The Prayer Book Rebellion saw another casualty. The Cornish language had been partly sustained by its use in church, and after 1549 it died a very rapid death. No longer were English-speaking officials greeted with '*Meea navidna cowzasawzneck*,' 'I will not speak English.' By 1700 the Cornish had no alternative.

In a strange footnote to the 1549 rising, the refusal of Bishop Jonathan Trelawny to sign the Toleration Act in 1688 (this allowed dissenters the right to worship in their own churches, though Catholics were excluded) gave Cornwall the nearest thing to a national anthem. When the bishop was threatened with execution for his refusal to agree to toleration, echoes of the Prayer Book Rebellion could be heard clearly in 'The Song of the Western Men':

> And have they fixed the where and when?
> And shall Trelawny die?
> Here's twenty thousand Cornishmen
> Will know the reason why.

Trelawny survived.

Around the same time when Cornish was waning, the use of the Gaelic language in Galloway was also withering, but some of the fierce piety of Ninian and the asceticism of his monks lived on. The Reformation in Scotland had created a very different church from that in England and Wales, and perhaps its most extreme and characteristic example was the phenomenon of the National Covenant and the popular movement of the Covenanters. The essence of both was the idea that a special contract or covenant existed between God and the nation of Scotland, the Kingdom of Christ. Just as the Jews believed themselves to be a chosen people, so sixteenth-century Scots divines developed the idea of a unique relationship between their newly reformed Christian nation and a Protestant God. They had no doubts at all about the proper relationship between religion and politics. In 1596 the reforming minister, Andrew Melville, memorably declared to James VI of Scotland; 'Thair is twa Kings and twa Kingdomes in Scotland. Thair is Christ Jesus the King, and His Kingdom, the Kirk, whase subject King James the Saxt is, of whase kingdome he is nocht a king, nor a lord, nor a heid, but a member!' For good measure Melville also reminded the king that he was but 'God's sillie vassal'. No wonder James never returned to Scotland after succeeding his cousin Elizabeth on the English throne.

When James's heir, Charles I, unwisely attempted to introduce the Book of Common Prayer to Scotland in 1637 and to conform the Kirk to the Church of England, there was outrage. In the graveyard of the Greyfriars Kirk in Edinburgh, the great and the humble appended their signatures to the National Covenant, which rejected the interference of a king in the affairs of Christ's kingdom and which was based, intellectually, on a determination to continue the special relationship between God and Scotland.

When the Civil War broke out in England, Oliver Cromwell appealed for help to the Covenanter army of the Scots. In return they drove a hard bargain which insisted that England, in essence, convert to Scottish Presbyterianism – a second attempt at the conversion of the south a thousand years after Aidan. Once the royalist army had been defeated and Charles I captured after his surrender to the Covenanter army, Cromwell felt strong enough to renege on the deal. After his death, and once the monarchy had been restored, the Scots were again betrayed. Although he had signed the National Covenant, Charles II had no hesitation in repudiating its contents when he was installed in London. He went even further, and attempted to reintroduce bishops into the Kirk. The Covenanters were appalled, resisted and then rose in rebellion. Having been thrown out of established churches, they held field services or conventicles in the hills and the more remote districts, which were attended by thousands. Nowhere in Scotland were the Covenanters more wholeheartedly supported than in Galloway.

Between 1662 and 1666, 550 Galloway Covenanters were forced to pay fines totalling £142,000, an enormous sum for the time. It broke the local economy and the ports of Kirkcudbright and Wigton were virtually closed for twenty years. There was nothing to export. In Kirkpatrick Durham, between Dumfries and Castle Douglas, Gabriel Semple held the first field conventicle in Scotland and Thomas Wylie of Kirkcudbright was the first of many ministers to hold communion in the open air, away from towns, disapproval and trouble. Wylie's service was repeated over three successive days because his huge congregation knew that dragoons were riding from Edinburgh to arrest their minister and they wanted a last communion from the old man. In 1670 the Black Acts outlawed field conventicles on pain of fines, imprisonment and death, and soldiers descended on communities intent on enforcing the new law by whatever means. But in Galloway the pious continued to rebel.

In 1678 the greatest conventicle ever held took place in the parish of Irongray, near Dumfries. Thousands attended and many Covenanters walked over the Lowther Hills from Clydesdale to join their brothers and sisters in Christ. At the first service 3,000 gathered on Skeoch Hill only four miles from Dumfries. Sentries and lookouts were posted to watch the north road, foot soldiers guarded the mass of the congregation and irregular cavalry patrolled further out, ready to engage any dragoons who appeared. On the following day another huge congregation of 3,000 gathered and was protected in the same way. This time government troops did appear, it being impossible to keep such an event a secret, but seeing how well armed and organized the Covenanters were, they did not attack and had to content themselves with glaring across the valley as prayers were said and hymns sung. On that occasion the minister was John Blackadder, and he must have smiled a grim smile to himself, for the theme of his sermon was 'Let Brotherly Love Continue'.

In 1684 great bands of five or six hundred homeless Covenanters still roamed the Galloway hills, living wild and scarting a meagre existence so that they could receive communion from their ministers without hindrance. Gilbert Wilson must have seen these groups and wondered at their devotion.

Gilbert Wilson was a farmer in the Galloway hills above Wigtown in the 1680s. Neighbours said that he doted on his daughters, but when Margaret was seventeen and Alice twelve they shocked their parents to the core by running away from home to join a band of Covenanters. Margaret and Alice stayed out for a year before hunger and the winter drove them into Wigtown. It was said later that Margaret brought her little sister to what she hoped was safety and that she herself planned to go back to the hills. They made the catastrophic error of knocking on the door of Bailie Patrick Stewart, one of the fiercest hunters of Covenanters in Galloway. He immediately put both girls in prison, and with an old lady named Margaret MacLachlan they were hauled before a court and summarily condemned to death. By that time Alice was thirteen and Margaret eighteen.

Gilbert Wilson watched the trial in horror, and once the verdict had been read his wife collapsed in a faint. Gilbert's reaction was to saddle his horse and ride like the wind to Edinburgh. At the Court of Session he obtained a conditional reprieve for Alice, on account of her age, and was promised that Margaret's would follow. Torn between waiting at Parliament House and knowing that the little girl's execution might take place any day, he sought and was given assurances that the second reprieve would be granted. Then he rode back the 150 miles to Wigtown.

Alice was quickly released but, ominously, a date was set for both Margaret Wilson's and Margaret MacLachlan's executions. They were to be drowned. In Wigtown harbour two stakes were to be driven into the sand and at low tide the women would be tied there to wait for the sea to drown them.

No reprieve arrived for Margaret Wilson and on the morning of the set date a huge crowd had gathered around the harbour and its jetties. Meanwhile, the onlookers noticed that the dragoons had put one stake much further out, at a place where the beach shelved steeply into the Irish Sea. The second had been driven in very close to the harbour wall. Margaret MacLachlan was led out through the silent crowd and taken down to the farther stake where the soldiers bound her facing landward. Margaret Wilson was tied to the stake by the shore, facing the sea. Apparently the authorities hoped that the dying screams of the old woman would move the young girl to recant. But the water was ice-cold and as the tide washed in on Margaret MacLachlan she fainted and was drowned in silence. With the waters rising to her breast Margaret Wilson began to sing Psalm 25:

> Let not the errors of my youth
> Nor sins remembered be
> In mercy, for thy goodness' sake,
> O Lord remember me.

The crowd implored her to recant. She prayed as the waves lapped around her neck. Before she was engulfed a soldier leaped into the water to hold her head up so that she still might say something that could be interpreted as a renunciation of the Covenant. The crowd begged her to speak and Major Windram, commander of the troops, offered to administer the Abjuration Oath which would allow her to be released. 'I will not,' she replied, 'I am one of Christ's children. Let me go.'

As the reformed church split into smaller groups like the Covenanters, the Welsh and the Cornish embraced Methodism with extraordinary fervour. The ideas of John Wesley first arrived in Wales in the 1750s, and within 100 years the established church had lost most of its congregations. Nonconformist sects of various sorts were passionately supported, and the power of the *hwyl* was first heard. Meaning literally 'mood' or 'spirit', it was particularly applied to preachers who had an intense and hypnotic style of delivery, something inherited, incidentally, by politicians like David Lloyd George, Aneurin Bevan and Neil Kinnock. Always conducted in Welsh and strikingly different from the staid solemnities of the Church of England, the rise and power of Nonconformity gave the language a new authority. Now, it was possible to talk to God in Welsh. The revivalism reached its zenith in the nineteenth century, and between 1800 and 1850 a chapel opened in Wales every eight days. It took many strange, ecstatic forms. For example, celebratory jumping must have been bewildering to outsiders. Done in heavy clogs on wooden floors specially strengthened to take it, it was a self-conscious imitation of the various sorts of dances done in the Bible as well as a form of physical trance. Visitors came from England to see it. In the last great revival of 1904 it was claimed that 100,000 were converted. Convictions for drunkenness convictions were halved in a year, and it was said that pit ponies stopped working because miners had given up swearing.

By 1851 Methodism had claimed 60 per cent of the population of Cornwall as converts and, as in Wales, chapels were built on many corners. At Gwennap, between Redruth and Falmouth, there is a remarkable testament to Cornish fervour. To accommodate a demand for mass worship beyond the capacity of any building, a huge pit was dug in the ground. With grass seating ledges arranged in concentric circles, it could take 4,000 people, and in one day John Wesley is said to have preached five services at Gwennap.

While in the Western Isles a grim Presbyterianism gripped the souls of the Gaels, it seemed that in the nineteenth century a Celtic church had found the Sea Kingdoms once more. Partly as an enthusiastic rejection of the Church of England and partly because the reformed churches almost always embraced Welsh or Gaelic, it turned back to the old simplicities. In the reformed religious life of the west there is little sense of hierarchy, little fuss or decoration, a genuine commitment to the priesthood of all believers, a belief in the ability of men and women to choose to live a virtuous life, and a passion in worship which contrasts vividly with the oddly bloodless rituals of the Church of England. Perhaps because they have lived a harder life on the cold, Atlantic edges of Britain, the Celts have chosen a hard God. That itself may be a memory of a long distant past when the gods were harsh and needed a constant stream of gifts, sacrifice and propitiation. Outside the walls of the chapels and churches, beyond the warmth of the hearthside and the comfort of shelter, there are places in the west of Britain where the old gods are close.

SEVEN

The Sons of Death

AT THE END OF THE EIGHTH CENTURY what medieval historians called 'a shower of hell' burst on the Sea Kingdoms. Blown westwards across the North Sea by greed and a need for adventure, the dragon-ships were first seen by the terrified monks of Aidan's monastery at Lindisfarne off the Northumbrian coast in 793. Roared on by their sea lords, the Vikings rowed hard for the beaches and ran their ships up above the tide-line. Jumping from the *dreki*, they made straight for the defenceless monastery and stole as much portable loot as they could cram onto the open decks of their ships.

A year later the Vikings rounded Cape Wrath, the turning point, and raided the northern Hebrides, where they may have attacked the coastal monasteries founded by St Donan and St Maelrubai. The converted Picts saw these places as sacred, in need of no special protection, and they must have appeared as open invitations to the pagan Vikings. In 795 they descended on Iona and carried off all they could find of two centuries of gifts and enrichments. Iona must have housed a large store of treasures, both as the focus for the cult of St Columba and as a focus for pilgrimage, and the Vikings knew it. They called the monks the 'followers of White Christ', and in turn the raiders were known as 'the Sons of Death'.

Iona was attacked again in 798 and 802, and in 806 the Vikings slaughtered sixty-eight members of the community of brothers and lay workers. The abbot, Cellach, had no option but to make plans to abandon the island, the place made sacred by Columba and his successors.

It must have been a heartbreaking decision, but the following year work began on a new inland foundation at Kells in Ireland, far from the sea. Some of Cellach's brothers found the loss of Iona impossible to bear and small groups went back, despite the danger. Some time before 825 a monk from an aristocratic background called Blathmac left Ireland to go and live at the old monastery, never to leave it. Blathmac knew the terror that would come from the sea, and he embraced it. A near contemporary account written in Reichenau in southern Germany makes it clear that the monk went to Iona precisely because he realized that the Vikings would almost certainly return. Blathmac actively sought martyrdom and he was not to be disappointed. It may be that he felt a blood sacrifice in defence of the sanctity of Iona and the memory of Columba, in defiance of the savagery of the raiders, might assure him of a place in glory with the saints. Nothing could have prepared Blathmac for what was to happen to him.

When the Vikings came, it was at dawn. But it was no surprise. Watchers in the night had sent the abbot advance warning and he sent away those monks whose courage failed them 'by a footpath through regions known to them'. Screaming their war cries, the Vikings broke into the abbey precinct and slaughtered everyone they could find, except Blathmac. In search of the treasures of Columba's shrine, they questioned the monk. When he refused to tell them where it was hidden, the Vikings did a strange thing. They rounded up four of the island ponies and brought them to the monastery. Ripping off Blathmac's habit, the Vikings threw him to the ground and tied ropes to his ankles and wrists. And then each rope was harnessed to one of the ponies. Before the animals moved the Vikings no doubt asked the terrified monk one last time where Columba's treasure was buried. When he shook his head, they smacked the ponies hard on the backside and they tore off Blathmac's limbs. The force probably severed his spinal cord. If it did not, then Blathmac will have died a slower and even more hideous death.

The Vikings showed an unrelenting thirst for blood. In November 869 they captured King Edmund of East Anglia and killed him with the agonies of blood-eagling. Intended as a human sacrifice to the war-god Odin, a victim was tied face-first to a stake or a pillar and the clothes torn from his back. While the pagan Vikings invoked their grisly god, a sea lord stepped forward with his sword drawn. With it he hacked Edmund's ribs away from his spine, and while the King was still living he pulled them outwards like the wings of an eagle and then ripped out his lungs.

This was not an isolated incident. These terrible rituals were carried out in Orkney and there are records of blood-eagling in the twelfth century. The Vikings lived by such savagery, and when monkish records express repeated horror at their deeds and trembling fear of their return, they are not merely creating propaganda and exaggerating events as a result of the raiders' fondness for attacking churches. They really were terrified. Perhaps because the dragon-ships were so fast and adaptable, consistently giving the Vikings the power of surprise, their onslaughts were truly frightening. During the summer sailing season lookouts were posted at vulnerable points, but in the grey hours before dawn it was difficult to make out shapes against the horizon, or tell the splash of oars from the play of seals or the wash of the waves on the shore. The only tell-tale sound was the rhythmic thud of wooden oars against the rowlocks, and by the time a lookout had heard that, the dragon-ship was only minutes away from rasping up the beach.

The first phase of Viking contact with the Sea Kingdoms seems to have been entirely piratical, and the raiders returned to Norway and Denmark with their portable loot. Although it is dated much later, in the thirteenth century, and tells of a man based not in Norway but in Orkney, this passage gives a good account of how these men thought of their work:

> This is how Svein used to live. Winter he would spend at home on Gairsay, where he entertained some eighty men at his own expense. His drinking hall was so big, there was nothing in Orkney to compare with it. In the spring he had more than enough to occupy him, with a great deal of seed to sow which he saw to carefully himself. Then when that job was done, he would go off plundering in the Hebrides and in Ireland on what he called his 'spring trip', then back home just after mid-summer, where he stayed until the cornfields had been reaped and the grain was safely in. After that he would go off raiding again, and never came back till the first month of winter was ended. This he used to call his 'autumn trip'.

When men embarked on these trips the younger and less wealthy might take only an axe or a spear, hoping to acquire more weapons or the means to acquire them. A sea lord might also carry a sword, bow and arrows and a shield. When Vikings put to sea they arranged their shields in a characteristic way on the gunwales of the ship in an attempt to keep dry in choppy weather. Usually round, each had a metal boss in the middle with a bar behind it for holding and protecting the hand. Swords were one-handed and double-edged for slashing. Very little Viking body armour has yet been found and no helmets with horns sticking out of either side. These were nineteenth-century Wagnerian products of the fertile imaginations of theatrical costume designers. Such helmets as have been turned up are rounded, and some are made of leather rather than iron.

The first waves of raiders were eventually followed by settlers who brought ploughshares as well as swords and who dealt in trade as well as blood. Shetland and Orkney were first landfall for those sailing 'west-over-sea' from Scandinavia; they became the mostly intensively colonized of all the islands, and were the heartland of the Viking sea kingdom. Neither remote nor isolated, they were the hub for voyages to the north, west and south out of Norway and Sweden. Both archipelagos stayed in Norwegian hands until 1468 when it was arranged that James III of Scotland should marry Margaret, daughter of Christian I, King of Denmark and Norway. As part of her dowry the Danes pledged Orkney and Shetland to the Scottish crown, but actual sovereignty was never transferred. Technically the islands still belong to Denmark because their king has never renounced his right to redeem that pledge.

Culturally they retained a Scandinavian atmosphere for much longer, and in some important senses, still do. Norse was spoken in a Shetlandic dialect called Norn until the eighteenth century and it still survives, just, in the language of fishermen. Because the sea is so capricious and dangerous the habitual superstition and conservatism of sailors often persuaded them to persist in the use of old languages, particularly when they were at sea: the Cornish and Manx languages were last heard as a spoken vernacular on the decks of fishing boats. In Shetland, the survival of Norn took an unusual turn – it is used as a cover tongue. Certain words in English are believed to be deeply unlucky by the Shetlandic fishermen, and, in order not to test fate too far, they use Norn equivalents instead. So that their use did not chase them away from the nets, the English words for fish are translated: cod is *drolti*, mussels are *knoklins* and halibut is *da glyed*, and in a twist of Viking memory, ministers and churches are thought to be taboo words and the deckhands called them *upstaar* and *munger-hoose* respectively. When they hear the cadences of Shetlandic English, some philologists believe that they can hear the way the Vikings spoke.

The harsh ethos of the Vikings was remembered in another custom which faded in the nineteenth century, and for good reason. Every three or four years Shetlandic crofters would 'ride the Hagri'. On their tough little ponies, the crofters went around the boundaries of their common grazing land that lay beyond the dykes of their in-bye (home) fields. At each boundary stone a young boy 'got a sair treshin sae as he soud mind weel whaur do hagmets stude', or he 'got a sore thrashing so as he should remember well where the boundary stones were'. Different boys were beaten at each stone and these indelible memories were printed on their memories in what was called 'the whipping custom'.

Shetlandic boats also reveal a clear line back to the raiders from across the North Sea. The sixern is a sea-going rowing boat whose shape and sea-handling are like a small dragon-ship and which, as its name shows, took six men to row. The islands and the voes they rowed between all have Norse names, and a significant echo of the Scandinavian past can be heard when local people climb aboard the ferries at Lerwick and Kirkwall. They talk of 'going to Scotland'.

The Vikings called Orkney and Shetland the Nordreys, or Northern Isles, which explains why such a northern county as Sutherland was thought to be south. It depends on where you stand or where you sail, and to the Vikings it was certainly to the south. Having colonized Caithness as well, settlers carved out farms in the Outer and Inner Hebrides, which they called the Sudreys. In the formal episcopal title of Sodor and Man, the name is still current, as are thousands of Norse place names which show a pattern of Viking occupation down the western edge of Scotland, in Galloway, Man and down the Irish coastline from Dublin to Wicklow, Wexford and Waterford. Sometimes these new colonies acted independently and at other times they were under the direct control of the King of Norway. Magnus Bareleg, the king who dragged his boat overland at Tarbert to prove Kintyre an island, mounted an expedition in 1098 to reassert his authority over the Viking sea kingdom. His court bard, Bjorn Cripplehand, describes a ferocity undimmed over the three centuries since the first raid on Iona, and conveys a powerful sense of how the Vikings understood where and what was theirs:

In Lewis Isle with fearful blaze
The house destroying fire plays;
To hills and rocks the people fly
Fearing all shelter but the sky.
In Uist the king deep crimson made
the lightning of his glancing blade;
The peasant lost his land and life
Who dared to bide the Norseman's strife.

The hungry battle-birds were filled
In Skye with blood of foemen killed,
And wolves on Tiree's lonely shore
Dyed red their hairy jaws in gore.
The men of Mull were tired of flight;
The Scottish foemen would not fight
And many an island-girl's wail
Was heard as through the Isles we sail.

On Sanda's plain our shields they spy:
From Islay smoke rose heaven-high,
Whirling up from the flashing blaze
The king's men o'er the island raise
South of Kintyre the people fled
Scared by our swords in blood dyed red,
And our brave champion onward goes
To meet in Man the Norseman's foes.

The story of Viking settlement in the places listed (and omitted) in Cripplehand's blood-soaked poem is often difficult to disentangle. Not only did the raiders fight with the indigenous Celts they found in the west, they also fought with each other. Norwegian and Danish Vikings vied for control of the Sea Kingdoms and their riches, while sometimes Scandinavian-based royal fleets sailed to engage in battle the ships of the colonists. After a generation or two, Viking and Celtic lines mingled to produce men with Celto-Norse names and mixed loyalties, blurring the picture even more, and amongst the scatter of dates, raids and battles a very interesting pattern emerges.

Over the winter of 840–41 a Viking called Turgesius attacked places deep in the green heart of Ireland. Sailing his dragon-ships into the mouth of the River Shannon and north through the network of lochs he came to the wealthy monastery of Clonmacnoise. He added insult to slaughter and pillage by placing his woman on the altar of the church and having her recite pagan oracles. Less shocking but more important was the establishment of what the Vikings called a ship-camp, a *longphort*, at the mouth of the Liffey at a place they called Blackpool. Better known as Dublin, the name comes from *Dubh-linne* which means dark pool. Forty years after the raids began, the choice of Dublin as the first place to over winter was instructive. As much an economic as a strategic choice, the Vikings knew that their palisaded ship-camp straddled the western route from Norway to Biscay, Spain and Europe, and it was close to being the best position for an entrepôt for all of the Sea Kingdoms. If a conventional understanding of Dublin's hinterland is reversed from landward to seaward, then the Vikings' choice is better understood. North Wales, Man, Cumbria and Galloway were its immediate maritime hinterland, and beyond that lay Cornwall and the Hebrides.

In 851 Danish Vikings sailed into the Irish Sea to attack the Norse-Irish Vikings of Dublin. They wanted a share, if not control, of the profits of the trade that was beginning to be transacted through the colony, particularly the lucrative business of slavery. Perhaps as many as 300 dragon-ships joined battle in Strangford Lough, south of what is now Belfast. It seems that the Danes gained a victory which allowed Ivar to become King of Dublin and begin to plan an even greater coup, the conquest of England, but a short time later he was supplanted by Olaf, a Norwegian king, who ruled in Dublin between 853 and 871. He campaigned a great deal in Scotland and laid an unprecedented four-month siege to the Rock at Dumbarton on the Clyde, the capital of the Old Welsh-speaking kingdom of Strathclyde. The Rock was captured and the Vikings took 'very many captives' to feed their slave traffic.

One of Olaf's sea-lords was Ketil Flatnose (the Vikings loved nicknames), and his family took the story of the Sea Kingdoms on a fascinating journey. After the victory at Dumbarton, it seems that Ketil and Olaf quarrelled and that Olaf's wife, Aud the Deep-Minded, became involved. She left her husband and sailed north with her father, Ketil, to sulk in the Hebrides. At some point after 871 Aud had a boat built, and in it she took her people and sailed further north to Shetland, on to Faroe and finally to Iceland to establish what is regarded as the first colony on the island. For cultural reasons the Icelanders have always emphasized an overriding Scandinavian influence but it is probable that Aud the Deep-Minded reached the island before anyone from Norway or Denmark because her ships were guided by men who knew the way and had been there before – men she took on board when she left the Hebrides. The fact that Iceland was originally colonized by Vikings from the west of Scotland has been insufficiently understood. There is clear evidence of Celtic and Christian influence in Iceland which was overlaid after the tenth century by later settlers, most of whom came from Scandinavia.

Many of the earliest settlers had Celto-Norse names, and while Iceland remained pagan until the eleventh century, because it was colonized slightly later from pagan Norway, an underlying Christian influence from the Hebrides was unquestionably present. Aud the Deep-Minded set up crosses at Holar, and since she could find no properly consecrated ground for her grave, she chose to be buried in the sands of the Icelandic beaches. Her son-in-law Helgi Bjolan had a Norse-looking Gaelic nickname which comes from *beolan*, meaning 'little mouth', and he was also an occasional Christian. Happy to worship Christ at home and even name it after him, Kristnes or Christ's Headland, 'he was very mixed in his faith. He put his trust in Christ and named his homestead after him, but yet he would pray to Thor on sea voyages, and in hard stresses and in all those things that he thought were of most account to him', according to the twelfth-century Icelandic *Book of Settlement*, the *Landnamabok*. In the late ninth century Helgi acquired a Christian neighbour, a Viking from the Hebrides called Orlygur Hrappson. He had a church built in Iceland that seems to have been dedicated to Kolumkilli, or more recognizably, Calum Cille, St Columba of Iona.

Other, more distant, sources support a discovery of Iceland made in a Hebridean Christian atmosphere. Dicuil, an Irish monk at the Carolingian court in France, compiled his *World Geography* in 825, fifty years before Aud the Deep-Minded sailed. Probably a monk who had fled from her ancestors and their attacks on Iona, he wrote about Faroe and a place he called Thule, which is clearly Iceland. Dicuil knew about the pack ice which lay to the north of Thule and a great deal more about the North Atlantic because he had talked to people who had been there. Before the Vikings rediscovered Iceland, there were people at Iona who had sailed far to the north, and come back to tell the tale. As Tim Severin showed in his curragh, the skin boat, the alleged fantasies of

St Brendan the Navigator were rooted in fact. It seems that hermit-monks, in search of *diseartan* in the vast wastes of the North Atlantic, had rowed and sailed their fragile boats to these uninhabited and bleakly beautiful islands. From Iona to Iceland there is a clear trail of place names based on the Irish Gaelic word for the monks, *papar* or *papa*, which means father. The word also appears in Pabbay and Bayble in the Hebrides, Papa Westray in the Orkneys and Papa Stour in Shetland. They all point north to Papey, an island off the south coast of Iceland. Later Icelandic chroniclers confirm that Viking settlers on Faroe and in Iceland came across Irish monks in what might have been a summer colony. The weather was kinder in the second half of the first millennium and there are further hints that Celtic monks developed a store of nautical lore which the Vikings used in their voyages further west. When Erik the Red sailed to found a colony on Greenland between 982 and 985, he took with him a Celtic Christian from the Hebrides, perhaps as a pilot who knew the waters. When Erik's son, Leif, took ship for Vinland, around 1000, to establish the short-lived settlement at L'Anse les Meadows in Newfoundland, he may have acted on information provided by people who could point him in the right direction. *Erik's Saga* tells of conversations with American natives at L'Anse les Meadows during which casual mention was made of 'foreigners' who had arrived long before the Vikings landed. They were men who wore long white robes, and marched in procession bearing long poles to which cloths were attached, yelling loudly as they did this. The Icelandic *Landnamabok* tells of reports of a country 'which some called Ireland the Great. It lies west in the sea near Vinland the Good.' The Vikings called their American colony Vinland for the everyday reason that they found vines growing there. There are two further mentions of encounters with Irish monks in the *Landnamabok*, and since at the time these were probably thought less than remarkable, they are given only passing attention.

A substantial body of documentary, place-name and practical evidence points to a discovery of the islands of the North Atlantic and the mainland of North America by Gaelic-speaking hermit-monks in the early eighth century, and the subsequent use of their maritime knowledge by the Vikings in the ninth century. When the first raiders plundered Iona they slaughtered those who stood in their way and stole whatever they could carry, but they were careful not to destroy something which, as seamen, they found immediately useful – knowledge of the oceans and of navigation. Across the arc of the North Atlantic there flickers the faintest shadow of Celtic Christianity.

Much easier to find than Greenland or Newfoundland is the Isle of Man. Sitting at the centre of the Irish Sea it was an obvious target for Viking colonists and soon after Turgesius overwintered at Dublin in 840–41, the dragon-ships appeared in the waters around Man. By the end of the ninth century these warrior-farmers had appropriated the most productive parts of the island, particularly in the north. Still stubbornly pagan, their great men were sent to meet their fierce gods in the impressive and economically very wasteful ritual of the ship burial. There is an elaborate example at Knock y Doonee in the north of Man. A ship burial or cremation aboard a burning ship was a signal of great honour and only accorded to lords or kings. A foreign merchant saw the preparations being made for a ship burning and he left a record which both fascinates and repels. The dead man was laid out in his finery and many of his most prized possessions arranged around him inside the ship. Sometimes horses and pets were killed and set in death as they had been in life, at their master's side. Under the mound at Knock y Doonee excavators found a sword, shield, spear, battleaxe, fishing gear and a hammer and tongs but also the skeletons of a horse and a dog. The belief that all were aboard a ship bound for a final voyage to Valhalla was very strong. So strong that the foreign merchant recounted how one of the dead Viking lord's slave girls volunteered to be killed so that she could travel with him. Apparently she was given powerful potions to drink and then allowed each of the lord's leading warriors to have sex with her. Then she cut off the head of a live chicken and went into the tent where she was to be killed. An old hag stabbed her to death while others around them roared and shrieked so that no-one could distinguish the screams of the slave girl as she died.

Ship burials on the Isle of Man became rarer as the gradual conversion of the Vikings diverted them away from such barbarities to more peaceful Christian practice. In their way, the surviving results of this cultural switch are as dramatic as the ships under their earth mounds – the Viking adaptation of an aboriginal habit of carving gravestones is an astonishing thing. Up until 850 simple funerary slabs had been made on Man, many with only an incised cross. Later a little decoration crept in, but when the Vikings began to commission these, a remarkable series of stunningly beautiful sculptures was created, known as the Manx Crosses.

The first Western European artist from the post-classical era to achieve a clear historical personality was not Giotto, Cimabue or any of the early Italian masters. Between 930 and 950 – a very early date, given the development of the fine arts in Continental Europe – a series of sixteen stone crosses was carved in the Isle of Man by Gaut Bjornson. This is not a matter of conjecture, attribution or confirmation from a separate documentary source. There is no doubt that Bjornson carved the sculptures – he signed some of them.

All of the crosses which are certainly by him, even at a distance of a thousand years, show a complete integrity of style and technique. Gaut was not master of a school which turned out hackwork blocked out by apprentices and finished by him – he did all the work, possibly even the initial excavation. He invented the instantly recognizable ring chain pattern of interleaving which he used to decorate both cross and background. Later pieces show him developing new styles of relief work, using natural forms like tendrils, and also growing in confidence. On the cross-slab of Kirk Michael there is even arrogance: 'Gaut made this and all in Man'. This is clearly not true since 160 crosses have been found, with the earliest dating from the fifth and sixth centuries. The sculptor was probably claiming that, as a lone artistic pioneer, he had created a new style of carving.

Crosses at Muncaster and Gosforth in Cumbria show less assured examples of his work and their location suggests that he began his career there, before moving to Man. On another, later, cross the signature is expanded to 'Gaut Bjornson of Kuli', which not only shows an increasing self-confidence but also confirms that he was the son of a Viking who probably lived at the village now called Ballacooley.

Gaut preferred to work on large rectangular cross-slabs rather than the more characteristic, free-standing sort. They varied in height from 2 feet 6 inches to 11 feet and were generally 15 to 24 inches wide and 2 to 4 inches thick. Some of Gaut's and many of the other contemporary crosses are round-headed or have a cross cut in the middle of a circle. Looking back at the tradition of Celtic carving which preceded them, it is possible to detect an interesting and surprising process at work. It shows that, contrary to popular assumption, these early crosses had nothing to do with the crucifixion. In the first half of the first millennium this was not a popular symbol amongst Christians, since it recalled a particularly Roman form of execution suffered by common criminals. In the first Manx examples and a handful found near Whithorn in Galloway, there are signs of a very different origin for the crosses which Gaut later carved so beautifully and which found their most monumental expression in the great Celtic high crosses of Ireland.

Christianity was fond of cryptic codes, because it was often a persecuted religion in the Roman Empire. Even now one of the earliest symbols, a stylized fish, is still in currency, and car-stickers for self-advertising believers often incorporate it. The key to this is in the Greek word for fish. Using the Roman alphabet, it reads 'Ichthus', which is an acronym for the name of the Redeemer: Iasos Christos Thiou Huios Sowtare. Or, Jesus Christ, the Son of God, our Saviour. Even more cryptic was the Chi Rho monogram. Written like a capital P with a cross cut through the stem, it is a device made from the first two Greek alphabet letters of the name of Christ, and from this the early Celtic crosses developed. The vestigial loop of the Rho, written like a long-stemmed version of the Roman capital P, is clearly apparent in early Manx and Galloway crosses. It had faded out by the time Gaut Bjornson took up his chisels but it may be the main reason why the characteristic Celtic cross has a circle around it. The usual provenance argued for the presence of the circle – that it represents the sun as a homage to Druidical beliefs – is unconvincing. Christian missionaries may have adopted holy wells and other places of pagan sanctity to set up the first churches, but their iconography was not a matter for compromise or an eclectic decorative exercise. It was central to their faith and not something which could happily accommodate the pagan beliefs the early missionaries fought so hard to defeat.

The free-standing Celtic high crosses of Ireland developed from around 800 onwards, and later examples insert a figurative representation of the crucified Christ in the circle of the Chi Rho. By that time the memory of the Roman Empire was far distant. Irish historians argue that part of the reason for the appearance of these huge and beautiful objects (the largest, at Monasterboice, is 21 feet tall) is that they were too heavy for Vikings to carry off. It may indeed have been a lesson handed down by Turgesius, the man who desecrated an altar with his wife and her pagan utterances, because a school of cross carving was based at Clonmacnoise, the monastery he attacked. Unlike Gaut Bjornson, who limited himself to abstract pattern, the unknown sculptors of the Irish high crosses chiselled out figurative scenes almost exclusively from the Bible. Many were set near the foot of the upright so that those kneeling in front could see them clearly, and they were brightly painted. All of the Irish crosses were free-standing and to be found in monastic enclosures or near churches.

The slab crosses of Man, used as markers for burials, allowed Gaut to carve decorative backgrounds, and, probably as important for him, to sign his name and carve a dedication on the edge of the slab. Gaut wrote in runes. Like the Ogham script found all over Celtic Britain, the runic alphabet consisted only of straight lines. It was designed to be cut rather than written in the kind of cursive styles we now understand by the term 'writing'. This supposedly primitive language of limited use allowed his identification as an artist. Yet, outside the Isle of Man, Gaut's achievement is virtually unknown and the beauty of what he made goes unrecognized.

The names of Gaut's patrons are also inscribed, as they are on crosses made by other artists. Typical dedications are on the Braddon Cross: 'Thorleif Hnakki erected this cross to the memory of Fiacc, his son', or on the Mal-Lumkin Cross: 'Mael-Lumchon erected this cross to the memory of Mal-Mura, his foster-mother, daughter of Dugald, the wife whom Athisl had'. Many carry the names of patrons with Celtic names like these, and in general they show a society with an astonishing degree of sophistication – and duality. The men who paid for, encouraged and appreciated the innovative creativity of Gaut Bjornson also continued to perform the barbarity of blood-eagling.

When the Vikings took control of the western seaways between 800 and 1100, they effectively ended the Irish intellectual hegemony of Europe. Had they been more numerous, more fortunate and acted in a better organized and concerted manner, Britain and Ireland may have become part of the Norse-speaking orbit of Scandinavia. Battles rarely settle more than short-term issues, but when King Brian Boru defeated a coalition of Vikings at Clontarf, now buried under the streets of Dublin, in 1014, he showed that Celtic Ireland was vigorous and determined not to surrender its identity. And when King Harold Godwineson defeated and killed King Harold Hardrada of Norway at Stamford Bridge near York in 1066, he effectively ended the possibility of the Danish dynasty of Cnut reasserting its claim to the throne of England.

By contrast, the Vikings remained a distinct political phenomenon in western Britain for a long time. Not until the Treaty of Perth in 1266 when Haakon IV of Norway sold his title to the Hebrides and Man did their involvement in the Sea Kingdoms really begin to decline, even though they held on to Orkney and Shetland for another 200 years. Although Norse was still spoken in Lewis until the fifteenth century, the re-emergence of Celtic culture and political power in the Hebrides and Man began much earlier. The Sons of Death were ultimately defeated not by the force of arms but by something much more effective. They integrated. The Gaelic culture of the Sea Kingdoms was strong and it absorbed the ferocious fighters who sailed 'west-over-sea', but it never forgot them and the Viking was never far from the Celtic surface. On the edge of the din of battle at Bannockburn, Culloden and many a foreign field, the war cries of the sea lords could still be heard.

EIGHT

The Lords of the Isles

ARDTORNISH IS A RUINED CASTLE on the southern tip of Morvern, barely discernible on the shore horizon, opposite the island of Mull. When I opened the Ordnance Survey to find the best way to approach it, I discovered that there was no road, only a vague track which led to a farm and fell far short of the castle site. I parked at a net-drying station on the southern shore of Loch Aline and began what promised to be a long hike. The track was walkable, but it had potholes which would have broken the axle of a wheeled vehicle, even a 4x4, and in places it had simply cracked and fallen apart. Clearly not many people went to see Ardtornish Castle, and I was beginning to wonder if I had taken the correct route.

I came across some cottages by the trackside, almost opposite the village of Lochaline on the other shore, but these were serviced by a small jetty. As often in the western Highlands and the west of Ireland the shortest and easiest route was by sea. If those in the cottages needed to buy something urgent in Lochaline, they could row across the narrow neck of the loch in ten minutes, whereas the journey by foot on the track and then car on the road would have taken five times as long.

The track pulled away uphill from the jetty and the Sound of Mull opened out before me; the sight of the Lochaline ferry on its way in the sunshine to Fishnish made me wonder if I should have enquired after a water-taxi rather than undertake what was proving to be a very long walk. Rounding a corner I saw the castle for the first time, sitting squat on its promontory, staring out to sea. By the time I had reached a derelict farmstead and walked through the fields towards the ruin, I could see that it was a perfect place to put a sea castle. Around it are fertile fields watered by streams, while below there is a large but sheltered bay with a shingle beach for easy landing and careful beaching. From the tower of the castle itself, the views to seaward are breathtaking: Ardtornish watches the Sound of Mull, a busy sea route, and looks down to Duart Castle, and beyond to the ancient forts at Dunstaffnage and Dunollie, while the town of Oban is clearly visible on a bright day. The castle sits at a marine crossroads, commanding the hub of the Inner Hebrides.

No-one remembers what happened within its tumbled down walls where only the sea birds perch. There is no plaque or board at Ardtornish Castle, no sign from the main road, and the men working at the net station, local people, had no idea that the place was even of much importance. The garden at Ardtornish is more notable now, and sometimes visitors stop to look at the flowers, breaking their journey to Lochaline and the ferry to Mull.

Yet in 1462 two powerful men signed the Treaty of Westminster–Ardtornish. One was Edward IV of England and the other was a man whose kingdom has entirely withered and is forgotten. All roads lead to Westminster today, but to Ardtornish there is barely a track.

Once, this was a place of huge power. John MacDonald of Islay, the Lord of the Isles and King of Man, was co-signatory to the treaty with the English King. On his accession he mustered 10,000 soldiers at his castle and 250 galleys in the sea loch below. After the English and Scottish kings, John was the greatest landowner in Britain. His will was done from the Butt of Lewis to the Calf of Man and all the islands and coastline between. These were not the barren, windswept places they are now. His riches were immense: Islay alone produced annually 720 merks of silver, 1,420 cows, 5,040 sheep, and 3,960 bolls of malt and meal. The bards remembered the power that pulsed across the Sea Kingdoms from Ardtornish:

> Without Clan Donald there is no strength,
> Without Clan Donald there is no joy.

John ruled an Atlantic principality which commanded resources enough to threaten the King of Scotland, and his treaty with Edward IV guaranteed him half of the kingdom if the boy king, James III, could be deposed.

But it all fell out differently. It was John who was forced to forfeit his vast estates and in 1493 he became a captive pensioner of the royal household. Others claimed and fought over the remnants of the old lordship and Clan Donald's great dominion began to disintegrate.

The Lordship grew out of the old Viking sea kingdom of the west of Britain, and it also looked back self-consciously to the Gaelic society of Dalriada, Columba and the kindreds of the Eastern Irish, but its story remains shrouded in Hebridean mist and misunderstanding. The Lords of the Isles were great sea kings who built an empire that stretched south to Man and sent generations of soldiers to fight in Ireland. Initially uninvolved in events on the mainland, and not comfortably accommodated in Scottish or Manx history, the Lordship has often been ignored by historians whose gaze is fixed on the attempts of succeeding kings to impose themselves and their dynasties on Scotland. The Kings of Alba, of Scotland, seem to represent a progressive force which ultimately resulted in the polity we recognize today. In fact, the struggles of mainland kings, particularly in the eleventh century, also had much to do with the Dalriadic past and less than is usually supposed with any progressive project. Their doings provide a useful background against which the emergence of the Lords of the Isles can be better understood.

Later history and a famous later fiction allude to these influences but also obscure them with anachronistic assumptions. William Shakespeare made a Demon-King out of a Gaelic king. He lived by blood, betrayal and reckless courage, and for 400 years audiences have shuddered at the thought of a kingdom ruled by Macbeth. The Scottish play was written at a time when James VI of Scotland was determined to curb the power of the Highland chiefs, and to bring the Gaidhealtachd properly into royal jurisdiction. As James I of Great Britain, he also wanted to promote the idea of a modern state which had left behind the barbarities of the likes of Macbeth. In this he was greatly aided by the progressive blackening of the tragic hero's character by Scottish historians anxious to please the Stewart dynasty. In the fourteenth century, John of Fordun miscalled Macbeth a usurper and Andrew de Wynton accused him of murdering King Duncan, whereas in fact he killed him in battle. Hector Boece added a domestic dimension to the tale when he transformed Queen Gruoch into the ruthless Lady Macbeth. This propaganda eventually found its way into the researches of Raphael Holinshed and, through his

Chronicles of England, Scotlande and Irelande (1577), into Shakespeare's imagination.

Although William Shakespeare wrote a masterly fiction to fit the temper of the times, the play contains much about Gaelic Scotland and has a real historical conflict built into its core. The evil and ambitious Macbeth is based in the north, and, while gentle King Duncan was his guest, he stabbed him to death in order to gain the throne for himself. In reality, when he killed his rival, by whatever means, Macbeth only did as much as Duncan's predecessor, Malcolm II macAlpin, when he murdered his cousin, King Kenneth III in 1005 to become undisputed king, and indeed much less than Duncan himself. The stately old man who remarked that Macbeth's castle had 'a pleasant seat, the air nimbly and sweetly recommends itself unto our gentle senses' probably murdered one claimant to the throne the day before his coronation, and another after it.

To Shakespeare, the royal court and his audience at the Globe Theatre, the murder of Duncan was a heinous crime. They believed that eldest sons succeeded their fathers as kings, and could not conceive of a Gaelic world 500 years before where this principle was not accepted. And in the play, the audience sides with the rightful heir, the murdered Duncan's son, Malcolm, when he comes from the civilized south to destroy the usurper from the barbaric north and to restore peace. The image of the historical King Macbeth was so distorted by the needs of early-seventeenth-century politics because he represented a Gaelic past which the English and English-speaking Scots wished to reject as backward.

The truth about Macbeth is, of course, very different. His real significance is that he brought the long and successful macAlpin dynasty to an end. Partly to put themselves out of range of the Vikings, the eighth century had seen the Dalriadic kings of Alba move into the centre of Scotland, to establish themselves at Scone. From there Kenneth Mac-Alpin and his successors ruled Scotland north of the Forth.

Malcolm II reigned for twenty-nine years, and was a tough and uncompromising warlord whose axemen cut a Northumbrian army to pieces at the Battle of Carham in 1014, pushing the frontiers of Scotland further south and ultimately establishing the eastern Border on the River Tweed – but this did not ensure that his eldest son succeeded him. In 1034 Malcolm was murdered at Glamis by his leading noblemen and the man probably behind the coup – his grandson – Duncan I, seized the throne.

When sweet old Duncan I succeeded Malcolm II, he embarked on a series of ill-starred expeditions to continue the expansion of his kingdom to the south. After he repeatedly failed to win more territory, his credibility at home may have begun to wither. Equally, Macbeth had as good or a better claim to the kingship of Gaelic Scotland. Royal succession in Celtic society was not arranged around ideas of primogeniture but was instead kin-based. Custom held that a king could be succeeded by his sons, his grandsons and even his great-grandsons. In practice this allowed the fittest and most ruthless of the extended royal family to assume the throne, not necessarily the first-born son of the king.

Once Macbeth had killed Duncan at a skirmish near Elgin, he was politically able to make himself king and sustain his position because he had made an alliance with Thorfinn, the Viking Earl of Orkney, and because he had his own power base in the Kingdom of Moray in the north. So vigorous and persistent were the efforts of the Moray dynasty to win the Scottish throne permanently that in the twelfth century David I was forced to send loyal settlers to supplant the local population. Their influence can still be heard either side of a linguistic boundary at the village of Auldearn. To the west, around Inverness, the standard English of people whose original speech was Gaelic is spoken, while to the east a strikingly different Scots is the everyday tongue. This is not a native dialect but one introduced by people who came from the south to live here after 1150.

The claims of the Kings of Moray were repeatedly pursued in rebellions until 1230, when a group of knights loyal to Alexander II went in search of a baby. After they had found the little girl who was heir to Moray and its pretensions to the throne, they rode into Forfar with her. Taking the lass by the heels, the knights had 'her head . . . struck against the column of the [market] cross and her brains dashed out'.

Once he had established himself and his wife, Gruoch, King Macbeth reigned between 1040 and 1057, and was secure enough in 1050 to leave his kingdom to go on pilgrimage to Rome where, it was said, he 'scattered money like seed'. In 1054 another character in Shakespeare's play, Earl Siward of Northumbria, moved to install Malcolm, son of Duncan, as ruler of Lothian and Strathclyde, while Macbeth retreated northwards to his heartland in Moray. Three years later there was a decisive battle in north-east Scotland and Macbeth was killed. His stepson, Lulach, took over the throne and was King of Alba for the year 1058. Then, the man whom history would call Malcolm Ceann Mhor had Lulach killed and he, in his turn, became king.

King Macbeth and King Lulach (some historians refuse to award them their titles presumably out of vestigial feelings of disapproval instilled by Shakespeare's play) are both buried on Iona, in the Reilig Oran, but their successor, Malcolm III, is not. Even though he took the Gaelic nickname, Ceann Mhor or Great Chief, Malcolm's attention was drawn to the mainland of Scotland, and to the south. His decision not to lie with the kings in the ground of Iona marks a break with the Dalriadic past, which removed the traditional focus away from the west, and also allowed an independence of thought and action to flourish in the lands of the original kindreds of the Eastern Irish. Another great Sea Kingdom of the west was to come into being.

Some time after 1103 and the death of Magnus Bareleg, the Norwegian king who led a punitive expedition down the western seaboard, a charismatic leader of a resurgent Gaelic Scotland emerged. The origins of Somerled, the man who took the title Rex Insularum, the King of the Isles, were obscure and possible even humble. Tradition tells that the people of Morvern and Ardgour were suffering under the attacks of Vikings and lost their chief in a raid. They went to Somerled to ask if he would lead their warriors, and found him fishing at a pool of the Gear-Abhainn, a stream which flows into Loch Aline near Ardtornish. Somerled had been trying to hook a wily old salmon, and when the men of Morvern asked him to assume command of their warband, he agreed to do it – but only if he could catch the fish. He succeeded, the omens were good, and Somerled's salmon can still be seen on the arms of the MacDonalds of Sleat. Assembling his warriors, he used a series of ruses to give an impression of a larger force and then waited until the Vikings returned to their beached dragon-ships:

> Withal he exhorted his warriors to be of good courage and to do as they would see him do, so they led on the charge. The first whom Somerled slew he ript up and took out his heart, desiring the rest to do the same, because the Danes were not Christians ... So the Danes were put to flight and many of them were lost in the sea endeavouring to gain their ships.

Behind the myth-history it is possible to read the story of a man not born to lead but rather chosen. Much later, bards recited Somerled's genealogy, which included the Gaelic names of his father, Gille-Brigde (servant of St Bride) and his grandfather Gilleadomnan (servant of St Adamnan). Going back six generations, it seems as though he was descended from Godfrey, who lived in the first half of the ninth century and styled himself Toiseach Innse Gall, the Chief of the Isles. Through a Christian male line, Somerled could fairly claim to be a Gael, but his personal name complicates the picture, for Sumar-Lidi means Summer Raider, or more directly, Viking, and popular history has labelled him tautologously as Somerled the Viking. The most reasonable assumption is that he was a Gaelic-speaking Celto-Norse chieftain whose early exploits in defeating a Viking raiding party thrust him into prominence.

In the early twelfth century the Hebrides, the Isle of Man and Dublin were controlled, at least nominally, by King Olaf of Man who reigned from 1113 to 1153. Somerled joined him on an expedition to raid the Isle of Skye and also married his daughter, Ragnhilde, some time before 1150. This was not his first marriage and he had already fathered several children by other relationships. It may be that Somerled followed the old Celtic custom of handfasting whereby a couple lived together for a year on a trial basis. An alternative explanation is that Somerled may have been polygamous, imitating the habit of Irish kings who married early and often. The monkish *Chronicle of Man* attacks his father-in-law, Olaf, for having 'many concubines' and being guilty of 'domestic vice'. Divorce in Celtic society was also not difficult and either partner had clear grounds in law for obtaining it. Whatever Somerled's circumstances, his bountiful progeny ensured that he was followed by many heirs who competed vigorously for their patrimony.

By 1140 that patrimony had already grown large: Somerled had made himself master of Knapdale, Lorne, Argyll and Kintyre. His relationship with the dynamic King of Scotland, David I macMalcolm, seems to have been cordial, and on at least one occasion Islemen fought in a royal host, but Somerled's dynasty made no attempt to forge links with the macMalcolms and the mainland. Theirs was a Sea Kingdom and the important political tool of marriage was used to strengthen relationships on the western seaboard, particularly with the kingdom of Man. Somerled could sail from Lorne to Man much more easily than David macMalcolm could ride from Stirling to Roxburgh, and would almost certainly have had most frequent contact with those powerful men whose territories were accessible by sea.

With the accession of David I's grandson Malcolm IV in 1153, Somerled turned his gaze to Scotland, where he saw an opportunity. The right of eldest sons to succeed through their father's line was still not accepted, and Somerled supported the claims of his brother-in-law, Malcolm MacHeth. Malcolm IV was a sickly child and the chance to remove him seemed very real. MacHeth was smarting from a twenty-three-year imprisonment at Roxburgh Castle (as far from his allies in the Hebrides as it was possible to get without leaving Scotland), where he had to endure the humiliation of being hung over the walls in a cage for public display. David I did not dare to have him put to death because of the trouble it might spark, and therefore it can be safely assumed that MacHeth's claim to kingship was strong. Somerled's fleet sailed up the Clyde and into the heart of Lowland Scotland to support it, but he and MacHeth were unexpectedly defeated, leaving Malcolm IV to continue his unsteady tenure of the throne.

Much more promisingly, Somerled next steered his warships through the North Channel and out into the Atlantic. King Olaf of Man, his father-in-law, had died in 1153, and this time the opportunity was not wasted. On the night of 5 and 6 January in 1156, off the island of Colonsay, Somerled's fleet of eighty galleys engaged the Manx fleet of Olaf's successor, King Godred II, and heavily defeated them. This was a signal moment. The King of Man was forced to concede the southern Hebrides and Somerled added Islay, Jura and Mull to his mainland possessions. Although Godred retained Lewis, the Uists down to Barra and the Isle of Skye, the fact that Somerled's power base lay between them and Man fatally loosened his hold on the northern Hebrides – what the Manx called the 'Out Isles'. It also produced an anomaly. The Manx parliament's legislative body is called the House of Keys, but its name has nothing to do with locks or doors. Keys comes from the Manx for twenty-four, *kiare as feed*, which is the number of members elected to the house. It contained sixteen members for Man and four each for Lewis and Skye. Even though the Out Isles passed formally out of the possession of Man in 1266, the House of Keys refused to accept the loss as permanent and continued to elect proxy members for Skye and Lewis. In the darkest days after 1707 when Scotland lost her parliament, few knew that part of Scotland was still represented in Man.

In 1158 Somerled and Godred quarrelled again and this time the outcome was even more decisive. Appearing off Man, near Ramsay, with fifty-three warships, Somerled chased Godred out of his kingdom and plundered the island for several days. In effect this victory underwrote the title Rex Insularum, because all of the islands and coastline from the Butt of Lewis to the Calf of Man were under Somerled's control. He owed his stunning rise to power to opportunism, no doubt, but also to invention.

When he took Islay from the Kings of Man, Somerled made his headquarters at Dunyvaig, 'the fort of the small ships'. Although the tactical details of the great sea battles planned there have been lost, it is clear that Somerled was a great admiral. No-one understood the waters off the west of Scotland and how to control them better than the Vikings and yet this new Gaelic-speaking sea lord expelled their descendants both from the southern Hebrides and the Isle of Man.

Somerled began a programme of building sea castles like Ardtornish. By 1450 there were thirty throughout the Lordship, as it had become known by the fourteenth century, and each commanded a natural harbour where galleys could be safely beached and a natural vantage point where sentries could watch for raiders on the tide. They are also very modern. While twelfth- and thirteenth-century Norman barons mostly contented themselves with wooden stockaded motte and bailey castles, the Lords of the Isles were building sophisticated stone structures on difficult sites. Their impressive sea castles generally have massive curtain walls and perch on rocky outcrops. Kismuil Castle in Castlebay off Barra is typical. The obvious course would have been to build on the island itself, but the strategists of the Lordship preferred a very awkward site on a tiny islet in the bay. Dunvegan Castle on Skye was accessible only by sea until the eighteenth century and several others have very difficult access by land. Some, like Ardtornish, might be on the Scottish mainland, but they have no road leading to them, only a safe harbour. Many of the sea castles are positioned within sight of each other to allow signals to be quickly sent down the chain. The point about them is simple: they were designed to watch over stretches of sea and not tracts of land. They are a powerful reminder that these truly were Sea Kingdoms.

In 1164 Somerled mounted another challenge for the throne of Scotland. This time he backed no rival claimant and was not simply taking an opportunity that happened to present itself. Malcolm IV had subdued the Gaelic-speaking kingdoms of Galloway and Moray and driven their ruling families into exile. His strategy was one of encirclement where powerful, loyal, magnates such as the Stewarts, Bruces and de Morvilles were given lands neighbouring the sub-kingdoms and, like the Welsh Marcher Lords, licensed to act unilaterally against the King's enemies for their own material benefit. When Fergus, Lord of Galloway, was defeated and expelled, Somerled believed that he and his huge domain could suffer the same fate. Although it is difficult to see how a Sea Kingdom could be encircled without significant naval power, the fact is that he felt threatened and led another enormous fleet up the Firth of Clyde to attack the Stewart possessions in Renfrew. They landed at Greenock and advanced towards Malcolm IV's army. After some inconclusive negotiation, it appears that Somerled was betrayed by a kinsman and stabbed to death in his tent. The Islesmen were shattered at the inglorious and treacherous loss of their charismatic warlord, a man who had built an empire out of almost nothing. Without offering battle, they returned to their galleys at Greenock, pushed them out, rowed them into the deeper waters of the Clyde and set their sails for the west and the Hebrides. Somerled was permitted burial at Iona, but his grave is unmarked, just as his great dominion is now almost forgotten.

Celtic society was fatally wedded to the concept of partibility: when a powerful man died, his legacy was divided equally between his sons. For centuries the Welsh kingship was crippled by partibility, and no dynasty ever successfully unified Wales for any length of time. It was also a tradition that worked against the principle of primogeniture in the succession of the Scottish kingship. When Somerled died, his Sea Kingdom was divided amongst three sons: Ranald, Dugall and Angus, whose branches of the family became known as the MacDonalds, the MacDougalls and the MacRuaris. Depending as much as anything on distance from royal power as a guarantee of independence, the descendants of Somerled behaved like great magnates, skilfully playing off threats of interference against each other. Until 1266 and the Treaty of Perth, the Islesmen claimed that they were not at all subject to the will of the Scottish Crown, but to Norway. It was a useful argument deployed adroitly until the new treaty left no doubt about the legalities.

By the end of the thirteenth century the Scottish crown was in turmoil and concerned only with its own survival. Alexander III had died in an accident in 1286 without leaving a male heir, and Edward I of England was determined to conquer and control Scotland just as he had done Wales. When Robert Bruce eventually emerged as the most likely successor to Alexander and the main focus of resistance to the English, the MacDonalds chose to support him, and the MacDougalls opposed him. For the latter it was a crucial miscalculation.

Angus Og MacDonald led a large contingent of Islesmen to fight at Bannockburn in 1314. Robert Bruce kept the MacDonald soldiers in reserve during the first part of the battle, but when the tight formations of Scottish spearmen began to turn back the heavy English cavalry in confusion, Angus Og raised his broadsword and roared the war cry 'Clann Domnhaill' and his men plunged into the crush of mounted knights. Swinging their Lochaber axes and the great two-handed claymores, the Islesmen cut the English to pieces, and over the wrack of dead horses and dying men, they forced Edward's army backwards until it broke and fled.

Angus Og did not fight at Bannockburn for the idea of Scotland. His goal was his dynasty's unhampered control of the Isles through a secure alliance with King Robert and his descendants. So long as the Scottish crown kept its side of the bargain, the prospects for the MacDonald principality were good. For the MacDougalls, Bannockburn was a disaster. After the battle Robert Bruce kept his bargain with Angus Og, confiscated the MacDougall territory and rewarded the MacDonalds with the bulk of it. The dominion of Somerled was beginning to reassemble. John of Islay, Angus Og's son, was the first formally to take the title, Lord of the Isles. In 1346 the last chief of the MacRuaris died leaving no heir except his sister, Amie, and since she was married to John MacDonald of Islay, the MacRuari lands of Garmoran, the coastline and the islands between Ardnamurchan and Skye, came back into the Lordship 180 years after Somerled's death. The huge Sea Kingdom began to pass down generations of MacDonalds and stayed united through the eventual acceptance of primogeniture. It was during this relatively peaceful period that the institutions of the Lordship developed.

The administrative centre of the Lordship lay at Finlaggan on the island of Islay, although, like most medieval kings, the Lords of the Isles moved around and took their government with them – by sea. While they were essentially autocratic, there was a council of state which occupied itself with dynastic issues – the succession, marriages of policy, defence and the principles of land ownership. Between twelve and sixteen men sat on the Council. There were four great men of the royal blood of Clan Donald: Clanranald, MacIain of Ardnamurchan, MacDonald of Kintyre and MacDonald of Keppoch. Then four great noblemen: Maclean of Duart, Maclean of Loch Buie, MacLeod of Harris and MacLeod of Lewis. And then four thanes also sat in Council: MacKinnon, MacNeil of Barra, MacNeil of Gigha and one other great man who probably took his seat by rotation. The Bishop of the Isles and the Abbot of Iona also attended. While the Council advised the Lords of the Isles on matters of state, the law was administered by brieves or judges whose office was often hereditary and whose knowledge of custom, practice and precedent was passed on down the generations.

This was not the sort of law that we understand, concerned with crime and its punishment, but a Celtic code of conduct which preferred reparation rather than judicial revenge. Fines reckoned in kind and in cash were far more likely to be imposed than hands or heads cut off. Irish law tracts of the seventh and ninth centuries offer a sense of how the law operated throughout Celtic Britain. There was no distinction between civil and criminal cases. Suits were brought to a judge by the injured party and both sides had to swear to abide by a decision before any proceedings began. For example, in matters of defamation the procedure was simple and the formal language eloquent. *Enech* meant honour or face, and an insult and the payment required to compensate for it was *enechruicce*, which means face-reddening. If a man failed to meet a charge of *enechruicce* or failed to honour a pledge if he was found to be guilty, then he faced the attentions of the bards. Through the 'law of the face' they had the power to mock him publicly and ensure that his *enech* fell in front of his peers. Three actions could wash away the 'dirt' of such offences. First 'the pumice stone' of publicly admitting a fault, then the 'water' of payment for any damage caused and finally the 'towel' of a penitential. This last practice is particularly interesting. Penitentials were lists of sins and fixed penances, such as fasting, which probably first appeared in the early Welsh church. The idea spread to Ireland, where it developed because it accorded well with the Irish legal theory that an offence carried a fixed price, determined by a tariff organized in relation to the seriousness of the misdemeanour and the status of the injured party. This produced a clear cause-and-effect concept of a Christian life which could be readily understood by new converts and ordinary people. Sins could be washed clean when the appropriate penance for their commission was applied. While this arrangement acted as a deterrent, certainly for the poor who would probably have been unable to afford the time or the goods involved, it also helped to develop the mechanism of absolution and forgiveness inside the early Celtic church. Penitentials spread from Ireland to the rest of Latin Christendom, and, along with the work of the gospel copyists and the missionaries, are a highly significant Celtic contribution to religious life.

Celtic law also dealt at length with issues of resource management. Surviving Irish and Welsh codes have much to say, for example, about the proper husbanding of swarms of bees. One codex runs to thirty pages on the subject, with much detail on how to determine the original location of queen bees, and where skips (the old straw hives) might be placed, and so on. Because it was the only sweetener available, honey was valuable, and because the insects who made it moved around and swarmed as they wished, issues surrounding the ownership of bees exercised Celtic lawgivers very much.

During the rule of the MacDonalds the economy of the islands and coastline also flourished. Tiree was the granary of the Isles and Islay produced a rich annual income. Disorder was kept to a minimum, partly due to a tradition of seasonal mercenary soldiering which grew up in the west in the Middle Ages. In a practical sense, the Lords of the Isles exported the potential for trouble every summer.

These mercenary soldiers were known as the Gallowglasses and they found Ireland to be a regular source of employment. Gallowglass comes from Gall-Oglaigh meaning 'foreign warriors', but since no Irishman would ever call a brother Gael from Scotland a Gall or 'foreigner', the name needs a little more unpacking. The Vikings who settled in the Hebrides and further south got the odd name of Gall-Gaidheal, the Stranger-Gaels, and this is what Gall-Oglaigh refers to. These Celto-Norse warriors were the descendants of the Vikings and the Irish recognized that mixture as different, even foreign.

Regiments of Gallowglasses sailed to Ireland for the summer campaigning season and the Irish kings employed them to help roll back the twelfth-century English invaders to enclaves based around the towns and centred on Dublin. The Pale came into being as a thirty-mile-wide screen of territory around Dublin and the English, in a telling phrase, began to think of Gaelic society as something beyond the Pale. Officered by their own chieftains, contingents of Gallowglasses were very effective against heavy cavalry. These Hebridean soldiers put up the first sustained and reliable resistance in western Europe to armoured knights. Firstly, they were highly disciplined professional infantrymen who had the confidence to stand their ground against a charge. Horses will instinctively wheel away from what they believe to be immovable and from men arranged in a well-organized line of battle, if they show sufficient resolve. Secondly, they were experienced men who went into battle for a living and never failed to show iron discipline or to enforce it. If only one or two men lost their courage, broke and fled, that left potentially fatal gaps in a battle-line which might spell defeat and death for all.

Irish kings valued these tough mercenaries greatly and were careful to ensure that they were properly equipped. Here is a no-nonsense record of how this was done for one of the Gallowglass groups in the fourteenth century, the MacSweeneys:

> This is how the levy was made: two gallowglasses for each quarter of land, and two cows for each gallowglass deficient, that is, one cow for the man himself and one for his equipment. And Clann Sweeney say they are responsible for these as follows, that for each man equipped with a coat of mail and a breastplate, another should have a jack and a helmet: that there should be no forfeit for a helmet deficient except the gallowglass's brain (dashed out for the want of it).

Contemporary illustrations show that Gallowglasses generally wore a round iron helmet to keep their brains intact, a protective collar piece and a long coat of mail which reached down to the knees. A jack was a padded leather coat of the same length sometimes worn if no mail could be afforded. Below this the Gallowglass wore knee-length boots which got the famous name 'jackboots', and when the long jack was shortened so that it could be comfortably worn on horseback, it was called a jacket.

In the 1500s the Englishman Sir Anthony St Leger noted that Gallowglasses carried double-headed axes, so that like Angus Og's men at Bannockburn they could get in amongst cavalry and attempt to cut the horses' hamstrings, and also a strange-looking weapon with an axe-head fixed onto a spear-length. These were called poleaxes and were highly effective in withstanding a charge and attacking horsemen still in the saddle, or cutting their reins and harness. Gallowglasses also used the great two-handed broadsword, the claymore, which is often confused with the single-handed basket-hilted sword wielded by the charging Highlanders at Culloden. St Leger was even more impressed by the flinty fighting qualities of the Hebridean mercenaries: 'these sorte of men be those that doo not lightly abandon the fielde, but byde the brunt to the death'.

Clans of MacSweens or MacSweeneys and other direct descendants of the Vikings, as well as MacDonalds and MacDonnells, eventually accepted grants of land in payment for their services and settled in Ireland, particularly in the north. William Shakespeare had also heard of the fearsome reputation of the Gallowglasses. In Act 1, Scene II of *Macbeth*, a sergeant describes the tragic hero's valour in what seems like a recent, and faulty memory of the Lordship of the Isles:

> The merciless Macdonwald,
> Worthy to be a rebel, for to that
> The multiplying villanies of nature
> Do swarm upon him, from the western isles
> Of kerns and gallowglasses is supplied;
> And fortune, on his damned quarrel smiling,
> Show'd like a rebel's whore: but all's too weak;
> For brave Macbeth, well he deserves that name,
> Disdaining fortune, with his brandish'd steel,
> Which smoked with bloody execution,
> Like valour's minion carved out his passage
> Till he faced the slave;
> Which ne'er shook hands, nor bade farewell to him,
> Till he unseamed him from the nave to the chaps,
> And fixed his head upon our battlements.

In reality, the Lordship of the Isles was a force for peace and stability in the Middle Ages, but when it fell in 1493, the ensuing disorder obscured that fact. When John of Islay concluded the Treaty of Westminster–Ardtornish in 1462, it was intended to remain a secret arrangement between himself and Edward IV of England, but in 1474 the plan to depose James III and partition the kingdom became known, and the Lord of the Isles was indicted for treason. After a series of internecine quarrels which weakened his position even further, John of Islay was forced to accept the forfeiture of all his estates and become a captive pensioner in the royal household, ultimately dying in Paisley Abbey. It was a humiliating end felt very keenly in the Isles. There were six armed rebellions which attempted to restore the Lordship, culminating in the 1545 campaign of Donald Dubh. Like the others it failed, and the Atlantic principality of the MacDonalds began to disintegrate. Great power sometimes begets good writing, and the ethos of the great sea kingdom of Somerled, captured in this poem of 1310, began to fade from memory:

> Tall men are arraying the fleet, which swiftly holds its course on the sea's bare surface: no hand lacks a trim warspear, in battle of targes, polished and comely ... They have a straight stern wind behind them ... their dappled sails are bulging, foam rises to the vessels' sides.

Few of the institutions of the Lordship survived in any recognizable form, except one surprising legacy that surfaced in Skye in the 1580s, although the likelihood is that it was much older than the sixteenth century. The MacCrimmons were hereditary pipers to the Macleods of Dunvegan, and until 1801 they maintained a school of piping which ensured that what the Gaels called Piobaireachd (Anglicized as Pibroch) developed into one of the most sophisticated musical traditions in western Europe.

From earliest times bagpipes were common to many cultures. There are records of the Roman Emperor, Nero, playing the pipes as well as the fiddle and the ladies of the medieval French court played the cornemuse as a refined social accomplishment. Henry VIII had five sets of bagpipes, but as high society became more and more indoor after 1500, they were played less and less. Although smaller domestic sets using a bellows arrangement rather than lungpower did maintain some popularity, the bagpipes were seen, along with the drum and horn, as an outdoor instrument. In only one country did they avoid modification for the drawing room. The great Highland bagpipes of the Scottish Gael retained their loudness and power and with them the Ceol Mor, the Great Music, was created.

Unlike bellows-driven pipes the bagpipe is mouth blown. The reeds work best when slightly damp, and to keep a set of pipes in good working condition they need to be played almost every day. This led to a creative virtuous circle. Because the pipes were played so often, composition began to develop and skills improved with good tuition and practice. Pipers had particular roles, and certain styles and tunes were eventually thought to be appropriate to each. In the morning they played reveille and in the evening they welcomed guests, as they still do at modern weddings. Like buglers, pipers were also important in warfare. They relayed battle orders to an army in action, and at the battle of Falkirk in 1746, the Jacobite army failed to press home its advantage because the pipers had given their instruments to their servants and gone in with their swords. That meant that Lord George Murray and the other commanders were unable to communicate readily with their troops.

The single most important impetus to the creation of pipe music as an art form of great beauty was the Skye college of the MacCrimmons. More than any of their predecessors, they understood how best to adapt the special qualities of the Highland bagpipe. Because the chanter which plays the tune is attached to the bottom of the bag and is not in the mouth, there can be little loud/soft variation, and there is no break in the music since the three drones make a continuous sound. Good players take a long time to tune the single bass and two tenor drones and often play informal preludes in order to work their instruments into a stable state.

At the MacCrimmon college, pipe music was divided into two classifications: the Ceol Mor, or Great Music, and the Ceol Beag or Small Music. Grander pieces in the Ceol Mor tradition tend to be laments, salutes or gatherings, while the Ceol Beag is found in dance music like reels, strathspeys and jigs, or marches and slow airs. In the Ceol Mor there is a classical structure which involves laying down a theme or *urlar*, the Gaelic word for a 'ground'. This is followed by variations and ends with the *crunluath*, which restates the principal notes of the melody embellished with grace notes. Most pieces of Ceol Mor last ten to fifteen minutes.

Tunes were composed and taught by mouth in a syllabic language called *canntaireachd* which uses vowels for principal notes and consonants for grace notes. When a piper shows great skill, a Gael will say that he can '*seinn air a phiob*', 'sing on the pipes'. A fully trained player in the eighteenth century had learned between 100 and 200 pieces of Ceol Mor by ear and could play them immediately from memory. All live pipe music is still played without a sheet of music, and most is heard in competition – like the Welsh eisteddfodau these have been crucial to keeping standards high. There are around 300 classical Ceol Mor tunes in all, but sadly little new material is composed nowadays because the principles of composition were never committed to paper, and they await rediscovery.

Few other legacies of the Lordship of the Isles have been as enduring as the Great Music. Because it possessed the unifying and controlling institutions of a state, the MacDonald principality could insist on and enforce peace in the Highlands, but this fact has been obscured by later events. When the Council of the Isles met at Finlaggan on Islay, its adjudications on disputes were made to stick because the corporate power of the Lordship lay behind them. When that power withered after the forfeiture conceded by John of Islay in 1493 and finally died with the rebellion of Donald Dubh in 1545, the Scottish state did not replace it with any effective alternative. When the MacLeans of Duart quarrelled with the MacDonalds of Dunyvaig on Islay in 1562 over the ownership of part of the island, the Council of the Isles attempted to reconvene, and a large group of chiefs met over a period of fourteen days in an attempt to resolve the dispute. But they could not bring both parties to agree, and could not enforce a decision themselves. A power vacuum had appeared in the west that would soon fill with disorder and occasionally anarchy.

Even Clan Donald itself began to disintegrate. In the sixteenth century there were MacDonalds of Sleat, MacDonalds of Keppoch, MacDonalds of Glengarry, Clanranald, MacDonalds of Glencoe, MacDonalds of Ardnamurchan and MacDonalds of Islay. Other famous names became prominent: MacLeods of Lewis, MacLeans of Duart, MacNeils of Barra, and in the old territories of Somerled in Argyll, Clan Campbell grew in stature through a mix of alliance and audacity. As clan rivalries sparked into skirmish and conflict, the sixteenth century became known in Gaelic as Linn nan Creach, the Age of the Raids.

Bards believed that Gaelic Scotland had entered a new heroic age that could rival the tales of Cuchulainn and Finn MacCool. Certainly there was plenty of action and much material for them to work on: like the recorders of the Celtic oral tradition, the bards loved dispute and violence, and constant change. It was much easier to make something grand out of clan battles than it was to sing of the merits of peace, stability and economic growth.

There is an unmistakable sense of looking backwards in what was reported and the manner in which it was reported. After a clan battle at Carinish in North Uist in 1601, a MacDonald warrior lies bleeding in the arms of a woman who sings:

> Your noble body's blood
> lay on the surface of the ground.
> Your fragrant body's blood
> seeped through the linen.
> I sucked it up
> till my breath grew husky.

Blood drinking was by no means unique to the Highlands of the early seventeenth century, but it does sound anachronistic, and it harked back to a set of pre-Christian beliefs which also survived in Ireland. When the Irish chief, Murrough O'Brien, was hung, drawn and quartered for rebellion at Limerick in 1580, the English Renaissance poet, Edmund Spenser, witnessed the spectacle with horror. Having advocated genocide for the Irish and not baulked at the sight of Murrough O'Brien having his bowels pulled out and burned while he still lived, Spenser was not squeamish, but it struck him as barbarous when 'an old woman, which was his foster-mother, took up his head whilst he was quartered, and sucked up all the blood running thereout, saying that the earth was not worthy to drink it'.

James I and VI wanted to consolidate the Elizabethan conquest of Ireland and he began to bring Border Scots, themselves guilty of long-term disorder, and others to settle as the first Plantations, particularly in Ulster. This affected the situation in the former Lordship of the Isles, since it cut off the Gallowglasses, the Celto-Norse mercenaries who campaigned in Ireland in the summer, from the source of their employment. After the Plantations and the defeat of the Irish Kings, the Gallowglasses stayed at home and became another unstable ingredient in the combustible mixture that was brewing in the Highlands.

Perceptions have always had a great influence on political decisions and it matters little that they are often based on very partial realities. From the late fourteenth century onwards, and perhaps even before that, the Highlands and Islands and Gaelic culture had not only grown apart from the Scots-speaking Lowlands, but had also become the Badlands, a dangerous, incomprehensible region populated by various sorts of savages. The major reason for complaint in the south was that the Highlands were lawless and disordered. Under the Lordship of the Isles, this was patently untrue in the west, but a man whose fearsome reputation has come down to us did his best to make it appear to be true. The Wolf of Badenoch was the nickname given to the Earl of Buchan. By 1382 he had made himself a powerful man in the north, with lands around the Moray Firth, and south into Badenoch and Buchan. He came into conflict with another powerful man, the Bishop of Moray, who accused Buchan of committing adultery. Apparently he had left his wife and was living with a woman called Mairead, the daughter of Eachann of Strathnaver. This insult prompted a furious response, and in 1390 Buchan destroyed the Bishop's town of Forres and burned his cathedral at Elgin, acquiring the famous nickname in the process. He hired mercenary soldiers known as *caterans*, who were notorious and utterly ruthless, and not the disciplined Gallowglasses who fought in Ireland. The Wolf's behaviour did much to stain the image of Gaelic Scotland in the Lowlands, which is ironic, since his given name was Alexander Stewart – he was the brother of King Robert III, and he was by no stretch of a genealogist's imagination a Gael. Like many of the Norman-Irish barons who colonized Ireland after the twelfth-century invasions, Alexander Stewart went native and consciously took on what he believed were the characteristics of a Highland warrior.

In 1396 an even more notorious related event took place on the North Inch, an island in the River Tay at Perth. Partly as a result of the failure of Stewart and other barons to keep order in the north, two rival clans claiming the same piece of territory could not find a peaceful means to resolve their differences. A judicial trial by combat was arranged – long after such things had become outmoded in the rest of Britain. Grandstands were erected and pavilions pitched on the North Inch to accommodate spectators, who included King Robert III and English, French as well as Scottish noblemen. The identity of the two clans involved is not clear but they were probably Camerons and Clan Chattan

– the latter a federation of clans dominated by the Mackintoshes. Each side chose thirty men who were to fight to the death to resolve the dispute. No quarter to be given and none asked. They armed themselves with swords, double-bladed Lochaber axes, dirks and crossbows with three bolts each. So that the contest would be decisive, no body armour or helmets were allowed. As both sets of warriors faced each other on the river island, and the spectators in the grandstands strained to get a better view of the promised slaughter, one man lost his nerve and swam across the Tay. While the opposing sides glared across the grass at each other, a replacement was found. Watched by a large and excited audience, each warrior loaded his crossbow and fired at the men doing the same thing only a short distance away. Those who survived the three deadly volleys then charged at the undefended wounded and those left standing. Men were hacked to pieces and blood ran red on the grass. All but two of Clan Cameron were killed and only ten or eleven of Clan Chattan survived this barbaric event.

Every contemporary Scottish chronicler mentions the Battle of the Clans, and some English writers also report it. As much as any greater political movement, it illustrates the gulf that was growing between Gael and Gall in Scotland. Put brutally, the slaughter on North Inch appeared to involve bands of sub-human savages whose lives were cheap and whose death agonies could provide gory sport for the more peaceable and civilized southerners sitting watching in the grandstands. It is powerfully reminiscent of gladiatorial contests in imperial Rome.

The policy of the Stewart kings towards the Highlands developed alongside a growing racist antipathy, and it is difficult to separate one from the other. Chroniclers had described the Highlands as barbarous and disordered since the 1380s, but by the 1530s opinionated description had given way to abuse. Alexander Montgomerie was a poet at the court of James VI who wrote a beautifully ornamented poetic allegory called 'The Cherrie and the Slae' which represented the triumph of reason over emotion. Probably set to music and taking the form of complex rhyming stanzas, it was a thinly veiled hint to James VI that he should return Scotland to the Catholic church. In an extraordinary contrast to the charming delicacies of 'The Cherrie and the Slae', Montgomerie produced a succinct appraisal of where he thought the Gaels stood in relation to Lowland Scotland:

How the first Helandman
Of God was maid,
Of a horse turd,
In Argyle,
It is said.

Adding to insult, the Stewart kings began to create legal means of exerting control over the Highlands. They demanded that each chief or leading gentleman should produce documentary evidence for the ownership of the lands settled by their people. Oral tradition was no longer enough. Title deeds were insisted upon, and failure to produce them resulted in the loss of land and its settlement by government colonists. Not only did these arrangements bring the Highlands into conformity with the rest of Scotland, they also asserted the Stewart kings as feudal superiors over the whole country, since deeds all implied that ultimate ownership lay in royal hands. In a literal sense, this demand marked a clear turning aside from an oral tradition. The fact that ownership of land or a particular use of it had long been *said* to be so was not enough. Word of mouth handed down through the generations was mistrusted precisely because it formed a central part of Highland tradition. Words on paper, an import from the south and Anglo-Norman models of administration and government, have now almost entirely taken over how the law views ideas of ownership. This insistence on written title prompted a frenzy of fakery and forgery, and a great deal of rummaging around. Many genealogies were invented at this time, and much that was dubious was converted into concrete fact. But royal policy produced a more profound crisis in Highland clanship which resulted, finally, in its destruction.

The origins of the clans were much more diverse than romantic myth-history allows. Behind what seems to have been a Gaelic-speaking and tartan-wearing homogeneity, there were, in fact, four distinct original groups. The surnames themselves illustrate this well. MacAulay from Mac-Olaf is a good example of the Celto-Norse element to be found particularly on the islands. By contrast, the MacDonalds portrayed themselves as a self-consciously Gaelic dynasty when the family were Lords of the Isles. They saw their identity as a matter of politics as much as genealogy. Their great rivals, Clan Campbell, claimed descent from the line of Diarmaid and from the Old Welsh speaking kings of Strathclyde. The Welsh language did not die in Scotland until the twelfth century and Campbell, which means 'twisted mouth', might be an early reference to a non-Gaelic language. The Anglo-Norman clans were established in the early middle ages when some penetrated as far north as the Moray Firth coast as an act of deliberate policy aimed at gaining a measure of control over Macbeth's old kingdom of Moray. The Fraser clan badge remembers that this most Scottish of surnames derives from *fraises*, the French word for strawberries, while the name of Grant probably derives from the French *Le Grand* simply meaning great or large.

As all these groups developed their identities in the Middle Ages, the idea of a clan society began to emerge. It found its clearest expression in the word *duthchas*. This means the collective heritage of a clan, with the emphasis on the word 'collective'. Broadly, it stood for the right to settle territories over which a particular warrior-chief and his leading men could provide protection. Much of the extent and effectiveness of this depended on geography and how well the sea lochs and coastlines allowed, or inhibited, communication.

The personal authority of a chief was recognized by all clansmen in a particular territory and as time went on, the habit of taking his name as a common surname became widespread. The word 'clan' is from *clann* and it meant 'children of' – in the sense of a group of people, or family, being under the protection of a chief and his warband. Under this system the question of the ownership of land was ambiguous. *Duthchas* implies a collective ownership, while the chief was owed obedience, certain services and, eventually, rent paid in cash. Whether or not the chief as an individual or the chief and the whole clan owned the land was an open question, although it is difficult to see a circumstance where the territory could be sold or disposed of by either party acting alone.

When the Stewart kings began to insist on clan chiefs having written title to clan lands, the idea of *duthchas* started to wither, and gradually it was replaced by a competing concept. *Oigreachd* literally means 'inheritance', and it became applied exclusively to the clan chief and his family. Title deeds named the chief and his descendants as outright owners of the land inhabited by his clansmen. Chiefs were free to dispose of the territory in whatever way they saw fit, although in practice very few did so until the early modern period. When the Scottish crown resided in Edinburgh, it was possible for important chiefs to attend the king and to spend time with their clansmen in the Highlands at other times in the year. After 1603, when James VI of Scotland ascended the British throne and moved the court, much of the government and the source of royal patronage to London, long absences grew quickly into permanent severance. A clan chief who never saw his clan lands and who dealt with his people through agents found it much easier to dispose of what he came to regard as his personal property without scruples. Another crucial cultural change occurred at the same time. The Tanaistear, the heir to the chief, was increasingly assumed to be his eldest son. In the days of *duthchas*, the chief's eldest son could be set aside if he was not suitable – a poor warrior or an inept leader – and another chief found amongst the leading men of the clan. But by 1600 chiefs were regularly followed by their eldest surviving sons, further reinforcing the replacement of *duthchas* with *oigreachd*.

Other traditions died harder. The practice of fostering gave tremendous social cohesion to the clan. The children of leading families were often removed from their mothers at birth and raised by their relatives and not their natural parents. This forged two sets of social bonds of immense intensity. It was not regarded as exceptional for foster children to sacrifice their lives to protect their chiefs just as natural sons might do. Since clans fought side by side as family units, there were few occasions when anyone took a step back. This made for a military culture of great cohesion and ferocity. In the visceral roar of a battle cry and the adrenaline rush of a Highland charge, few were in any doubt about what they were fighting for. Running through the heather towards the ranks of their enemies, broadswords raised, side by side with brothers, uncles and cousins, clansmen fought to the death for each other. Since many of their war cries were also place names like 'Cruachan!' for the Campbells, they were also fighting for the lands of their people.

Although *duthchas* never died completely as an idea, the universal acceptance that rents should be paid to the chief effectively conceded that ownership of the land was primarily his. Rents were collected by Tacksmen. This is a Scots word and originally a 'tack' was a rent or a lease. It is the origin of tax and taxman in the modern sense. Usually members of the lesser gentry of a clan, Tacksmen operated a basic unit of economic management which attracted the name *baile* or 'township'.

A *baile* could include as few as four but never more than sixteen families. It depended on the quality of the land. The families in a *baile* had individual holdings for which they paid rent but, in essence, they worked the land communally. In modern crofting townships there persists a powerful sense of this at peat-cutting time and harvest and in a general willingness to share machinery and lend a hand when needed.

Tacksmen also mobilized the clan host in time of war. Now adopted by another, highly disreputable clan, the Ku Klux Klan, the muster signal of the fiery cross was passed around each *baile* and men were expected to take up their weapons immediately and quickly gather at the standard of their chief. One of the main reasons why so many rebellions originated in the Highlands was the speed with which clansmen could mobilize into an army, but often the Tacksmen raised the host for social and ceremonial purposes. In the summer, when farming demanded less time, chiefs kept their clansmen away from the temptation of banditry by organizing hunts where hundreds of men beat the heather or chased the deer. Virile sports were also organized, which have come down to us as Highland Games. Despite the enthusiasm of Queen Victoria and the annual attendance of the present Queen at the Braemar Gathering, these games are not something got up for the amusement of royalty but are genuinely old. Most of the events involve feats of strength rather than the more artificial emphasis of modern athletics on running and jumping. Tossing the caber and putting the weight did not entirely succeed in preventing disorder. And when the Stewart dynasty made repeated efforts to re-establish itself on the British throne, it is more than ironic that its members always sought the help of the war-like clan society that they had done so much to attack.

The story of the Lordship of the Isles is one of a Sea Kingdom which crossed current national boundaries and flew in the face of several traditional assumptions. It has tended to be marginalized by history at least partly due to the warfare which seduced the bards of the Linn nan Creach, the Age of the Raids, and amused the Lowland sophisticates of seventeenth- and eighteenth-century Scotland. The bards loved the endless series of clan battles because they provided rich food for poetry, and the Lowlanders enjoyed feeling superior to the illiterate savages who babbled, squabbled and fought in Gaelic, and occasionally had to be dealt with when their surprising enthusiasm for Stewart kingship boiled over into rebellion. The prime casualty of this selective historical memory is the remarkable institution of the Lordship of the Isles. All that can now be seen of its power and achievements are the ignored and isolated ruins at Ardtornish, Tioram, Mingary and elsewhere: lonely, rarely visited, windswept places. The sea-borne civilization that built them is no more and the warships that gave them purpose have left no trace on the face of the mighty Atlantic.

In 1947 the Lord Lyon King of Arms recognized Lord MacDonald as High Chief of Clan Donald, who is far more properly the inheritor of the Lordship of the Isles than the current holder of the title, Prince Charles. Under Lord MacDonald were to be the Chiefs of the Mac-Donalds of Sleat, of Clanranald and Glengarry. But these are only big names now. The present High Chief is Lord Godfrey MacDonald, and he has been forced to sell off the last few morsels of what was once a great patrimony. Now he runs a hotel in Skye with his wife.

NINE

The Long Riders

HIGH ON A RIDGE in the Border hills a posse of six riders suddenly appears against the horizon. Their leader carries a flag fluttering in the morning breeze, and as their silhouettes move slowly against the sky and the horses carefully pick their way through the heather, a fearful memory stirs. Once off the ridge and threading their way down a diagonal path, with the flag framed against the green hillside, hundreds of riders flood into view behind the posse. Sometimes a metal bit or a silver browband glints in the sunshine. From a mile away, without any obvious detail of the twenty-first century, the image of the horsemen is somehow not comfortable and, in open country, perhaps even threatening. As more and more riders breast the ridge, they create an indelible impression of something very ancient.

Once at the bottom of the hillside, the riders disappear from view down onto the valley floor. Before they are seen again, the drumming of hoof beats can be heard. First the gold tip of the flag appears, then the standard bearer and his followers thunder through the grass, racing across the centuries to meet their waiting supporters. When they gallop nearer, they are smiling and not screaming war cries. They kick on their horses, stand up in the saddle with horsewhips held in the air, yelling hurrahs at the hundreds of people who have come to cheer them on. Those who listen closely to the hoof beats can hear the noise of history.

On the first Friday after the second Monday in June every year a forgotten part of British Celtic culture comes alive for a morning in the Scottish Border country. Celebrated for at least 500 years and probably another 500 before that, the Selkirk Common Riding remembers passions and skills much prized by the Celtic warriors who exploded from their heartlands in central Europe around 750 BC. Horses were at the core of early Celtic culture, and one of the few deities whose images are regularly identified was Epona, goddess of horses. She is almost always shown seated on a horse, often side-saddle, and her name may be the derivation of the word 'pony'. The armies who defeated the Romans and the Greeks did not march to victory against the legionaries and hoplites. They rode.

On 16 June 2000, the Standard Bearer of the Royal Burgh of Selkirk led 420 riders around the boundaries of the common land belonging to the town. An annual inspection of the boundary markers of territory is by no means unique in Britain, but what happens nowhere else but in the Scottish Borders is the gathering of very large numbers of riders to complete the rituals. These ceremonies have only recently become that – four years ago the resemblance between the modern Selkirk Common Riding and a force of light cavalry patrolling the hills was no resemblance at all. That is exactly what it was.

In the 1120s David I, King of Scotland, recognized that Selkirk had common land, and between 1315 and 1536 this grew into a huge area, more than 11,000 acres to the north and south of the town. Adjacent landowners constantly tried to occupy parts of it and to move the boundary markers ever inwards. These threats gave rise to the ancient purpose of the Common Riding – to chase off the grazing sheep and cattle of neighbouring lairds, and to check at least once a year that the boundary markers had not been moved. Streams, stones and cairns were and are still used to mark where Selkirk's land lies. Sometimes big hardwood trees formed part of the boundary, and the Selkirk men would cut or beat the bark to mark it so that they could recognize the same tree again next summer. It is the origin of the phrase 'beating the bounds'.

Protecting Selkirk Common was often dangerous. The town's Provost, John Muthag, and his fellow baillie, James Keyne, were ambushed and killed while riding to Edinburgh to the Court of Session to prove Selkirk's ownership of its land. During the seventeenth century the townspeople were often forced to take up their weapons and ride out to fight the retainers of the encroaching landowners who surrounded them. The common was very valuable – as a source of winter and summer pasture, as arable land, for the digging of peat and for stone and turf for building. In 1606, 340 townspeople rode and walked out to drive off the sheep and cattle of the lairds who had tried to take over the south common, and a few years later the Scottish Privy Council, which contained many titled names, wrote to the Provost of Selkirk to insist 'that in the riding of their marches, they behave themselves in a peaceable, modest and comely manner'. Selkirk ignored the letter and went on fighting for its rights. By 1681 the human and legal costs began to take their toll and a compromise was reached. In return for relinquishing their claim to all of the land, the surrounding lairds were given part of the common in a final settlement. From that time onwards the Common Riding became less of a paramilitary exercise and increasingly more of a ceremony.

Selkirk may well be the oldest common riding, but it is not the only one with ancient roots. At Hawick, Lauder and Langholm huge cavalcades of riders are led by a Cornet and his Right and Left Hand Men, and in other Border towns there are several younger or revived versions of essentially the same ceremony. Flags are everywhere and the military atmosphere unmistakable, but the rituals also express the quintessence of these towns' identity, and these places are never so much themselves as when the riders clatter out on a summer morning to beat the bounds. In Hawick the crowds roar after the Cornet as he gallops with colours flying, 'Aye in common!', 'Always held in common!', and at Langholm a man stands up behind a sitting rider on the rump of a strong horse and cries the ancient rights of the Langholm Fair. It is a defiant list of what the townspeople have the right to do and where they have the right to go. The cheering is deafening.

The common ridings are intensely political and repeatedly assert the freedom of communities to act in concert against powerful magnates, against central government and against any who would challenge their rights. On these summer mornings emotions are near the surface. At the commemorations of world wars and ancient battles fought half a millennium ago many people weep openly for their dead, and in the still centre of the ceremonies there are silent moments filled only by the tick, tick, tick of memory. Cornets and Standard Bearers have ridden the marches for hundreds of years, and every midsummer they go where their fathers, mothers and grandfathers went before them, in exactly the same way and at exactly the same time. These little towns forget nothing. Distilling more than a thousand years of shared experience into the shape of a journey on horseback, they use the common ridings like an invisible clock.

The roots of these ceremonies are partially datable and traceable, but it is the ethos of the folk memories and the sense of unselfconscious, living tradition which means that these remarkable ceremonies must be included in the story of Celtic Britain. As in Padstow with the 'Obby 'Oss on 1 May, there is real abandonment at the common ridings, widespread drunkenness and a sense of a huge party to which everyone is invited but which is also unintelligible to outsiders. Uniquely in the Borders, the link with the Celtic past is not through people alone, but through people and their horses. The ubiquity of these in a Border summer ceremonies is a vivid reminder of the Celtic culture of Britain in a place not thought to be Celtic at all. In fact, the Scottish Border country has a profoundly Celtic past, but what initially perplexes is the fact that it was not a Gaelic past. Even though Gaelic-speaking dynasties came to the Scottish throne and ruled north of the Tweed until the fourteenth century, the Celtic culture of the Borders has almost nothing to do with their influence. It is much older and has powerful links not with the Highlands or central Scotland, but with Wales and the Welsh language – exemplified by the fact that the native population spoke P-Celtic, a version of Old Welsh. The Celts left behind a rich cultural legacy which was obscured by later shifts of people and power, and has been almost entirely forgotten.

As often, the ground is strewn with clues and memories and, providing the correct lexicon is to hand, these can quickly be seen for what they are. Place names such as Kelso, Peebles, Penicuik, Dalkeith and even Edinburgh and Glasgow are all Welsh in origin, and some of them, like Dalkeith, which sounds so Scottish, describe the landscape as it used to appear to P-Celts. Dalkeith is from the Old Welsh, Dol-coedd and it means 'the field by the edge of the wood'. In the early seventh century, when Anglian war bands entered the Tweed basin, they changed some names to suit themselves but left many to speak of the P-Celtic peoples they settled amongst, and over whom they gained political control.

Defeated peoples rarely have a voice, but 600 years after the Anglian takeover, the Celts of the Borders found a bard to remember and record something of their vanishing culture. True Thomas, Thomas of Ersildoune, perhaps best known as Thomas the Rhymer, was composing poetry in English eighty years before Geoffrey Chaucer. Because manuscript versions of his work did not appear until the fifteenth century, his early appearance has sometimes gone unremarked, or been confused. Thomas cast himself in his stories and has often been thought a mythic figure as a result, but he was real enough, living some time between 1210 and 1290, witnessing legal documents and holding land near the Border village of Earlston, called Ersildoune in the medieval period. He got the name True Thomas because he claimed to be a seer, a prophet who predicted the death of Alexander III in 1286, the Wars of Independence that followed and much else. Very consistent in the body of oracles is his wish to see the defeat of the Sais, the Saxons, and the return of the Celtic peoples to the thrones of Britain. Some of this is probably an adaptation of older prophecies to new politics, as, towards the end of Thomas's life, Edward I of England attempted to drag Scotland into the Plantagenet empire, but, as a prophet, Thomas stands squarely in a clear Celtic tradition and his utterances would not have been out of place at the court of a Welsh prince or an Irish king. Much later the Gaelic Highlands unexpectedly adopted him as a messianic figure whom they redubbed Tomas Reumhair, Thomas the Wanderer.

His defining work is usually titled *The Romance of Thomas the Rhymer*, and it concerns a journey to Elfland. Out hunting on the Eildon Hills near Melrose on Hallowe'en, or Samhuinn Eve, Thomas meets a beautiful woman riding a white horse in splendid harness. She fixes him with a bewitching eye and points out three roads.

> Oh see ye not yon narrow road
> So thick beset with thorns and briars?
> That is the path of righteousness,
> Though after it but few enquires.
>
> And see ye not yon braid, braid road
> That lies across yon lily leven?
> That is the path of wickedness
> Though some call it Heaven.
>
> And see ye not that bonny road
> That winds about the fernie brae?
> That is the road to Elfland
> Where you and I this night maun gae.

Full of triple choices and hinging around a lightly disguised sexual relationship between Thomas and the Elf Queen, this is a tale of a Celtic Otherworld seen by a prophet who slipped through a crack in time on Samhuinn Eve, on Hallowe'en, when the barriers between the earthly and spiritual worlds are lowered. It is more than an echo of the Celtic past of the Scottish Border country: it is a clear link to that past. Thomas of Ersildoune may have been a collector of stories and prophecies from the remnants of an Old Welsh-speaking community still surviving in the up-country in the twelfth century.

His adventure with the Elf Queen began in a significant place, a place where the old gods were close. Around the summit of Eildon Hill North lies the circuit of a huge rampart and inside it are the remains of 300 hut platforms. This was a sacred site where Celtic festivals were celebrated on the quarter days, when fires were lit and people climbed the hill to be closer to the sky gods. When the Angles came to the Tweed valley, they observed the rituals of the Celts and called the hill Aeled-dun or Fire Hill. The Romans had a more prosaic name for the group of three hills that seemed to rise so suddenly out of the flatlands around them – Trimontium – and they built a large army camp and military depot at their foot. Having pacified and accommodated the horse-riding Celtic tribes they found in the Tweed basin, the Romans turned their attention to the troublesome Picts in the north. Hadrian and Antonine lent their names to walls which attempted to contain them but eventually, by the beginning of the third century, imperial strategists evolved a policy of supplying and sustaining the Celtic warriors based in the Borders as buffers between Britannia and Pictland. It worked reasonably well, but by 367 it had broken down and failed to staunch significant Pictish incursions into the southern provinces. To stiffen the buffer states of the Borders, Roman prefects backed by squadrons of cavalry were assigned to them. Hidden in the earliest kinglists are P-Celtic versions of their names: in the Strathclyde genealogies Cinhil was Quintilius and Cluim was Clemens, in Galloway Anhwn Donadd was Antonius Donatus and in the Tweed valley Padarn Beisrudd was Paternus Beisrudd. The last is particularly interesting because it is a Roman name with a P-Celtic nickname attached: it means Paternus, the Man with the Red Cloak – probably a serving Roman officer.

These prefects were important in that they helped to build a series of powerful military kingdoms in southern Scotland which later became a focus of resistance against the incursions of Germanic tribes after the Romans finally abandoned Britannia in 410. The expedition of one of their successors, Cunedda, is eloquent testimony to where important political decisions were made in fifth-century Britain. With a large cavalry force of perhaps 1,000 warriors, auxiliaries and spare remounts, Cunedda left the Tweed valley and rode down to Wales to expel the Irish who had invaded and settled in the Lleyn Peninsula and elsewhere in the north. It is the only example of anything resembling Roman statecraft in fifth-century Britain, and it originated not from the south-east of England but from the Borders, and crucially for this story it was accomplished on horseback.

In addition to these early traditions of cavalry prowess, there is persuasive evidence that Britain's most famous horse-riding hero, Arthur, or King Arthur as the romantics style him, also originated in the Tweed Valley and that he and his war bands beat back the Germanic invaders for a generation. Arthur is quoted as a byword for bravery in a long poem composed in Edinburgh in Old Welsh around the year 600. Known as *The Gododdin*, it tells the tale of 300 cavalry troopers who rode south to Catterick in North Yorkshire to confront the army of the Anglian kingdom of Deira. The bard, Aneirin, reserves some of his most highly coloured language for the snow-maned and swan-breasted horses of *The Gododdin*, but their beauty did not save them, and the Angles cut the Celtic cavalry to pieces in a victory so emphatic that a generation later they were in the Tweed valley installing their chieftains in old Gododdin fortresses. Arthur's spectacular base at Marchidun, near Kelso, got a new name as it was taken over by a man called Hroc and became Roxburgh.

The Angles fought on foot and their only interest in the cavalry traditions of the Scottish Border country can have been to neutralize them. This they unquestionably did, but they could not entirely obliterate an equestrian culture ingrained for almost a thousand years. It would reassert itself in incendiary fashion towards the end of the Middle Ages.

When Thomas the Rhymer prophesied the death of the childless Alexander III, he could not foresee how the consequences of dynastic failure would afflict the Borders. The Wars of Independence followed, and even though Robert Bruce established his family's right to kingship with a stunning victory at Bannockburn, it did not bring an end to conflict.

Scotland, and the Border in particular, continued to suffer appalling depredations throughout the fourteenth and fifteenth centuries. Terrible battles were fought – at Halidon Hill near Berwick in 1333 thousands of Scots were felled by the murderous hail of English arrows. Each generation seemed to suffer from disaster. In 1349 the Black Death decimated Carlisle's population and Roxburgh was occupied by an English garrison for more than 100 years. By 1483 Berwick had become permanently part of England. As armies crossed and recrossed, by 1500 civil order had broken down over a wide area on both sides of the frontier, and clanship began to present the only hope of security to many people. The days of the Reivers were dawning.

Clanship may be a slightly misleading term, since it implies a connection with the clans of the Highlands of Scotland, but even though the competing concepts of *duthchas* and *oigreachd* had a much more muted expression in the Borders, all their military and some of their social aspects were present in the south. A near obsession with genealogy was something shared both by Border families and Highland clans, and it was often seen by outsiders as a Celtic characteristic. When the Welsh flooded into London in the wake of the Tudor succession in 1485, Sir Thomas Overbury took a dim view of them, and particularly deplored their constant and bewildering references to kinship and ability to recite their pedigree and stated that 'he accounts none well descended, that call him not cousin'. What Overbury did not realize was that in Celtic society, the identity of a cousin was more than a mere family connection – it might be a matter of life and death.

In the Borders after 1500, it most certainly was. Border Scots phrases still in currency betray an attitude that has changed little since that time. These speak of the central importance of family, blood relationships and the necessity of precision in describing these. A Borderer who enquires if someone is 'freen tae oo' or 'friend to us' is not asking a question about fondness, but wanting to know if someone is related – a cousin, uncle or whatever. The modern innocence of the question remembers old enmities: to most sixteenth-century Borderers their only friends were family, and the only bonds that would bear the weight of trust were those of kinship. Spelling could be of the essence because sometimes it differentiated in a very specific manner between cadet branches of the same family, and one family at least required a mnemonic to aid recollection. T. S. Eliot would have been amused at the early use of poetry in such a hard-bitten Border family as his. This is how the Eliots remembered who they were and where they came from:

> The double L and single T
> Descend from Minto and Wolflee,
> The double T and single L
> Mark the old race in Stobs that dwell,
> The single L and single T
> The Eliots of St Germans be,
> But double T and double L
> Who they are, none can tell.

The verse reveals a vital accuracy about place of origin, and this is a habit which has also endured. Partly because of the wide currency of a few characteristic surnames such as Armstrong, Grieve, Graham, Murray, Scott, Elliot, Kerr and a few others, a place is often still attached to a surname for clarity – this also happens in Wales and the Highlands. Sometimes, the place can be a town, but that is not always sufficiently specific – Armstrong of Langholm covers a large group of people – more often a nickname added to a place provide sufficient accuracy for all. Everyone knows who Bindie McCombie of Kelso is, but no-one knows any more what Bindie means. Bangtail Irvine of Hawick got his name so long ago that everyone has forgotten how.

In the Scottish Border country there is a phrase which explains and excuses much. 'It's aye been,' or 'It's always been like this,' is not so much a comment, as a philosophy of life. In his novel *Weir of Hermiston*, Robert Louis Stevenson applied this form of social conservatism to all Scots, but his character was really talking about the Borders:

> This is the mark of the Scot of all classes: that he stands in an attitude towards the past unthinkable to Englishmen, and remembers and cherishes the memory of his forebears, good and bad; and there burns alive in him a sense of identity with the dead even to the twentieth generation.

If a profound interest in genealogy marks Border society as Celtic, it is its 2,500-year-old love affair with the horse that make it uniquely so. From its beginnings in central Europe, the horse had been at the heart of Celtic culture, and Epona, the mare-goddess, was widely revered. The link between horses and warfare was enduring and indelible in the

Borders. It reached across a millennium to connect the horse warriors of pre-Roman, and fifth- and sixth-century British Celtic society with the Border Reivers of the sixteenth century.

For all of the sixteenth century a huge tract of Britain, perhaps a tenth of the total landmass, became in essence a separate state. Between the Solway Firth and the North Sea, much of Galloway and Cumbria, almost all of Northumberland and the Scottish Border counties found itself the unchallenged domain of the Border Reivers, the cattle-rustling, horse-riding bandits immortalized by Walter Scott and others. Under their rule, the Borders became utterly ungovernable, a place where the writs of English and Scottish kings were ignored and where for more than 100 years no outsider ventured unarmed. Until 1603 and the Union of the Crowns, powerful families like the Armstrongs, the Carletons, the Scotts, the Fenwicks, the Elliots and the English and Scottish Grahams 'shook loose the Border' in their own phrase, and created an anarchic state on the edges of England and Scotland. In a series of shifting alliances the Reivers raided as far north as Edinburgh and as far south as York. These were the Badlands where concepts and words were introduced to the language like 'blackmail', 'red-handed', 'gear' and, most ominously, the word 'bereaved'.

Warlords like Walter Scott of Buccleuch, who could put 4,000 men in the saddle in a morning, organized their private armies on a kinship basis exactly like the Highland clans of the north, while the English Grahams had more loyalty to the Scottish branch of their family than anyone else, no matter their nationality. It was a cattle-based economy where herds were grazed on the open hills guarded by horsemen or lookouts from fortified tower houses. Only in the east and the Eden valley around Carlisle was arable cultivation carried on with any consistency. The Reivers lived not by farming or even by efficient stocks-manship, but by plunder.

Willie Armstrong of Kinmont and Auld Wat Scott of Harden were two of the most infamous Border Reivers. Both were active in the last quarter of the sixteenth century and unquestionably knew each other. Wealthy and resourceful warlords like these maintained fortified stone towers (many are still standing, now fortified by grants for restoration as dwelling houses) that could be quickly barred and defended for short periods. Armstrong had his tower at Morton Rigg, very near the border and about ten miles north of Carlisle. He was fond of raiding in Tynedale and in 1593 he gathered a force of 1,000 horsemen and rode over the hills and down into England to rustle 2,000 head of cattle from the farms in the valley. In common with other Reivers, Armstrong's gang took everything of value that could be carried or could be driven before them back to Scotland, and on a foray in 1584 they stole £2,000 worth of goods. The Border Reivers called this sort of loot 'gear', and have bequeathed the term to modern thieves.

By 1600 Armstrong had joined a band of outlaws called Sandy's Bairns. These were 'broken men' who had left their kindred groups for whatever reason and come together into the sort of gang famously found on the American frontier 250 years later. Armstrong was also active in blackmail at this time. The Reivers invented the word, if not the idea, and, nothing to do with the post, it comes from *mail*, meaning a rental payment. In essence, it was a protection racket run by men who had as little love for other families as they had for either government.

Willie Armstrong was a powerful man. He could raise 1,000 men to follow him at short notice and lived the life of a ruthless warlord, raiding on the Border for at least twenty years. And he probably died an old man and in his bed.

Auld Wat of Harden added some dark humour to the grim days of the Riding Times. Raiding out of Teviotdale on a smaller scale than Armstrong, he is said to have ridden past a haystack on the way home from a successful foray and said, 'Aye, if ye had four legs, ye would not stand there long.' Married to Mary Scott of Dryhope, a local beauty known as the Flower of Yarrow, Wat Scott had many quarrelsome sons, and when one of them was killed by a rival family, he locked them all in a dungeon to prevent any hot-headed vengeance, and then rode to Edinburgh to obtain a grant of the murderer's lands in redress.

These men were ruthless bandits and whatever romance was later woven, not least by Walter Scott, a descendant of Auld Wat, around their moonlit raids, nothing should obscure their savagery or mendacity. This period marked a reversion to ancient atavisms: it was a society not subject to murder and robbery, but organized around both. By contrast, people were murdered and robbed often in Shakespeare's London in the last quarter of the sixteenth century, but it was not accepted as a way of life. One Reiver left a unique testament that underlines the cold, hard facts of life on the Border at that time. Awaiting execution for his crimes, Geordie Burn gave this statement to Robert Carey, the March Warden, who wrote it down:

> He voluntarily of himself said, that he had lived long enough to do so many villanies as he had done; and withal told us, that he had lain with about 40 men's wives, what in England, what in Scotland, and that he had killed 7 Englishmen with his own hands, cruelly murdering them; that he had spent his whole time in whoring, drinking, stealing and taking deep revenge for slight offences. He seemed to be very penitent, and much desired a minister for the comfort of his soul.

Feuds between rival families were common, and ferocious. In Annandale the Johnstons and the Maxwells (aided by the Moffats, a troublesome bunch) killed and stole from each other for six generations. The Scottish crown deplored the lynch law that ignored the efforts of their sheriffs to impose justice. In the sixteenth century eighty punitive expeditions were mounted, and all of them failed. Even when a great Reiver prince was captured, it had little lasting effect. James V entrapped Johnnie Armstrong, Laird of Gilnockie, near Canonbie, at what purported to be a parley at Carlenrig Chapel in Teviotdale in 1529. When the King's men surrounded Armstrong and his thirty-six followers, the Reiver tried hard to talk his way out of the trap. When a noose was placed around his neck, the rope slung over a stout branch and he was set on his pony, Armstrong made a last, eloquent plea to James V, but the King turned his back and Johnnie shouted after him in anger, 'What a fool I was to seek grace from a graceless face.' And then a sergeant whacked the pony's backside.

In order to sort out disputes without bloodshed, regular Truce Days were arranged by the Scottish and English Wardens – these were royal appointments often held by notorious Reivers. In 1596 at Kershopefoot, twenty miles north of Carlisle, Willie Armstrong of Kinmont turned up, wanting to argue some matter or other which has gone unrecorded, but as he rode away north a group of English Reivers broke the truce and overpowered Armstrong before taking him to Carlisle Castle to claim reward from Lord Scrope, a new Warden sent by Elizabeth I.

News of the abduction spread like wildfire. In a century or more no truce had been so flagrantly broken. Occasionally fights had broken out but nothing so deceitful had ever been done before. Walter Scott of

Buccleuch was Keeper of Liddesdale and he wrote formally and, unusually, very courteously (his letter survives) to Lord Scrope. Even after a second, slightly more strained letter, no satisfaction was forthcoming.

Buccleuch decided to act. Carlisle Castle was one of the strongest in England but he reasoned that since an armed raid was the last thing Scrope would expect, that was exactly what should be done. First, Buccleuch gathered intelligence about the state of the castle's defences and exactly where Willie was being held. Then he contacted the English Grahams and the Carletons for help. Willie Kang Irvine acted as fixer and go-between and after some preliminaries a deal was struck. Even though the Carletons were actually Deputy Wardens of the English March, royal authority meant nothing to them, and Scrope was an unwelcome recent posting by Elizabeth I.

At Langholm Races, Lance and Thomas Carleton told Willie Kang that they had bribed some of the castle guard to open a small postern gate near Willie's quarters, but they also insisted that the raid be undertaken soon since they had serious worries about security. A date was hurriedly set and Buccleuch, a Border warlord who had thousands of horsemen at his command, chose to ride with a party of only eighty, including the notorious Gilbert Elliot and Auld Wat of Harden. In the bright moonlight the raiders picked their way carefully through the hills, even though the Grahams had guaranteed them safe conduct, and they went quietly, anxious not to raise any alarm. They approached Carlisle's walls under Stanwix Bank, which screened them from any sharp-eyed sentry. Then, taking only a dozen men, Buccleuch left the main body of his small force and stole into the town.

From a serving girl paid by the Carletons the raiders knew where Kinmont Willie was and, as important, he knew that they were coming. Buccleuch found the postern gate, got it open, crept up the stairs to the room, took hold of Willie, pulled him down, out and onto a spare horse before the alarm was raised. Then the raiders rode hard, clattering through the streets for the Irish Gate, which their comrades had forced open. Two hours after sunrise they were back in Scott territory with Kinmont Willie leading the celebrations. A ballad offers even more drama. When Lord Scrope gave chase, Buccleuch is said to have taunted him:

> He turned him on the other side,
> And at Lord Scrope his glove flung he -
> 'If ye like na my visit in Merry England,
> In fair Scotland, come visit me.'

Perfectly executed, with brio and bravery, the rescue of Kinmont Willie was a fitting end, the last great raid of the Border, the Reivers' last goodnight. Seven years later the Union of the Crowns abolished the frontier, and James VI and I hanged, imprisoned, deported and ennobled enough of the Reivers to bring this extraordinary period in Britain's history rapidly to a close.

1637 was an annus mirabilis on the Border. In all the marches, from Carlisle to Berwick, there were only thirty-seven executions. No-one could remember such a peaceful time. This happened because entire families, like the Grahams, had been removed from the Borders. Many were transported to Ulster, and from there sailed on to a new life in America, where they prospered. Eleven of the first fifteen presidents of the USA were Ulster Scots. The writer George MacDonald Fraser noted an extraordinary cameo in 1968 in his brilliant history of the Border Reivers, *The Steel Bonnets*, which provided a reminder of the hard men who had terrorized the Border. At the inauguration of President-elect Richard Nixon, there was a moment when he shook hands with Billy Graham. Beside him stood the outgoing President, Lyndon Johnson, while behind him was the figure of the astronaut, Neil Armstrong. All Border names of Border descent borne by the square-jawed, hard-bitten men whose families had been at the core of this amazing period in British history.

TEN

Keys of the Kingdoms

A BAKER'S SHOP is not an obvious place to find an understanding of Celtic culture, yet food and the ways in which it is prepared and eaten often has much to say about the history of a people. The Cornish pasty is more eloquent than most. Close to being a modern emblem for Cornwall (when the Cornish country rugby team contested two cup finals at Twickenham, their supporters hoisted a giant pasty over the crossbar), it originally evolved alongside the tin mining industry, whose now redundant, crumbling winding towers and chimneys are also powerful symbols. A meal of meat and potato wrapped inside a robust pastry casing was carried underground by the tinners and could be easily eaten from the hand with no need for the fuss of a knife or spoon. Some tin mines even provided ovens so that pasties could be eaten warm, and, in order to avoid confusion, women baked on their husband's initials at the left-hand corner. There are records of pasties being made in the sixteenth century and one of Henry VIII's wives, Jane Seymour, was said to be very partial to them. She did not need the combination of carbohydrate and fat that kept the hard-working tinners hacking away at the ore-bearing rock, but Jane's tastes do suggest a very long tradition of pasty-making.

Outside Cornwall all sorts of pale imitations are produced, many with the crimp, or wavy seam that holds the pasty together, along the top. This is not a proper pasty. So that the hungry tinners could eat with one hand, the crimp should always be on the side, and, just as important, the filling should never be cooked separately.

Sometimes miners saved the initialled corner of their pasty for a later snack, and some of the more superstitious left a corner on a shelf somewhere in the shaft. In Cornwall there was a persistent belief in mischievous, even malign, sprites or 'little people' who could cause all manner of ill fortune if they were not properly propitiated with offerings of scraps of pasty or other food. A clearly pre-Christian, Celtic habit, propitiation persisted particularly in areas of dangerous work, like fishing and mining, where the uncontrollable and unpredictable forces of chance could overwhelm even the most careful – and the most godly. These spirits of the deeps were the Tommyknockers, and many miners had an unshakeable belief in their existence and their power.

Cornish mineshafts can be eerie and otherworldly places where thoughts of the supernatural come easily. An old miner told me that when the shafts chased the seams of tin under the sea-bed, they sometimes became very echoic, and not just with the voices of miners and the clash of machinery. On stormy days the undercurrents of the sea above their heads rumbled the boulders like thunder on the floor of the ocean.

As workable seams of tin became more and more difficult to find and shafts were sunk to depths as low as 4,000 feet, often under the sea, safety was much on a miner's mind. Unlike coal seams there was little danger of fire from gas ignition, but much more from flooding. With such long shafts it was difficult to devise and maintain a reliable warning system until one mine superintendent hit on the idea of using eucalyptus oil. Barrels were placed at the head of each main shaft with an axe near at hand. When flooding in any part of the mine was reported, the foreman would pick up the axe, smash open the barrels of eucalyptus oil and pour it down the shaft. Eucalyptus is one of the most distinctive and pungent smells in the natural world, and when the miners sniffed it, they rushed to the surface as fast as they could. The early excavation of tin offered no such problems because it was not so much excavation as extraction. Nuggets of tin ore were first panned from Cornish streams and rivers and then the upland deposits were dug in open-cast mines. It was only when Cornishmen began to dig far underground that problems of safety came to the fore: the metal was very valuable, and risks were taken to win it from the ground.

From earliest times there had been a lucrative maritime trade with Mediterranean merchants who brought their ships to be loaded at

St Michael's Mount near Penzance. The medieval English crown shared this ancient enthusiasm for what the Cornish tinners produced and was prepared to grant them privileges in order to ensure a stable supply, although it was not so much the tin but the tax which interested the Exchequer. So important was this revenue that English kings reversed their expansionist policies for Celtic Britain and devolved significant powers to Cornish institutions. The Stannaries, from the Latin *stannum* for tin, began to formalize rights and privileges which had been evolving over a long period.

Written records begin in 1197 when the first Lord Warden of the Stannaries of Cornwall (and Devon, since tin was also mined across the Tamar), William de Wrotham, was appointed. The following year he convened juries of tin miners at the old county town of Launceston. They were asked formally to confirm 'the law and practices of the tin mines', and crucially for the crown, to agree the royal tax on tin. Stannary districts were also eventually agreed and ultimately these covered most of Cornwall and western Devon. Since the business of mining was often remote and carried on in country places, the collection of this lucrative tax needed careful organization. Five places were nominated as Stannary Towns: Liskeard, Lostwithiel, Truro, Helston and Penzance, and they also became known as the Coinage Towns. The description developed from the way in which the royal tax was collected. Once tin had been smelted and cast into standardized ingots, the taxman clipped off the corner, which was called by the French word *coin* or *quoin*. In time these small pieces of precious metal came to be known as just that, coins.

With royal approval and so long as the supply of coins held up, the Stannaries marked out Cornwall as a separate polity, legally not part of England. Its status as a duchy rather than a county also helped to maintain a real sense of difference. Prince Charles, as Duke of Cornwall, Prince of Wales and Lord of the Isles, seems to have accumulated enough titles to crown himself King of the British Celts.

Cornwall's self-image was also naturally sustained by the Cornish language. Proceedings in the Stannary courts must have been conducted in Cornish, since most of the medieval miners were monoglots. Tinners did not have to go to ordinary courts of law. They were tried by juries of their peers on all matters relating to their industry, and on those that were not the jury was half tinner and half outsider. The Stannaries received wide-ranging exemptions from general taxation, and when Westminster promulgated new legislation they carefully recognized their separate jurisdiction. Acts were either *'pro Anglia'* or *'pro Anglia et Cornubia'*.

By the early sixteenth century these rights had expanded dramatically and a Stannary parliament had been allowed to constitute itself with the right to veto laws made in London if they were deemed to affect Cornwall, and the tinners did not agree with their provisions. The Lord Warden convened the parliament from the major Cornish towns. Truro, Lostwithiel, Launceston and Helston nominated six Stannators and they acted with some authority, making new laws which were regularly given royal assent.

This surprising degree of devolution depended on one thing – a consistent supply of tin and the coinage tax it produced for the crown. When other sources of ore were found around the world and exploited, the ability of Cornwall to extract concessions began to wither. The Stannary parliament last met in 1752, the tin coinage was abolished in 1838 and the Stannary Court tried its last case in 1896. Like other constitutional redundancies in Britain, the Stannaries were never formally abolished. They simply stopped meeting. Most people in Cornwall had forgotten that they ever existed until Margaret Thatcher's Poll Tax sent historians scurrying back to the dusty documents in an attempt to recreate the old parliament in the 1980s. Shares in worked-out tin mines were offered at £1 apiece to qualify Stannators and jurors so that they could convene, re-establish the ancient constitution of Cornwall and vote down the hated Poll Tax, but Thatcher was removed before the tinners could attempt to reassert their rights and call her to account.

The defence of the Stannaries and a sense of Cornish difference were the sparks that ignited another, far more extraordinary, protest 500 years before the Thatcher Poll Tax. In 1497 two separate rebellions broke out in the south-west. The first was the more threatening and dramatic.

Henry VII persuaded parliament to vote him heavy taxes to sustain a war against the Scots, who at that time were supporting the pretender and impostor, Perkin Warbeck. A charismatic Cornish leader emerged in the shape of Michael Joseph, a blacksmith from St Keverne on the Lizard Peninsula. He gave loud and eloquent voice to resentment against the new taxes. Coming from the Cornish-speaking heartland, Joseph had the name An Gof, the Smith, and apparently he was an inspiring and confident speaker in the tradition of many figures in Celtic history. A Bodmin lawyer, Thomas Flamank, contributed political arguments to the growing unrest by insisting that the new taxes went against both the spirit and the letter of the Stannaries and were therefore illegal. The English court historian, Polydore Vergil, left this account of the beginnings of the first 1497 rebellion:

> For the men of Cornwall, who live in a part of the island as small in area as it is poor in resources, began to complain that they could not carry the burden of taxation imposed for the Scottish war. First, they accused the king, grumbling at the cruelty and malice of counsellors: then they began to get completely out of hand, threatening the authors of this great oppression with death, and daring to seek them out for punishment.
>
> While the people were thus in a ferment, two men out of the scum of the people, namely Thomas Flammock [sic] and Michael Joseph, a blacksmith, two bold rascals, put themselves at the head of the rising. When they saw that the mob was aroused they kept shouting that it was a scandalous crime that the king, in order to make a small expedition against the Scots, should burden the wretched men of Cornwall, who either cultivated a barren soil, or with difficulty sought a living by digging tin.

Although not well equipped, the rebel Cornish army had swollen to 15,000 strong. Meeting little or no resistance, they crossed the Tamar and marched clear across southern England to the outskirts of London. Henry VII had marshalled a defensive force but decided to wait for the Cornish to approach the city. They camped at Blackheath and looked out over London, a sight which few of them had ever seen the like of. Despite An Gof's oratory and exhortation, their nerve failed many, and when the battle-lines were drawn up on the morning of 17 June, it was seen that at least 5,000 had stolen away during the night. The remaining Cornishmen were not a fair match for the well-led and disciplined government army and were quickly defeated and scattered. As he fled the field, An Gof was captured and taken into London to stand trial for treason. The verdict was foregone:

> The court doth award that you be led back to the place from whence you came and from thence be drawn upon hurdles to the place of execution; And there you shall be hanged by the

neck, and being alive cut down. And your privy members to be cut off, and your entrails to be taken out of your bodies and you living, the same to be burnt before your eyes. And your heads to be cut off, your bodies to be divided each into four quarters to be disposed at the pleasure of the King's majesty.

An Gof and Thomas Flamank were taken from their cells in the Tower of London and tied upside down to a hurdle, and then dragged seven miles bumping through the streets and lanes to Tyburn where they suffered the cruel death prescribed by the court. The journey on the hurdle must have been appalling. Traitors were humiliated in this way so that bystanders could spit and urinate on them and empty buckets of ordure over their faces. But An Gof remained defiant, roaring at the crowd that he had only done what was right and that 'he should have a name perpetual, and a fame permanent and immortal'. He was not to get his wish, for few outside Cornwall have ever heard of the man or his vainglorious attempts to preserve the difference of a part of Celtic Britain.

In a more concrete way, An Gof's rebellion of 1497 (and the second, less dramatic uprising in support of Perkin Warbeck later the same year) was successful because it persuaded Henry VII prudently to placate the Cornish in 1508 with further grants of rights and the confirmation of the Stannary parliament. He needed the coins.

Elsewhere in the Sea Kingdoms there existed another ancient parliament and a man who died a traitor's death to defend its privileges. In the Isle of Man, the Tynwald is very old indeed, and may fairly claim to be the longest continuously held parliament in the world. The Icelandic Althing insists that it is older, having started in 930, but since the island was colonized by Celto-Norse families from the Hebrides and Man, it is unlikely that they did not take the framework of a pre-existing institution with them. The first recorded notices of Tynwald occurred in 979, but it is probably at least eighty years older than that. Primarily Norse in origin, the name Tynwald is Tynvaal in Manx and that more clearly shows the derivation from Thing-vollr. It means, literally, Parliament-field, or the place where assemblies were held out of doors. Like the word 'thing' for an object, it comes from the old Norse *thingian*, for 'to discuss', and hence create an object or cause for that discussion.

Modern Tynwald is arranged in two locations for its annual mid-summer meeting (for the rest of the year it meets indoors as the House of Keys), and these reveal how its functions evolved. At one end of a processional way sits the nineteenth-century rebuilding of St John's Chapel. This is a Christian substitute for a temple, probably to Thor, where the Norse King of Man met with his leading men to discuss the law and individual cases. Once decisions had been reached, the king and his men would process down the path to Tynwald Hill where, in the open air, in front of large groups who needed to hear and be clear about it, the law was spoken out loud. At this point in Manx history it only existed in oral form. This habit was not peculiar to Man or the Celto-Norse. When the seventh-century Anglian kingdom of Northumbria established a royal palace at Yeavering near the River Tweed, at the foot of a Celtic hill fort, they erected a wooden grandstand whose shape resembled a wedge of cake. There was seating for many people, tiered up on bleachers, but room at the bottom for only one or two to stand and speak. This was how pre-literate societies achieved quick and consistent communication of important matters – their rulers spoke once to many people at the same time.

At Tynwald there is a three-tiered circular hill at whose top the king sat and from where the chief justices of Man, the Deemsters, spoke the law, and swore to administer justice fairly. They still undertake to adjudicate 'between party and party so indifferently as the herring back-bone doth lie in the middle of the fish'. If the Deemsters had judgements on particular cases, the verdicts were enunciated and punishment was meted out immediately. At some Norse Tynwalds there was a Doom Ring where a body of jurors sat, either to witness or adjudicate. Deem and doom have the same root and originally doom meant a judgement.

Because part of the point of an open meeting of Tynwald was to allow justice to be seen to be fairly done, a practice developed which ensured that the judicial traffic was not all one-way. Anyone who sought redress for a grievance was encouraged to present a petition at Tynwald and the practice still goes on today. The Clerk of Tynwald 2000 received several petitions from Manxmen and women which described real issues important to those people. This was not a matter of ceremony but an example of government in action.

The Tynwald of July 1916 was particularly eventful. The Lieutenant Governor, Lord Raglan, was 'sodded' when a protestor threw a clod of grass at him. Raglan had resisted reform of the Manx parliament, even though there was clearly substantial popular support for change. Here is a report of the turbulent day from a journalist, Samuel Norris, who later became a member of the House of Keys:

Tynwald Day in 1916 dawned in all the glory of a midsummer holiday. Only once during the last 25 years had rain fallen during the annual ceremony of promulgation; this day was no exception to the rule, but in most other respects July 5th 1916, the 'Manx Day of Independence' was memorable for scenes and incidents which have probably no parallel in the Island's history and are, perhaps, never to be seen again . . .

When the Peel fishermen, in 1880, made a protest against the Governor's policy of taxing their fishing boats without providing harbour accommodation, they received Governor Loch as he arrived at St John's between their silent lines, and cheered him as he entered and left their ranks. The leaders of the demonstration in 1916 did not follow that or any other precedent. The main contingent in three horse-drawn 'roundabouts', holding about ten each, left Douglas at an early hour and took up positions in the field adjoining the path from the church to the Hill – using the vehicles as platforms, one near the church, one about mid-way, and one near the Hill.

From each of the three platforms large cards were displayed . . . bearing the following words in large type and red ink:

WE WANT A NEW GOVERNOR – TAXATION OF WEALTH – NO FOOD TAXES – REVENUE FROM THE CAMPS FOR WAR DISTRESS – REDRESS, RETRENCHMENT, AND REFORM!

'As the legislature marched to Tynwald Hill' said the *Isle of Man Times*, there was a hostile demonstration. The Governor was greeted with shouts of 'Resign!', the Council with cries of 'Reform!', and the House of Keys with cries of 'Dissolve!' Intermingled with these cries were demands for 'A New Governor', 'No Food Taxes', 'Direct Taxation', 'Old Age Pensions', 'Redress, Retrenchment and Reform'. There was also a considerable amount of booing, hooting and cheering.

'These demands and marks of disapproval of the Legislature's doings grew and increased in intensity as the procession made its way along the path to the Hill. The cheers were completely drowned by groans.'

In 1918, Lord Raglan was forced to cancel the Tynwald Day ceremony altogether because a general strike was called by the island's trade union leaders. Order was slowly restored and dissatisfaction met as reforms were put in place in the 1920s. These episodes clearly show that Tynwald is not simply an excuse for dressing up and solemnity, but something taken seriously as a functioning piece of government by the people of Man.

The annual ceremony now takes place on 5 July, but its traditional date was Old Midsummer. When the Westminster government ordered that the calendar in Britain be adjusted by eleven days to bring it into conformity with the rest of Europe in 1752, the Manx ignored the modernization and continued to hold Tynwald on the day they had always held it, even if the date had changed. As late as 1900 families in the more remote parts of Man stubbornly kept Christmas on 5 January, because it was the true date of 'the right Christmas'.

In 1651 the right liberties of the Isle of Man were at stake in a remarkable incident. By this stage in her chequered history the island had come into the possession of the Earls of Derby. They sat on the top of Tynwald Hill and had called themselves Kings of Man until 1504, and thereafter Lords of Man. James Stanley, the seventh Earl of Derby, was, not surprisingly, a royalist in the English Civil War. He squeezed the island hard to provide resources for the cause, and in autocratic fashion changed the land-holding arrangements heavily in his favour. When he left to fight, and be captured, at the Battle of Worcester, Derby was a hated man. Taking the opportunity presented by his absence, William Christian, called Illiam Dhone in Manx, became Governor of the island. He and Edward Christian, his immediate predecessor, are still the only native Manxmen to have held the office. At once recognized as a leader of real purpose, Dhone rallied a force of the disaffected and captured all the island castles except two of the strongest. A parliamentary regiment embarked at Chester to occupy Man, and with Dhone's help this was quickly achieved.

When Charles II was restored in 1660, the Earls of Derby were given back the Isle of Man. A general amnesty was announced for all who had supported Oliver Cromwell and the Commonwealth, but when Iliam Dhone returned to Man in 1660 he forgot that English law did not extend to the island. The Derbys immediately had him arrested, found guilty of treason and sentenced to death, unusually, by firing squad. Several members of the House of Keys were appalled at events and refused to support Dhone's condemnation. The Derbys had them summarily removed. In front of the muskets, Illiam Dhone refused a blindfold and made a moving speech vindicating his actions on behalf of the Isle of Man. Tradition insists that all but one of the soldiers shot in the air.

After the restoration of 1660, Tynwald did not meet regularly and the House of Keys, the legislative body that expected to govern throughout the year, lost much of its old authority as the Earls of Derby continued to act without consulting or even informing it. Partly because of their autocratic style, and partly because of the restrictive trade legislation enforced by the English parliament, smuggling began to flourish in Man. Customs duties were comparatively low on the island and a huge volume of goods was imported, far greater than the population could itself consume. Wine, brandy, rum, tea and tobacco were landed at Manx ports and then immediately transferred to small boats and run into England through the Lancashire coast, and also to Ireland and Scotland. With a shallow draught, the boats of 'the running trade' could easily be beached in small bays and refloated with the tide if necessary, and they could outrun the revenue cutters by sailing over the shallows and sandbanks of Morecambe Bay.

By 1765 the British government had lost patience as well as revenue, and it effected what amounted to a compulsory purchase of the island, but through a mixture of tradition, inefficiency on the mainland and Manx stubbornness, no MP was ever proposed for election to Westminster, and the House of Keys and Tynwald survived. Throughout the nineteenth century, the Manx parliament began to develop into its modern form, with some help from Britain. In 1863 the members of Keys did what many governments have longed to do and had a critical newspaper editor imprisoned. The British Privy Council had to intervene to quash the sentence and have compensation paid to the poor man. It took the Isle of Man many years to win a measure of meaningful independence from Britain and total control of all internal expenditure was only agreed in 1958. Manxmen also have tax-varying powers – set at a generous 21 per cent, their top rate of income tax attracts many incomers. This is devolution which evolved. No-one expressly voted for it – the House of Keys simply endured – and it was only in 1866 that the twenty-four members troubled to seek the endorsement of the Manx electorate.

In Cornwall the trend has been in the opposite direction. With the withering and ultimate abandonment of the Stannaries, its distinctive institutions and the substantial degree of self-government disappeared. Cornwall began to share only cultural ties with Man and the rest of the Sea Kingdoms. Aside from the excitements and profits of the smuggling business, there exists one other connection: the sound of a ball being struck by a hockey stick. Called *camanachd* or shinty in the Highlands of Scotland, hurling in Ireland and Cornwall, *soule* in Cornish and *cammag* in Man, it appears that the Welsh are the only Sea Kingdom not to share a passion for this ancient version of hockey. Hurling was probably exported from Ireland, some time in the middle of the first millennium, but never took root in Wales. Certainly it is very old. The Irish warrior-hero, Cuchulainn, was a hurler and could smack a ball prodigious distances, throw his stick after it and run and catch both before they fell. Up until the nineteenth century, shinty, *cammag* and hurling were frowned up by all sorts of authority as being no more than an excuse for disorder. In Cornwall the Methodist parsons particularly discouraged the game, and there is a circle of standing stones near Redruth called the Hurlers. It is claimed that they were caught playing on the Sabbath, and like Lot's wife froze into pillars on the spot. Rival teams of tinners from Camborne and Redruth played hurley with scant regard for any formal rules, and to preserve territorial neutrality, they agreed to hold their fixtures on a pitch in the parish of Illorgan. In the sixteenth century, hurley was played at all the festivals on Celtic quarter days, like the one at Morvah.

In Ireland, hurling very early took on a political complexion and English colonists were specifically banned from playing in the Statute of Kilkenny of 1366. Since it involved large assemblies of young men, the Elizabethans also disapproved, as did the church. The Sunday Observance Act of 1695 took the same dim view as the Cornish Methodists. It was in the late nineteenth century that the game became closely identified with Irish nationalism. In 1884 a teacher called Michael Cusack founded the Gaelic Athletic Association. Originally an enthusiast for cricket and rugby, Cusack grew increasingly unhappy with how socially exclusive these sports had become in Ireland and, typically for a Victorian, also believed that imported English games were bad for national morale. He decided to do something about it, and founded the GAA to promote the native Irish sports of Gaelic football and hurling, as well as traditional athletics. Almost at once, Irish nationalists saw the political value of the association, and two years after it was created they had gained control of the executive and forced the resignation of Cusack. In 1887 the first All-Ireland Championship Gaelic football was contested, and by 1900 huge attendances of more than 20,000 were common at fixtures. Hurling also became very popular and held its own All-Ireland Championship. Significantly for the national executive of the Gaelic Athletic Association, these peculiarly Irish sports had a mass following which not only underlined a powerful sense of difference from the cricketing and soccer-playing English, but could also quickly translate into a following for political expressions of Irishness.

In the Isle of Man *cammag* was once universally popular, but while hurling and shinty players were codifying rules and forming clubs in the nineteenth century, the sport died out on the island. The more significant fact is that, while aspects of its Celtic culture have withered, Man has tenaciously kept its own form of government in place. The House of Keys meets regularly, and with its Legislative Council and the boards or ministries, it is, to all intents and purposes, the government of an independent state. However, it is a deeply conservative body: in recent times its twenty-four members have voted to retain corporate punishment, by birching offenders, and it refused for some time to accept United Kingdom legislation on homosexuality. Perhaps no Deemster could be persuaded to speak the new provisions for consenting adults in private in front of the assembly of dignitaries at Tynwald. This survival of ancient government is important – it is not just about Ruritanian quaintness or the attractions of tax advantage. Despite the sad fact that there are now no native Manx speakers left, this fascinating survival has disproved the motto of the language pressure group Mec Vannin, '*Gyn cheangy, gyn cheer,*' which means 'Without the language there is no country.' It is not true. Amongst the Sea Kingdoms, Man has doggedly remained itself.

ELEVEN

Sons of Prophecy

THE WELSH NATIONAL ANTHEM is not quite 'Land of My Fathers':
'*Yr Hen Wlad fy Nhadau*' literally means 'The Old Land of My Fathers',
and the adjective is important, for the Welsh have lived on their part
of the British archipelago for a very long time, and a clear consciousness
of that is central to their sense of themselves. When the anthem's cres-
cendo builds through the steps of '*Wlad! Wlad!*' or 'Land! Land!' it stirs
a recognition common to all of us, Welsh or not. While the weary and
solemn dirges of 'God Save the Queen' or 'Scots Wha Hae' and many
others like them grind out references to monarchs and forgotten battles,
the Welsh anthem is about a simple thing: a love for the place, and the
Welsh sing of that love with an unequalled passion. Here is A. P. Graves's
English translation, where he substituted Wales for Land or '*Wlad*':

> O land of my fathers, O land of my love,
> Dear mother of minstrels who kindle and move,
> And hero on hero, who at honour's proud call,
> For freedom their lifeblood let fall.
>
> Wales! Wales! O but my heart is with you!
> As long as the sea
> Your bulwark shall be,
> To Cymru my heart shall be true.
>
> O land of the mountains, the bard's paradise,
> Whose precipice proud, valleys lone as the skies,

Green murmuring forest, far echoing flood,
Fire the fancy and quicken the blood.
Wales! Wales! etc.

For tho' the fierce foeman has ravaged your realm,
The old speech of Cymru he cannot o'erwhelm,
Our passionate poets to silence command,
Or banish the harp from your strand.
Wales! Wales! etc.

The crumbling Victorian resorts of the north Wales coastline and the
dereliction of the coalfields and the bulldozed factories of the post-
industrial south are home to most of the three million Cymry, and I
had always assumed that their love for the place was simply a stronger
and older mix of the same sentimental attachment we all share for home,
no matter how unprepossessing or unlikely. If the flaking stucco of
Bangor or the rainswept spoil heaps of the Rhondda were the *Wlad* that
had captured and swelled the heart of a nation, then perhaps their
passion should be admired all the more.

But it is not. There is another Wales, a place which is heart-piercingly
beautiful but where few people live and fewer visitors penetrate. It is a
Wales kept secret by winding roads, poor guidebooks and amateurish
publicity. Somewhere complained about as nowhere by bureaucrats and
businessmen who regularly have to travel from south to north Wales
and back. Somewhere complained about by kids who think there is
'nothing to do'. It lies between much denser populations strung along
the coast from Prestatyn to Caernarfon in the north and the sprawling
ribbons of the conurbation which hugs the hillsides of the southern
valleys. It is rural Wales. Punctuated by little towns with names few
outsiders have heard of and none can pronounce properly, it covers a
large geographical area and an even larger part of the emotional landscape of Wales. Llanuwchllyn, Llwynwril and Machynlleth are pleasant
enough in themselves but they do not in themselves say much about the
Wlad that rings around the Millennium Stadium on Cardiff international
days, or that so affects the expatriate Welsh with homesickness. That is
because it is the whole majesty of the place that is so striking.

Leaving the coast near Caernarfon, I drove up to Llanberis, a village
not visited for any beauty of its own but for the place where it sits. The
Llanberis Pass climbs up on the north-eastern shoulders of Snowdon,

the highest place in Wales, and then on past the great mountain into a landscape of smithereens. Everywhere there is stone. Lying in gulleys and on the flanks of the splintered mountains are millions of pieces of brittle, grey stone. Immediately above Llanberis quarries cut gigantic steps square out of the slate mountains, while in the pass itself the rock has been sheared by the freeze-thaw of countless winters. Broken pieces of the Old Land seem to lie about the traveller on every hand.

Looming above the splinters is Snowdon, a massive presence whose peak is harder to see the closer it is approached. Yr Wyddfa in Welsh, it means the throne, a place for kings and heroes. It is the bulwark mountain of all Wales, and for much of its history the throne of Gwynedd – of north-west Wales and Anglesey – was occupied by men who came to be seen as heroes. Llywelyn the Great and his grandson, Llywelyn Olaf, the last Welsh Prince of Wales, ruled Gwynedd and tried to extend their power all over Wales. Their bards called Snowdonia Eryri, a name which has survived and passed into English almost unchanged as 'eyrie'. The Place of Eagles was thought to be an impregnable redoubt. The early peoples of Britain knew that eagles lived a long time, occasionally for more than 100 years, and no doubt the bards of Gwynedd wove the stories of the great birds into praise for the rulers of Eryri.

From the top of the Pass of Llanberis the road winds down to the Llyn Gwynant, a truly beautiful place, and when the westering sun glints off the water, the passion of 'Land of my Fathers' comes alive. More than 60 per cent of the land mass of Wales is 500 feet above sea level and 25 per cent is at 1,000 or more. But these are not the statistics of a plateau. As the anthem says, Wales is precipitous, and the road down from Gwynant to Penrhyndeudraeth and sea level is steep and twisting before coasting on the flat for a few miles. Then it climbs back up into the mountains. Cadair Idris is circled before another descent into the Dyfi Valley and the old town of Machynlleth, and then on to the coast, Aberystwyth and wide Cardigan Bay. In Aberystwyth, Wales's first university town, the bookshops offer surprisingly little in the way of Welsh history in print. In one there is more shelf space devoted to Scottish history. What there is about Wales is mostly recent, and one book has an oddly evocative, even plaintive title. *When Was Wales?* by the late Gwyn Alf Williams asks a loaded question so basic and yet so enigmatic that outsiders might conclude something for the fact that it is asked at all. At the end of a brilliant essay, Professor Williams bleakly concludes that Wales has been the invention of the Welsh: a matter for deliberate choice, but a choice that looks increasingly limited, and increasingly difficult to define as Welsh. Even allowing for the fact that he was writing in 1985, after the overwhelming rejection of Welsh home rule in 1979 and before the narrow majority for it in 1999, and also in the shadow of the Thatcher years, Williams has some telling insights:

> The Welsh or their effective movers and shapers have repeatedly employed history to make a usable past, to turn a past into an instrument with which a present can build a future. It was once done in terms of myth, it has been recently and can be again done in terms of history . . . But in these days without precedent and without promise, I must confess that I often succumb to what Aneurin Bevan once called, in capital letters, The Invasion of Doubt.

It struck me that doubt would be dispelled, or at least diluted, if much, much more was written and read about the history of this old country. A better understood past could illuminate its future, and confirm its uniquely Welsh character.

After Aberystwyth, I drove down the long coast road to Cardigan and on to St David's, the place called Tyddewi in Welsh, the house of the patron saint of Wales. A strange place, it asks Gwyn Alf Williams' question in a different but more concrete way. St David's is Europe's only cathedral village. The sixth-century Celtic monk was attracted here by the elemental beauty of the place: a green headland with a rocky shoreline surrounded on three sides by the sea, laid out under the huge skies of the west. As at Iona and Whithorn, it is a good place to bear witness to the eternal simplicities of God's creation. But not good enough. Tyddewi, St David's House, was replaced in the twelfth century by a huge Romanesque cathedral staggeringly out of scale with its surroundings, and obliterating much of what was atmospheric about the little valley of the River Alun, the place where David built the walls of his *llan* and his chapel. The early medieval name for St David's was Mynyw, which derives from the Irish Gaelic *muine*, meaning a bush. It remembers how the valley looked when the first monks lived there: dense with bushes and trees. Now, a thundering Anglo-French cathedral has crushed these natural beauties, and immediately to the north-west there stands another monument to insensitivity, a bishop's palace larger than most modern city-centre hotels, but which is, thankfully, falling down. The only place where a fleeting sense of what David found still exists is in the car park to the west of the cathedral where the river flows through a birch wood on its way to the sea.

I spent less than an hour at the cathedral, having driven the length of Wales to see it. It is no different, no less or more interesting than dozens of other medieval survivals all over England and northern France, but it has little to do with the life and beliefs of the man to whom it was dedicated. And it supplies one sort of answer to the question 'When was Wales?' Wales was more Wales before the Anglo-Normans planted this monster of a Romanesque cathedral on Tyddewi.

The large-scale Ordnance Survey map offered an alternative. St Justinian, or Iestyn, was a near contemporary of David, and on the headland opposite Ramsey Island, there is a chapel dedicated to him. I parked by a white gate which leads to a lifeboat station tucked down below the cliffs, and to a large bungalow looking out over the sea. Near it stands a small roofless rectangular building inside the clearly visible perimeter of an ancient *llan*. 'This is private property!' roared a man out of the front door of the bungalow, but he relented somewhat and allowed me to walk around part of the grounds. St Justinian's belongs to an English millionaire fond of giving grand parties under marquees pitched inside the *llan*. The caretaker told me that David Essex and the Beverley Sisters had performed for his guests on that ancient headland. It is easy to imagine the ghosts of Justinian's monks shutting their gospels with a snap and shaking their heads indulgently, but it seemed to me a far better use of a Celtic site than the 800-year-old vandalism down the road at St David's.

After the end of the Roman province of Britannia in 410, Wales and the rest of P-Celtic Britain broke into a patchwork of independent kingdoms. The grumpy historian Gildas mentions some of them and complains about the sinfulness and the poor grasp of Latin of their rulers. Most were in what is now Wales, and two of them, Powys and Gwynedd, lasted for nearly a thousand years, long into the medieval period.

The expedition of Cunedda in 425 to expel the Irish invaders from north Wales established close and much-valued links between these kingdoms and the part of southern Scotland they called Yr Hen Ogledd, the Old North. Its vigour and durability allowed the Welsh to retain a meaningful sense of Britishness and to hope that they might again hear a king in London speak Welsh, and perhaps more important, to reassure themselves that they were not alone. For centuries historians have given the strong impression that early Wales was a historical cul-de-sac into which British Celts were driven by hordes of Anglo-Saxon warriors who either wiped out entire populations or pushed them relentlessly westwards. This view cannot begin to represent what really happened. When the war bands of Germanic tribes defeated native kings, they would have been foolish to destroy or even critically destabilize the agricultural labour force which fed the territory they had just shed blood to seize. Instead, a new military and political superstructure must have been imposed on a Celtic society which, over time, adapted, intermarried, learned Germanic languages, and above all, survived where it was. It may be that a Celtic elite fled west before the invaders, but by definition, those numbers must have been small. In the Old North there is a train of events described in a chronicle which gives a clear indication of how this happened. In 870 the Viking King Olaf, husband of Aud the Deep-Minded, brought a huge fleet of 400 dragon-ships to lay siege to Alcluid, the Rock of the Clyde at Dumbarton, and the principal stronghold of the P-Celtic British kingdom of Strathclyde. The Rock was taken after four months, but the kingship of the most enduring of the Welsh-speaking peoples of southern Scotland lingered for another twenty years. The Welsh chronicle, the *Brut y Tywysogion*, notes, 'The men of Strathclyde, those that refused to unite with the English, had to depart from their country and go to Gwynedd.' The natural route for migrations of this sort was by sea, in this case down the Firth of Clyde and across the Irish Sea, and if Celtic nobility from other parts of Britain also fled, they were as likely to make their escape to Wales in boats. When it is argued in modern histories that after the battles won by the Angles and Saxons at Dyrham near Bristol in 577, and Chester in 616, Wales was isolated, the conclusion is obviously incorrect.

The Welsh kingdoms of the so-called Dark Ages were in fact powerful. When Offa of Mercia contemplated building the huge dyke that bears his name, he was setting a limit on his own ambition as much as attempting to control access to his kingdom from the west. The line of the dyke, which runs from Prestatyn to Chepstow, much longer than Hadrian's Wall, shows signs of having been a negotiated frontier where sometimes Mercia benefited from its placing and sometimes the neighbouring Welsh kingdoms did. Even though areas to the east of the dyke were later reclaimed by the Welsh, particularly in the north, Offa defined the borders of Wales very early in her history.

Another, equally powerful definition of Wales is her flag. The Red Dragon may be the oldest national standard in the world, since there is a record of it being carried aloft by the Welsh king, Cadwaladr, in the seventh century. Its origins go further back than even that early date. When the Roman Emperor, Marcus Aurelius, was campaigning on the Danube in 175, he came across the cavalry of the Sarmatians, a tribe of barbarians from the Russian steppes. As part of the hastily patched together peace treaty (trouble was flaring in Syria at the same time), the Romans co-opted 8,000 Sarmatians for service throughout the empire, 5,500 of whom came to Britain and were ultimately stationed at Ribchester in Lancashire and on Hadrian's Wall. They brought with them something the Romans called a *draco*. This was a hollow, open-mouthed dragon's head attached to a lance with a long tube of red or white material attached to it so that when a horseman galloped, the whole thing would fill with air, like a windsock. For extra dramatic effect, reeds were inserted into the dragon's mouth, and when air rushed through it, it seemed to hiss. The *draco* was adopted by all Imperial cavalry squadrons by the fourth century, and when the usurper Emperor Magnus Maximus made his move from Britain into Europe in 383, he carried a dragon standard and took many British troopers with him on his quest for the purple. Later, several Welsh royal families chose Magnus Maximus, or Macsen, as a founder figure and adopted his standard at around the same time.

. It must have been an effective rallying point for the soldiers of Wales because they achieved something no other part of the Sea Kingdoms managed. In the ninth century they prevented the Vikings from establishing any significant permanent base on their long and vulnerable coastline. The Vikings attacked Welsh monasteries and set up a slave port at Bristol, but Wales remained comparatively free from their influence.

By the tenth century a Welsh king had succeeded in uniting most of Wales under his leadership. Hywel Dda, or Hywel the Good, is remembered as a lawgiver, and his was a powerful legacy. Along with a sense of cultural cohesion given by a common language, a commonly accepted code of laws was something much prized by the Welsh throughout their history. These were firmly in the Celtic traditions laid down in Ireland and adopted all over the Sea Kingdoms. Founded on the principles of reparation rather than retribution, they were bound to come into conflict with the wholly different conception at the root of English law.

That clash was made inevitable by a battle more decisive than most in British history. In the tenth century the King of Wessex, Athelstan, was a great warrior. He marched an army north to York, took it from the Danes and killed their king, Sygtrygg the Squint-eyed. The victory gave him power over most of England, and it galvanized his enemies. By 937 an alliance of several kingdoms was formed: Olaf Guthrifson, King of Dublin, joined Constantine II of Scotland, Owain macDomnhuill, King of Strathclyde, and Aralt, King of Man and the Isles. There is no mention of Hywel Dda, but during his reign a prophetic poem was composed which called for the Celts and the Vikings to fight together under the banner of St David to expel the English from Britain. The 'Prophecy of Great Britain', the 'Armes Prydein Fawr', is not only stirring, it must have represented Welsh policy.

The battle was fought at Brunanburh, which has probably become Bromborough on the Wirral peninsula, opposite the city of Liverpool – a good rendezvous for a series of converging sea-borne expeditions, but the location of a terrible outcome. Athelstan scored a brilliant victory, and five kings and seven Viking earls were killed. It was probably the last chance to check the advance of English power and ended any possibility that the Celts had of recovering control of Britain.

After Brunanburh the history of Wales concerns itself mostly with Wales, and the attempts of succeeding kings to impose themselves on their neighbours and gain the sort of pre-eminence enjoyed by Hywel Dda. But Wales mostly resisted pressure to unify, and three or four kingdoms in Gwynedd, Powys, Deheubarth (the south-west) and Glamorgan (the south-east) maintained their independence for much of the period before the Norman conquest of 1066. In the late eleventh century the Marcher Lords were carving out territory for themselves on the frontiers of Wales and in the south, striking deep into the heart of Glamorgan and Deheubarth, but as individuals, even though some had vast estates in England, they were insufficiently powerful to attempt the subjugation of all Wales without royal backing. The descendants of William the Conqueror remained busy with dynastic matters and affairs in France for 200 years before an English king would turn his gaze west, to Wales.

The Normans were natural colonizers. In the eleventh and twelfth centuries they took opportunities all over Europe to seize land and power and, more important, to retain it. Their conquest of England is the most famous, but in some ways is the least daring or surprising. William the Bastard knew a great deal about the place he coveted and what had to be done to conquer it, and he set out in 1066 from a secure base which was close at hand. When Robert Guiscard and his followers arrived in southern Italy and Sicily, they had no such reassurances, and yet they and their descendants established the Norman duchies of Apulia and Calabria and invaded the Saracen island of Sicily to create what became the Kingdom of the Two Sicilies, a polity which survived in various forms until the nineteenth century and Garibaldi's unification of Italy. Even further from Normandy, and much further east, the Crusader kingdoms of Jerusalem, Antioch, Acre and Edessa were sustained by Franco-Norman force of arms and stubbornness. It is a comment on the lasting impact made by these men that the generic Egyptian word for foreigner is *firengi*, which derives from the Frankish warriors who went to the Holy Land in the early Middle Ages.

Given the extent of this European and Near Eastern enterprise and expansion, it is surprising that it took the English kings so long to start the Anglo-Norman colonization of Celtic Britain, as is the length of time they took to complete it. Wales was first and nearest – and, apart from Cornwall, the smallest Celtic region to be comprehensively subdued. From the outset the outcome of the wars between English kings and princes of Wales was never in doubt. What was really at stake was the nature of the peace settlement and how well or badly it accommodated Welsh needs. In the event, it was a good deal worse than had been feared, largely due to the traditional inability of Welsh ruling families to agree amongst themselves.

By the early thirteenth century Llywelyn I, called the Great, of Gwynedd had built up a principality based on feudal tenets which covered most of the country, and which, in 1215, included the English town of Shrewsbury. Llywelyn was a powerful magnate, adroit at exploiting divisions in England for his own benefit and sufficiently influential to have Welsh clauses inserted into the Magna Carta. These protected the rule of Welsh law in Wales, Marcher law in the marches of Wales and English law in England. But he could not protect the rights of his chosen heir, his son Dafydd, to the principality he had so painstakingly compiled. Llywelyn knew that the tradition of partibility was potentially damaging to the ambitions of his dynasty and that his second son, Gruffudd, would have to be content with only a small inheritance. Gruffudd was not, and as soon as his father died he went to war with his brother, Dafydd. Henry III stepped in and with the help of Welsh armies who backed the disinherited son, he reduced Dafydd's power drastically. The point was rammed home when the English began to build more castles in Wales: two of the most important were at Dyserth and Deganwy in the north-east.

Despite this intervention, the grandson of Llywelyn the Great and son of Gruffudd began to build up his patrimony to equal that of the old man. By 1267 Llywelyn II, also called Llywelyn Olaf, the Last, had achieved legal recognition of his status as Prince of Wales from Henry III of England. This was a concession no previous Welsh prince had succeeded in extracting. The Treaty of Montgomery also confirmed that all Welsh lords should do homage to the Prince of Wales, who in turn acknowledged that he was a vassal of the King of England. It was an important understanding because it legally ratified the power politics of the past when successive Lords of Gwynedd had compelled Welsh magnates to do their will. By the terms of the treaty Llywelyn had secured the means to create Wales as a polity separate and distinct from England, but in only ten years his ambitions were to lie in ruins.

The trigger for Llywelyn's downfall came, as it had in the generation before him, from within his own family. His brother, Dafydd, was promised land in the Treaty of Montgomery, but it was only a gesture and left him far from content. He compiled an alliance with disgruntled vassals of Llywelyn and in 1274 a plot was hatched to kill the Prince. When it failed, Dafydd immediately fled to England where the new king, Edward I, gave him shelter.

As his brother, Dafydd was heir to Llywelyn's principality and his defection made marriage and the production of an heir a priority. Llywelyn contracted a proxy marriage with Elinor, the daughter of Simon de Montfort, the leader of the barons' revolt against Henry III. As Elinor sailed from France to Wales in 1275, Edward gave orders that her ship should be intercepted and that she should be imprisoned at Windsor. A crisis was developing.

Llywelyn had complaints about the behaviour of royal officials on the borders of Wales and Edward I demanded that the Welsh Prince come to court to do homage to him. Saying, reasonably enough, that he feared for his safety at a court where his wife was a prisoner and his disaffected brother was sheltered, Llywelyn refused to come. Finally, Edward denied the validity of the hard-won Treaty of Montgomery and, doubtless with Dafydd whispering in his ear, he insisted that Llywelyn's lands be divided according to Welsh law, that is, between his brothers. The Prince tried to find a solution to a worsening situation and suggested arbitration in these disputes by the King of France, but Edward would have none of it, and in November 1276 he declared Llywelyn a rebel and began to prepare for war.

The English military planners were extremely methodical. Resources were amassed and soldiers levied from as far away as Gascony. When it mustered, Edward's was a huge army: 800 armoured knights and 15,000 foot soldiers tramped along the coast road of north Wales to meet Llywelyn's forces. However, it should not be overlooked that between 8,000 and 9,000 of the infantrymen fighting for the English were Welsh. Resentment against Llywelyn and his impositions of taxes and other forms of exaction for the defence of his territories was allied to hopes of preferment in the wake of the inevitable English victory, as well as a natural wish to be on the winning side. Historically the Welsh were not alone in this apparent disunity – half of the government army at Culloden were Scots, and throughout the long history of the English colonization of the Sea Kingdoms, some Celts always fought with them. It is true to say that Edward I would have conquered Wales without the help of the Welsh, but he would have found it a great deal more difficult and even more expensive.

In the face of such overwhelming numbers, the Welsh sensibly fell back to the mountains of Eryri, a natural fastness which had never failed them. Until now. Edward had planned his campaign with meticulous precision and he had anticipated what Llywelyn would do. Provisioning his army by sea out of Dublin and Chester, he immediately made for Anglesey and its rich corn harvest. Called Mam Cymry, the Mother of Wales, it is a flat and fertile island. He landed 360 English reapers under escort to take the harvest and deny the armies of Llywelyn winter provisions. The high pastures of Snowdonia could not sustain flocks and herds, and therefore soldiers, for any length of time, and in November 1277 Llywelyn was forced to send word that he would submit.

Edward I confiscated or redistributed most of the Prince of Wales' lands but he was careful not to humiliate him completely. However, those who had conspired with and supported Edward soon began to complain loudly at the exploitive behaviour of his officials. It is more than ironic that a second Welsh rebellion was sparked by Dafydd, Llywelyn's brother and co-author of the disputes of 1276–7 with Edward I.

In the spring of 1282 Dafydd attacked English castles in the north-east and, showing some planning and coordination, there were also successful raids made in the south. Llywelyn was slow to join the revolt. His wife Elinor had died in childbirth only a few days before it started, and perhaps he saw little chance of success. However, by the end of June that year he may have concluded that he had no option but to throw in his lot with Dafydd, and he assumed command.

Edward I reacted immediately. Directing the progress of the campaign personally, he used the knights of his household as lieutenants whom he instructed 'in his own words'. Robert Tibetot, Otto Granson, Bogo de Knovill, Grimbald Pauncefoot and Roger Lestrange were ruthless professional soldiers who could reasonably hope to benefit from the colonization of Wales and were determined to bring Llywelyn to his knees once more.

They did not get the chance to see the Welsh Prince be humbled before Edward I. On 11 December 1282 Llywelyn was killed near Builth Wells, close to the marches of mid-Wales. He was apparently in combat with a Shropshire soldier who did not recognize him. His brother, Dafydd, fought on until June the following year when he was captured by 'men of his own tongue' and despatched to Shrewsbury, where he suffered the hideous death of a traitor.

The conquest of Wales was complete, but its colonization had only just begun. The two wars against Llywelyn had cost Edward I very dear, but he was about to commit a staggering amount of money to ensure that he never had to campaign in Wales again. Henry III had initiated the building of royal castles and Edward continued the policy, but with much greater urgency. In the heart of Gwynedd he caused huge and impressive castles to be raised at Conwy, Caernarfon and Beaumarais.

This was to be an iron ring around Eryri, and so determined was Edward to hold Wales fast that he spent £60,000 over twelve years to build them, a sum equivalent to £40 million in today's terms.

In addition to money, a new castle needed sophisticated organization. Transport of materials was of prime importance, and the logistics of this were eased by the decision to place each castle on the sea shore. Even so, it was clearly sensible to find a source of quarry stone as close as possible to the site. Wood was also required in great quantity for joists, flooring, roofing, stairs and for scaffolding for the masons and their labourers. Since nearby woods were almost certainly long depleted, it probably had to be brought great distances by barge or merchant ship. The most costly element was labour, and while building Beaumarais Castle on the south-east corner of Anglesey, the master mason, Jacques de St Georges d'Esperanches, wrote this mildly exasperated letter to the Barons of the Exchequer at Westminster:

Sirs, As our lord the king has commanded us, by letters of the Exchequer, to let you have a clear picture of all aspects of the state of works at Beaumarais, so that you may be able to lay down the level of work for this coming season as may seem best to you, we write to inform you that the work we are doing is very costly and we need a great deal of money.

You should know:

1. That we have kept on masons, stone cutters, quarrymen and minor workmen all through the winter, and are still employing them, for making mortar and breaking up stone for lime; we have had carts bringing this stone to the site and bringing timber for erecting the buildings in which we are now living inside the castle; we also have 1,000 carpenters, smiths, plasterers and navvies, quite apart from a mounted garrison of 10 men accounting for 70s a week, 20 crossbowmen who add another 47s10d and 100 infantry who take a further £6, 2s, 6d.

2. That when this letter was written we were short £500 for both workmen and garrison. The men's pay has been and still is very much in arrear, and we are having the greatest difficulty in keeping them because they simply have nothing to live on.

3. That if our lord the king wants the work to be finished as quickly as it should be on the scale on which it has been commenced, we could not make do with less than £250 a week

throughout the season; with it, the season could see the work well advanced. If, however, you feel we cannot have so much money, let us know, and we will put the workmen at your disposal according to whatever you think will be the best profit of our lord the king.

As for the progress of the work, we have sent a previous report to the king. We can tell you that some of it already stands about 28 feet high and even where it is lowest it is 20 feet. We have begun 10 of the outer and 4 of the inner towers, that is, the two for each of the two gatehouse passages. Four gates have been hung and are shut and locked every night, and each gateway is to have three portcullises. You should also know that at high tide a 40 ton vessel will be able to come fully laden right up to the castle gateway; so much we have been able to do in spite of all the Welshmen.

In case you should wonder where so much money could go in a week, we would have you know that we have needed – and shall continue to need – 400 masons, both cutters and layers, together with 2,000 minor workmen, 100 carts, 60 waggons and 30 boats bringing stone and sea-coal; 200 quarrymen; 30 smiths; and carpenters for putting in the joists and floorboards and other necessary jobs. All this takes no account of the garrison mentioned above, nor of purchase of materials, of which there will have to be a great quantity.

As to how things are in the land of Wales, we still cannot be any too sure. But, as you well know, Welshmen are Welshmen, and you need to understand them properly; if, which God forbid, there is a war with France and Scotland, we shall need to watch them all the more closely.

You may be assured, dear sirs, that we shall make it our business to give satisfaction in everything. May God protect your dearest lordships.

P.S. And, Sirs, for God's sake be quick with the money for the works, as much as ever our lord king wills; otherwise everything done up till now will have been of no avail.

Each of the three new castles in Gwynedd had a harbour by their walls (although despite d'Esperanches' efforts boats can no longer reach the walls of Beaumarais, since the sea has receded by some distance), both to supply the garrison and also for the use of the townspeople. Borrowing from the experience of pacifying and colonizing Gascony, where Edward I was duke, d'Esperanches built walled, *bastide*, towns which were attached to the castles. At Conwy in particular the walls are very impressive, enclose a substantial area, and are still largely intact. The walled towns were populated only by English settlers, with the Welsh permitted to enter during daylight hours to work at whatever menial tasks they were allotted, and at no other time. They were not allowed to trade and certainly not to bear arms. Edward's conquest had an unmistakably colonial air. Wales was to be under strict military control, exploited ruthlessly and the Welsh treated as foreigners, *forinseci* or 'mere Welshmen', in their own land. Ultimately, no Welshman could bring a legal case against an Englishman and the treasured laws of Hywel Dda began to retreat in the face of English Common Law and its different sense of justice.

Methodical as ever, Edward I laid down the framework for colonization in the Statutes of Rhuddlan in 1284. There was no mistaking the absolute nature of what had happened:

> The land of Wales [is] annexed and united ... unto our crown
> of the aforesaid realm as a member of the same body ... We
> have caused to be rehearsed before us the laws and customs of
> those parts ... which being diligently heard and fully understood
> ... we have abolished certain of them, some thereof we have
> allowed, and some we have corrected.

English exploitation and expropriation stretched far beyond the *bastide* towns and their looming castles. In hundreds of places Welsh farmers were removed from fertile land and, if they were given any thought at all, shoved somewhere up-country to break in ground that had only been good for summer pasture. Many of those involved in winning the wars against Llywelyn were rewarded with the possessions of the incumbents, and in the Vale of Clwyd two cooks who worked for the Earl of Lincoln were given estates, while Welsh families were evicted and found themselves on land high in the Hiraethog Mountains. The law, so well defined in the Statutes of Rhuddlan, and any concept of fair treatment were of no importance in this process. Wales was a prize won by war, and in the decades that followed the spoils were divided amongst the victors. Later, in the fourteenth century Wales was shamelessly and systematically milked for cash and resources, and after the Black Death of 1348 and the labour shortages it caused, the pressure was redoubled, although the process of disinheritance slowed.

Excluded from living in towns, the Welsh remained, in essence, a rural society for a very long time. In the tourist brochures Caernarfon and Conwy are painted as Welsh towns where the language is spoken and the culture lively, but in truth it is something of a fiction. With their enclosing walls and castles glowering over them, they are far more English than Welsh in feel, and as far as their role as bastions of native culture is concerned a closer examination is instructive.

Caernarfon Castle houses a permanent exhibition of the investiture of Charles as Prince of Wales in 1966. Portrayed as the most important event in the castle and town's history since the English built both, it is historically inaccurate (claiming that there were no Princes of Wales before the English came up with the title for the Black Prince), but worse it is a deeply obsequious piece of theatrical nonsense dreamt up, apparently, by the former Speaker of the House of Commons, Viscount Thomas of Tonypandy. A tenacious example of the neo-colonialism that still lingers in Wales, the exhibition is nothing less than a disgrace and should be replaced with something of historical honesty.

It was not until the eighteenth century that towns were built in what might be understood as a native atmosphere. Even when the Industrial Revolution rumbled over south Wales and the tendrils of ribbon development sprouted along the steep hillsides and valleys, the towns built quickly to serve the pit, mill and factory had, to no-one's surprise, the sort of utilitarian character to be found in Lancashire and south Yorkshire. It is in the countryside where a powerful sense of the uniqueness of Wales still lives and can be felt, and where the devotion of the Welsh to their hills, mountains, forests, valleys and streams is not merely a sentimental cliché from Victorian sheet music. *Hiraeth* in Welsh means the sort of longing associated with homesickness and is keenly felt by country people who find themselves displaced. Those born in large towns and cities look out on man-made horizons, and when they move away to other towns and cities the break is less sharp – they are not so different. But when a Welshman leaves a valley and its ring of mountains, he can find that horizon nowhere else.

The Gaels of Scotland have also remained an essentially rural people whose culture includes no towns or cities (there are many Gaels in

Glasgow, but it is hardly their town, and Stornoway is predominantly English-speaking and dismissive of those who live beyond the cattle-grids, the *maws*). During the nineteenth-century Highland Clearances, the pain of separation from the land was almost unbearable. In Gaelic such pain is known as *ionndrain*, which translates as something like 'missing'. In November 1852, 830 forcibly dispossessed crofters from Skye, Harris and North Uist boarded the emigrant ship *Hercules*, bound for Adelaide in South Australia. Here is an extract from a diary which says something about the heartbreak of *ionndrain* or *hiraeth*:

> The Cuillin mountains were in sight for several hours of our passage; but when we rounded Ardnamurchan Point, the emigrants saw the sun for the last time glitter upon their splintered peaks, and one prolonged and dismal wail rose from all parts of the vessel; the fathers and mothers held up their infant children to take a last view of the mountains of their Fatherland which in a few minutes faded from their view forever.

As much as the removal of the Welsh from their better agricultural land or the structural discrimination detailed in the Statutes of Rhuddlan, the creation and encouragement of racial attitudes towards the Welsh were an enduring legacy of the defeat of Llywelyn. Long after Edward's legal structures withered into disuse, these persisted and are prevalent today. The English still regard the Welsh as inferior and sometimes do not hesitate to say so in print. In a remarkable, but not unique, tirade in the *Sunday Times* in 1998, the restaurant and television critic, Adrian Gill, described the Welsh as 'stunted, bigoted, dark, ugly, pugnacious little trolls'. If he had written the same things about Asians or Afro-Caribbeans, his newspaper would not have published the piece, but they did not think twice about allowing a series of blatant racial slurs on Welsh. In March 2001 the quiz show host, Anne Robinson, was invited onto a BBC Television comedy programme to nominate things she would like to get rid of, to insert into the dustbin of history. She chose the Welsh because they were 'irritating', and in a tone of decided exasperation, asked, 'What are they for?' When Welsh commentators and MPs protested, the BBC reacted by repeating the programme. These attacks run with the grain of English attitudes, and not against it. The same sorts of things have long been said about the Scots and the Irish, again without much fuss. The historian Charles Thomas sums up a milder sort of English prejudice when he writes about Wales as 'the sunset-facing back room that John Bull so tolerantly and for so long has allowed his strange Celtic relatives to occupy'.

These are the archetypal attitudes of colonists and they gained full play when the British Empire collected together dozens of peoples inferior to the English. In some ways Wales has yet to recover from the defeat of Llywelyn, and the fact that it was a cataclysm did not escape the imagination of the bard, Gruffydd ab yr Ynad Coch:

> Do you not see the path of the wind and the rain?
> Do you not see the oaks beating together?
> Do you not see the sea scouring the land?
> Do you not see the truth preparing itself?
> Do you not see the sun sailing the heavens?
> Do you not see the stars fallen?
> Do you not believe in God, simple men?
> Do you not see that the world has ended?

For the Welsh it did not quite end in 1282. Before the nation sank into its supporting role, there was one more thrash left in the dragon's tail.

Born some time around 1356, Owain Glyn Dwr's life as a comfortably off Welsh country gentleman seemed destined to follow what would become a traditional pattern. He went to London to train in the Common Law which Edward I had promised would govern Wales, and spent seven years at the Inns of Court. Then Owain gained the appropriate rank, for an aspiring member of an underclass, of esquire and went to Berwick Upon Tweed in the military service of the King of England. When he returned to his property at Sycarth in north-east Wales, he settled down to several years as an unremarkable landowner. However, trouble flared from a predictable source. Lord de Gray of Ruthin was a Marcher baron who held large estates in England, and after the Edwardian conquest his family had been given even more land in Wales. Probably believing that he could act with impunity, de Gray allowed his men to seize a place called Croesau, a piece of common land over which Owain Glyn Dwr's family had traditionally enjoyed rights. This minor incident was to prove the small spark that set all Wales alight.

Because of his legal training Owain believed that he could use the courts to win back the use of the land, since he was certain that he could prove his hereditary rights. The case went as far as the Westminster parliament, but politics and prejudice exerted more pressure than the pleas of a mere Welshman. Lord de Gray was an advisor and supporter of King Henry IV and, above all, an Englishman. Here is a report of the judgement:

> Owen de Glendour, a Welshman who had been esquire of the Earl of Arundel, came to parliament complaining that Lord de Gray Ruthin had usurped certain lands of his in Wales, but no argument helped against Lord de Gray. The Bishop of St Asaph (John Trefor) gave counsel in parliament that they should not entirely despise Owen, as the Welsh might perhaps revolt. But those in parliament said that they cared nothing for the bare-footed clowns.

And so that Owain could not appeal to Henry IV personally (as an esquire in royal service expected to accompany the king when he was on campaign, he might have an opportunity to explain the circumstances of his case), Lord de Gray acted to cut off that possibility:

> When the king was preparing to hurry off to Scotland, amongst other things he sent letters, sealed with his own seal, to the said Owyn, for he was himself thought those days to be a fine esquire, that he should go with the king who would in no way excuse him. Lord Grey of Ruthin was appointed to carry these letters, but having accepted them he put off delivering them until the king's departure, and only handed them over the third day before the king left. Owain was completely taken aback, saying that it was much too late, too sudden and too unexpected a warning for such a journey, and briefly excused himself, as it was quite impossible to go to Scotland. Lord Grey left him in Wales, and went to the king in Scotland as fast as he could, and made the worst of it in telling him that the said Owyn despised his letters and held his commands in contempt.

Perhaps because he felt utterly frustrated, certain that his status as a Welshman would always leave him at the mercy of English high-handedness, and perhaps because the bards had woven an aura of expectation around him with their prophesies and praise poems, Owain

Glyn Dwr rose in rebellion. He and his men immediately attacked the hated English towns at Ruthin, Denbigh, Holt, Rhuddlan, Hawarden and Flint. Oswestry and Welshpool were burned to the ground. On his return from Scotland, Henry IV came to Shrewsbury and began a punitive expedition through Wales to Gwynedd. Owain's forces had been badly beaten by those of an English landowner, Hugh Burnell, near Welshpool, and it looked for a moment as though the revolt might quickly fizzle out. But then news came that Anglesey had been taken by Owain's cousins, Gwilym and Rhys ap Tudur, and they felt strong enough to attack Henry IV and drive him into Beaumarais Castle to seek safety.

During the winter of 1400–1401 little was heard from Owain, but in the spring he began campaigning again. The Tudur brothers took Conwy Castle with only forty men on 1 April, although they were forced to surrender it again on severe, punitive terms. Events were finely balanced when Glyn Dwr found himself trapped with only 120 men on a hill at Hyddgen in the uplands near Cardigan. Surrounding them was an army of 1,500 that included many Welshmen and Flemings. Against these odds and with a courage born of despair, Owain and his handful of men cut them to pieces, leaving 200 dead on the hillside. It was an astonishing victory. Entirely unreported in English sources, it turned the course of the rebellion and immensely boosted Glyn Dwr's prestige. Thousands flocked to the golden dragon-standard of Uther Pendragon which had been adopted by the insurgents. The English parliament was told that

> the Welsh scholars who have been living at the Universities of Oxford and Cambridge have departed for their own country; and also the Welsh labourers, who have been living at various places in the realm of England, have suddenly retreated from the said realm to their own land of Wales, and have provided themselves with armour, bows and swords.

In Wales news of the revolt crackled around the countryside like wildfire as bards moved from place to place speaking of Owain's deeds.

1402 to 1404 were the years of victory. English castles were in poor repair and not the impregnable bastions intended by Edward I. The English Exchequer was strapped for cash, and Henry IV had problems on every side. Meanwhile, Owain was declared Prince of Wales by his peers and hailed as Y Mab Darogan, the Son of Prophecy. He was much attracted to the world of seers and poets (he refused to campaign between

Gower and Carmarthen because it had because it had been foretold that he would be captured there under a black flag), but he was also a realist. When his offer of talks with the English was summarily refused, he attempted to build a string of diplomatic relationships between the Celtic nations, with the Irish kings and Robert III, King of the Scots. He wrote letters reminding them of their common descent, and also contacted the Bretons for help. Under Jean d'Espagne, a French fleet attacked Caernarfon Castle on Owain's behalf but its positioning and design was such that, even with only a small garrison, it held out.

Inland, the Welsh operated in the classical manner of guerrilla fighters. Using Eryri as a base, and the place where he kept captives for ransom, Owain struck out with forces which could be deployed with amazing speed. They rode on small and nimble Welsh mountain ponies capable of carrying the soldiers and their minimal baggage very long distances without any loss of condition, and which knew how to survive on the tussocky grass of the windy uplands.

All down the western edge of Britain there are remnants of the breeds of hardy ponies which provided horsepower for both military and peace-time use. In Cornwall and Devon there are Exmoor and Dartmoor ponies and several herds are now allowed to run wild as far west as Bodmin. The Manx pony died out in the nineteenth century, but the shaggy Highland pony, mostly grey in colour, is still much in demand, especially for riding schools, such is its reliable temperament. On the island of Eriskay, at the foot of the Hebridean chain, there is a small herd of island ponies, but they are probably the last of the breed. In the Scottish Border country the Reivers did not ride great snorting chargers of the sort still seen prancing down the Mall on ceremonial occasions – their ponies were called hobblers, the origin of 'hobby-horse'. Most famous are the Shetlands. Originally used for riding and also carrying packs, these little ponies rarely exceeded 9 hands in height, or 3 feet from the foreleg hoof to the withers. In those days no-one cared if their feet dangled way below the horse's belly – what was important was not to be doing the walking. Sir Walter Scott was very struck by a habit he encountered on a visit to Shetland. Because the ponies ran wild and were never taken in or fed, ownership was unclear. Shetlanders wanting to make a journey would catch one near at hand, put a halter on it, ride it to wherever they were going and then simply let it go. Known as Shelties, they were very hardy indeed, living off seaweed in winter.

After growing a deep, shaggy coat to survive a bitter northern winter, Islanders let the ponies graze the spring grass at least until mid-June so that they could recover their condition and be fit enough to help with carrying away the peat cut from the moors in summer. In the nineteenth century Shetland ponies became very popular, and with the introduction of bigger stallions the average height gradually rose to 12 or 13 hands. They were used in coal mines and for pulling carts in farms and towns. Now these notoriously bad-tempered little horses are mostly kept for show and competition carriage driving.

For Owain Glyn Dwr his ponies were a military weapon capable of delivering him and his men quickly into unexpected places. His tactics had been brilliantly successful, and by the summer of 1404 he was in control of most of Wales. At the centre of his territory, at the heart of rural Wales, is the town of Machynlleth. A sign announces that it is the ancient capital of Wales and an old rectangular stone building explains the reason for the roadside boast. In 1404 Owain Glyn Dwr called a parliament at Machynlleth. Formally proclaimed Prince of Wales, he had climbed to the peak of his powers. The new state was organized along English lines, with a Chancery and seals of office, and Glyn Dwr began to develop a foreign policy to match. So that the support of the French could be maintained, the allegiance of the Welsh church was switched from the Roman papacy to the schismatics at Avignon, who were French puppets. No doubt under the influence of the scholars who left Oxford and Cambridge to join the revolt, plans were made for the foundation of two Welsh universities, one in the south and one in the north. Owain's most significant and hopeful initiative was the formation of an alliance with two powerful but disgruntled English magnates. In a relationship immortalized by William Shakespeare in *Henry IV Part One*, Glyn Dwr contacted Harry Hotspur, Earl of Northumberland, and converted his captured enemy, Edmund Mortimer, into an ally. In 1405 at Bangor, the three men met to sign the Tripartite Indenture. Under the terms of this agreement, so-called because the paper was divided up by a zigzag, or indented, line cut to give jagged edges which could later be matched up by each party so that there was no possibility of forgery, Owain, Hotspur and Mortimer were to partition England and Wales between them. Shakespeare has Hotspur complain about the size of his share while advising the boastful Glyn Dwr 'to tell the truth and shame the devil'. Just as the division of Scotland seemed an attainable aim in the Treaty of Westminster–Ardtornish, this was considered a possible outcome in the circumstances: Henry IV was weak and broke and could have been toppled. Much in character, Owain Glyn Dwr had used prophecy to help determine the boundaries of what was called Greater Wales. Where the frontier extended into England it reached a place near the sources of the Mersey and the Trent in the Peak District, which the Welsh called 'The Ash Trees of Meigion'. A Welsh king, Cadwallon, had fought and won a seventh-century battle at Meigion and Merlin had prophesied that it would be won by the Welsh again.

The three conspirators never had to fit together the jagged edges of the Tripartite Indenture. The English king gradually reasserted himself. His Gwynedd castles had never fallen and battles began to be lost. The historian Gruffudd Hiraethog wrote:

> [There was] a slaughter of the Welsh on Pwll Melin Mountain, near Usk, where Gruffudd ap Owen was taken prisoner. It was now that the tide began to turn against Owen and his men. At this time Glamorgan made its submission to the English, except a few who went to Gwynedd to their master.

Despite the loss of his son and many men at Pwll Melin, Owain continued to fight and in 1409 there are mentions of him still campaigning. But soon after, he disappeared. In 1412, Dafydd Gam, a Welsh soldier who supported the English and had attempted to assassinate Owain, was captured and ransomed, confirming that the rebel leader was occasionally active. He was thought to be in hiding somewhere in north Wales, probably in the mountains of Snowdonia. The new king, Henry V, offered Owain a pardon but his overture was met by silence and by 1415 there was a report that he was dead: 'Died Owen Glendower . . . and in the night season he was buried by his followers. But his burial having been discovered by his adversaries, he was laid in the grave a second time; and where his body was bestowed no man may know.' There is another chronicler who detailed Owain's movements up to 1415 and then wrote: 'Very many say that he died; the seers maintain that he did not.'

Almost immediately, a legend began to grow. No bard wrote his elegy because, like Arthur, he never died. Glyn Dwr sleeps and waits for Wales. For once the romance is not spurious: what he did was extraordinary. He was clearly 'not in the roll of common men', and was a charismatic man with tremendous personal magnetism as well as cool and rational head. He sustained a rebellion against the English for fifteen years, an unprecedented length of time. He had the support of all Wales, and unlike Llywelyn was immediately accepted as Prince of Wales. There was no challenge to his authority and during his long periods in hiding, no-one betrayed him. As far as it can been judged from a distance of 600 years, he fought not for personal gain but for Wales.

After the passing of the Son of Prophecy, English oppression deepened, and the bards redoubled the intensity of their efforts to keep Wales alive in the popular imagination. The landed classes who had supported Glyn Dwr attempted to forget him but his legend lived on in the minds of lesser people and it was the re-emergence of these stories in the eighteenth century which installed him as a national hero.

The power of the great poetry that followed the fall of Owain still resonates: '*Dwg Morgannwg a Gwynedd/ Gwna'n o Gonwy i Nedd*', 'Bring Glamorgan and Gwynedd together/ Make us one from Conwy to Nedd', '*Gwae ni ein geni yn gaeth*', 'Woe unto us, born into slavery' – and a great deal more in this dramatic vein. Excluded from power of any sort, the fifteenth-century Welsh were forced to live in the imagination, in the poetry of their history and the hope of their prophecy. Wales existed in the dream of things rather than in the temporal world. In the late sixteenth century observers in north Wales reported great gatherings of people on the hillsides collecting to hear prophecy, to sing, recite their genealogies, listen to hero-tales and the lives of their ancestors, and the myth-history of Merlin and Taliesin. For a people for whom there seemed to be nothing but a mean future, there were always the ancient glories of their past, when Wales was Britain and the Sais were nothing.

TWELVE

Imagineering

EDWARD WILLIAMS LIVED IN HIS DREAMS. Born in 1747 in Glamorgan, he left Wales as an experienced stone mason to find work in London, and began to imagine the history of his native place rather than simply remember it. Unlike most romantics, Williams was also a man of action as well as invention. The *Gentleman's Magazine* of October 1792 reported an unusual event for 23 September:

> This being the day on which the autumnal equinox occurred, some Welsh Bards, resident in London, assembled in congress on Primrose Hill, according to ancient usage . . . The wonted ceremonies were observed. A circle of stones formed, in the middle of which was the Maen Gorsedd, or Altar, on which a naked sword being placed, all the Bards assisted to sheath it.

Since there was no existing stone circle available on Primrose Hill, Edward Williams had thoughtfully brought along some pebbles in his pocket and laid them out on the grass. And at this allegedly ancient ceremony, he informed the assembled bards: 'I am giving you the Patriarchal religion and theology, the Divine Revelation given to Mankind and these have been retained in Wales until our own day.' Meaning ancient British or Druidic by Patriarchal, Williams was forty-five when he announced that he knew what it was, and more, that he believed what he was saying was true. In fact it was mostly nonsense: brilliant, passionate, artful and confusing nonsense. Using his profound knowledge of medieval Welsh manuscripts, Williams had made most of it up.

Edward Williams came from an interesting background: his father was also a stone mason and a man much interested in literature and the life of the mind, and his mother had family connections to a line of Glamorgan bards. Edward's belief that he was passing on traditional British Druidic and bardic learning had some slight substance, for his native part of Wales still supported working bards akin to those who had composed verses for Owain Glyn Dwr, Llywelyn Olaf and kings and princes before them. But he took these meagre foundations and erected on them a tottering but remarkably resilient edifice.

Some time before the first 1792 Gorsedd on Primrose Hill, after a mind-clearing spell in a debtors' prison in Cardiff, Edward Williams had emerged a changed man. He became Iolo Morgannwg, or Iolo of Glamorgan, and first he asserted that the Glamorgan bards had somehow preserved in their ancestral memory a perfect recollection of the ancient wisdom of the Druids. He then set about proving it. Because he had made himself the most learned and energetic Welsh scholar of the late eighteenth century, Iolo managed to bring off a string of convincing textual forgeries which underwrote his contention that the Glamorgan bards, primarily himself, had remembered real lore and rituals. Using the authentic poetry of the late medieval bard Dafydd ap Gwilym as a guide and a literary base, Iolo combined some that was genuine with much that was invented. So intertwined and so well made are his forgeries that it has taken entire academic careers to sort out what is really old from what he made up. Those scholars, such as G. J. Williams, who spent an academic life exposing Morgannwg's chicanery, came in the end rather to admire him. The *Oxford Book of Welsh Verse* has gone further and now happily includes a poem formerly passed off as the work of Dafydd ap Gwilym with the name of the real author, Edward Williams, attached to it – such is its quality.

Described as a shabby little man in a black hat, with a canvas sack of books and manuscripts slung over his shoulder, Iolo tramped all over Wales to collect, write down and preserve fragments of the Welsh oral tradition, as well as to embellish it. It is said that he chose to walk out of respect for his horse. He was also a fine hymn-writer, a lexicographer and a grammarian, but is for the invention of the Gorsedd and its spurious texts that Iolo will chiefly be remembered. After the first meeting at Primrose Hill in 1792, he managed to persuade the revitalized National Eisteddfod to adopt the ceremony. Eisteddfodau are genuinely ancient, perhaps more than a thousand years old, and they were important for the regulation and accreditation of wandering bards, for keeping standards high and organizing competitions. In 1819 the Carmarthen Eisteddfod allowed Iolo to mount his Gorsedd of Bards as part of the three-day event. In the garden of the Ivy Bush Hotel, he arrived with another pocketful of stones, set them in a circle and began the solemn rituals. These involved Druids in strange costumes, the Ceremony, the Prayer, the Traditional Rites, the Invocation of Peace, the Symbol of the Ineffable Name and other early nineteenth-century paraphernalia with faint tinges of freemasonry attached. The Gorsedd is clearly a powerful idea, and it even survived this description by Matthew Arnold who happened to be in Llandudno at the right time in 1855. He observed a day of

> storms and winds, clouds of dust, an angry, dirty sea ... the Gorsedd was held in the open air, at the windy corner of a street ... The presiding genius of the mystic circle, in our hideous nineteenth century costume relieved only by a green scarf, the winds drowning his voice and the dust powdering his whiskers, looked thoroughly wretched; so did the aspirants for bardic honours.

It is striking how strongly the Welsh want to believe in the Gorsedd. Even when it was exposed as an invention, they still wanted to believe in it. As the passage of time made the nineteenth-century costumes of sheets, oaken crowns, *lunulae* and Excalibur look progressively dafter, they continued to insist on its popularity and place at the heart of their culture. The bogus solemnities, bardic crowning and heavy furniture are now seen as traditional, and at 200 years' distance from Edward Williams and his pocketful of pebbles, they even seem old in themselves.

At the Gorsedd held at the National Eisteddfod of 2000 at Llanelli, the stone circle had been set up in a newly bulldozed and reclaimed area of the town, site of the heavy industry that used to characterize south Wales. The stones had been set up a few days before the ceremony was due to take place, enough time for graffiti to appear, including the comment, 'Fuck Off Pricks'. By the time the white-, blue- and green-robed celebrants processed into the circle, the offending words had been scrubbed and painted over. The ceremony was extremely good-humoured, with many jokes and comments from the Archdruid as he

Three warders, or rooks, from the Lewis chessmen.

St David's Cathedral dwarfs the stream that formed the original focus of the Celtic monastic community.

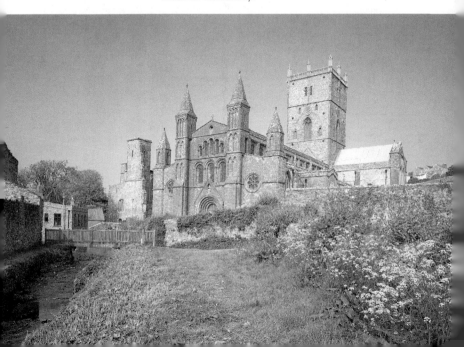

Edward I of England with bishops and clerics.

ABOVE LEFT A portrait of General Sir Gregor MacGregor by J S Rochard which shows him, surprisingly, without decorations or medals, but in possession of a splendid hat.

ABOVE Henry Joy McCracken.

LEFT Theobald Wolfe Tone in the uniform of an Adjutant General of the French army.

RIGHT Captain Swayne pitch-capping a victim. The background shows that women were not exempt from this type of extreme cruelty.

BELOW Rebels piking prisoners on Wexford Bridge in 1798. Note the contrast between the simian faces of the Irish rebels and the saintliness of their victims.

The amazing Dr William Price of Llantrisant pictured in a 'suit of scarlet merino wool with green silk lettering' for the frontispiece of one of his books, published in 1871.

BELOW The serious faces of Dowlais Temperance Choir from South Wales at the Crystal Palace in 1895, when they won the national choral competition.

Known as 'Caradog', the formidable Griffith Rhys Jones conducted the South Wales Choral Union to Glory at Crystal Palace in 1872 and 1873.

ABOVE LEFT Tynwald in session. The wigged figure in the centre of the picture is a Deemster.

ABOVE A cross standing by St Columba's Abbey on Iona looks out over the sound to the Isle of Mull.

LEFT A seagoing curragh photographed off the Irish coast.

RIGHT Cornish wrestlers competing at the Royal Cornwall Show.

ABOVE The Padstow 'Obby 'Oss.

BELOW A funeral at Dalmore on the Isle of Lewis.

crowned each of the bards who moved into the centre of the circle. The applause was particularly warm for a Japanese professor who had achieved a distant eminence in Welsh cultural studies.

Afterwards I spoke to James Nicholas, the Recorder of the Gorsedd, and his quiet passion about the importance of the Order of Bards was unquestionably impressive. Wearing long white robes, white leather boots, a head-dress of oak leaves and carrying a staff, he cut a frankly ridiculous figure, but in some ways this made his commitment all the more striking. Leaning forward and pointing a schoolmasterly finger, he told me that Iolo Morgannwg, or Edward Williams, was a heroic force, a genius who had done more than anyone to save the Welsh language. For Mr Saunders the Gorsedd was the core and fount of the language's health, and therefore of Welshness. The costumes and the ceremonies might seem arcane, even daft, but that did not matter. 'They are ours, and ours alone,' the old man declared.

The stone circle of the Gorsedd had been set up some way from the main pavilion of the Eisteddfod, and unfortunately the Llanelli police would not allow me to bring my car into the park so that I could drive the elderly Mr Nicholas the mile or so he needed to go. Instead, we caught a bus. Dressed in his Druidic finery, Mr Nicholas stepped on board, and all of the passengers burst out laughing, and no-one laughed harder than the Recorder of the Gorsedd. Then, having got over the Pythonesque incongruity, they cheered and applauded the old man, and slapped him on the back as they passed. Mr Nicholas introduced me to a man sitting quietly near the front with a shopping bag on his knees. He had been crowned the National Bard of the Eisteddfod a few years before and was the writer of some of the best lyric poetry in Welsh 'since the War'. The man smiled nervously at the grandiloquence and asked me if I was enjoying the Eisteddfod. It struck me how oddly self-effacing Welsh language culture could be, and how rooted in every-day life it appeared to be.

When we arrived at the main pavilion, I quickly found a seat inside the huge structure. Thousands of people were crammed into one of the largest tents I have ever seen. The ceremonies began with a procession of the Druids from the stone circle, and then representatives from the Gorsedds of Cornwall and Brittany were introduced, and also guests from Scotland, Ireland and Man. The National Eisteddfod of Wales is one of the few occasions when Celtic Britain is formally and clearly recognized as such, and I found it very moving to hear the six Celtic languages spoken in one place and the guests cheered by the audience, and heartening that the simultaneous translation was not into English. The ceremonies are immensely long and the report of the chairman of the panel of judges on the entries for the bardic competitions seemed set to go on into the evening. But the verbose and intricate arcana of modern bardic practice are as nothing compared to what happened in the nineteenth century.

As it developed, the Gorsedd and modern Druidism in general gave birth to more eccentricities and more forgery, but perhaps their most astonishing child was the amazing Dr William Price of Llantrisant. He lived in Glamorgan, like Iolo Morgannwg, just as it was beginning to industrialize, and in his practice as a GP he seems to have treated patients on a unique basis. If he failed to cure someone, he charged them, and refused on principle to treat people at all if they smoked. A vegetarian, a republican and a pursuer of lawsuits of all kinds, he was also very fond of dressing up. On the frontispiece of one of his books, there is a remarkable photograph of Dr Price at the age of seventy-one. Holding a staff with a crescent moon stuck on it, he stares earnestly into the middle distance dressed in what appears to be a romper suit. Barefoot on a leopard-skin rug, his rig-out is described as a suit of 'scarlet merino wool with green silk lettering'. In an aquatint published elsewhere, Dr Price wears another eye-catching outfit. This time he has on a vaguely military green jacket and trousers with a basket-hilted sword held in place by a red sash and is carrying a crescent moon in one hand and a lighted rope torch in the other. But it is his hat which draws most attention: a fox pelt with the head balanced on the crown of the doctor's head and the forepaws folded on his forehead, it most closely resembles something Davy Crockett wore on the wild frontier.

However odd his dress, Dr Price did something that changed the world. At the age of eighty-one, he showed commendable stamina and began living with a much younger woman whom he refused to marry because he was of the view that marriage was only a form of legalized slavery. Showing even more stamina, they had a son in 1884. Naming the boy Iesu Crist, his father predicted an epoch-making future for him. The child would remember 'the lost secrets of the Druids' and re-establish them in Wales. Tragically, a future was never to be realized, for the baby died aged only five months. Because Price held that his son had been destined for great and mysterious things, he built a pyre in a field above Llantrisant and, accompanying the ceremony with incantations, he burned the little boy's body. Wearing scarlet romper suits was one thing, but this latest episode appalled the sober people of Llantrisant. Some thought that the baby had been burned alive and a mob outside Dr Price's house had to be discouraged with a show of firearms. The police then appeared and arrested the old man for disposing of a body in an illegal manner. As in all his cases, Dr Price conducted his own defence and, dressed in a white linen smock with fancy cuffs, he argued his way to a signal victory. The court judged that Price had acted legally and its decision made cremation legitimate all over the British Empire. When the doctor himself died in 1893, tickets were distributed to those who wished to witness his cremation, and thousands turned up to see the old man go out in a blaze of glory.

Iolo Morgannwg and William Price were not merely lone eccentrics fiddling at the edges, anxious to embrace a culture that never existed – they were supported and understood by very many Welshmen and women who saw their and others' efforts as part of a national renewal. The fact that much of it was myth-history seems to have been less important than a powerful need to identify with a past that was quintessentially Welsh and profoundly un-English. These tenuous threads connecting to a Celtic, pre-English Britain were not confined to Wales. Indeed, the process of converting the past into comforting entertainment may have begun in Scotland.

In 1968 Neil Armstrong took a piece of tartan to the Moon. His small step for man was also a giant leap of the romantic imagination. Armstrong was not the son of a Highland family, and he only visited Scotland after he had been to the Moon. In fact, his people were originally Border Scots from near the small town of Langholm, and may have been evicted when James I and VI dealt with the problems of the Reivers after 1603. After the Moon landing, he was invited to the town, where the delighted councillors conferred the freedom of the burgh on him. Even though no-one was quite sure what that freedom actually involved for an American who lived thousands of miles away, Neil Armstrong declared that, somehow, he felt that he had come home. He felt that the connection between him and Langholm was strong, and for him the most potent and portable symbol of Scottishness that he could have about him on the lunar surface was a piece of tartan, even though the reality is that tartan had absolutely nothing to do with the Border origins of his family. Given the long history of antipathy between Highland and Lowland which had culminated in the 1745 Jacobite rebellion, the Border adoption of tartan and much of the iconography of the Gael is a remarkable reversal of attitudes.

In the immediate aftermath of 1746 and Culloden, the Highlands suffered an eighteenth-century form of ethnic cleansing where whole populations were terrorized and often worse. Much was done to dismantle the social and military structure of clanship, and in an obviously symbolic measure, the wearing of tartan was banned amongst the civilian population. Like the bagpipes and the Gaelic language, it was seen as a badge of rebellion which marked out the Gaels as different from loyal, Lowland Scotland. Highland soldiers in government service were still permitted to wear the kilt, but when soldiers came home on leave, that privilege no longer obtained and the indignity of trousers or trews had to be suffered. The Gaels even had to coin a new word for this alien garment: *brioghais*, probably a borrowing into Gaelic from the Scots word 'breeks', or trousers. As early as 1739 the independent Highland companies who made up the Black Watch had begun to dress in a standardized design of blue, green and black. At the battle of Fontenoy in 1745 against the French, the regiment had gained its nickname by conducting a gallant rearguard action. For ever after it was called 'the Black Watch of the Battles, first to come and last to go'. The right to wear the tartan had been granted after the Jacobite uprising because the removal of the kilt from such a valued and formidable fighting unit might have damaged their morale. It was also a uniform instantly recognizable to the enemy, and one which was undoubtedly feared. The Black Watch is still sometimes called the government tartan and has been adopted by Clan Campbell as their own. It may be the oldest sett, or pattern, still worn.

By allowing Highland regiments to continue to wear tartan, the government unwittingly sustained a long tradition. War dress for medieval Highlanders was the *leine croich*, a long pleated coat which covered the shoulders and came down below the knees. Several tombstones and engravings show warriors wearing the *leine croich*, a pointed metal cap, chain mail across the shoulders and holding a spear and a claymore.

This was a two-handed broadsword and not the basket-hilted short sword with which it is often confused. When soldiers campaigned, they almost always slept outdoors and used the *leine croich* as a blanket. In Gaelic the word for blanket is *plaid*, now used by Americans to mean tartan. When called to muster in the morning Highlanders put on the *leine croich*, or what came to be known as the *feileadh mor*, or big kilt, by lying down. First they set their belt on the ground and laid the pleated plaid lengthwise on it, always allowing enough material below the belt to cover their backsides. Then the soldier lay down and folded the shorter end of the plaid around his front and buckled his belt. When he stood up, he put on his jacket and arranged the surplus material around his shoulders in a number of variations. The *leine croich* did restrict movement, and when it was sodden with rain it must have been difficult to manage. In warfare, it was sometimes dispensed with entirely. In 1544 a clan battle between the Frasers and the MacDonalds got the name Blar na Leine – 'the Field of Shirts' – because warriors fought in them, having thrown off the *leine croich*.

Around 1730 an English ironmaster from Lancashire leased the Forest of Invergarry from the Chief of the Clan MacDonnell. In the early Industrial Revolution manufacturers were more concerned about the lack of efficient transport than the location of their factories and several moved close to the sources of fuel. Thomas Rawlinson recruited workers around Invergarry to fell the trees and feed his furnaces at the ironworks. He noticed that the long plaids of the men were causing difficulty. Not only did the folds of tartan make for warm work near the furnaces, but they might be dangerous in this semi-industrial business. Rawlinson wanted no impediment to his ability to make money, so he consulted the tailor at the army garrison at Inverness and together they designed a short kilt. It covered only the lower half of the abdomen and down to the knee, thus doing away with the surplus material which needed to be secured over the shoulder. The *feileadh beag*, or 'small kilt', quickly became popular with both civilians and soldiers but it was conveniently forgotten that the central icon of Scottishness was developed into its present form by an Englishman. Adding lexical insult to cultural injury, the word 'kilt' is not derived from Gaelic. It is related to the Danish word *kilte*, meaning 'to tuck up'. The *leine crioch* never completely died out and it became known as the *feileadh mor*, or the 'big kilt'.

After the defeat at Culloden, the small kilt survived solely for military use until 1782, when the ban was lifted. During that period and later, several dress conventions were established by Highland regiments. All kilt jackets have shoulder straps because soldiers originally needed them for epaulettes, and in the early nineteenth century army tailors began to sow rows of metal buttons up the sleeves of military kilt jackets to discourage soldiers from wiping their noses on them. The short kilt jackets are not only designed to show off the pleats at the back of the kilt, but are another legacy from the military. Regimental dress jackets worn with trousers or breeches are similarly cut short. As late as the 1960s white stockings were adopted in a self-conscious imitation of the *cath dath*, the red-and-white diced pattern known as 'war colours'.

Tartan was unbanned in 1782 partly through pressure from the London Highland Society, and partly because of the reaction to a sensational new publication. In 1760 James MacPherson brought out his *Fragments of Ancient Poetry Collected in the Highlands of Scotland and Translated from the Gallic or Erse Language*. It reprinted rapidly over several editions. The preface suggested that there still existed an oral tradition of very old and unrecorded poetry in the Highlands. After the success of the first edition, MacPherson was dispatched on a tour to gather more material, but he had a problem. His understanding of Gaelic was actually fairly poor, and he was forced to rely on translations of such fragments as he found made by other scholars. There is also more than a suspicion that MacPherson missed a few subtle ironies in certain of the taller tales he was told. In return for a welcome coin or two, some Gaels may have elaborated or invented what they claimed they could remember, and the enthusiastic MacPherson wrote it all down. His lack of good Gaelic showed in the texts which he ultimately produced and cast great doubts over the authenticity of his next publication, *Fingal: an Ancient Epic Poem*, which appeared in 1761. With its hero as the doubtful inspiration for the naming of Fingal's Cave, the story dealt with his journey to Ireland to fight at the side of the great warrior Cuthullin against the Norse King Swaran. Although they are different in time and place, the tale of Fingal resembles the genuinely early Fenian and Ulster Cycle poems, some of which deal, far more authentically, with the boy-hero Cuchulainn. These poems provided ready models of mood and sources of phrasing and vocabulary, but MacPherson insisted that he had translated an ancient epic poem which he had pieced together from what old people could recall. He ascribed authorship of the epic to Fingal's son, the warrior-poet Ossian, and the stories came to be named after him. The poem was a huge success. It was hailed as a Scottish *Iliad* and proof that a heroic past had indeed existed in the Highlands, where the romantic scenery seemed to demand it. Mac-Pherson consistently claimed that he had translated something genuinely ancient, and it was in turn translated into several European languages. Figures as diverse as Goethe in Germany and Napoleon Bonaparte read it and believed absolutely in its antiquity. It is said that Napoleon kept a translation by his bedside during all his campaigns. The Ossian poems exerted a great influence on European thought and sowed the seeds of the romantic movement with its tales of wild places, the power of nature and primitive but noble savages. Ossian was probably based on fifteen or so genuine fragments but, like Iolo Morgannwg, MacPherson invented much new material and tailored the whole to suit eighteenth-century tastes and expectations. Even so it is difficult to sift out the nuggets of older poetry from the fabrication.

Despite this forgery, Ossian radically altered attitudes to the Highlands of Scotland. From the aggression and outright racism of the seventeenth century, these became sympathetic, interested, patronizing and much more subtly racist. The popular view of the Highlands moved from barbarity to quaintness in the early nineteenth century with extraordinary rapidity. At the same time, crucially, the telling of the history of the Gaels became disconnected from any knowledge of the Gaelic language.

This was a determining shift. No British historian of France, for example, would ever presume to attempt a history of that country without a knowledge of French, but after MacPherson, few would feel any inhibition in writing about the Highlands without a working knowledge of Gaelic. What this meant in practice was a near-complete absence of authoritative Highland voices in those histories until very recently, and that there was no effective brake on the translation of myth into history.

The success and the fakery of Ossian may well have amused one contemporary. Living in Edinburgh in the 1760s and working as a member of the city's police force was Duncan Ban MacIntyre. His genuinely great Gaelic poetry was of no interest to the monoglot literati eager to celebrate Ossian as a Scottish Homer. Duncan Ban could neither read nor write: he composed in his head and then recited, like a traditional bard, to a friend who acted as his amanuensis. In the rush to read the romantic Ossian no-one noticed a man who was a genuine descendant of the Gaelic oral tradition, and one of the greatest Gaelic poets who ever lived – an eloquent commentary on how romance wilfully diverged from reality.

The remaking of the Highlands begun by James MacPherson was taken further by the historical novels of Walter Scott. A Borderer with no Gaelic at all, he rewrote much of the history of the Gael in a series of dazzling novels. Published in 1814, *Waverley, or, 'Tis Sixty Years Since*, tells the story of an eponymous hero who first deserts the government army in 1745 to join Bonnie Prince Charlie and then deserts the Jacobites to rejoin the redcoats. Scott's novel sold in unprecedented numbers, was translated widely and reprinted regularly. Although it was presented as a novel, *Waverley* mixed fictional and historical characters and was generally understood as a version of what really happened in the 1745 rebellion. Scott followed this success with *Redgauntlet*, *Rob Roy* and other stories. He was a consummate story teller, and his books helped to foster a deeply romantic set of attitudes to Highland history which have largely persisted and remain dominant today. Quaintness, loss, political conservatism, mysticism, mañana and much more suffuse Scott's broadly sympathetic but often unilluminating view of a people whose language he did not understand.

Scott's prose found surprising expression in 1822. George IV came on a state visit to Edinburgh, the first British monarch to do so since Charles I in 1633. Critics called it 'a Highland extravaganza' and complained that Walter Scott, the organizer of events, had 'made us appear as a nation of Highlanders'. The centrepiece of the King's welcome was a royal genealogy which began with him and traced his lineage back to Fergus Mac Erc, King of Dalriada, and, without a trace of awkwardness, the plump figure of George IV appeared in a remarkable rig-out. Wearing flesh-coloured tights, he entered the city in a short kilt of Stewart tartan. The romance of Ossian and *Waverley* had made it possible for the Hanoverian King to forget the rebellion of seventy years before and put on the clothes of his enemies, the Stewarts. Political necessity had persuaded the portly King into this theatrical daftness, as by allowing Scott to make him a neo-Highlander with a Gaelic genealogy, German George at last attached a sense of much-needed Britishness – or at least Celtic Britishness – to his dynasty.

At Balmoral, also festooned with Stewart tartan on the walls and

windows, his niece, Victoria, managed the same trick of association. The
Queen and Prince Albert first visited Scotland in 1842, only four years
after her coronation. They explored Perthshire and read Walter Scott's
Lay of the Last Minstrel. The Prince tried deer stalking and for both the
visit was the beginning of a life-long love affair with the Highlands. As
a remote descendant of the Stewarts, Victoria's adoption of tartan, porridge and whatever else best met her notions of Highland identity was
no dafter than the general interest in things Gaelic evinced by many of
her subjects who had consumed Ossian and Scott. She may also have
sensed Scotland's alienation, which was partly the result of residual
Jacobite sentiment and political mismanagement after the Act of Union
in 1707, and perhaps hoped to redress it by creating a Scottish identity
for the royal family. In any case, the sincerity and constancy of her
affection for the Highlands cannot be questioned. The 1842 visit became
an annual event, as it still is. In 1848 the Balmoral Estate was first rented
and then purchased, and by 1852 the building of Balmoral Castle had
begun. From this base, Victoria and Albert set out on frequent and
sometimes arduous excursions throughout the Highlands. After the early
death of Prince Albert in 1861, Victoria spent more time in the Highlands.
She clearly loved the place, and she probably also fell in love with a
Gael. John Brown was a Gaelic-speaking crofter's son from Craithenaird,
near Balmoral. A lifelong bachelor, he became Victoria's constant companion. His fondness for whisky and for bluntness were both well known.
While fastening the Queen's cape, he was once heard to remark, 'Wum-
man! Can ye no' haud yer heid up!' Brown's loyalty and Victoria's
devotion to him were unwavering, and she took to her grave a portrait
of him on her wrist. In 1867 the Queen published her *Leaves from a
Journal of our Life in the Highlands*. It was an enormous success. She
produced *More Leaves* in 1883, which was dedicated to her 'beloved
friend, John Brown', as well as sketches and paintings of the scenery she
loved so much. This royal output did even more to publicize the Highlands than Scott's novels. Royal patronage became a new feature of
Scottish life, and numerous monuments were unveiled and exhibitions
opened.

Not only had Gaelic Scotland been blown to bits at Culloden, but
after MacPherson and Scott it also became a figment of a British imagination in love with a past that had never existed. Far more than the musket
balls of 1746, this remaking of the Highlands caused what really remained

to be ignored and to wither into near-extinction. It was perhaps providential that Duncan Ban died in 1812, ten years before George IV stepped off the boat at Leith Harbour to steal a part of his heritage. He would have shaken his head at the daftness and the cleverness of it all.

In the months leading up to the royal visit of 1822, the Highland Society was deluged with requests from Lowland notables for details of correct Highland dress. George IV could not be seen wearing the only kilt in Edinburgh. And later when Queen Victoria came to Balmoral and attended Highland gatherings, held balls with reels and strathspeys, and espoused everything tartan so profoundly that she could declare, without a trace of irony, that in her heart she was a Jacobite, the headlong rush into the never-neverland of myth-history carried on unabated. Shawl and tweed weavers from Paisley to Brora owed their livelihoods to the Queen's love of tartan.

Cloth manufacturers must have rubbed their hands with glee. The royal visit of 1822 and the standardization of regimental tartans had combined to establish the custom of linking particular setts with a particular clan name. This was reinforced by more fakery. In 1842 the self-styled Sobieski-Stuart brothers published a beautifully illustrated but entirely spurious book called the *Vestiarum Scoticum*. They claimed to be the grandsons of Bonnie Prince Charlie and alleged in the book that the recent association of particular setts with clans was in fact very old. Deriving its information from an old Gaelic manuscript which seemed never to be available for inspection, the *Vestiarum Scoticum* was clearly a figment of the brothers' imagination, and the instrument of their commercial success. Many of today's clan tartans are based on their illustrations.

While the royal family, cloth makers and charlatans like the Sobieski-Stuarts were substituting tartan for history, Gaelic Scotland was dying. The Highland Clearances of the nineteenth century saw the removal of many thousands to the cities of Scotland's central belt or across the ocean to the New World. The emigrations meant that the landscape fitted the new myth even more exactly. The empty, lonely and windswept wildness which delighted the romantics also inspired Victorian painters. Thomas Faed's *The Last of the Clan* is more than simply a canvas of tragedy – it seems to transpose the Gaels into another dimension. All of Faed's carefully posed figures more closely resemble actors rather than real people – in fact, they probably were actors. In Edwin Landseer's quintessential painting *The Monarch of the Glen*, the Highlands have been entirely depopulated, leaving only the majestic stag in charge of the bens and the glens.

Some of what happened to Gaelic Scotland also happened across a nineteenth-century Europe searching for identity and comforting traditions, but much of the disconnection between myth and reality in Scotland was specifically related to the suppression and withering of the Gaelic language. Its deeper history remained unknown to all but those who spoke Gaelic. In telling contrast, in Wales both culture and language were held together in the Eisteddfodau and, very significantly, more than 8,500 books were published in Welsh in the nineteenth century. In Scotland, language and culture were severed, and Gaelic is dying while the iconography of the Gael has never been so popular. Kilts and tartan are now regularly reinvented in stylish fashions aimed at a young market. Unless something radical is done urgently, Alba will be no more. Perhaps Neil Armstrong's piece of tartan on the Moon was an appropriate and depressing metaphor – a remnant of Gaeldom in an empty and arid landscape.

In nineteenth-century Wales and Scotland, Celtic history was reduced to quaintness, local colour and comforting entertainment. In Ireland, it was the stuff of politics. After the forced union with Great Britain in 1800, Gaelic-speaking Catholic Ireland remained disenfranchized and discriminated against across the whole spectrum of society. Daniel O'Connell, the son and eventual heir of a Catholic landed family that had managed to hang onto its estate in County Kerry, became leader of the movement for the repeal of the Act of Union. To demonstrate the scale of support for his nationalist views as well as an opportunity to enunciate them, O'Connell held a series of what were called 'monster meetings'. Attended by hundreds of thousands of people, they were orderly, well organized and impressive. They were held in places where the memories of Celtic Ireland swirled around O'Connell and his audience, as they listened to passionate speech-making. The largest meeting of all took place on the Hill of Tara and an even larger one was planned at Clontarf, now part of Dublin but in 1014 the site of the battle where King Brian Boru defeated the Vikings. The colonial authorities saw the Clontarf meeting as too threateningly symbolic, and, since it was to be held in the city, too dangerous to tolerate so close to all the symbols and mechanisms of British rule. Daniel O'Connell was dedicated to a policy of legality and non-violence, and in October 1843 he agreed to call it off.

In 1845 *Phytophthora infestans* entered Irish history. Potato blight wiped out huge proportions of the staple crop, and the effect was utterly devastating. The scale of the disaster was such that few reliable official statistics were kept, but recent scholarship puts the number of dead at 1 million. More died of disease than starvation, and both the elderly and the very young were acutely at risk.

The Great Famine changed Ireland completely. In 1841, 8,175,000 people lived on the island; most spoke Irish Gaelic every day and many had no English at all. In rural communities from which few travelled, there was little need to learn it. By 1851 the direct effects of the famine and the mass emigration to Britain, North America and Australia had reduced the population to 6,500,000, while many of those who remained had left the land and drifted into cities in search of work. After 1851 the Irish language began to wither, with only 25 per cent of the population able to speak it and 5 per cent using it as their sole language. Drastic social change was wiping away much of what was Irish about Ireland and drawing it ever closer to the booming economy of late-Victorian England.

Nationalists knew that the neutered fate of Gaelic Scotland and Welsh Wales awaited if a powerful cultural revival was not initiated quickly and sustained. Alongside Michael Cusack's Gaelic Athletic Association, a society dedicated to the promotion of the Irish language came into being in 1893. It was known as the Gaelic League, and it hoped to revive Irish as a spoken vernacular and as a literary language. Like the GAA, it was almost immediately politicized. Between 1890 and the final achievement of independence for the south of Ireland in 1922, cultural matters were not merely a compartment of life where fine thoughts could be filed or found – culture was politics and politics expressed itself through Irish culture. This unusual fusion is well caught in the life, beliefs and actions of an extraordinary man, P. H. Pearse.

Born in Dublin to an Irish mother and an English father, Padraic Pearse was not a native Gaelic speaker and only began to learn when he was fourteen, but like many who choose to espouse a culture they are not born to, he became its passionate advocate. In October 1896 the young Pearse joined the new Gaelic League, and at the age of nineteen was co-opted onto the Executive Committee where he met many highly politicized figures such as Eoin MacNeill and Douglas Hyde. The latter was an academic, a collector of Irish vernacular music and a theatrical collaborator with W. B. Yeats, and in 1938 became the first President of Ireland. Padraic Pearse himself began to write poetry and became the editor of *An Claidheamh Soluis*, the journal of the Gaelic League. Like many minority-language activists, he realized that education was the key if Irish was to survive and thrive, and in 1908 he founded St Enda's School on the outskirts of Dublin. So far as it was possible pupils were taught an Irish curriculum of history, literature, sport and the arts, and the school operated bilingually. Significantly for what Pearse was to do in the future, he caused a fresco to be painted of the boy-hero, Cuchulainn, with a motto inscribed below in Irish. It read: 'I care not if my life has only the span of a night and a day if my deeds are spoken of by the men of Ireland.'

When the First World War began in 1914, many Irish nationalists saw Britain's distractions in Europe as an opportunity for their ambitions. Padraic Pearse had joined the Irish Republican Brotherhood and the Irish Volunteers and soon became an influential member of both organizations, and an eloquent advocate of independence. In 1915 the body of Jeremiah O'Donovan Rosa, an activist who had spent many years in British prisons, was brought home to Dublin for burial. Pearse wrote and delivered a passionate eulogy which showed the directions in which his thinking was moving:

> Life springs from death; and from the graves of patriot men and women spring living nations ... The Defenders of this realm ... think they have pacified Ireland ... the fools, the fools, fools! They have left us our Fenian dead, and while Ireland holds these graves, Ireland unfree shall never be at peace.

Throughout the rest of 1915 and into early 1916 arguments in the nationalist movement over tactics arrived at no unified conclusion, and as the war in Europe wore on some, like Pearse, began to fear that the chance for action that it presented might slip away. In any event, some Nationalists actually supported the war and advocated a policy of imperial loyalty as a better prelude to a negotiated settlement. John E. Redmond, leader of the Nationalist party at Westminster, supported recruitment and even saw his brother killed in the trenches in 1917.

However, Pearse and the IRB were determined to act. A landing of a large shipment of arms supplied by the Germans was planned for early April 1916, and since this would give thousands of men all over the country a rifle, a rebellion was planned for Easter. But the German ship was intercepted and scuttled, and within the Republican movement there arose profound disagreement over what course of action to adopt in the circumstances. Pearse was determined: along with James Connolly and others he believed that the momentum for Irish independence needed nothing less than a blood sacrifice – that the ancient cult of dead heroes, of martyrdom needed to be fed in as spectacular a fashion as could be managed.

Accordingly, on the morning of Easter Monday 1916, more than a thousand volunteers, not all of them armed, met at Liberty Hall in Dublin. Detachments were despatched to seize key points around the city while Pearse and Connolly marched down Sackville Street with 150 men to set up their headquarters at the General Post Office for Dublin. After they had barricaded themselves in, Pearse stepped out onto the busy street clutching a piece of paper. Usually a powerful and confident orator, he seemed nervous and uncharacteristically restrained. As the bemused bank holiday crowds milled around the classical pillars of the post office portico, Pearse read out this proclamation:

> Irishmen and Irishwomen: In the name of God and of the dead generations from which she receives her old tradition of nationhood, Ireland, through us, summons her children to her flag and strikes for her freedom.
>
> Having organised and trained her manhood through her secret revolutionary organisation, the Irish Republican Brotherhood, and through her open military organisations, the Irish Volunteers and the Irish Citizen Army, having patiently perfected her discipline, having resolutely waited for the right moment to reveal itself, she now seizes that moment, and, supported by her exiled children in America and by gallant allies in Europe, but relying in the first on her own strength, she strikes in full confidence of victory.
>
> We declare the right of the people of Ireland to the full ownership of Ireland, and to the unfettered control of Irish destinies, to be sovereign and indefeasible. The long usurpation of that right by a foreign people and government has not extinguished the right, nor can it ever be extinguished except by the destruction

of the Irish people. In every generation the Irish people have asserted their right to national freedom and sovereignty: six times during the last three hundred years they have asserted it in arms. Standing on that fundamental right and again asserting it in arms in the face of the world, we hereby proclaim the Irish Republic as a Sovereign Independent State, and we pledge our lives and the lives of our comrades-in-arms to the cause of its freedom, of its welfare, and of its exaltation among the nations.

The Irish republic is entitled to, and hereby claims, the allegiance of every Irishman and Irishwoman. The republic guarantees religious and civil liberty, equal rights and equal opportunities to all its citizens, and declares its resolve to pursue the happiness and prosperity of the whole nation and of all its parts, cherishing all the children of the nation equally, and oblivious of the differences carefully fostered by an alien government, which have divided a minority from the majority in the past.

Until our arms have brought the opportune moment for the establishment of a permanent National Government, representative of the whole people of Ireland and elected by the suffrage of all her men and women, the Provisional Government hereby constituted, will administer the civil and military affairs of the Republic in trust for the people.

We place the cause of the Irish Republic under the protection of the Most High God Whose blessing we invoke upon our arms, and we pray that no-one who serves that cause will dishonour it by cowardice, inhumanity or rapine. In this supreme hour the Irish nation must, by its valour and discipline, and by the readiness of its children to sacrifice themselves for the common good, prove itself worthy of the august destiny to which it is called.

Signed on behalf of the Provisional Government, Thomas J. Clarke, Sean MacDiarmada, Thomas MacDonagh, P. H. Pearse, Eamonn Ceannt, James Connolly, Joseph Plunkett

They knew that they had also signed their own death warrants. The readiness of all of these men and several others to sacrifice themselves for Irish independence was clear. From the outset neither Pearse nor Connolly entertained any hope that the Easter Rising would, in itself, succeed. As they marched down Sackville Street on the fateful Monday morning, a young volunteer asked Pearse what the chances of victory were. 'None whatever,' he replied, almost cheerfully. And when Pearse's mother asked a similar question earlier, her son said, 'The day is coming when I shall be shot, swept away, and my colleagues likewise.'

No other fate was politically possible after the rebels at the GPO shot dead four British cavalry soldiers who charged down Sackville Street on the Monday afternoon. For a week a full-scale military action took place in Dublin and more than 3,000 people were killed, many of them uninvolved civilians, and much of the centre of the city was destroyed by fire or bombardment. By Friday 28 April the GPO was ablaze, and having held out long enough for the rebellion to register on world consciousness, Pearse and a badly wounded Connolly escaped. At a shop in nearby Moore Street, they met the other leaders to discuss what action should be taken next. Pearse and his brother, Willie, had seen a family of civilians waving a white flag shot by British soldiers and to avoid further bloodshed the leadership finally agreed to an unconditional sur-render. On Saturday 30 April, Padraic Pearse walked up Moore Street to meet the British commander to bring the action formally to a close. He knew what would happen next.

He also knew that his martyrdom would take the cause of indepen-dence further than he could hope to do in life. As some of the insurgents were led away to prison, Dublin crowds booed them, but in less than a week that mood would change for ever.

At his court martial Padraic Pearse felt history pressing on him: 'You cannot conquer Ireland. You cannot extinguish the Irish passion for freedom. If our deed has not been sufficient to win freedom, then our children will win it by a better deed.' At dawn on 3 May, with Thomas Clarke and Thomas MacDonagh, Pearse was taken out into the stone-breaking yard at Kilmainham Goal and shot by firing squad. The execution of the sixteen leaders of the Easter Rising went on every morning until 12 May, when the wounded and dying James Connolly was carried out tied to a chair because he could no longer stand to face the firing squad. The Dublin and Irish public were horrified at what went on, particularly at the callous treatment of Connolly. Pearse's policy of willing blood sacrifice ultimately succeeded because it came directly out of the store of Celtic memory. The choice of the fresco to Cuchulainn and its motto at St Enda's School was no accident – it showed a clear understanding of what needed to be done.

THIRTEEN

1798

THE CRY OF THE BANSHEE has chilled the hearts of Irish men and women for many centuries. In an eighth-century poem, *The Cattle Raid of Fraoch*, recited as a foretale to *The Great Cattle Raid of Cooley*, death is announced by the Mna Si or the Otherworld Woman – the Banshee in modern Irish Gaelic. In the 1930s, collectors for the Irish Folklore Commission archives in University College Dublin recorded a story told, in Gaelic, in County Waterford. A young man had been out visiting:

> He was coming home this night late as usual. Just as he was coming in the gate of the boreen [track] which stretched for about half a mile to the house, the most awesome, unnatural sound that anyone had ever heard struck his ears. Like a bullet it went headlong by him in the direction of the house and it scattered the mud of the road over the hedges like the winter wind.
>
> He was halfway along the boreen when the second roar hit him. This really put him in a frenzy and he ran faster and faster, the loneliness of the sound and some other element of strangeness in it he could not describe, almost taking his breath away.
>
> He was at the door when she screeched again, and, if she did, John screamed at her in great terror, and with such severe fright that he woke every one of us. At the same time he began to kick in the door as hard as he could until my father got up in a rage. But when he unbolted the door the 'corpse' fell 'stone-dead' in on the floor.

239

Then the hullabaloo started as we all thought he was beyond help from anyone in this world. It was not long until he heaved a sigh and then another one. Then we saw him opening the eyes and looking around. Finally he spoke and these are the words he said: 'Oh God save us, am I alive or dead?' He gradually quietened down, and we teased out of him what had happened to him.

The old man, Tomas Toibin, who lived next door to us was told about the terrifying thing that had happened. He listened to the very end without uttering a word and then he said: 'It was the badhb [Banshee] and she is coming for me. It will not be long now.' He was right. He died the following day.

Many hundreds of stories like this and dozens of traditions surround the phenomenon of the Banshee. The name has a simple derivation: *si* pronounced 'she' means a spirit or a ghost, and *ban* is a prefix which makes it female. For example, *righ* in Gaelic means king, while *banrigh* means queen. Like Mna Si, Banshee means Otherworld Woman, and its origins clearly lie in a pagan Celtic past. While many claim to have heard the wail of the Banshee, fewer witnesses have actually seen her. Even so, there is a remarkable degree of general agreement about her appearance: an old woman with long white hair worn loose, wearing white clothes and sometimes found sitting on a rock by a stream. In County Waterford the Banshee is known as the Baidhbe, and on modern maps there is a place called Carraig na Baidhbe, the Rock of the Banshee. In Tipperary, Mayo and Limerick she gets another alternative name, Am Bean Chaointe, the Keening Woman, and the Gaelic verb *caoin* is the origin of the English 'to keen' or wail at funerals or wakes.

The Banshee is almost always heard at night, and more precisely in the grey hours of the late evening and the time just before dawn. In Ireland and other parts of Celtic Britain there is a general belief that barriers between the Otherworld and the visible, temporal life are blurred in darkness, and there are stories in the Scottish Gaidhealtachd which underline this understanding. In the late nineteenth century in Glengarry a young woman hurrying home very late one night was confronted by an apparition which explained the situation succinctly, '*Biodh an latha agadsa, ach an oidche againne!*', 'You may have the day, but we will have the night!'

As the Waterford story confirms, the Banshee was only heard as a

harbinger of death, but it was an old-fashioned passing that she anticipated. When country people died at home, instead of lingering in
hospital, her cry would help to anticipate events and act as a herald for
a whole community. When death was not a private event managed by
doctors and with pain-killers, out of the sight of people, but something
which could be eased by the help of a clutch of friends and neighbours,
the recognition that it was coming soon could be comforting. Equally,
in some country districts, terminally ill people believed that they could
not die unless and until the cry of the Banshee was heard.

But apparently some in Ireland were deaf to the wail of the Otherworld
Woman. Researchers from University College Dublin have compiled a
long list of the surnames of families who have reported incidents, and
it turns out that the names of English and Scottish settlers who came
to Ireland in the seventeenth century and afterwards are entirely absent.
It appears that the Banshee only screamed in Gaelic. This detail may
seem minor, but it is symbolic of a growing cultural rift. Successive
groups of incomers followed the twelfth-century invasions of Richard
fitz Gilbert Earl of Pembroke, known as Strongbow, but they had
gradually been absorbed into Gaelic society so profoundly that they
became 'Hiberniores Hibernis ipsis', 'more Irish than the Irish themselves'. In the lists of families who heard the Banshee there are
Fitzmaurices, Fitzsimons and Fitzgeralds and many other Anglo-Irish
names. By contrast, after 1600 the families which came from Scotland
and England maintained a distinct and aggressive identity, rarely
learned Gaelic or became involved in Gaelic culture, and their political
ambitions created divisions and tensions which have never lost their
sharpness. In the late sixteenth century Ireland began to take on
more of the characteristics of a colony and a bard began a descriptive
historical poem with a one sentence summary which is hard to argue
with: 'The land of Ireland is Sword-Land.'

In response to Elizabethan pressure, a scion of the ancient Ulster dynasty
of the O'Neills, Hugh Earl of Tyrone, rose in rebellion in 1595. He
compiled an alliance of Gaelic noblemen and won an encouraging victory
at the Battle of the Yellow Ford. His coreligionists, the Spanish, were at
war with England at the time, and they sent O'Neill an army which
landed at Kinsale on the south coast in 1601, but their combined forces

were badly beaten in a pitched battle with a government army. Hugh O'Neill eventually surrendered in 1603, only a few days after the death of Elizabeth I and the informal accession of that great enemy of the Gael, James VI and I. A treaty was signed suspending hostilities on reasonable terms but, four years later, O'Neill felt so seriously threatened that he took the fateful decision to go into voluntary exile. Accompanied by Rory O'Donnell, Earl of Tyrconnell, Cuchonnacht Maguire, Lord of Fermanagh and many followers, Hugh O'Neill sailed from Donegal to France and thence to Rome where he died in 1617. 'The Flight of the Earls' effectively ended substantial opposition from the Gaelic-speaking Irish nobility, and when their extensive properties, mainly in Ulster, were confiscated, it opened the way for the Plantations, marking a pivotal point in Irish history.

Ulster had been the most Gaelic of Ireland's provinces. Both Scotland and, probably, the Isle of Man had been colonized from Antrim and Down. The old city of Armagh was the prehistoric centre of Ard Macha, the seat of the Kings of Ulster, and the place chosen by St Patrick as the focus of his mission. Hugh O'Neill's ancestors, the Ui Neill, had been one of the most ancient and powerful clans in Ireland, and the pastoral economy which had sustained them had remained unchanged for centuries. All that was to change for ever, and after two generations only remnants of Gaelic Ulster would survive.

The six counties of Armagh, Cavan, Donegal, Fermanagh, Derry and Tyrone became the property of the crown, and in 1609 'orders and conditions' were promulgated which became the framework for the Ulster Plantations. It was a systematic and well-organized programme of direct colonization intended to make a significant difference in the management of Ireland, and there is absolutely no doubt that it did, and does.

Sir Josias Bodley first surveyed and mapped the land confiscated from the exiled Earls and their supporters, and it was parcelled into lots of 2,000, 1,500 and 1,000 acres. English planters were granted most of the best land, with Scottish settlers not far behind and tending to make up the largest group, often as tenant farmers. James VI and I used the Ulster Plantations to solve other British problems. After the Scottish and English border had been pacified, he ordered the wholesale deportation of the notorious Graham family. With their customary ruthlessness, they carved out a new domain in Ireland and other Border families followed in their wake.

The political and strategic importance of Derry was recognized, and the Irish Society of London was formed to fortify the town and plant its hinterland. King James and his ministers put pressure on the City of London guild-companies to invest in the Irish Society and what quickly came to be called Londonderry. The Society controlled customs, the administration of towns and the management of fisheries, while the rest of the landward part of the county was divided between the guild-companies. Between 1614 and 1618 the formidable walls of Londonderry were built and by 1630 there were nearly 2,000 British settlers in the county, and more than £140,000 was invested in development and infrastructure. The Irish Society and the companies made profits for many years until a mixture of political agitation and economic pressure forced the London guilds to sell their land in the nineteenth century, although the Irish Society itself only disposed of its last substantial asset, the Foyle Fisheries, in 1952.

The new Planters were compelled to build substantial castles where they could, and developed tightly knit communities highly conscious of their own security where they could not – a legacy that has never faded. The Flight of the Earls and the seizure of their land left large and dangerous bands of soldiers at large in the north of Ireland. These were known as Idlemen and the English governor, Sir Arthur Chichester, immediately transported 6,000 of them to Sweden to fight as mercenaries in the armies of Gustavus Adolphus, but many other soldiers remained and, living lives of banditry, they raided and menaced the Plantations. Getting the name Woodkernes, or Forest-Bandits, they fuelled a primitive stereotype by appearing suddenly out of the wilderness to despoil order and cultivation: in one view, the wild men of the woods were Gaelic-speaking and Catholic, while the hard-working, robust and civilized farmers spoke English and worshipped in the Protestant faith. The line between reality and the workings of a fearful imagination became ever more blurred as the Plantations took root. By 1630 around 6,500 adult British males had settled in the territory of the Earls, and as they expanded and others joined them over time, the political goals of the settlement were at least partly achieved. Catholic Ireland had been physically diluted by Protestant Britain, and the ever-present English fear of an alliance between Catholic European kings and the disaffected Catholic lords of Ireland had been mitigated. A fault line that has divided Irish politics for almost 400 years was created.

In 1641 Gaelic Ireland rose in a bitter rebellion against the Plantations and on behalf of the royalist faction in the English Civil War. The menace of the Woodkernes was fulfilled when at least 4,000 Protestants were massacred, many in an infamous drowning at Portadown. But like the King's cause, the rebellion failed, and ultimately Cromwell himself arrived in 1658 to direct a brutal subjugation of the native population. In attitude, behaviour and policy, England's relationship with Ireland mirrored that with Wales in the Middle Ages – except in the degree of violence. The Irish were often described by English commentators and officials as subhuman and treated accordingly. On many occasions the cruelty meted out to the Irish was as appalling as it was unthinking. Like Wales before it, Ireland was quickly becoming a second English colony.

Emblazoned on Loyalist banners in the Ulster marching season are many references to the Battle of the Boyne. Exhortations such as 'Remember the Boyne!' are potent rallying cries to the Unionist faithful. Fought on 1 July 1690, it was in fact a British drama played out on Irish soil. After his dethronement in 1688, the hopelessly incompetent James II first sought help in Scotland, and when that failed he sailed to Ireland to rally the Jacobite cause. King Billy – King William III – came from Britain to lead the government army in person, and they took up a position on the River Boyne, twenty miles north of Dublin. Although a national myth has been founded on it, the reality was that the battle of the Boyne was itself indecisive. At 1,000 on the Jacobite side and 500 for the Williamites, casualties were relatively light. The myth was instead fuelled by the image of brave King Billy in the thick of the fighting astride a grey horse, in contrast with the frankly cowardly behaviour of James II, who fled the field at the first sign of difficulties.

The following year, the Williamite army engaged and defeated the Jacobites at a far more decisive battle at Aughrim in County Galway. This time the slaughter was very great, with 7,000 fleeing Jacobites cut down in the aftermath. Aughrim effectively ended serious opposition to the English colonization of Ireland for more than a hundred years, and the Treaty of Limerick formalized the political settlement with a bargain which made it workable. Patrick Sarsfield was the most able and success-ful Irish commander in the Jacobite army. Having gained invaluable experience in modern warfare in the service of the Kings of France, he fought with tenacity and a resolve which contrasted sharply with the spinelessness of James II. In a mixed appraisal, Sarsfield was said by a contemporary to be 'a man of huge stature, without sense, very good natured and very brave'. Events were to show that he was in fact fairly astute. In the Treaty of Limerick he agreed to surrender the city in return for safe passage to France for all of his soldiers. Since it concluded the war and exported the potential for future trouble, it was an arrangement readily acceptable to the government. Patrick Sarsfield embarked with 16,000 soldiers who left Ireland for ever, ultimately to form the Irish Brigade in the French army. They soon became known as the Wild Geese. Although they fought on foreign soil for a foreign employer, the Irish Brigade was never so fired as when they engaged the British army. At the battle of Fontenoy in 1745, where the Black Watch won their name, the Duke of Cumberland's forces overpowered the French centre, but in a ferocious and headlong charge they were thrown back by the Irish Brigade under the command of Charles O'Brien, the disinherited Viscount Clare. Fontenoy has always been seen by Irish nationalists as a proxy victory over the English.

The eighteenth century also saw the beginnings of substantial emigrations of civilians from Ireland. Penal legislation disabling Catholics from taking part in civil life became increasingly oppressive. Restrictions on land-holding, participation in public office, education and religion were enacted, and since these were directed at the overwhelming majority of the total population, instead of some hapless minority, the atmosphere they produced was inevitably both pervasive and poisonous. Intolerance was also focused against the substantial and dynamic community of northern Irish Presbyterians, many of whom were of Scots origin and had settled in the era of the Ulster Plantations. This distinction within Irish Protestantism has sometimes been ignored or underestimated, and it was to prove an important factor in the Irish Rebellion of 1798.

Although the religious restrictions of the late seventeenth and early eighteenth centuries were eased for Presbyterians by the Toleration Act of 1719, many continued to resent the economic levies imposed on them for the maintenance of the Anglican Church of Ireland. They were forced to pay for a faith they did not adhere to. Emigration from Ulster to the North American colonies began to grow and in the five years between 1769 and 1774 as many as 40,000, both Catholic and Presbyterian, sailed across the ocean to begin a new life in religious freedom. This created a network of transatlantic family ties which was backed by a close commercial relationship between Belfast and New York and Philadelphia. So influential were the Presbyterian immigrants to the early USA that eleven of the first fifteen Presidents were of Ulster Scots extraction. When Benjamin Franklin visited Ireland in 1771, he met similar frustrations to those simmering in America:

> I found them disposed to be friends of America, in which I endeavoured to confirm them, with the expectation that our growing weight might in time be thrown into their scale, and by joining our interests with others, a more equitable treatment from this nation [England] might be obtained for them as well as for us.

At the same time when common ties of family and unhappiness with the English colonial regime grew between Ireland and America, the population of the island began to increase at an extraordinary rate. Reckoned at 2.5 million in 1741, it had doubled to 5 million by 1800, compared with a population of 10 million in the whole of Britain. This naturally led to pressure and competition for land. Violence first flared in County Tipperary in 1761 when a group of vigilantes called the Whiteboys attacked farmers who had enclosed common land. In Irish Gaelic they were known as Buachailli Bana, the White Shepherds, because they wore white smocks and had a direct interest in preventing the loss of their pasture. In County Armagh, where there were equal numbers of Protestants, Presbyterians and Catholics, agrarian disturbances took on a sectarian character. The Peep O' Day Boys, who operated in the dawn hours, raided Catholic farmhouses and the Catholic Defenders responded in kind. In 1795, at a clash known as the battle of the Diamond, a crossroads near Loughall in County Armagh, a sect of the Peep O' Day Boys who had taken to calling themselves the Orange Boys occupied a strong hilltop position from where they beat off a force of Defenders, killing thirty of them. The victors marched to Loughall, where they repaired to the inn of James Sloan and met to establish what became known as the Orange Order. It was dedicated to the 'glorious and immortal memory' of King William III and his triumph over the Catholic Jacobites at the battle of the Boyne. The name of the order has an obscure provenance. Prior to his accession to the British throne, William Prince of Orange was Stadtholder of Holland and Zeeland, but in the distant past his family had owned the Provençal town of Orange on the banks of the River Rhone. In the midst of Catholic France and only a few miles from the palace of the schismatic popes at Avignon, the town was Protestant in character until Louis XIV suppressed the Huguenots in 1703 – the name of the Orange Order was unconsciously emblematic of a place where a Catholic and Protestant struggle had been played out a hundred years before. In the July marching season, on the anniversary of the battle of the Boyne, the Orangemen don their fringed orange collarettes and bowler hats to remember King Billy, and raise a loyal toast of sorts: 'To the glorious, pious and immortal memory of the great and good King William, who saved us from popery, slavery, knavery, brass money and wooden shoes. And a fig to the Bishop of Cork!'

With many Ulster-born Presbyterians in the van, the American Revolution finally broke out into open warfare in 1776. The Westminster government was appalled and quickly sent reinforcements across the Atlantic. This critically diminished the Irish garrison and as a direct result produced a surprising phenomenon. Instead of seizing an opportunity for rebellion, the Irish formed a huge Volunteer force to defend the island against French or Spanish attentions – the fear of Catholic takeover was clearly greater than a wish for radical action in pursuit of independence. There seems at the time to have been a general identification of Catholicism with despotism at the time. At its height the Volunteer force included 100,000 men under arms, some of them Catholics, and while it provided a convincing deterrent to invaders, it also began to make London politicians uneasy. It was run as a private army loyal to the crown but not controlled by it. The Volunteer leadership soon recognized their political potential and began to make demands. Forming up in companies in unmistakable shows of force, they persuaded the British government to lift a number of restrictions on the Irish parliament and allow it a semblance of power. For some commentators this was the moment when the gun entered Irish politics, and it was also the beginning of a popular tradition of civilian paramilitaries. The name of the UVF, the Ulster Volunteer Force, is a deliberate connection to the past.

However, the concessions made by the London government turned out to be much more apparent than real. As dissatisfaction grew in Ireland, a second revolution broke out, this time closer at hand. The overthrow of Europe's most powerful monarchy in the French Revolution of 1789 also changed Ireland's political landscape. First and most important, it showed that a Catholic country was not necessarily wedded to despotism. In fact it could, and had in France, created a new society which embraced freedom and toleration. In 1790, on the first anniversary of the Fall of the Bastille, a huge force of Ulster Volunteers marched in Belfast to celebrate and fire three *feux de joie* with their muskets.

For once, the pen seemed mightier than the gun in Ireland. A young Protestant barrister from Dublin, memorably named Theobald Wolfe Tone, wrote a pamphlet in 1791 which had the potential to change the way in which influential Irishmen thought. Entitled 'An Argument on Behalf of the Catholics of Ireland', it took the view that the reforms demanded by the Volunteer movement in the 1780s had failed because they were too narrowly based. Perhaps influenced by the doctrine of '*Egalité, Fraternité et Liberté*' drummed abroad by the French revolutionaries, Tone insisted that the framework for political change had to include the Catholic majority. The reforms of 1782 had 'left three fourths of our countrymen slaves as it had found them'. The options facing Protestants were stark:

> on the one hand, reform and the Catholics, justice and liberty; on the other, an unconditional submission to the present and every future Administration ... who may indulge with ease and safety their propensity to speculation and spoil and insult.

The government was appalled at the prospect of political union between Catholics, Protestants and Presbyterians, and believed, undoubtedly correctly, that it could not hold Ireland if it came into being. Surprisingly, given more recent history, Belfast developed as the centre of radical Irish nationalism at the end of the eighteenth century, and events began to gather pace when Wolfe Tone rode north to join in the town's celebration of Bastille Day in 1791. Plans for a new political society which would embrace the ideas in Tone's pamphlet, the American Declaration of Independence, Tom Paine's *The Rights of Man* and the writings of the French revolutionaries were put quickly in train. In October 1791, the new club first met in Belfast, invited Wolfe Tone from Dublin to join and immediately accepted his proposal for a name. They were to be called the United Irishmen, and their manifesto combined the new radical thinking with the native patriot tradition:

> – the promotion of constitutional knowledge, the abolition of bigotry in religion and politics and an equal distribution of the

Rights of Man throughout all sects and denominations of Irishmen;

– a brotherhood of affection, an identity of interests, a communion of rights and a union of power among Irishmen of all religious persuasions;

– immediate, ample and substantial justice to the Catholics and when that is attained, a combined exertion for a reform of parliament is the condition of our compact and a seal of our communion.

These incendiary ideas were promulgated widely through pamphleteering, meetings of the Society of United Irishmen, the opening of other clubs in Dublin and elsewhere and the publication of the *Northern Star*, a radical newspaper founded in Belfast in January 1792. Later that year, the new alliance with the Catholic majority formally became a reality when Wolfe Tone himself became assistant secretary of the Catholic Committee in Dublin – a group of aggressive, middle-class reformers who believed that emancipation should be a right, and not a reward for deference to the English government. Two years of agitation produced concessions from London that once again appeared to be much more than they actually were.

Meanwhile, war had broken out between Britain and France, and the government began to clamp down on radical politics which seemed to be in sympathy with those of the enemy. Assemblies were outlawed, the Volunteers disbanded and the Catholic Defenders in particular were ruthlessly suppressed. In 1795 in County Meath a schoolmaster, Laurence O'Connor, was condemned to death as a Defender and suffered the hideous fate of a traitor. With the Viceroy in attendance as a witness, he was hung, disembowelled, beheaded and his body quartered. It seemed as though nothing at all had changed for hundreds of years. More subtly, the government moved to support the Orange Order in an attempt to stall the aims of the United Irishmen. These aims had clearly developed far beyond a domestic agenda and a programme of campaigning to persuade the government to legislate or repeal the penal laws, or even act within the constitution. Wolfe Tone was actively considering armed insurrection and making practical plans to involve the French. These came to light with the arrest of the Rev. William Jackson in 1794. He was an agent of the French government and amongst his belongings was a paper written by Tone which dealt with the prospects for and logistics of French military aid. Considering the dreadful fate of Laurence O'Connor, the consequences of this discovery could have been fatal, but with an extraordinary eloquence and charismatic charm, Wolfe Tone argued his way out of the hangman's noose and agreed to go into voluntary exile to the USA. This allowed him to act as an envoy of the United Irishmen and seek military aid from the Americans, and finally to persuade the French to become involved in the destinies of Ireland.

Before his departure on 13 June from Belfast, Wolfe Tone met his fellow United Irishmen Henry Joy McCracken, Thomas Russell and a small group of other men. They climbed Cave Hill, behind Belfast, and scrambled over to a prehistoric site known as McArt's Fort. Bleak and windswept, with sheer cliffs on three sides and a commanding view south over the city and Belfast Lough, the fort has an ethereal quality: it is a place of heroes and high ideals that looks down on the traffic at its foot. In that ancient place, where the memories of an independent Ireland were close, they swore an oath: 'never to desist in our efforts until we subverted the authority of England over our country and asserted our independence'.

Ultimately making his way to Paris, Tone once again demonstrated how charismatic he could be. Having arrived in the melting pot of revolutionary France, with few connections, no friends and little understanding of French, he quickly made himself familiar with the shifting contours of the volatile political landscape. He correctly saw that the key decision maker was Lazare Carnot, the Director with responsibility for war, and set about persuading him to help the United Irish cause. By June 1796, the Directory in Paris had approved plans for a French invasion of Ireland. A force of 14,450 soldiers was to be shipped from Brest to Bantry Bay, where it would create a bridgehead before joining with the forces of the United Irishmen to march on Dublin and Belfast. A military band was included in the expedition, with instructions to teach the Irish to sing 'La Marseillaise'. The fleet sailed on 16 December and made its way through the winter seas to the south coast of Ireland. On 22 December a landlord named Richard White ventured onto his terrace in a terrible storm and looked out over Bantry Bay. He was amazed to see dozens of warships attempting to make landfall, and because of the appalling weather failing to get the French army ashore. In the uniform of a French Adjutant-General, Tone stood on the bridge of a warship as the sea raged about him. For eleven days the captains tried to land, but were finally driven back by the storm. 'We were near enough to toss a biscuit ashore,' wrote Tone, 'England has not had such an escape since the Spanish Armada.'

Bantry Bay electrified the English government, and in 1797 it began a reign of terror in Ireland whose terrible memory has never faded.

Political history stays vividly alive when it is also family history, and although the events of 1798 have clearly outrun living memory, they are not beyond the reach of personal genealogy and a powerful inherited memory. In my own family in Scotland there are only four conversations between my experience and that of William Moffat, my great-great-great-great-grandfather, who was born in 1763 and died some time after 1851. A literate and aware young ploughman, he rejoiced, along with many Border Scots, at the American victory at Yorktown in 1781. Perhaps he knew people who had relatives fighting in the revolutionary armies. My grandmother, Bina Moffat, knew that story and passed it on to me. These were ordinary country people who had lived and died in the same district for uncounted generations, and they not only knew their genealogy but also saw it as a means of understanding the past. In exactly the same way the Rebellion of 1798 remains vivid for many Irish families. What happened to their ancestors feels close and is painful to them – it is not interpreted as past history and forgiven as such.

By 1796 Britain's European war and the removal of many regiments to the West Indies had drastically reduced the garrison of regular soldiers in Ireland – there were only 3,500 regular cavalry and 1,600 regular infantry based there. To supplement this meagre force a Yeomanry was formed on the basis of the counties and its strength stood at 20,000. It was officered by Protestants who were considered reliable. There was also a county militia with 18,000 part-time soldiers, and 9,000 fencibles were brought over from Scotland, the Isle of Man and Wales. Fencibles were an eighteenth-century version of the Home Guard and they tended to consist of men rejected or too old for regular army service. It was an unreliable, unprofessional and combustible mixture.

After the bad scare of Bantry Bay the government had no hesitation in turning loose these amateur soldiers on the countryside. Their mission was to root out rebels and disarm them in whatever manner seemed suitable, and their methods were appalling. Torture was used on a widespread and virtually indiscriminate basis. Suspects were tied up and subjected to pitch-capping: a tar-soaked skullcap was placed on their heads and set alight. Many confessed and supplied names, any names. Others were hung up by the heels on a twisted rope which was let go so that it spun them around violently as it unwound, while soldiers stood around lashing the victim's body. Half-hanging and flogging were carried out in the market places of villages and towns all over Ireland, and because these excesses were committed by amateur soldiers who lacked proper leadership and discipline, they were ineffective as a deterrent, while the information gained was often confused, summary and patchy.

The government probably did not much care about the superficial aims of the terror – the identification and disarming of rebels – because its real purpose was to provoke rather than deter. Edward Cooke, the Under Secretary in the English administration responsible for intelligence, welcomed the prospect of open rebellion: it is 'really the salvation of the country. If you look to the accounts that 200,000 are sworn in a conspiracy, how would that conspiracy be cleared without a burst?' Other influential figures in the government echoed his view. Cooke was very aware of the oaths that had been sworn and conspiracies created because he had been active in setting up a network of informers who had penetrated the organization of the United Irishmen very deeply. He knew that plans for a rebellion in May were brewing and the identity of its leadership.

Cooke could hardly fail to recognize at least one prominent United Irishman. Much the most attractive and powerful military figurehead in the movement was Lord Edward Fitzgerald, the youngest son of the Duke of Leinster. He had become entranced by the idealism and the romance of the French Revolution. He married a Catholic, the daughter of Philippe Egalité, the Duke of Orléans – but nevertheless a French revolutionary leader. Fitzgerald must have felt great affinity with him. He cut his hair short in the French style, and like many in the 1790s with the same sympathies he was called a Croppy. Refusing to use his carriage, Fitzgerald walked everywhere in Dublin and was said to wear a red-white-and-blue cravat. For all the seeming affectation, he was a powerful figure. Trained as a professional soldier, with an understanding of logistics and personally very brave, his role in the plans of the United Irishmen was absolutely central – he was to lead the Rebellion as military commander. But on 19 May Fitzgerald was betrayed. His hiding place in Dublin was revealed to the government by an informer, and after a savage fight in which one man was killed and Fitzgerald badly wounded, he was taken and imprisoned. Other leaders were rounded up and it seemed as though the prospect of imminent insurrection had receded. Certain that attempts would be made to rescue Fitzgerald, the government set a secure guard right around Dublin and posted soldiers at key points in the city.

In fact, the rebellion did go ahead on the agreed date, but as the government kept prisoners in custody there were no incidents in Dublin and it was largely leaderless. The signal to United Irishmen all over the country was to be the interception of the mail coaches outbound from Dublin, and on the night of 23–4 May they were stopped. The Rebellion of 1798 had begun.

Although Dublin was quiet there were dozens of skirmishes in many parts of Ireland on the morning of 24 May. Bands of United Irishmen, most armed only with pikes or pitchforks, attacked garrisons and detachments of soldiers, but in almost every case they were heavily defeated. Some groups sustained hundreds of casualties. Military commanders had orders to take no prisoners, and when engagements took place in villages or other centres of population, the government forces indiscriminately killed civilians as well as rebels. At least half of all those who died were non-combatants. When 300 rebels attacked the town of Carlow, William Farrell recorded what happened:

> The soldiers opened on them a most tremendous fire of musketry. The rebels flew like frightened birds. Some forced in the doors of thatched cabins to hide themselves. The army advanced firing volley after volley till they came up to the cabins. They set every one of them on fire and all that were in them, men, women and children, innocent and guilty, even all burned together in one common mass. I knew one man myself, as peaceable and inoffensive a man as any in town, who ran out his bed in his shirt and an infant in his arms and was shot dead at his own door – for the orders given out were to spare no man that was not in his regimentals.

From the very outset the rebellion was sporadic, had no overall coordination, and pitched undisciplined, poorly armed rebels in battle against well-equipped troops who had at least some experience of soldiering. Only in Leinster did the rebels have some success. The United

Irishmen in the south-east had not been extensively penetrated by informers, partly due to luck. At a crucial meeting of all of the United Irish organization in Dublin, at which an informer was present and listening, the Leinster delegate failed to turn up because he had become unavoidably detained in a nearby public house. This gave Leinster the advantage of surprise.

Led by Father John Murphy of Boolavogue, a force of rebels ambushed government troops in Leinster and destroyed them. A young man called Myles Byrne took part in the rebellion; he eventually escaped to France to serve in the French army with Napoleon and at the end of a long life wrote his memoirs, which were published in 1863, a year after his death. Here is his description of the first victory of the rebels in open field at Oulart, ten miles north of Wexford:

> The King's troops were commanded by Colonel Foote and Major Lombard, and as soon as they came within about two muskets shot of the Insurgents they deployed and prepared for action, but became enraged when they saw the Insurgents retreating back to the top of the hill; however they followed quickly, knowing that the hill was completely surrounded by the several corps of yeomanry cavalry, and that it was impossible for the Insurgents to escape before they came in with them. Father John allowed the infantry to come within half musket shot of the ditch, and then a few men on each flank and in the centre stood up, at the sight of which the whole line of infantry fired a volley. Instantly Father John and all his men sallied out and attacked the soldiers, who were in the act of recharging their arms; and, although they made the best fight they could with their muskets and bayonets, they were soon overpowered and completely defeated by the pikemen, or, rather, by the men with pitchforks and other weapons; for very few had pikes at this battle on account of having given them up by the exhortations and advice of the priests.
>
> Of this formidable expedition, which was sent from Wexford, on the 27th of May, to exterminate the Insurgents, very few returned to bring the woeful tidings of their defeat, and the glorious victory obtained by the people over their cruel tyrants.

The rebels went on to capture the towns of Enniscorthy and Gorey, and after another surprise attack on government troops they took the city of Wexford. Against a background of almost total failure across the rest of Ireland, it was a stunning achievement. Clearly showing the influence of the French Revolution, the rebels declared a Republic of Wexford and appointed a Committee of Public Safety, with equal numbers of Protestants and Catholics serving on it.

Without any central direction and, it seems, any overall strategy in hand, the rebels hoped that continuing success would help to ignite support in the rest of Ireland. On 6 June the Wexford army attacked the town of New Ross. Straddling the border with Kilkenny, it was an important tactical target, and if the rebels could capture it then the south of Ireland might rise and join them. After some ferocious street fighting where the advantage ebbed and flowed, the government forces finally beat off the attack and held the town with heavy losses on either side. As it retreated, the Wexford army passed through the village of Scullabogue, where more than a hundred loyalist prisoners were held in a barn. In a rare atrocity on the rebel side, the barn was fired and all within, including some women and children, were asphyxiated or burned to death.

At exactly the same time the United Irishmen in Ulster rose in rebellion, but enjoyed little success and were quickly forced to give up any gains they had made. When the town of Ballymena was retaken without a fight, there was massive desertion and the leader of the Ulster rebels, Henry Joy McCracken, was forced to flee. With only ninety-seven men, he climbed Slemish, a volcanic plug east of Ballymena, which offered panoramic views of the countryside and any movement of government troops along the roads. Later, for greater safety, they moved on to another hill, Little Collin. There they received a letter from John Magill warning them that their whereabouts were known. Magill was a member of a company of veterans based in Carrickfergus commanded by Sergeant 'Fogy' Lee, and they were known as 'The Old Fogies'. McCracken knew that his chances of evading final capture were slim.

At Wexford, the government forces were also closing in, and on the bridge over the Slaney Estuary, the rebels committed another atrocity. Loyalist prisoners had their arms pinned and were surrounded by three or four pikemen. They stabbed the prisoners and hoisted them in the air to suffer dreadful deaths, impaled on the points of their weapons. Father Murphy led the Wexford army to Enniscorthy to establish a camp on Vinegar Hill, just to the north of the town. On 21 June they were almost completely surrounded by a massive government army and were raked by an intensive artillery bombardment, but many escaped through a gap in the encirclement, and marched to the north west. They made their way through the Wicklow Mountains and aimed to cross the River Boyne near Clonard. Loyalists had fortified Tyrrell House, which guarded the bridge, and even though only forty marksmen were faced by 2,500 rebels, they managed to hold out long enough to be relieved and to inflict many casualties. A young boy called Willie Doyle ran away after the battle and hid in a potato field until nightfall. In the immediate aftermath he was hidden and fed by local families, and when the rebellion ended he was given odd jobs by local farmers. Ultimately he married a local girl, and his descendants still live near Clonard.

Willie Doyle was lucky. As they marched through Meath the Wexford soldiers dwindled in number as they were attacked or made their escape. Many men were buried where they fell, laid in shallow graves known as Croppy Graves by local people. Some are still marked at the roadside with whitewashed stones but many have been lost, overgrown or moved.

While the insurgents marched and counter-marched in the south, Henry Joy McCracken was finally arrested after having been recognized near Belfast on 7 July. He had been hiding up on Cave Hill, the place where he and Wolfe Tone had sworn a brave oath in 1795. Taken into Belfast, tried and condemned to death, the last few days of McCracken's life were documented by his devoted sister, Mary:

> I took his arm and we walked together to the place of execution, where I was told that it was the General's orders that I should leave him. I peremptorily refused. Harry begged I would go. Clasping my hands around him (I did not weep till then) I said I could bear anything but leaving him. Three times he kissed me and entreated I would go; and looking round to recognize some friend to put me in charge of, he beckoned to a Mr Boyd, and said, 'He will take charge of you' ... and fearing any farther refusal would disturb the last moments of my dearest brother, I suffered myself to be led away.

Wolfe Tone was captured near Lough Swilly, and, on being denied a military execution by firing squad, he botched his suicide. He failed to sever his carotid artery and cut his windpipe instead, lingering for six days of agony before his death.

Perhaps the most poignant incident in the aftermath concerned someone whose part in the Rebellion of 1798 has remained entirely anonymous: the story of an ordinary man trying to find his way home. A priest from Portlaoise recalled a story told to him when he was young by an old man who was himself a boy in 1798:

> According to Father McCrea, the old man told him that ... a man called to his father's house asking for some food and a place to rest. The man was taken inside the house but, before entering, he left a sack, containing something, outside the door. The boy's curiosity got the better of him and he peeped inside the sack where he found the body of a boy.
>
> The man was a Wexfordman and had fought at the battle of Clonard together with his fourteen-year-old son. The boy had been killed there and the father said that he was carrying the body back to Wexford so that he could bury it with his own people. The man was travelling by night and resting by day.

While stories of incalculable sadness and great cruelty were pouring out of Ireland in the months after the Rebellion of 1798, the Celts of Scotland and Wales were becoming part of a quaint cultural landscape. While 30,000 Irish men, women, and children were being killed with inhuman savagery, the reading public of Britain was being entertained by stories of noble savages, Edward Williams was taking pebbles out of his pocket to lay out a stone circle inside which magical rituals could unfold, and Walter Scott was dreaming at Abbotsford of mist-shrouded glens and Jacobite heroes. By 1798 a fundamental disconnection had taken place between Celtic Britain and Ireland, which was compounded by the appearance of regiments of Scottish, Manx and Welsh fencibles to deal with the rebellion. Just as many Scots had fought on the government side at Culloden in 1746, they attacked Gaelic-speaking rebels in Ireland with great ferocity. Two of the most notorious groups were the Manx Fencibles and a Welsh regiment who awarded themselves the unconsciously ironic title of the 'Ancient Britons'.

In essence, what had taken place between the end of Owain Glyn Dwr's rising in 1415 and 1800 was the invention of Britain; and England had started to acquire her empire, beginning with Wales, Ireland and Scotland. After the Union of the Parliaments in 1707 and the intellectual exertions of the Edinburgh Enlightenment, Scotland had become nominally north Britain, but was in reality north England. Despite the unfortunate Jacobite episode in 1745, that process of assimilation with England gathered pace throughout the eighteenth century. Scotland emphasized her Englishness and downplayed her Gaelic origins and character, consigning them to an old-fashioned and increasingly romantic supporting role, and almost entirely forgot her pre-medieval Old Welsh-speaking kingdoms. Wales, on the other hand, had in essence become an integral part of England after 1415 and the memory of distant and often imaginary glories from the ancient British past offered a little harmless consolation.

A century of wars between England and Catholic France had, to some extent, galvanized Protestant Britain into a closer union, and after the conclusion of the Seven Years War in 1763 Britain won an enormous empire which offered apparently limitless opportunities for English, Welsh and Scottish businessmen, manufacturers and colonists. When Britain acquired Canada, large tracts of India, much of the West Indies and parts of West Africa from the French, as well as Manila and parts of the East Indies from the Spanish, there were compelling reasons to adopt the new badge of Britishness and forget the old labels and the old languages.

Ireland fell outside much of this. Ancient links were forgotten by the British Celts, and Britain treated her more and more like just another troublesome colony peopled by truculent natives, which happened to be near at hand. More than that, Ireland was a largely Catholic nation whose capacity for treachery had been clearly demonstrated by the attempted French landing at Bantry Bay in 1796.

This is not to insist that the imperial project sundered old Celtic alliances and shared political ambitions. These scarcely existed at any point in history. Rather, the eighteenth and early nineteenth centuries saw Celtic Britain submerged, and in 1798 brutally suppressed, and the cultural experiences shared by Scotland, Wales, Man, Ireland and Cornwall were largely forgotten, or worse, trivialized.

FOURTEEN

The Revenge of the Disnamed

THE STORY OF CLAN GREGOR is a mirror to the modern story of Gaelic Scotland, and perhaps a guide to its eventual fate. With its turns of savagery, romance, excess, brio and futility, it epitomizes what happened to Celtic Britain in the eighteenth and nineteenth centuries, and helps to explain why it is hard to see this clearly. The MacGregor clan badge carries a grand motto, ''S Rioghall Mo Dhream', which means 'My Race is Royal' and refers to a traditional claim of descent from Griogair, the third son of Alpin, father of Kenneth macAlpin, King of Alba. While this sounds unlikely, it was the source of a powerful sense of self-worth, even arrogance, which informed the actions of MacGregors and never left them.

In the medieval period Clan Gregor held three glens at the head of Loch Awe in Argyll. Glenstrae, Glen Orchy and Glen Lochy all eventually fell into the area of influence of the powerful and ambitious Clan Campbell. Anxious to gain territory and to please whoever wore the Scottish crown, the Campbells fulfilled both aims by attacking the hapless MacGregors, who had taken to cattle rustling in a big way, thereby providing a justifying excuse for Campbell expansionism. Finally, the clan lost almost all of its lands and was forced to live almost exclusively on the proceeds of crime. Like their fellow cattle thieves in the Borders, they operated protection rackets, and, living in the southern Highlands, were handily placed to raid the fertile flatlands of eastern Perthshire, Angus and Stirling.

In 1604, the quintessential enemy of the Gael, James VI and I, intervened decisively, and enacted a remarkable piece of legislation designed to curb the lawlessness of the so-called royal race of Alpin. In essence he deprived the MacGregors of the use of their name. It was to be 'altogether abolished'. By making it a crime to be called MacGregor, the King attempted to dissolve the identity of the clan and make it difficult for its members to act in concert. Once again James I showed how well he understood Gaelic Scotland, because through this simple device he almost succeeded in wiping Clan Gregor off the historical record. Even though the new legislation made it legal for anyone to hunt and kill a MacGregor without recrimination, some still refused to renounce their name. Without it, they were nothing and they preferred to suffer death. The chief of the clan, Alasdair MacGregor, was brought to the Mercat Cross in Edinburgh's High Street with five of his leading men and all of them were hanged for the crime of bearing a surname. Clan Gregor scattered. Some took to the hills as outlaws, while others adopted pseudonyms such as Murray, Grant and even Campbell.

Many MacGregors settled in Aberdeenshire and used the abbreviated form Gregory. In the seventeenth century this branch of the disnamed clan founded an extraordinary dynasty of an entirely different and unexpected sort. Best known was James Gregory, who became a professor of mathematics at both St Andrews and Edinburgh Universities. He was immensely talented: he produced the first proof for the fundamental theory of calculus, and created series expressions for trigonometric functions, a new, abstract and sophisticated mathematical language. If the technology of the day had been equal to his theories, he could have invented the most advanced reflecting telescope to date. Isaac Newton was greatly influenced by James Gregory and adapted much of his work, but retained most of the intellectual credit. Dying at the early age of thirty-seven, Gregory was a largely unsung scientific and mathematical pioneer. His older brother, David Gregory, was also intellectually talented and invented a cannon which was much superior to any other contemporary artillery, but once again Isaac Newton took a hand and ordered the model for it to be destroyed. It is said, somewhat implausibly, that he was horrified by its destructive potential. David Gregory also had other talents and fathered no less than thirty-two children. His enormous extended family were professors and regents at Scottish universities for almost two centuries. There were Gregorys at Edinburgh, Aberdeen, St Andrews and even Cambridge and Padua until the late nineteenth century.

Because James I disnamed the MacGregors, few have recognized the close connection between the cattle rustlers of Glenstrae and one of the inventors of calculus, or realized that if the clan had kept their name the Gregory dynasty might never have flowered. At the period when Lowland abuse of Gaelic Scotland as chronically barbarous and dis-ordered was at its height, a substantial group of Gaels under assumed names had made their way out of the Highlands and into the centre of European intellectual life – the difference between the two realms was cultural, not genetic.

While his distant cousins were teaching at St Andrews University, the most famous MacGregor of them all was becoming skilled at the use of the two-handed broadsword, the claymore. His long arms and great strength made him a notable swordsman. Rob Ruadh MacGregor got the nickname because he had red hair, and in English he became simply Rob Roy. No portrait of him was ever painted from the life, although several have been wrongly assumed to be of him. One hangs in the Glasgow Art Gallery at Kelvingrove, but it is probably a likeness of another Highlander. Much more reliable are the memories of the elderly people who knew Rob Roy when they were children who gave verbal descriptions of him to Sir Walter Scott. Most of them are in agreement: Rob was around 5 foot 6 inches tall – slightly above average height for the times; he had very broad shoulders and thickly muscled legs which were tufted with red hair; but his most striking physical characteristic was the length of his arms. Highlanders who spoke to Walter Scott said, with a wink, that he could pull up his stockings without bending down. With no Gaelic and less common sense, Scott wrote down what the old men said, and it gained something in the translation and passed into history as an undisputed fact. In reality, Rob's arms were so long and powerful that no-one could take anything from him without help, and it was said that he could hold down a stag by the horns, although why he would want to do such a dangerous thing remains a mystery. Rob Roy's hair and beard turned from red to auburn in later life, and his manner was said always to be direct and open. However, certain facts about Rob fit none of the stereotypes of swashbuckling legend and noble savages. Not only could he read and write fluently in Gaelic and English, but some of his letters actually survive. He was also a subscriber to a limited edition of Bishop Keith's *History of the Scottish Reformation*, and had a wide appreciation of literature. His elder brother went to Glasgow

University and Rob probably followed him to matriculate in the years 1683–5.

Immortalized first by Walter Scott in his novel of 1817, and then much later, twice by Hollywood, first in the shape of the English actor Richard Todd and then the Irishman Liam Neeson, Rob Roy became simply the most famous Highlander in the world. Walter Scott awarded Rob a romantic supporting role in a novel which, although it bears his name, is really about an Englishman called Francis Osbaldistone. Since the story also includes Bailie Nicol Jarvie, one of Scott's most brilliant creations, the story of Rob is implicitly understood by readers rather than clearly set out. His function was to move the plot along by fighting with people. One of the highlights of the novel is Rob Roy's dramatic clash with government troops after the Jacobite rebellion of 1715 and his subsequent dispatch of the dastardly Rashleigh, Francis Osbaldistone's greatest enemy. Walter Scott draws Rob almost exclusively as a noble warrior and man of action, which is why the story appealed so much to film-makers. The Richard Todd version downplays the nobility and introduces a twinkle with a giveaway title. The film was called *Rob Roy – the Highland Rogue* and that twinkle was probably the only authentic touch of the production. By contrast, Liam Neeson had the luxury of an intelligent screenplay written by a Scot, Alan Sharp, and it far more clearly reflects the real story of MacGregor. Unusually for a historical piece, the film had the confidence to rely not on confected romance but on the facts, considering them sufficiently interesting to hold an audience.

Rob Roy first came to the notice of contemporaries when he fought at the battle of Killiecrankie near Pitlochry under Viscount Dundee in 1689 in the first Jacobite rebellion in support of James II. Rob was only eighteen when Dundee deployed his clansmen on the crest of a hill to the west of the government troops. Both armies eyed each other uneasily for two hours, but despite artillery fire the Highlanders made no move and were ordered to sit on their shields. Dundee was waiting for the westering sun to move behind his men so that when they finally charged, the government army would be blinded. The tactic worked well, and although Dundee was killed as he tore down the hill with his Highlanders, Rob Roy and his comrades tasted victory.

In 1694 the ban on the name MacGregor was renewed and Rob began to call himself Campbell. He bought land at Craigroyston and at

Inversnaid, on the eastern shore of Loch Lomond. When he rented grazing in the beautiful glen of Balquhidder in Perthshire, he had become a prosperous cattle dealer. Anxious to expand his operations, he raised £1,000 in 1711 from the Duke of Montrose and others to buy and collect new herds, but his chief drover, a MacDonald, absconded with all of the letters of credit. Rob Roy was blamed, gazetted as an outlaw and evicted from his house at Craigroyston. He then had no option but to begin a life of cattle rustling and lawlessness.

Rob Roy raised the remnants of Clan Gregor for the Jacobite cause in 1715 but seems to have used it mainly as an excuse for raiding on his own account. He was at the battle of Sheriffmuir with his clan but he seems to have taken no active part in the fighting, although he was later convicted in absentia of treason. Despite being declared an outlaw, losing his name and becoming a traitor, Rob still managed to pursue a busy and unhindered life in the southern Highlands, raising cattle and renting property. By 1725 he had submitted to the English commander, General Wade, and having been converted to Catholicism, he died in his bed in 1734 at Inverlochlarig at the head of the Glen of Balquhidder. He was sixty-three.

Rob Roy's grave is clearly marked in the kirkyard at Balquhidder township and each year tens of thousands of visitors come to see it – it is almost a shrine. Close to Stirling Castle in 1975 a bronze sculpture of Rob was unveiled. The likeness is doubtful but the words on the plaque beneath are unequivocal:

> My foot is on my native heath
> And my name is Rob Roy MacGregor

After Rob's death, stories of his exploits quickly took on the stature of legend. He twice escaped imprisonment: when captured near Stirling, he was mounted on a pony tied behind one of his captors, but while crossing the River Forth at the Fords of Frew he cut the belt that held him and plunged into the river to swim and scramble to freedom. These adventures are partly what immortalized Rob Roy and persuade people to make the journey to Balquhidder to see the place where he is buried, but he was in reality a very minor figure whose exploits were unremarkable – he is venerated more due to his role in fiction than his role in history. Not surprisingly, many of the complexities of history have been omitted from his story, but nevertheless the overall impression left by his legend is very instructive. Living amid the heather, outside the law, appearing from nowhere and then retreating into invisibility, he comes from a half-forgotten pantheon of Celtic warrior-heroes rather than from the politics of eighteenth-century Scotland. He has a powerful sense of menacing marginality: he is a figure from the edges of history and not someone from a major, sophisticated culture.

This was the era when Highlanders were fading fast into myth-history and Gaelic Scotland – Alba – was becoming more a state of mind and less a real place. And after 1745 the energy of Alba began to dissipate fast. A curious episode which occurred only two years before the last Jacobite Rebellion demonstrates that the Scottish Gaels were beginning to be seen like reservation Indians. In 1743 George II decided that he wanted to see for himself something of the martial prowess of the savage Highland clans which so worried his generals. After making enquiries, royal agents in Scotland summoned Gregor Drummond and his cousin James to Perth, where they were bundled into a stagecoach and driven south to London under military escort. Forced to adopt the surname of Drummond by the proscription of the name MacGregor, Gregor the Beautiful, Griogair Boidheach, was a tall, extremely good-looking and proud young man considered by the chiefs and leading men of the southern clans to be a great warrior. His cousin James came nearest to matching him in martial contests at the annual gatherings in the Perthshire glens.

At St James Palace they were taken by a company of mitred redcoats to an inner courtyard, and below the windows of the royal apartments each was first given a claymore. As George II looked down from a safe distance the young Highlanders wielded the six-foot double-handed broadswords in a dazzling display of strength and swordsmanship. Surrounded by nervous government soldiers, Gregor and James exchanged the claymores for Lochaber axes, which they swung and threw with breath-taking skill.

Impressed, George II invited the young warriors up to his staterooms, under heavy guard, where he complimented them on their skill and then gave each a golden guinea. Partly because all three shared a poor grasp of English, but mainly because Gregor and James fought for honour and not for money, they were puzzled and offended at the King's behaviour. When they left the royal presence they showed their disgust at such disrespect and gave the golden guineas to the amazed flunkeys who opened the stateroom doors for them.

The eldest son of Rob Roy, James Mor, inherited the MacGregor good looks and fiery temperament, and also a substantial measure of Celtic eloquence. With his younger brother, Robin Og, he was accused of murdering one of the MacLaren clan, cattle rustling and breaking out of prison, but so skilfully did he conduct his defence, in what must have been his second language, at the Court of Session in Edinburgh that the charges were found not proven.

James Mor was captain of the MacGregor regiment at Culloden where he fought beside his cousin Gregor the Beautiful. After escaping another conviction in 1752, this time for assisting in the abduction of a wealthy and handsome widow, Jean Key, who later married Robin Og of her own free will, James arrived in Paris as an outlawed exile. There he tried to seize the Jacobite agent, Alan Breck Stewart, in order to exchange him for a pardon from the British parliament, but ultimately he died in exile and in great poverty.

In 1774, the proscription of the name MacGregor was finally lifted. Twelve years later, on Christmas Eve 1786, Gregor MacGregor was born in Queen Street in Edinburgh. Grandson of Gregor the Beautiful, he was one of the first male children to bear his right name for 175 years. From his Gaelic-speaking nurse he imbibed the history of his clan – the earliest known Gaelic song is '*Grioghal Cridhe*', 'The Heart of Gregor' – and from his father he heard of the genocide begun by Butcher Cumberland after Culloden and continued by greedy landlords, many of them chiefs absent in London or Edinburgh, who were clearing the Highlanders off their ancient territory to make way for the great sheep ranches of the early nineteenth century. By the time Gregor reached manhood, he could recite his genealogy. He knew who he was.

When Napoleon Bonaparte imposed his brother Joseph on the Spanish throne and closed the Iberian ports to British trade, an expeditionary force was despatched under the command of Sir Arthur Wellesley, later to become the Duke of Wellington. At its core were the infamous Highland Companies, men recruited to fight in foreign wars after the Disarming Act of 1746, intended to pacify the Highlands after the Jacobite Rebellion. William Pitt promoted this process to George II, 'I sought for merit wherever it was to be found ... and I found it in the mountains of the north. I called it forth and drew it into your service, an hardy and intrepid race of men.' General James Wolfe, who fought against the Highlanders at Culloden and with them at the Heights of Abraham at Quebec, had a more brutal assessment which betrays the reality of contemporary English thinking about Gaelic Scotland: 'They are hardy, intrepid, accustomed to rough country and no great loss if they fall. How can you better employ a secret enemy than by making his end conducive to the common good?'

Wolfe met his own end at the Heights of Abraham after the Highlanders had charged the French and rescued the battle for him. How far he thought that conducive to the common good is not recorded. In this calculated way the military sting was drawn from the clans and their warriors' blood was given to the all-consuming drive for Empire and the domination of Europe. Most feared were Am Freiceadan Dubh, the infantry companies combined into the Black Watch, wearers of the 'government tartan' and winners of 172 battle honours, more than any other regiment of foot.

Like his ancestors, Gregor MacGregor was a martial man, and at the precocious age of twenty he gained the King's commission in the 57th Regiment of Foot. When Wellington embarked for the Peninsula, Gregor was with him. In the bitter winter of 1810–11 the French attempted to drive the British off the Iberian Peninsula and into the sea, but they were thwarted by the lines of Torres Vedras forty miles north of Lisbon. From a network of forts, ditches, walls and gun emplacements, Wellington sent sallies out to harry the army of Marshall Massena, eventually forcing it into a ragged retreat back across the Pyrenees. Chief amongst the tormentors of the French were the companies of the 57th Foot, whose ferocious charges scattered even the most hardened veterans of Napoleon's campaigns. Amongst the reckless and battle-hard clansmen one young officer distinguished himself again and again for bravery. Gregor MacGregor was ultimately summoned to the presence of the King of Spain and Wellington where, to his astonishment, he was knighted.

A glittering military career beckoned: the Napoleonic War was to rumble on across Europe for another four years and opportunities for advancement would come quickly to Sir Gregor. But he refused them, turning his attention and his ambition to the other side of the world. The agents of Simon Bolivar, the great liberator of Latin America, were active amongst European armies, recruiting experienced men to fight in the wars of independence which were just beginning. The enfeeblement of Spain and Portugal and the engulfing war in Europe had encouraged Bolivar, San Martin and the other revolutionary leaders to act quickly. They needed men like Sir Gregor MacGregor, and by 1811 he was in Caracas.

At first the Creole forces he commanded were defeated by the Spanish and Gregor suffered personal as well as military setbacks: in the great earthquake of 1811 he lost all he possessed, but slowly the tide turned and the liberation of the northern part of South America gradually began to succeed. Under Bolivar and San Martin, Gregor was steadily promoted until in 1816 he became Commandant General of the Cavalry in the Army of the Republic of Venezuela. He was invested with the new Order of Liberators and he married Bolivar's niece, the beautiful Doña Josefa.

The New World had made Gregor MacGregor: by the age of twenty-seven he was one of the most powerful men in Latin America; feted, decorated and with expectations of wealth, he had succeeded brilliantly. And yet his soul was not requited. Instead of building on his reputation as a successful young general and remaining in South America, where further opportunities would doubtless have presented themselves, Gregor's restless ambition led him elsewhere. Having fought hard for the sake of others, for their land and freedom, Gregor wanted something for himself. He knew that in Scotland his kinsmen were being cleared off their ancient *duthchas* by greedy landlords. Burned out of their houses and herded down to the rocky seashore to scrape an impossible living, many took the coffin ships to the Americas, Canada and the newly independent USA. Some even found their way to Latin America.

In 1816 Gregor MacGregor was in Baltimore and Philadelphia, where he met representatives from the governments of Mexico, Venezuela, Rio de la Plata (Argentina) and Nuevo Granada (Colombia). After what must have been a complicated, as well as speculative, negotiation, a document was finally signed on 31 March 1817 that gave Gregor a commission to attack and capture Amelia Island from the Spanish. It lay off the coast of Florida and was thought to be a strategically important springboard for a successful invasion of both East and West Florida, as they were then known. Having acquired legitimacy through his paper commission, MacGregor set about organizing his expedition. One of his first acts was a portent of things to come. At Charleston in South Carolina he began to advertise the sale of land in Florida, at one dollar an acre, even though he had not yet conquered it. It seemed like a bargain to some, and 30,000 acres were sold. Gregor also received an offer of $150,000 to finance his expedition. America must have seemed like the land of unlimited opportunity.

In the event Gregor needed something money could not buy and which he demonstrated again and again that he had in abundance – sheer, brazen cheek, even arrogance. On 29 June 1817 his ship dropped anchor, with Doña Josefa on board, and he and seventy-three men rowed to the coast of Amelia Island and quietly slipped ashore. Unfortunately more than fifty of his mercenaries deserted immediately, but with only twenty soldiers at his back Gregor convinced the commander of the strongly defended Spanish forts that he was both out-numbered and out-gunned. With barely a shot fired, Gregor accepted the surrender and hoisted the flag of what he called the 'Green Cross Republic' on Amelia Island.

However, promised reinforcements from New York and Charleston failed to arrive and immediate plans for the invasion of Florida were set aside. Instead, he created a miniature state. Styling himself 'Citizen Gregor MacGregor, Brigadier-General', he printed currency and organized a market for pirates. Captured booty was brought in by ship and in return for a commission of 16.5 per cent (plus costs), it could be sold to unscrupulous merchants under the doubtful auspices of the government of Amelia Island. To add some much needed dignity and legitimacy, medals were struck to celebrate Gregor's victory, fourteen of which survive. On one side is a representation of the Green Cross flag and on the obverse is an adaptation of a famous Latin phrase: 'Amelia, I came, I saw, I conquered.' Gregor seems to have had a sense of humour.

The Amelia Island government also issued letters of marque, for a handsome fee, to pirates operating in the Caribbean. These were licences permitting the fitting out and arming of a ship so that it could attack cargo vessels deemed to be enemies of the issuing government. In the case of Amelia Island that could mean almost anyone, and the trade in letters of marque was brisk.

Gregor MacGregor had cordially informed the United States government that once the Floridas had been captured from the Spanish he was prepared to sell them at what he called 'a bonnie price'. Early State Department papers make it clear that Secretary Adams believed that overtures had also been made to the British government. Gregor was obviously planning to conduct a lucrative international auction, but when reinforcements from the Carolinas failed to appear and the Spanish counter-attacked, Gregor promptly sold Amelia Island on 10 September 1817 for $50,000 to a pirate, Luis Qury, who operated under letters of marque from the Mexican government.

Between 1817 and 1819 various schemes aimed at carving territory out of the crumbling Spanish empire came to nothing, but then an idea began to form in Gregor's mind. Gathering together a group of exiled Highlanders and some Creoles from Caracas, he and Donna Josefa persuaded the revolutionary government to co-fund an expedition which would carry the war against Spain into the Caribbean. Gregor knew that Spanish control of Central America had collapsed, and in particular that the Captaincy General of Guatemala was in chaos. With only two small ships and 150 men he and his wife sailed out of Caracas harbour with a commission to liberate the Creole and Indian populations from colonial rule. In reality, however, Gregor was looking to found a new nation with himself at its head. He was the man who would be king.

At first he enjoyed tremendous success. With his small force he captured Portobelo, an important trading post on the Panama isthmus which had once fallen to Sir Francis Drake, but since it was one of the best defended fortresses on the Spanish Main, Bolivar's agents followed Gregor and unwittingly frustrated his secret goal. Portobelo was simply too close to Venezuela for the comfort of either party, and he decided to sail on up the east coast of what is now Nicaragua. What came to be known as the Mosquito Coast stretches 500 miles north to the British colony of Belize. Between 1730 and 1786 a handful of Scottish logwood cutters had worked timber there, but under the terms of a treaty between Spain and Britain they were forced to quit their tiny settlement at the mouth of the Black River. When Gregor's ships dropped anchor, the jungle and mangrove swamp had obliterated all trace of the loggers' settlement. The Indians were still there, and after a dangerous moment or two Gregor finally made contact with Frederick Augustus George, King of the Miskito Indians who controlled the area and gave the coastline, and hence the insect, its infamous name.

On 29 April 1820, Gregor and the old man made a deal over a bottle of whisky. In return for some vague promises and a chestful of medals, a huge concession of territory was obtained. The Miskito King gave away around 70,000 square miles along the valley of the Black River, an area which became known as Poyais. MacGregor then sailed away to London to carry out his greatest coup, one of the most brilliant confidence tricks of the nineteenth century, and a stupendous act of revenge on the society that had humiliated Clan Gregor for more than two centuries.

The clan motto, 'Royal is my Race', was more than a historical curiosity to Gregor MacGregor. It came from an ancient belief that he and his kinsmen were descended from Griogair, third son of Alpin and brother of the great King Kenneth MacAlpin, an early overlord of both Picts and Scots. 'The Seed of Scotland', in Gaelic '*Siol na h'Albainn*', was, in Gregor's mind, more than simply a metathetical version of '*Siol na h'Alpin*'. He believed that he was descended from royalty, even if those kings had reigned more than a millennium before. This absolute belief made Gregor's later claims sound both convincing and seductive. When he landed in London as His Serene Highness Gregor I Prince of Poyais, with the charming Princess Josefa at his side, he carried off the role to the manner born.

Old, ill and daft, George III had died early in 1820 a few months before the Poyaisan ships arrived. The new political atmosphere was promising: George IV and his courtiers had painted a picture of optimism and growth; an outward-looking Britain, fresh from crushing victory over Napoleon was anxious to exploit and augment its already vast Empire. George IV immediately agreed to receive the exotic Prince Gregor and accept his credentials in the staterooms of St James Palace where his grandfather had insulted Gregor's grandfather with a golden guinea. It was fitting that that the usurper House of Hanover should greet a MacGregor prince as an equal – and astonishing. It was exactly the start that Gregor needed.

With legitimacy conferred so easily, Gregor then began to enact the details of his carefully worked out plan. A Poyais Loan was quickly floated on the London Stock Exchange and land offices were set up in London and Edinburgh for the purpose of selling off 'baronial estates' to prospective settlers, none of whom had any idea what conditions were really like on the Mosquito Coast.

Gregor hit on the idea of issuing banknotes and exchanging them for British currency held by those settlers who planned to take up land grants in Poyais. Soon, presses in Edinburgh were busy printing Poyais currency on which was inscribed in Gaelic the boast of the Seed of Alpin, ''S Rioghal mo Dhream'. They were the first and only Gaelic banknotes in history, and it is a sad but oddly appropriate reflection that from the moment the ink was dry they were absolutely worthless. Prince Gregor's Chargé d'Affaires prepared a brochure on Poyais with remarkable speed in order to satisfy the curiosity of a somewhat mystified public, and coloured engravings were sold displaying the wonders of Prince Gregor's capital city. It lay on a river, near its mouth on the Caribbean coast, and contained bridges and domes, streets lined with trees and an opera house. The brochure explained that the country was rich in timber – redwood, cedar and mahogany – while the plains groaned beneath herds of cattle, crops and all manner of fruit trees. Most seductive of all were those passages hinting at the existence of 'very many gold mines'.

MacGregor's agents were mesmerized not only with the possibility of becoming exceedingly rich, but also with the medals and titles that he handed out. Throughout the summer of 1822 the Poyais Scheme was hyped to fever pitch by these men, even to the extent of handing out in the streets copies of a promotional song composed by a gullible Glasgow clerk who had been promised 'a cornetcy of lancers' in the Poyaisan army. A book entitled *Sketch of the Mosquito Shore, Including the Territory of Poyais*, was written by Thomas Strangeways, who took the title 'Captain 1st Native Poyer Regiment, and Aid-de-Camp [sic]'. It was published in 1822, and extolled in glowing prose the virtues and limitless opportunities to be found in the Poyais territory. Strangeways presented such an exaggerated picture of the Miskito coast's potential for settlement that one cynical reviewer wrote that Poyais seemed to be a paradise, 'where all manner of grain grows without sowing, and the most delicious fruits without planting; where cows and horses support themselves, and where ... roasted pigs run about with forks in their backs, crying "come, eat me!"' Despite the cynicism, Gregor's scheme raised the colossal sum of £200,000 on the London Stock Exchange. When he and Princess Josefa favoured Edinburgh with a visit they had their portrait painted, while the douce and greedy burghers hastened to pledge over £70,000 of good Scottish currency for Poyaisan banknotes.

By now more than half believing the mirage which he had single-handedly created, Gregor opened legations in Europe's capital cities. He sent ambassadors to London, Paris and Madrid and had plans to open more in Amsterdam and Vienna. The project had begun to get out of hand, and would soon take on altogether darker tone. The practical and human consequences of Gregor's confidence trickery quickly unfolded as hundreds of colonists queued up to book their passages to 'the emerald shores' of Poyais, and on 10 December 1822 the first party of sixty men and women set sail from Gravesend on the *Honduras Packet*. A month later they were followed by the *Kinnersley Castle*, which departed from Leith with 160 emigrants on board.

This should have been Gregor's cue to gather up his gains and make himself scarce, but instead he continued to live in style and state in London. Perhaps he wanted people to know that he had deceived them, and exploited their avarice, and maybe, most of all, he wanted to display his contempt. There is an unmissable swagger and Celtic arrogance in all that Gregor did.

Few of those on board the *Honduras Packet* could have anticipated the sight that would greet them as they dropped anchor off the Mosquito Coast. There was of course no town at the mouth of the Black River, no fields of sugar cane, no signs of settlers waiting to greet them and no opera house. As far as the eye could see there was only mangrove swamp and dense tropical forest.

Undaunted, still believing, still fuelled by greedy dreams, the emigrants began to offload provisions and hardware under the direction of Colonel Hector Hall, who had been appointed Governor by MacGregor, but the disembarkation started very badly. As barrels of supplies were unloaded, they were rolled through the salt water and their contents spoiled. Then total disaster struck when a sudden storm blew the *Honduras Packet* off its inshore anchorage out to sea with three quarters of the provisions still on board. The captain rode out the storm and then set sail eastwards, away from Poyais and the stranded settlers, to sell the remainder of the settlers' property and supplies at his first port of call.

Those left on shore were now in a desperate situation. Colonel Hall decided that they should clear a patch of forest by the Black River and erect temporary shelters. Then they should try to manage as best they could and await the safe arrival of the *Kinnersley Castle* from Leith, a much larger ship with more people and more provisions on board. Matters deteriorated very quickly. Some of the settlers, unprepared for and unable to bear the intense heat and the endless misery caused by the insects, committed suicide. Others wandered off, completely unequipped, into the interior in search of gold mines. They were never seen again.

Weeks passed with no sighting of the second ship. Eventually, a desperate Colonel Hall set off on foot along the coast to get help from the Miskito King, who lived 100 miles to the east at Cape Gracias a Dios. When Frederick Augustus George heard that Gregor MacGregor had declared himself Prince of Poyais and was selling off tracts of the Miskito kingdom, he was enraged. He summarily nullified the grant and demanded that the settlers swear allegiance to him. The King returned with Colonel Hall to the Black River to find that the second ship had arrived, but once again the captain had made off with most of the provisions. Some of the Scots settlers tried to escape, and while most them were cut down by Frederick Augustus George's warriors, some made it to the British colony of Belize by canoe.

The Superintendent of the colony immediately sent a rescue party, one of whom later described what they found:

> Most of the people were lying on the ground under a few leaves and branches thrown across some stakes, which it would be a violation of truth to call houses. Many were in a state of ague and fever, and absolutely unable to crawl to the woods for the common offices of nature.

The Belize Superintendent was a Scotsman named John Young. He sent a devastating report to London.

The Poyaisan Disaster created uproar. A London bank rocked at the news from the Miskito Coast and the newspapers fulminated against Gregor MacGregor. He treated it all with a lofty disdain and instructed his Chargé d'Affaires to issue a strongly worded rebuttal which, surprisingly, was published without comment in *The Times*. However, as more reports filtered back and the truth behind the fancy banknotes became ever clearer, Gregor and Princess Josefa sensibly withdrew to their residence in Paris. Astonishingly, in 1825 a French expedition set out across the Atlantic for Poyais. Gregor had raised another massive sum on the French Bourse by issuing more banknotes: £300,000 this time, even more than in Edinburgh and London.

Again he made a tactical retreat, back across the Channel, but on this occasion matters caught up with him, and it appeared that he had overreached himself for he was flung in prison and made the subject of the vicious cartoonists of the day. But like his fellow clansman, Rob Roy, Gregor was not the sort of person a prison could hold for long, and through deception he extracted himself and fled again to France. After another brief period of captivity he emerged to find that his resources had dwindled alarmingly. When he completely ran out of money he simply submitted a memorandum to the government of Venezuela explaining his difficult circumstances. Mindful of all that Gregor had done in their recent struggle for independence, the Venezuelans welcomed him and his wife back with great ceremony and honour in 1839. He was granted a generous pension by a grateful nation. He died six years later, a much feted and honoured citizen of the country he had helped to liberate.

As Gregor MacGregor sat on the verandah of his villa, sipping a glass of rum punch, looking out over the warm and balmy Caribbean, he will have reflected on a remarkable life. Displaying a dazzling repertoire of Celtic characteristics – reckless courage, arrogance, eloquence and excess, he had risen like a rocket and fallen to earth in darkness. He achieved nothing lasting, and his story is almost entirely forgotten.

Although Gregor's career was founded on a series of sustained fictions – it appears that even his knighthood may have been an invention, as there is no mention of it in any heraldic records – it also rode on an even greater series of romantic illusions about Celtic Scotland, sustained by Walter Scott's novel *Rob Roy*. When Scott insisted that, on his pageant-like visit to Edinburgh, George IV be escorted by the MacGregor clan as his bodyguards, the outlaws whose name had been restored only forty years before, he forgot history entirely. In place of understanding, and political reality, he substituted colourful theatricality. Against that background of fantasy, it is perhaps no more than fitting that Gregor MacGregor's greatest achievement was not his part in the liberation of South America, but a brilliant confidence trick, the creation of another grand illusion.

Despite the human cost of his deceptions, it is difficult not to feel sorry, both for the waste of talent, energy and courage, and for the fact that, among the thousands more worthy and respectable achievers cast abroad from Celtic Britain, there was a general sense of great loss and dissipation. The nineteenth century saw millions running from Europe to the New World. Often leading the charge were many whose ancestors had raised their spears and broadswords against both the English and those who would be English.

Celtic Britain is harder to see now, because so much of it has long gone and is no longer British, because it is so clogged with the sticky fantasies of myth-history, and because it seems to have retreated back into the dream of things.

FIFTEEN

Beyond the Circle
of Firelight

KELPING IS A NEAR-FORGOTTEN INDUSTRY. Journalists attempting
to add some colour and context to the unexpected war for the Falkland
Islands in 1982 referred to the islanders as 'the kelpers'. They worked at
an industrial process involving the gathering and treatment of seaweed
and the extraction of chemicals from it. It seemed a suitably bleak and
windswept business for the place described by the American Secretary
of State, General Haig, as a pile of rocks in the South Atlantic.

The passing mention of kelping stirred bitter memories elsewhere.
Between 1780 and 1820 Scottish and Irish Gaels were driven off their
land and forced to live on the seashore – the more rocky and barren
the better – so that landlords could press them into labouring at the
lucrative business of kelping. After the defeat in 1746 at Culloden, many
Highland landlords began to replace crofting clansmen with *na caoraich
mora*, 'the big sheep'. These were Cheviots and Blackfaces, and huge
herds of them, sometimes accompanied by Border shepherds, were introduced over a short period. The Highlanders hated *na caoraich mora*
because they could easily see how much more money and how much
less trouble they would make for the landlords. 1792 was known as Am
Bliadhna na Caoraich, the Year of the Sheep, and as shepherds hefted
their flocks to the Highland hills, some were attacked by groups of
crofters. This made little or no difference: by 1800 there were 50,000
head of sheep in Inverness-shire alone, and by 1850, 600,000.

Landlords began to clear large numbers of their tenants off the land, and while the Cheviots and Blackface were herded up the fertile glens, the people were herded down to the infertile seashore. Kelp was promised as their salvation. While new houses were built on the coast and earth was brought down in baskets to establish beds in the machair and scrubland for growing potatoes and whatever else would survive in the wind, the gathering and processing of seaweed became a primitive but highly profitable business for landlords.

Kelp, or brown seaweed, contains several valuable chemicals such as sodium, potassium and magnesium, which were essential for the manufacture of glass, soap and other products. When European supplies of these chemicals were cut off by the Napoleonic Wars, the price of kelp rocketed to £22 a ton, and the pace of clearance in the Highland glens quickened.

The process of making kelp was simple but harsh. The best seaweed was known as red wrack, sometimes also called yellow, black and prickly tang. Collecting started in mid-November, when it was hoped that winter gales had loosened large quantities and driven it ashore onto the beaches. When the wrack was still attached to the rocks by its holdfasts, collectors had to wade out into the freezing water and cut it, sawing with toothed sickles, sometimes working with their hands under water for long periods. Gathered seaweed was dried on raised wooden steethes, and then it was burned. Kelp kilns were dug in the machair, or in the sandy scrub above the high-water mark and they were usually coffin-shaped ditches measuring 5 by 3 by 2½ feet deep: 24 tons of seaweed was needed to make 1 ton of ash. The fires burned for a long time and then had to be left for weeks before the lumps of chemical-rich ash could safely be lifted out. It was an exhausting and poorly paid business for the displaced crofters but very lucrative for the landlords. In the peak years of production between 15,000 and 20,000 tons of kelp left the Highlands at the end of the collecting season.

When the European wars concluded and normal trading conditions resumed, the price of processed kelp fell dramatically and the final clearance of people from the land entirely began to gather pace. Many families fled south to the cities of central Scotland, and, being nearest to the Highlands, Glasgow was a favoured destination. Urban folklore still remembers the arrival of the impoverished crofters, and the railway bridge over one of the main streets is called 'the Hielandman's Umbrella'.

For those who wanted to go further, some landlords provided assistance with a passage across the Atlantic, but others were utterly ruthless. Gordon of Cluny wanted to sell Barra to the government as a convict island and he drove 1,500 people off his land, whipping them onto the boats. When crofters from Lewis boarded too slowly on one ship, advice was sent on to the next point of embarkation 'to push them on without their luggage'. Even when what seemed like a safe passage to North America had been found, the crossing could be appalling. This extract is from the journal of one of a group of crofters cleared off the estates of the Duke of Sutherland:

> The old and the children could not stand the hardship of the voyage, every day one of more of our group was buried at sea. After tossing on the Atlantic for eleven weeks we came to the coast of Canada. Each day we had to pay for our food and as some of us had some money left, the Captain cruised up and down for three weeks before landing us penniless on the Canadian shore. We were taken by bullock wagon to Toronto. There we stayed in sheds put up for the emigrants. Smallpox was raging and carried off many who had survived the voyage. Then we were given an Indian guide, a sack of maize-meal, a sack of seed potatoes and a plough. We marched a hundred miles and were left in the middle of a forest to make our homes. We had to burn down the trees before we could plant the potatoes. For six months we had nothing to eat but maize-meal and water.

In the nineteenth century Celtic Britain lost enormous numbers of her people. The statistics are worth listing: 8 million left Ireland between 1801 and 1921; 18.5 million left Scotland between 1814 and 1914; many Manxmen and Welshmen left through Liverpool where, between 1815 and 1914, 15 million people from Britain and Northern Europe sailed to the USA and Canada. Only in Wales were matters different. The huge human needs of the rapid industrialization of the southern valleys meant that the population there more than doubled between 1801 and 1901, and it was second only to the USA as a destination for immigrants.

It is surprising that, even though there were no assisted passages, no protection from the British Empire and its colonial administration and initially many fewer Scots, Irish, Cornish or Manx communities to welcome them, an overwhelming majority preferred to go to the USA. Of the 18.5 million who left Scotland in the nineteenth century, 13 million went to America and most of the 8 million from Ireland did the same. The USA was the Land of the Free, and a place where the Celts of Britain could at last escape the domination of the English.

However, it is fruitless to believe that Celtic Britain is somehow living in exile in America and part of the cause of that country's immense flowering. The St Patrick's Day parades and the Highland Games at Grandfather Mountain are days out of place and time, and an opportunity to remember something whose roots have long since shrivelled. Those who left the Irish and Hebridean shore tended not to take much of their Gaelic culture with them to the New World. They were not inward-looking refugees. These men and women suffered privation, took brave decisions and risked everything not to become expatriates but to become Americans. For many Irish and British Celts the future lay not in hanging on to what little they had, but in helping to invent a new country. For many 'the dream of things' became an American dream, and what was left behind became mostly figments of wish-fulfilment and cliché: emerald and tartan lands lost in a mist of tragedy and heroes, quaintness and 'customs', big names, genealogical societies and little ruins by the seashore.

Confusingly, the reality of Celtic Britain does in fact contain all of those elements, and rather than straightforwardly segregating myth and history, this journey between Stornoway and Penzance has tried to avoid the summary dismissal of cliché and has attempted to understand what lies behind it. The best antidote to conventional 'wisdom' has been the business of travelling to places in Celtic Britain, and being open to what could be found or experienced there.

At Maughold Head, on the easternmost tip of the Isle of Man, there is a beautiful little church much loved by the villagers who live around it. The mountain of North Barrule sweeps up behind it, massive and stately, giving scale and casting a mighty shadow. Inside the church stands a medieval sandstone cross, powdery with age, showing the earliest example of the triskelon, the three-legged emblem of Man, while outside, sheltered by a dusty porch, are dozens of ancient stones. Some are complete Manx cross-slabs, while others are only fragments and the oldest, perhaps 1,500 years old, is an uncut stone with a simple cross scored on it. The churchyard rises up gently behind the church, towards the cliffs of Maughold Head, and in the far corner, hard by the retaining dry-stone wall, are the remains of an old Manx *keeil*. Only two or three courses of split slate stone mark out a small rectangle in the grass between the rows of modern headstones. The same word as the Irish place-name prefix *kil*, deriving from the Latin *cella* for a 'small room' or 'cell', *keeil* is the Manx Gaelic word for the earliest Christian churches on the island. Traces of hundreds of them can be seen almost everywhere. Against the corner of the *keeil* is an old well shaft with an iron grill bolted over it. Peering through the darkness, it is possible to see the glint of a few silver coins in the water at the bottom.

In the late evening the high summer sun makes Maughold churchyard glow in a warm yellow light, and across the broad bay below the headland the sea shimmers. But as soon as the bottom part of the sun dips below the horizon, the effect is startlingly immediate. As the yellow light departs the ground and climbs up the walls of the church, a grey-green gloaming rises behind it. On the bay the shadows begin racing seawards, and the glowering mass of North Barrule looms over the water. Maughold churchyard quickly becomes a place of shadows, and what was vibrant grows cold and lifeless. The outline of the *keeil* melts into the ground and the carving on the crosses in the porch needs fingers and hands to make it out.

Telling the stories of the losers in the War for Britain is like chasing the shadows at Maughold churchyard. What seems graphic and clear cut can quickly become blurred and near-impossible to catch. This is not a history punctuated by turning points, decisive battles and clear signposts, rather it is a series of overlapping processes: rising and falling, shining and fading or forgetting and remembering. Very little of this has left concrete, tangible remains, in the reassuring way of ruins, roads, old towns and the like. The boast of the Romans, '*Si monumentum requieris, circumspice,*' 'If you need a monument, look around yourself,' could never apply to Celtic Britain. There are no grand monuments to see, no Parthenon, no pyramids or Valley of the Kings, and no mighty castles, moated and crenellated, impose themselves. There are a few texts, a little reliable archaeology and a mountain of misconception about the history of Celtic Britain. The stories of Celtic England deserve far more than the small space that they have been allowed here, and even if it had been possible to include more, there are very few historians who accept that such a concept as Celtic England is either possible or appropriate, and there are even those who doubt the usefulness of applying the word Celtic to anything or anyone at all. Nevertheless, English identity is unquestionably part Celtic, just as Celtic identity is certainly part English. Most Britons have a Celtic influence at some stage in their immediate genealogy.

What banishes this overwrought academic anxiety about definition and terminology is a simple thing: a long journey. I have travelled south from Stornoway through all the Hebrides to Ulster, to Galloway, to the Isle of Man, southern and western Ireland, Wales and finally to Cornwall. I can report that there is such a place as Celtic Britain, that it shares a common culture, an intimately related history and strikingly similar geography, and also that its story can be found in these places. What is elusive or confusing in a library or in the labyrinth of the internet springs to life under the scrutiny of the naked eye and the tramping of the feet. It is in places, not always the obvious places, where the stories of Celtic Britain can be heard, whispered in the air and atmosphere of a place where there is sometimes nothing obvious to see at all.

The sea is different. Inscrutable, pitiless, silent and elemental, it leaves no trace, no memory of the people who crossed it, fished it and fought on it. It stands at the centre of the Sea Kingdoms, is ever present but never less than mysterious. No-one I met, at least no-one with any sense, claimed to know the sea intimately or even to have much affinity with it. On the day I drove down to the Isle of Whithorn, I blundered into the funeral of the young seamen of the *Solway Harvester*, lost off the Isle of Man in 2000. The official enquiries have produced no reason why the fishing boat went down with all hands, but many believe that it was rammed by a huge steel container floating half-submerged in the sea. A modern monster put there by careless men. The funeral dwarfed the village, the grief was silent and palpable, and even the tabloid photographers and journalists were kept back at a respectful distance by it. Beyond the rooftops, beyond the breakwater, stretching farther than can be imagined, was the ceaseless, mighty surge of the sea.

There can be no conclusions to the story of the Sea Kingdoms. It is in not a discrete narrative with easily recognizable limits and a clear, unifying narration. Best to offer an interim report, and a little advice on what to look for and where to find it.

Llanwnda, St David's, Wales

Although it appears in a Welsh Heritage pamphlet entitled 'Saints and Stones', Llanwnda is hard to find. Near Fishguard, where the car ferries load for a four-hour journey across the Irish Sea to Rosslare, the little church lies at the end of a maze of single-track roads on the headland to west of the port. As with many atmospheric places in the west of Britain, it is difficult to know where to start. There is little or no signage, nothing obviously central and a general air of detachment. A farmstead stands to the south of an open space where the road peters out into a grass track, and to the north there is a small grey church sat in an overgrown cemetery.

Llanwnda gets its name from St Gwyndaf, an early Breton holy man. His origins immediately bring to the fore its maritime background, for religious contact between the sea kingdoms was close and frequent. It would not have been unusual for a P-Celtic-speaking Breton to establish a *llan*, a sacred enclosure, in a place like this. The Welsh Heritage pamphlet notes that the church was heavily restored in 1881, but there are five inscribed stones incorporated into the exterior walls. One of them is very arresting. Simply known as 'the Llanwnda Stone', it is a slab carved in relief showing a head surrounded by three heavily incised borders and set on a pointed stone or stake. 'Saints and Stones' wants it to be a Christian artefact but it clearly recalls the early Celtic fascination with the head – for them it was the place where the soul resided and an object of great magical power. The eyes of the Llanwnda head are closed, which suggests the decapitated head of a dead man – something the Celts and their Druids collected with enthusiasm. Despite the description of it as an early representation of Christ, 'a head in the style of a pantocrater', there is little doubt that the church of Llanwnda has part of a Druid ghost fence built into the wall of the south transept.

St Gwyndaf is said to have had an altercation with St Aidan, which offers a tentative date for Christian settlement at Llanwnda of some time around 630 to 650. It confirms contact between Iona, Lindisfarne and the Welsh and Breton saints – even if it was not harmonious. As with many of the nursery-rhyme-style stories associated with Christian saints, there is a faintly daft episode where St Gwyndaf is supposed to have fallen off his horse when it spooked at a fish jumping in a nearby stream.

Unlikely though that may sound, the story makes some sense when the stream itself is found.

For in the centre of the open space at Llanwnda, very easy to miss, there is a small, Celtic holy well and a stream flowing from it. Bubbling out of the ground amongst bramble bushes, it has been built around in earlier times, because there are several overgrown cut stones arranged at the source. There were two old rags tied on to the bramble bushes when I came across it, and through the peaty water some coins could be seen. St Gwyndaf is said to have cursed the stream where the fish allegedly jumped, but he may simply have cursed the stream because it still attracted the pagan veneration of the people who lived near his new Christian *llan*.

Llanwnda was a sacred place for a long time before St Gwyndaf arrived from Brittany. To the south of the holy well, behind the farm, is Carreg Wastad. The name may mean 'the Watching Rock', and it commands panoramic views of the sea and the land on either side. Near the top of the rocky hill there is a dolmen. Prehistoric peoples made these megalithic tombs by raising a large and often very heavy flat stone off the ground and wedging a smaller stone underneath to keep it propped up and stable. The effect is strange. The dolmen at Llanwnda looks as though it is a door to the underworld which stands permanently ajar. And indeed, that may have been what the makers intended. The Celts believed that holy wells were portals to the Otherworld, and if they lifted their heads to look up the hill at Carreg Wastad, they may have seen another way in.

Llanwnda is unquestionably a sacred place and has been so for millennia. Sanctity, and not of a Christian sort – that seems as dormant at Llanwnda as in an empty city-centre church – still hovers in the air. Like other powerfully atmospheric Celtic sites, it feels literally otherworldly – somewhere one might easily slip through a crack in time.

Beyond the church there stands a house, perhaps the old rectory or vicarage, and some outbuildings. These last had been painted with large, brightly coloured flowers in the style of Sixties hippies, and a car has been parked next to them, which is covered with hundreds of small Dinky Toy cars that have somehow been attached to the bodywork. Between a telegraph pole and its wire guy rope, someone had constructed an elaborate string and twig sculpture of what might have been a human form, which looked as though it could have been made 2,000 years ago.

At the foot of Carreg Wastad is a cottage constructed partly from green corrugated iron sheets. Since it stood at the edge of the rocky hill, it seemed polite to ask permission to walk up to the dolmen. The afternoon sun shone brightly through a large window on several large women watching daytime television. A notice on the garden gate warned callers about large dogs, but when I knocked on the door the lady who answered could scarcely have been more polite. And yet the atmosphere around the little cottage felt decidedly otherworldly.

Llanwnda is not merely an interesting place, or a nice place to be, or a place where anything much is clear. In fact there is menace in the air, a sense of the smallness and insignificance of life, and most of all, a strong notion that the corporeal, temporal, tangible, observable life that we all basically agree on could be turned inside out in an instant. The old gods are close at Llanwnda.

Glendalough, Wicklow Mountains, Ireland

The porter at the Glendalough Hotel told me that the bar did not open for another half hour, 'Sure now, it won't take you long to wait half an hour.' I must have looked nonplussed. 'Why not go over the road and have a walk around the old churches?' he prompted. I asked if the precinct was open, unlike the bar. 'Now, when would God ever be deaf to the prayers of a poor sinner like yourself?' The old man smiled at me and went about his business.

Glendalough is deep in the Wicklow Mountains in the south-east of Ireland, far from what the Gaels call Abhainn Mor an t'Sluaigh, the Great River of People. More than a thousand years ago the simple monastic foundation of St Kevin had grown into what the Irish called a monastic city. There were three others as big at Kildare, Armagh and Clonmacnoise, and all four were centres for pilgrimage. The cemetery at Glendalough was, like Iona, thought to have a purifying soil and many wished to be buried there. In Gaelic the Irish called it *ruam*, a Celtic rendition of Rome, another holy city. When pilgrims arrived they must have thought Glendalough a beautiful place, with two lakes and a broad strath in a steep-sided glen, now patterned with mercifully irregular plantations of pine trees. There are some interesting monastic ruins and a complete pencil-shaped tenth-century tower reaching high into the mountain sky, but it is what happened out of doors at Glendalough, in the midst of God's creation, which catches the attention. The monastic city was a centre of manuscript copying, and for many of the monks the best light for their intricate work belonged to God: on fine days they worked outside their dark and windowless cells on boards resting across their knees. There is an Irish manuscript in the Swiss monastery of St Gall which was probably produced at Glendalough, and in the margin of one page there is a beautiful lyric poem which offers a tangible sense of what life was like for the monks in the monastic city in the mountains:

> Over me green branches hang
> A blackbird leads the loud song;
> Above my penlined booklet I hear a fluting bird-throng.
>
> The cuckoo pipes a clear call
> Its dun cloak hid in deep dell;
> Praise to God for this goodness
> That in woodland I write well.

The beauty of Glendalough and the sanctity of its founder brought many pilgrims into the mountains from as early as the ninth century and probably before that. A large part of the motivation for undertaking long and arduous journeys to shrines like St Kevin's, or St David's in Wales, was the need to serve a penance for sins committed. Not only was the idea of a list of penances appropriate to each category of sin originally an Irish idea, but the concept of a personal confessor also began its life in places like Glendalough. The early Christian church made the doing of penance a matter of public recognition by physically separating those who had sinned from the body of a religious community and forbidding them access to the holy sacraments until penance was completed. In Ireland the innovative use of a personal confessor changed this. It encouraged a frequent, and perhaps more open, confession of sins to someone called in Gaelic an *anmchara*, a 'soul friend'. Lists of penitentials were still consulted by a soul friend but the transactions between him or her and a sinner became private. Irish Christianity was very influential in shaping the habits and practices of the early European church, although, in the apparent remoteness of Glendalough, it is easy to forget that.

Because it was difficult to reach the monastic city, it remained unharmed by outside or malign influences for 800 years. The continuity of sanctity at Glendalough is striking, and it was only broken when the English attacked the monastery in 1398. There are few details of the raid itself but no doubt that the buildings suffered a good deal of damage.

When the English and others attacked Irish churches, they often had to break through a strange charm, something physically attached to the architecture, although more castles than churches had them stuck to their walls. These were little sculptures known as the Sheela na gig, and they were certainly pagan in origin. Very crudely carved, all of them show a naked female form with exaggerated breasts and often openly displayed and pulled apart pudenda. The term Sheela na gig might derive from the combination of a personal female name with the Gaelic *na gcioch*, meaning 'of the breasts'. They are a very surprising thing to find attached to the walls of churches and they witness a powerful continuity from the pagan past literally grafted onto Christianity.

The pilgrimages to Glendalough, called 'patterns' in Ireland, also took on some of the characteristics of Celtic festivals. They were widely seen as occasions for taking a good deal of strong drink as well as enjoying all sorts of other licence. The Victorian Catholic church became so alarmed at the drunkenness and debauchery of the Glendalough patterns that, in 1863, they were summarily cancelled. Pilgrimage continued nonetheless, and the power and attraction of St Kevin was not diminished. The Glendalough Hotel thrives on the pilgrimage business but keeps the consumption of strong drink indoors and on the premises. That is, when the bar is open.

Niarbyl Beach, Dalby, Isle of Man

The grassy heights above Niarbyl Beach are not particularly elevated, but on a bright day it is possible to see clear across the Irish Sea to the Mountains of Mourne in Northern Ireland, and north to the Galloway Hills. From South Barrule, the mountain dominating the south of the island, the low farmlands of Anglesey can be made out, and sometimes even Snowdon, rising mighty behind them, while from Maughold Head in the north the Cumbrian Fells are often visible. From Man – the Midway Island – the shores of five of the sea kingdoms can be seen, and this fact of geography makes an eloquent point: the Irish Sea was a Celtic lake until the Vikings sailed through the North Channel, and after their time passed the Lordship of the Isles and Man ruled these waves.

The views across the sea from the Isle of Man show a clear world picture. The merchant sailors, fishermen, holy men and adventurers who passed Niarbyl Beach understood this picture well – everyone who ventured on the Irish Sea understood where and in what direction the land lay. It was a world far more cosmopolitan than that of rural inland Britain, outside which very few stepped in the course of their entire lives. Even though the Celts of the west of Britain seemed to be pushed out to the margins, crushed up against the mountains and the sea, their horizons were huge and their world no small and incidental place.

The name Niarbyl refers to a spit of rocks reaching out into the sea from a headland sheltering a small beach. The rocks are submerged most of the time and are of concern only to sailors making safe passage by coasting from Peel in the middle of the west coast of Man down to Port Erin or Castletown in the south. The beach itself is not visible from landward and is reached by a steep path down from fields and pasture which give no hint of its existence. From the seaward side the spit of rock and the small headland it leads from give shelter from the wind and a shallow but safe haven. Because Niarbyl Beach is hidden but close to fertile and settled countryside, it was precisely the sort of place where Vikings chose to beach their boats and mount surprise raids.

On 5 July 2000 I watched a Viking dragon-ship come into Niarbyl. Out in the open sea the *dreki* was little more than a speck amongst the choppy waves. The swell was sufficient to hide the ship and its black sail completely before it bobbed back up again. Through binoculars I could see that the crew were rowing hard to bring their boat around into the waves bow first and not broadside. They were getting very wet. After what seemed to be only a short time they rounded Niarbyl Rocks and appeared in the calmer waters of the bay. It was an awesome sight: exactly what the terrified monks of Lindisfarne and Iona fled from and what lookouts on western headlands hoped never to see. The progress of the dragon-ship was silent, making no sound that was different from or could be heard above the wash of the waves, except when the steers-man asked for hard rowing at a quicker clip, and the sound of the wooden oars banging against the rowlocks beat across the water. With the steerboard carefully turning this way and that, and a man leaning out over the bow searching the water for submerged rocks, the dragon-ship glided closer and closer to the beach. Suddenly it looked huge, as its dragon-head prow slid quickly up the shoreline.

The oarsmen from Peel dress up as Vikings and do a great deal for charity, and also for fun. Their ethos is like that of a boisterous rugby team, but each of them has square shoulders and the biceps of a weight lifter. Last year they rowed forty-four miles across the Irish Sea to Ardglass in Ulster to raise cash for Manx charities. Sometimes the sea ran with them as the tide washed out, and sometimes against them. It took a whole day and most of a night to get to Ardglass, but when the men from Peel rowed into the harbour there was a huge crowd, a brass band and the local mayor waiting to greet them. Having pulled hard in a last flourish, they slumped breathless over the oars at the quayside to a terrific roar, and when they climbed up onto the jetty, everyone wanted to shake their hands. Apparently it was an agonizing round of congratulation, since each man's hands were badly calloused and bleeding. 'All we had to do was lift a glass of beer that night,' said one of the oarsmen, 'but a thousand years ago these boys rowed for days and then had to jump out of the boat and fight. Hard men, and brave.'

Glencoe, Highland Region, Scotland

Beside the road across Rannoch Moor, where it climbs up to an empty landscape of heather, bracken and moorland lochs and lochans that still looks inhospitable on a sunny summer's day, there is a sign in Gaelic. It reads *'Failte do'n Gaidhealtachd'*, 'Welcome to the Highlands'. Beyond the sign the road stretches on towards one of the most disconcerting and ineffably sad landscapes in Britain. At the head of Glencoe stands its massive mountains of Stob Dearg and Buachaille Etive Mor, while down to the right lie the solitary white buildings of the Kingshouse Hotel. For miles there seems to be nothing: it is a trackless wasteland of grey-green mountains and moorland – majestic but empty. Welcome to the Highlands.

As the road winds its way through narrow defiles, between the shoulders of the mountains, it is difficult to imagine how travellers negotiated the corkscrew paths and tracks on foot or ponies, particularly in the bad weather for which Glencoe is notorious. Eventually the mountains retreat, and straths and fields open out. There are some ruined crofts and modern houses, and, as the road comes within sight of the sea loch, a few buildings cluster at Glencoe village.

In February 1692 a massacre took place here. It was a deliberate and planned act of genocide designed to act as a deterrent to rebellion, and it was authorized along a clear chain of command, with the orders countersigned by King William of Orange himself. It is important to be precise about the origins of the Massacre of Glencoe, since centuries of government embarrassment at what occurred and its consequences intentionally obscured the truth. For example, the events of February 1692 have sometimes been presented as an episode in the long-running rivalry between Clan Donald and Clan Campbell. This is nonsense: Glencoe happened because the Edinburgh and London governments wanted it to happen.

After 1688 and the removal of James II, William and Mary's government was understandably anxious about the political stability of the Highland clans. All chiefs were required to swear and sign an oath of loyalty by 1 January 1692, and after consulting with the exiled King almost all complied. MacIan of Glencoe did not sign on time, but it was not for the want of trying. Through the depths of a bitter winter the old chief made his way to what is now Fort William to discover that he was in the wrong place. The commander of the garrison, Colonel Hill, was not empowered to administer the oath, and in any case MacIan should have gone to Inverary, a long way to the south. When he finally arrived, it turned out that the Sheriff was absent on holiday after the New Year celebrations. After a wait, MacIan did eventually sign the oath of loyalty, but it was not enough to save himself, his wife, his family and his clansmen.

The Master of Stair, John Dalrymple, was Secretary of State for Scotland and he decided that the lateness of the Glencoe MacDonalds' oath was pretext enough to make an example of them. On 1 February two companies of soldiers were billeted with the families who lived in the glen. They had not paid their taxes and were therefore liable for this sort of imposition. The commander, Robert Campbell of Glenlyon, had orders to secure both ends of the glen and pen in the MacDonalds and 'fall upon the rebels . . . and put all to the sword under seventy'. On the morning of 6 February the massacre began. MacIan, his wife and two of their sons had their throats cut, and in a short time thirty-eight men, women and children had been murdered. Many more slipped through the military cordon only to die of exposure in the snow-filled passes above the strath. There is more than a suspicion that some of the soldiers under Glenlyon's command had little stomach for the massacre and allowed people to get away.

The Massacre of Glencoe was not the first slaughter in Highland history, but it was probably the most cold-blooded and callous. It shows how profoundly Scotland had split into two places by the end of the seventeenth century, and how Highlanders were seen as dangerous sub-humans to be disposed of without remorse. It also marks how low the fortunes of Clan Donald had sunk. MacIan was a scion of the same family who had been Lords of the Isles and masters of an Atlantic principality.

High above the village where the massacre took place there are the three rocky buttresses of Bidean nam Bian, known as the Three Sisters. An opening in one of them is now called Ossian's Cave, after the alleged composer of James MacPherson's epic poem of ancient Celtic Highland heroes. It is accessible by a rock climb called Ossian's Ladder, and the whole area is very popular with rock-climbing enthusiasts.

St Keverne's, Cornwall

In 1999 John Angarrack wrote an angry book. Called *Breaking the Chains – Propaganda, Censorship, Deception and the Manipulation of Public Opinion in Cornwall*, it fulminates in a fine rage about the ignorance of Cornish language and history in Cornwall. Naturally, Angarrack has a good deal to say about the Cornish rebellions of the fifteenth and sixteenth centuries, and in particular about the leader in 1497, Michael Joseph, known as An Gof:

> On the 500th anniversary of the slaughter of our ancestors the people of Cornwall attempted to have placed in St Keverne village square (An Gof's home village) a statue to the memory of the fallen. Although many who had recently moved to the area were enthusiastic, a selection of brainwashed Cornish quislings, diehard Royal British Legion members and old-school Church of England types objected.

The memorial was ultimately erected, but, as John Angarrack bitterly complains, it sits halfway out of town near a bus stop. With only the faintest of memories of 500-year-old martyrs to call on, the cause of the Cornish can seem literally bloodless, and certainly marginal. Yet what Angarrack and those who support him want is simply an understanding that Cornwall is different from the rest of England, and for that difference to be recognized in civic society, education and local government. Lest his efforts, or those of the Cornish separatist group, Mebyon Kernow, the Sons of Cornwall, be thought overblown, eccentric or vainglorious, sceptics should remember that popular Cornish culture, in unguarded moments, celebrates those differences.

When the Cornish rugby team won the county championships at Twickenham in 1991 and again contested the final in 1992, 40,000 Cornish men, women and children, more than 10 per cent of the whole population, went to London to support their team. In the pre-match caperings ordinary people came up with a popular iconography: Cornwall fans wore the black and gold Cornish kilt while carrying a giant pasty around the ground. There was a huge inflatable Cornish chough bouncing over the heads of the crowd and replicas of the Padstow 'Obby 'Oss danced on the pitch. The black and white flags bearing the cross of Cornwall's patron saint, St Piran, seemed to flutter everywhere, along with banners proclaiming '*Kernow Bys Vyken*', 'Cornwall For Ever'.

Thoroughly intoxicated by the determination and desire of the Cornish team, a radio commentator, describing a try scored by a Cornish player who carried several Yorkshiremen on his back as he charged for the line, shouted into his microphone that 'he dived for the line, festooned with Saxons'. After Cornwall reached the final again the following year, the *Western Morning News* of the following Monday morning basked in the warm afterglow of achievement, if not triumph (the Cornish lost in 1992), transcending not only rugby but the unionist realities of 1992 of John Major's Britain. The leader writer gathered all of his Cornishness about him when he boomed that the fans 'carried the Cornish cause into the capital of foreign England' and declared that 'in the reorganization of power in Britain that must surely come, Cornwall must keep its own identity, and should have enhanced power'. While sport is often the blue touchpaper that ignites this sort of popular nationalism, the notable ingredient for the Cornish is a strong memory of their Celtic history. The English are Saxons, and the Cornish are not, at least in the minds of the fans travelling to the match.

Because the numbers of Cornish speakers and Cornish nationalists are small, it is tempting to be dismissive and to believe that their passion is no more than mild eccentricity and is in itself a small thing, but that cannot be fair. John Angarrack is surely more than justified in his insistence on a proper memorial to An Gof. War memorials to the fallen in the War for Britain deserve their place beside those for Flanders and the Second World War.

On the Isle of Man, where the Manx language was all but extinct, with the last native speaker, Ned Maddrell, dying in 1974 without a word of his native language being said or sung at his funeral, there is also passion – of an incendiary sort. In protest at the Anglicization of Man and the withering of Manx, two angry young men began a campaign of arson directed at the half-built houses of wealthy incomers. They were caught and sent to prison for substantial terms. Tynwald was surprised and alarmed, and with some haste appointed a Manx language officer and encouraged the establishment of Gaelic play groups. The next census will show a rise from 160 speakers to more than a thousand.

Now, these achievements are hard won and represent repeated acts of stubborn dedication by devoted people. They are not a band of weird, woolly, quaint or daft impossibilists attempting to roll back the mighty tide of English. They have no illusions that Manx or Cornish will re-establish themselves as first languages used as vernaculars in the streets of Penzance or Douglas, but they do believe that a knowledge of these old languages can only be good, and can only inform an interest in their history and culture.

In Scotland the transition of Gaelic from a vernacular language describing the lives of most people in the Highlands and Islands to a lexical curiosity spoken only by enthusiasts is currently underway. At the beginning of a new millennium it is important to face the fact that Gaelic Scotland has become, like the story of Rob Roy, marginal and romantic, or, like the story of Gregor MacGregor, dazzling but unknown. Although the new Scottish parliament in Edinburgh has decorated its buildings with bilingual signs and has debated once in Gaelic, the bitter truth is that there is now no meaningful sense in which Gaelic Scotland lives. The figures from the census returns are utterly unequivocal. When the population of Scotland was first asked the question 'Do you have Gaelic?' in the census of 1881, 231,934 people answered yes. In 1991 only 65,978 did. The prospects are very bleak, and the language is rapidly on the way to extinction as a community vernacular within the next twenty years. One statistic drives the point home. In 1991 only 357 children under the age of five spoke Gaelic.

In Wales and Ireland Celtic languages have government backing and in the case of Welsh its decline was reversed by a massive act of collective effort. The Welsh understood well was the correct answer to an oft-repeated question. What is the practical use of Gaelic or Welsh? Everyone who speaks a Celtic language speaks English, so if you want to go to all the trouble of learning a language then why not learn something useful like French or Spanish? The answer is simple. French will not teach you more about Ireland, but Gaelic will. Spanish will not add to anyone's knowledge of Wales, but Welsh certainly will. These marginal and threatened languages are necessary for a deeper reading of history and a better understanding of these nations' identity. If they are lost then a large part of ourselves dies with them.

Stonehenge, Wiltshire, England

At the summer solstice of 2000, on 21 June, English Heritage allowed access to Stonehenge to anyone who wanted to celebrate the turning point of the millennial year. For a long time such gatherings had been forbidden. About 6,000 people braved the driving rain to dance, sing and play music around the ancient stones. Many journalists also turned up to watch, including John Vidal of the *Guardian*:

> But for those who have embraced romanticism, paganism and the many strands of druidism and the counter culture, the stones hold a symbolic and physical power of place. 'Scum and germs ... remember your culture', cried Helen, self-styled Lancastrian mistress of the night, dressed somewhere between Simon Bolivar and an Italian traffic cop – but with specs and a three foot horn which she blew frequently to the four winds ... 'It's a return to the spirit of the free festivals of the 1970s,' said Tim Sebastian, whose title – Archdruid of Wiltshire, Chosen Chief of the Secular Order of Druids, Conservation Officer for the Council of British Druid Orders and Bard of the Gorsedd of Caer Abiri (Avebury) – defied any state-conferred nobility in its arcane absurdity. 'We are seeing a return to Celticity.'

This sort of harmless fun can easily be seen as the fate that befell Celtic England: a jumble-sale of big names and little understanding. Like John Vidal, the readership of the *Guardian* will undoubtedly have seen the Stonehenge rituals as something marginal and weird, and of virtually no use in compiling a meaningful definition of Englishness. This last is no longer of interest only to cultural historians and leader writers in the broadsheets who occasionally worry about football hooliganism or the north/south divide. Now that political power has devolved to Wales, Ulster and Scotland, English identity, and what it means and needs, has become central to a general debate about government. London has a sufficiently strong sense of itself to have acquired a measure of autonomy, but what of the English regions? The Midland police force had to go back 1,300 years to Offa to find a suitable name when they retitled themselves the Mercia Police. It is doubtful that meant much to anyone, even those living in Walsall or West Bromwich.

To some extent the revellers at Stonehenge are the descendants of Iolo Morgannwg and the amazing Dr William Price of Llantrisant, but they lack the learning and the language to back their eccentricities. Sadly, they show how meaningless and diffuse the idea of Celtic culture has become. No wonder the 'Obby 'Oss men of Padstow say 'Bollocks!' when it is suggested that they are taking part in a Celtic festival. And no wonder that historians and other commentators remain deeply suspicious of any narrative that incorporates 'Celtic' in the label.

POSTSCRIPT

THIS BOOK IS an extended definition of what 'Celtic' might usefully mean to anyone who wants to think about Britain and Ireland in a more expansive way, about a Britain and Ireland that do not take London as their starting points, unlike so many academic histories. And, including Stonehenge, all the places noted in the last few pages offer a shorthand version of that definition. They are all named in Celtic languages, and for 2,000 years were described exclusively in Gaelic or Welsh. All communicate a pungent sense of loss, and sometimes some anger at that loss. The people of Celtic Britain fought and died for their sense of themselves, and to retain an identity which was not overwhelmingly English. Often, the only way of discovering what happened in Celtic Britain was to deduce the action from the English reaction – from massive structures such as Caernarfon Castle to less obvious, but no less important, measures such as the Statute of Kilkenny.

Many of these places also share a sense of sanctity, as much imparted by the place itself as by anything of human hand that remains there. They are illuminated by a combination of pagan and Christian holiness that derives both from the sea and the land. They look and feel similar, and while that should be no great surprise, given their situations and the impression made on our geography by the mighty Atlantic, it is striking nonetheless.

In addition to these connections there are others in the west which are surprising and quirky: for example, wrestling is contested in several variants of the same Celtic style, and a version of hockey (hurling, shinty and *cammag*) is played in places are far apart as Inverness and Redruth, while in the west several breeds of hardy ponies worked at everything from carrying peat to carting tin ore.

But the main links in this long and complicated chain are historical: it is a history not of shared alliances, or even of a common purpose, but one of similar concerns and cultural inclinations. Most of all it is a shared history, because for 1,500 years the islands of Britain and Ireland have been shared with the English. Throughout, I have tried to avoid value judgements and show only that Celtic culture has its own history, and that it is different from that of the English. Not better, just different. To claim better would be to lose the threads of this story in the labyrinth of myth-history which has twisted itself around the Celtic west for far too long.

Despite artificial national borders, and the academic histories which made the formations of these countries of Britain and Ireland seem inevitable, there is a clearly discernible cultural unity through all the Sea Kingdoms of the western edge of Britain and Ireland: another way of seeing ourselves, another country inside the one we think we know.

BIBLIOGRAPHY

Set out at the end of a book in neat lists, bibliographies can look deceptively prescriptive, like a list of ingredients for a recipe. They confer a sense of pattern, forethought and planning on a process which, in reality, often exhibits none of these characteristics. For the spine of this book was not a long reading list but a journey, a sequence of ferry timetables rather than a set of references.

However, not everything is visible to the naked and uninformed eye, and before I pointed my old car westwards I spent a long time reading and thinking about what I might look for. Most refreshing and encouraging was Norman Davies' brilliant history of Britain and Ireland, which he scrupulously titled *The Isles* (1999). The cover, featuring a seventeenth-century maritime chart of the Irish Sea, and the dedication to 'Richard Samson Davies (1863–1939), English by birth, Welsh by conviction, Lancastrian by choice, British by chance' reflect Davies' own misgivings about the focus of traditional 'British' history. *The Isles* expands that focus decisively westwards and understands the whole of Britain and Ireland as a combination of different, and often competing, cultures.

In its simple insistence on looking at the Atlantic coastline of Europe from seaward instead of landward, Barry Cunliffe's *Facing the Ocean* (2000) is more than a revolutionary *aperçu*, it is a persuasive thesis which demands a wholesale reconception of European history. *The Celts* by Nora Chadwick (1971) helps define terminology and a timetable. By sharpening the focus on Britain and Ireland, Charles Thomas' excellent *Celtic Britain* (1986) offers the beginnings of a historical chart through the difficult waters of the Sea Kingdoms, but to the reader's (and the author's) chagrin, *Celtic Britain* only reaches the eighth century.

Anyone seriously interested in a truly encyclopaedic view of British history should invest in *The Oxford Companion to British History* edited by John Cannon and published in 1997. My copy is dog-eared from constant use.

In compiling this bibliography I have tried to limit entries to books still in print and therefore available to an interested reader. For ease of use I have arranged the list in regional compartments – this is not a reflection of the structure of the book itself.

GENERAL

Bond, Janet and Colin Bond, *Mysterious Britain*, 1971
Costley, Sarah and Charles Kighty, *A Celtic Book of Days*, 1991
Ellis, Peter Beresford, *The Ancient World of the Celts*, 1991
Frere, Sheppard, *Britannia*, 1967
Gardiner, Robert, ed., *The Sea and History*, 1996
Green, Miranda, *Dictionary of Celtic Myth and Legend*, 1992
Green, Miranda, *The Gods of the Celts*, 1986
Hutton, Ronald, *The Pagan Religions of the British Isles*, 1991
Laing, Lloyd and Jennifer Laing, *Celtic Britain*, 1995
McMahon, Agnes, ed., *The Celtic Way of Life*, 1976
Piggott, Stuart, *The Druids*, 1968
Ross, Anne and Michael Cyprien, *A Traveller's Guide to Celtic Britain*, 1985
Sharp, Mick, *Holy Places of Celtic Britain*, 1997
Whitrow, G. F., *Time in History*, 1989
Yeats, W. B., *The Celtic Twilight*, 1893
Zaczek, Ian, *Chronicles of the Celts*, 1996

CORNWALL

Angarrack, John, *Breaking the Chains*, 1999
Carman, Philip, *The Western Rising, 1549*, 1994
Earle, John, *Walking in Cornwall*, 1996
Filbee, Marjorie, *Celtic Cornwall*, 1996
Jenkin, John, *A First History of Cornwall*, 1984
Payne, Robin, *The Romance of the Stones, Cornwall's Pagan Past*, 1999
Payton, Philip, *Cornwall*, 1996
Rawe, Donald R., *Padstow's 'Obby 'Oss*, 1971
Soulsby, Ian, *A History of Cornwall*, 1986
Whetter, James, *Cornish Weather and Cornish People in the 17th Century*, 1991
White, G. Pawley, *A Handbook of Cornish Surnames*, 1972

WALES

Barber, Chris, *In Search of Owain Glyn Dwr*, 1998
Davies, John, *A History of Wales*, 1990
Davies, John, *The Making of Wales*, 1996

Davies, R. R., *The Age of Conquest, 1063–1415*, 1987
Henken, Elissa R., *National Redeemer, Owain Glyn Dwr in the Welsh Tradition*, 1996
Hodges, Geoffrey, *Owain Glyn Dwr*, 1995
Jones, John, *Welsh Place-Names*, 1979
Lofmark, Carl, *A History of the Red Dragon*, 1995
Morris, Jan, *Wales*, 1984
Rees, David, *The Son of Prophecy*, 1997
Smith, J. Beverley, *Llywelyn ap Gruffudd*, 1998
Williams, Gareth, *Valleys of Song*, 1998
Williams, Gwyn, A., *When Was Wales?* 1985

MAN

Kermode, P. M. C., *Manx Crosses*, 1907
Kinvig, R. H., *The Isle of Man*, 1944
Stowell, Brian and Diarmid O'Breaslain, *A Short History of the Manx Language*, 1996

Programme of Tynwald, 2000

IRELAND

Bardon, Jonathan, *A History of Ulster*, 1992
Bartlett, Thomas and Keith Jeffrey, *A Military History of Ireland*, 1996
Bartlett, Thomas, Kevin Davison and Daire Keogh, *Rebellion – A Television History of 1798*, 1998
Cahill, Thomas, *How the Irish Saved Civilisation*, 1995
Doyle, Eamon, *March into Meath*, 1997
Duffy, Sean, *An Atlas of Irish History*, 1997
English, Richard, *A History of Ireland*, 1991
Furlong, Nicolas, *Fr. John Murphy of Boolavogue 1753–1798*, 1991
Gahan, Daniel J., *Rebellion!* 1997
James, Michael, *Mythic Ireland*, 1992
Jenner, Michael, *Ireland Through the Ages*, 1992
Kenny, Michael, *The 1798 Rebellion*, 1996
Keogh, Daire and Nicolas Furlong, eds, *The Women of 1798*, 1998
Lysaght, Patricia, *A Pocket Book of the Banshee*, 1998
Lysaght, Patricia, *The Banshee*, 1986
McCoy, G. Hayes, *Scots Mercenary Forces in Ireland (1505–1600)*, 1937

O'Brien, Jacqueline and Peter Harbison, *Ancient Ireland*, 1996
O'Brien, Maire and Conor Cruise O'Brien, *Ireland: A Concise History*, 1977
O'Croinin, Daibhi, *Early Medieval Ireland*, 1998
O'Meara, John, trans., *The Voyage of St Brendan*, 1976
O'Shaughnessy, Peter, ed., *Rebellion in Wicklow*, 1998
Severin, Tim, *The St Brendan Voyage*, 1978
Sheedy, Kieran, *The Tellicherry Five*, 1997
Stanley, Jo. ed., *Bold in Her Breeches, Women Pirates Across the Ages*, 1995
Stewart, A. T. Q., *The Summer Soldiers*, 1995
Whelan, Kevin and Thomas Bartlett, eds, *Memoirs of Miles Byrne*, 1997
Zaczek, Ian, *The Book of Kells*, 1997

SCOTLAND

Brown, Raymond Lamont, *Scottish Folklore*, 1996
Darwin, Tes, *The Scots Herbal*, 1996
Dey, Joan, *Out Skerries*, 1991
Donaldson, Gordon, ed., *Scottish Historical Documents*, 1970
Fenton, Alexander, *The Northern Isles*, 1997
Finnie, Mike, *Shetland, An Illustrated Architectural Guide*, 1990
Fraser, George MacDonald, *The Steel Bonnets*, 1971
Graham-Campbell, James and Colleen E. Batey, *Vikings in Scotland*, 1998
Gregg, Richard T., *Gregor MacGregor, Cazique of Poyais*, 1999
Hunter, James, *Last of the Free*, 1999
MacDonald, Donald, *Lewis*, 1978
Macdonald, R. A., *The Kingdom of the Isles, 1100–1336*, 1997
MacLean, Malcolm and Christopher Carrell, eds, *As An Fhearann*, 1986
MacLeod, Mona, *Leaving Scotland*, 1996
MacNeill, Seumas and Richardson, Frank, *Piobaireachd and its Interpretation*, 1987
McCulloch, Andrew, *Galloway*, 2000
Prebble, John, *Culloden*, 1961
Ritchie, Anna, *Viking Scotland*, 1993
Roberts, John L., *Lost Kingdoms, Celtic Scotland and the Middle Ages*, 1997
Robertson, John F., *The Story of Galloway*, 1963
Ross, Stewart, *Ancient Scotland*, 1991
Stratford, Neil, *The Lewis Chessmen*, 1997
Watson, W. J., *The Celtic Place-Names of Scotland*, 1926
Williams, Ronald, *The Lords of the Isles*, 1984

ACKNOWLEDGEMENTS FOR QUOTATIONS

Glenalough poem, trans. Maire MacNeil, from *Ancient Ireland* by
Jacqueline O'Brien and Peter Harbison, Weidenfeld, 1996
Poem by Bjorn Cripplehand, trans. Alfred P. Smyth, from *Warlords and Holy Men: Scotland AD 80–1000*, Edinburgh University Press, 1980
Winter poem, trans. Brendan Kennelly, from *Celtic Way of Life*, ed.,
Agnes McMahon, O'Brien Press, 1976

Tain Bo Cuailgne, based on *The Cattle Raid of Cooley*, trans. Winifred
Faraday, Nutt, 1904

INDEX